Leading and Managing Change for School Improvement

Nadire Gülçin Yildiz
Istanbul Medipol University, Turkey

A volume in the Advances
in Educational Marketing,
Administration, and Leadership
(AEMAL) Book Series

Published in the United States of America by
    IGI Global
    Information Science Reference (an imprint of IGI Global)
    701 E. Chocolate Avenue
    Hershey PA, USA 17033
    Tel: 717-533-8845
    Fax: 717-533-8661
    E-mail: cust@igi-global.com
    Web site: http://www.igi-global.com

Copyright © 2024 by IGI Global. All rights reserved. No part of this publication may be reproduced, stored or distributed in any form or by any means, electronic or mechanical, including photocopying, without written permission from the publisher.
Product or company names used in this set are for identification purposes only. Inclusion of the names of the products or companies does not indicate a claim of ownership by IGI Global of the trademark or registered trademark.

Library of Congress Cataloging-in-Publication Data

Names: Yildiz, Nadire Gülçin, editor.
Title: Leading and managing change for school improvement / Nadire Gülçin
  Yildiz, editor.
Description: Hershey, PA : Information Science Reference, [2024] | Includes
  bibliographical references and index. | Summary: "The book has been
  purposely planned to enable school leaders and administrators to have a
  better understanding of how schools are changing and how such changes
  could be managed so that they can provide effective leadership"--
  Provided by publisher.
Identifiers: LCCN 2021061503 (print) | LCCN 2021061504 (ebook) | ISBN
  9781799839408 (hardcover) | ISBN 9781668435021 (paperback) | ISBN
  9781799839415 (eBook)
Subjects: LCSH: School management and organization. | Educational
  leadership. | Educational change.
Classification: LCC LB2805 .L3446 2022 (print) | LCC LB2805 (ebook) | DDC
  371.2/011--dc23/eng/20220215
LC record available at https://lccn.loc.gov/2021061503
LC ebook record available at https://lccn.loc.gov/2021061504

This book is published in the IGI Global book series Advances in Educational Marketing, Administration, and Leadership (AEMAL) (ISSN: 2326-9022; eISSN: 2326-9030)

British Cataloguing in Publication Data
A Cataloguing in Publication record for this book is available from the British Library.

All work contributed to this book is new, previously-unpublished material.
The views expressed in this book are those of the authors, but not necessarily of the publisher.

For electronic access to this publication, please contact: eresources@igi-global.com.

Advances in Educational Marketing, Administration, and Leadership (AEMAL) Book Series

ISSN:2326-9022
EISSN:2326-9030

Editor-in-Chief: Siran Mukerji, IGNOU, India; Purnendu Tripathi, IGNOU, India

MISSION

With more educational institutions entering into public, higher, and professional education, the educational environment has grown increasingly competitive. With this increase in competitiveness has come the need for a greater focus on leadership within the institutions, on administrative handling of educational matters, and on the marketing of the services offered.

The **Advances in Educational Marketing, Administration, & Leadership (AEMAL) Book Series** strives to provide publications that address all these areas and present trending, current research to assist professionals, administrators, and others involved in the education sector in making their decisions.

COVERAGE

- Governance in P-12 and Higher Education
- Academic Pricing
- Educational Marketing Campaigns
- Direct marketing of educational programs
- Marketing Theories within Education
- Academic Administration
- Enrollment Management
- Technologies and Educational Marketing
- Faculty Administration and Management
- Educational Management

IGI Global is currently accepting manuscripts for publication within this series. To submit a proposal for a volume in this series, please contact our Acquisition Editors at Acquisitions@igi-global.com or visit: http://www.igi-global.com/publish/.

The Advances in Educational Marketing, Administration, and Leadership (AEMAL) Book Series (ISSN 2326-9022) is published by IGI Global, 701 E. Chocolate Avenue, Hershey, PA 17033-1240, USA, www.igi-global.com. This series is composed of titles available for purchase individually; each title is edited to be contextually exclusive from any other title within the series. For pricing and ordering information please visit http://www.igi-global.com/book-series/advances-educational-marketing-administration-leadership/73677. Postmaster: Send all address changes to above address. Copyright © 2024 IGI Global. All rights, including translation in other languages reserved by the publisher. No part of this series may be reproduced or used in any form or by any means – graphics, electronic, or mechanical, including photocopying, recording, taping, or information and retrieval systems – without written permission from the publisher, except for non commercial, educational use, including classroom teaching purposes. The views expressed in this series are those of the authors, but not necessarily of IGI Global.

Titles in this Series

For a list of additional titles in this series, please visit:
http://www.igi-global.com/book-series/advances-educational-marketing-administration-leadership/73677

Preparing Students for the Future Educational Paradigm
Fatima Al Husseiny (Lebanese International University, Lebanon) and Afzal Sayed Munna (University of Sunderland in London, UK)
Information Science Reference • copyright 2024 • 358pp • H/C (ISBN: 9798369315361) • US $285.00 (our price)

History and Educational Philosophy for Social Justice and Human Rights
Jahid Siraz Chowdhury (Lincoln University College, Malaysia) Kumarashwaran Vadevalu (University of Malaya, Malaysia) A.F.M. Zakaria (Shahjalal University of Science and Technology, Bangladesh) Sajib Ahmed (Universiti Malaya, Malaysia) and Abdullah Al-Mamun (Sunway University, Malaysia)
Information Science Reference • copyright 2024 • 300pp • H/C (ISBN: 9781668499535) • US $235.00 (our price)

Promoting Crisis Management and Creative Problem-Solving Skills in Educational Leadership
Afzal Sayed Munna (University of Sunderland in London, UK) Uzoechi Nwagbara (University of Sunderland in London, UK) and Yahaya Alhassan (University of Sunderland in London, UK)
Information Science Reference • copyright 2024 • 321pp • H/C (ISBN: 9781668483329) • US $215.00 (our price)

Strategic Opportunities for Bridging the University-Employer Divide
William E. Donald (University of Southampton, UK & Ronin Institute, USA)
Information Science Reference • copyright 2024 • 329pp • H/C (ISBN: 9781668498279) • US $225.00 (our price)

Enrollment and Retention Strategies for 21st Century Higher Education
Rayshawn L. Eastman (Mount St. Joseph University, USA)
Information Science Reference • copyright 2024 • 300pp • H/C (ISBN: 9781668474778) • US $215.00 (our price)

For an entire list of titles in this series, please visit:
http://www.igi-global.com/book-series/advances-educational-marketing-administration-leadership/73677

701 East Chocolate Avenue, Hershey, PA 17033, USA
Tel: 717-533-8845 x100 • Fax: 717-533-8661
E-Mail: cust@igi-global.com • www.igi-global.com

Table of Contents

Preface xii

Chapter 1
Leading Effectively for K-12 School Improvement 1
    Raymond J. John Schmidt, Escuela Internacional Sampedrana,
        Honduras

Chapter 2
Making Schools Effective: 21st Century School Leaders' Agenda 26
    Reginah Ndlovu, University of Zimbabwe, Zimbabwe

Chapter 3
Organizational Change in Educational Organizations 51
    Özcan Doğan, Eskişehir Osmangazi University, Turkey
    Damla Ayduğ, İstanbul Gedik University, Turkey

Chapter 4
The Impact of Distributed Leadership on Effective Professional Development
via Organizational Innovativeness 75
    Ramazan Atasoy, Harran University, Turkey
    Mehmet Tufan Yalçın, Çankırı Karatekin University, Turkey

Chapter 5
Walking a Mile in Their Shoes: Understanding Students in Poverty 99
    Queen Ogbomo, Tennessee Tech University, USA

Chapter 6
Transforming School Organisational Culture Through a Contextually
Relevant Change Leadership Approach Within a Pakistani Urban Private
School 121
    Venesser Fernandes, Monash University, Australia

Chapter 7
Project for the Global Integration of Meaningful Learning of English in Early
Childhood Education 146
    Antonio Daniel Juan Rubio, Universidad de Granada, Spain

Chapter 8
Adaptive Primary School Design: Post-Pandemic Reuse Projects for Adana
Former Archeology Museum..173
    Orkan Zeynel Güzelci, Istanbul Technical University, Turkey

Chapter 9
Digitalization of Education in a School on the Basis of Microsoft Teams
Platform: Effectiveness of Synchronous and Asynchronous Learning..............198
    Olena H. Hlazunova, National University of Life and Environmental
        Sciences of Ukraine, Ukraine
    Valentyna I. Korolchuk, National University of Life and Environmental
        Sciences of Ukraine, Ukraine
    Tetiana V. Voloshyna, National University of Life and Environmental
        Sciences of Ukraine, Ukraine

Compilation of References 235

Related References.. 260

About the Contributors 282

Index.. 287

Detailed Table of Contents

Preface xii

Chapter 1

Leading Effectively for K-12 School Improvement 1
Raymond J. John Schmidt, Escuela Internacional Sampedrana,
Honduras

This chapter explores six key principles essential for school leaders to effectively spearhead transformative initiatives. Central to this discourse is the understanding that successful change management necessitates collaborative efforts, stakeholder engagement, clear communication, and a focus on continuous professional development for educators. Moreover, fostering a culture of innovation, embracing evidence-based practices, and leveraging technology are imperative for addressing the multifaceted challenges faced by K-12 schools. Drawing upon seminal works by Darling-Hammond, Fullan, Kotter, and Senge, among others, this chapter elucidates a comprehensive framework for leading change that encompasses vision setting, capacity building, and sustainable implementation strategies. By synthesizing theoretical perspectives with practical insights, this chapter underscores the critical role of visionary leadership and effective management practices in driving meaningful improvements in K-12 educational environments.

Chapter 2

Making Schools Effective: 21st Century School Leaders' Agenda 26
Reginah Ndlovu, University of Zimbabwe, Zimbabwe

The 21st century dispensation has brought a lot of challenges in developing countries such as Zimbabwe that have resulted in schools becoming ineffective. The study was prompted by the need for schools to prepare students to meet the demands of an emerging digital world. The change management theory was used with the aim to inform the changes which are taking place in 21st century schools. The corpus of the study has been published works for the years 2011 to 2014. The Nziramasanga Commission, which informs the basis of Zimbabwean education, was also studied.

Chapter 3
Organizational Change in Educational Organizations 51
    Özcan Doğan, Eskişehir Osmangazi University, Turkey
    Damla Ayduğ, İstanbul Gedik University, Turkey

Change is an inevitable fact of life from birth to death, affecting cultures, countries, and societies. Especially today, change is happening faster than in the past, and this causes societies and organizations to face much more change that they need to keep up with. Organizations can only survive if they change themselves by adapting to these rapid changes. In this study, definitions of organizational change were given, and the factors that cause organizational change were described. Then, the theories of change were mentioned depending on the reason for the change and the changes it brings about in the organization. Then, resistance to change, management of organizational change, and organizational change in educational organizations were examined.

Chapter 4
The Impact of Distributed Leadership on Effective Professional Development
via Organizational Innovativeness 75
    Ramazan Atasoy, Harran University, Turkey
    Mehmet Tufan Yalçın, Çankırı Karatekin University, Turkey

This chapter aims to explore to what extent distributed leadership affects effective professional development of teachers mediating organizational innovativeness in the sample of the countries participating in the TALIS 2018 survey. Accordingly, the sample consisted of 15,980 schools and 261,429 teachers from 48 countries participating in TALIS 2018. The study found that teachers' gender, education level, and experience have a significant, albeit low, effect on their thoughts on the effectiveness of professional development activities. Another important research finding has shown that school principals' distributed leadership behaviors contribute to the effectiveness of professional development activities by promoting organizational innovativeness. Based on the findings of this study, the identified variables should be considered in the development of policies and practices for teacher learning. Future research could explore multilevel models that would examine the potential impacts of various leadership styles and teacher attributes on teacher learning.

Chapter 5
Walking a Mile in Their Shoes: Understanding Students in Poverty..................99
    Queen Ogbomo, Tennessee Tech University, USA

This study examined the impact of a poverty simulation project, an experiential learning procedure on preservice teachers' perception of elementary students living in poverty. Thirty undergraduate preservice teachers from two cohorts in a public university in the southern part of the United States were asked to participate in a poverty simulation activity to expose them to the lived experiences of people living in poverty. An early analysis of the debriefing session after the simulation project showed that students viewed this simulation project as an engaging learning experience. Means and standard deviations of scores in relation to pre-test and post-test personal bias toward poverty, understanding individuals in poverty, effort in teaching students living in poverty, and responsibility for students living in poverty were obtained. While there was no significant difference from the paired sample t-tests, there was a slight difference in three of the four areas measured.

Chapter 6
Transforming School Organisational Culture Through a Contextually Relevant Change Leadership Approach Within a Pakistani Urban Private School 121
Venesser Fernandes, Monash University, Australia

This chapter focuses on the transformative journey of a K-12 Pakistani urban private school in moving from autocratic-charismatic leadership practices to distributed-strategic leadership practices through the use of a total quality management change leadership approach integrated over two years. This study found that distributed educational leadership practices are developed at the school level through contextually relevant change leadership approaches that focus on sustained and continuous school improvement. The chapter provides insights into possibilities for further developing school organisational culture through emphasis given to collaborative and strategic decision-making practices amongst senior-level, middle-level, and teacher-level leaders in urban private schools in Pakistan.

Chapter 7
Project for the Global Integration of Meaningful Learning of English in Early Childhood Education 146
Antonio Daniel Juan Rubio, Universidad de Granada, Spain

This study is based on the premise that learning English has become a necessity in an increasingly globalised world, and that its teaching is simpler and more effective from an early age, offering better results. Based on studies related to the subject, this project has been conducted on various aspects such as current teaching in so-called "bilingual schools" or the influence of the family and new technologies on the use of routines in the teaching of pupils in the early childhood education stage. This chapter defends the application of a leading project based on new methodologies that share an eminently practical and interactive approach and that manage to involve all the agents related to the education of pupils, incorporating the necessary resources to facilitate linguistic immersion. All of this is aimed at achieving an improvement in the results of language teaching. The general objective of this chapter is to present a globalised teaching project that generates significant learning capable of achieving comprehensive training in English in early childhood education pupils.

Chapter 8
Adaptive Primary School Design: Post-Pandemic Reuse Projects for Adana
Former Archeology Museum 173
  Orkan Zeynel Güzelci, Istanbul Technical University, Turkey

This chapter explores the strategies for adapting existing buildings in a way that respects both cultural and environmental sustainability. It specifically focuses on the adaptive reuse of the Adana Former Archaeology Museum, exploring its transformation into a primary school in response to post-pandemic needs. The primary goal is to demonstrate the potential of adaptive reuse of heritage buildings for contemporary educational purposes while preserving their cultural essence. The methodology involves a teaching experiment (case study) with undergraduate interior design students, who develop various scenarios and spatial designs for the museum's transformation. This case study offers practical insights into the challenges and opportunities of adaptive reuse in architecture and interior design. The chapter highlights adaptive reuse's major implications for educational leaders, emphasizing the importance of creating dynamic, flexible, and adaptable learning environments.

Chapter 9
Digitalization of Education in a School on the Basis of Microsoft Teams
Platform: Effectiveness of Synchronous and Asynchronous Learning 198
  *Olena H. Hlazunova, National University of Life and Environmental
      Sciences of Ukraine, Ukraine*
  *Valentyna I. Korolchuk, National University of Life and Environmental
      Sciences of Ukraine, Ukraine*
  *Tetiana V. Voloshyna, National University of Life and Environmental
      Sciences of Ukraine, Ukraine*

Educational institutions need a transformation in the methods and tools of organizing education. It is caused by technological evolution and external challenges, such as pandemics or wars. Effective organization of synchronous and asynchronous learning at school based on the Microsoft Teams platform is key to a successful transition to a distance (blended) format. The chapter presents modern approaches and methods of using Microsoft Teams to organize the learning process in synchronous and asynchronous modes. Models for the organization of synchronous and asynchronous interaction in schools are proposed. Criteria and indicators for evaluating the Microsoft Teams environment as a tool for synchronous and asynchronous interaction in modern conditions have been developed: functionality, reliability, effectiveness, interaction, availability, security and privacy, technical support, and assistance. The results of an experimental study evaluating the effectiveness of using Microsoft Teams for synchronous and asynchronous training are presented.

Compilation of References 235

Related References 260

About the Contributors 282

Index 287

Preface

Welcome to *Leading and Managing Change for School Improvement*, a comprehensive reference book crafted to address the evolving landscape of educational institutions in the 21st century. In a world that is in a constant state of flux, the role of educational leaders becomes paramount in navigating the complexities and dynamics of schools.

Curated by Nadire Gülçin Yildiz, this book is designed to equip school leaders and administrators with the knowledge and insights necessary to meet the challenges of leading institutions in an ever-changing environment. The contents of this book encapsulate modern ideas, providing a profound understanding of the complex nature of schools, the dynamic school environment, cultural nuances, the type of instructional leadership required, and effective techniques for sustaining improvement.

The primary objective of this book is to empower teachers, school leaders, and administrators to comprehend the ongoing changes in schools and to guide them in effectively managing these transformations.

Delving into the intricacies that make schools multifaceted entities, the book aims to help readers understand the complex nature of schools. It further examines the diverse contexts within which schools are established, offering insights into fostering a conducive culture for effective schooling. The book also provides strategies for schools to adapt and respond to the dynamic shifts in the educational landscape and explores ways to improve schools, making them more effective in the face of continuous change.

This book is not only relevant but also timely, as it addresses the pressing need for educational leaders to stay abreast of the evolving educational landscape. It serves as a guide for navigating the challenges posed by change, offering practical and insightful perspectives on effective leadership.

Leading and Managing Change for School Improvement is not limited to a specific audience; rather, it caters to a diverse readership. It is a valuable resource for school leaders and administrators, education officers, circuit supervisors, educational leadership researchers, and postgraduate students specializing in Educational Leadership and Management. The comprehensive topics covered in this book also

Preface

make it a suitable reference for school inspectors and training officers seeking a deeper understanding of effective school management in the 21st century.

We believe that this book will serve as a valuable tool for those invested in the field of education, offering practical guidance and thoughtful insights to navigate the ever-evolving landscape of schools and educational leadership.

ORGANIZATION OF THE BOOK

This edited reference book, *Leading and Managing Change for School Improvement*, presents a diverse collection of chapters that delve into crucial aspects of educational leadership and change management. Each chapter offers a unique perspective, combining theoretical insights with practical applications to guide school leaders, administrators, and educators in navigating the complexities of the evolving educational landscape.

Chapter 1, titled "Leading Effectively for K-12 School Improvement" by Raymond J. Schmidt, explores six key principles essential for school leaders to spearhead transformative initiatives successfully. Emphasizing collaborative efforts, stakeholder engagement, clear communication, and continuous professional development, the chapter synthesizes theoretical perspectives from influential authors like Darling-Hammond and Fullan, providing a comprehensive framework for visionary leadership and sustainable implementation.

In Chapter 2, "Making Schools Effective: 21st Century School Leaders' Agenda" by Reginah Ndlovu, the focus shifts to the challenges faced by schools in the 21st century, particularly in developing countries like Zimbabwe. Using change management theory, Ndlovu explores the need for schools to adapt to the demands of an emerging digital world, referencing the Nziramasanga commission as a basis for Zimbabwean education.

Chapter 3, titled "Organizational Change in Educational Organizations" by Özcan Dogan and Damla Aydug, provides an in-depth exploration of organizational change in the context of educational institutions. Covering definitions of organizational change, factors driving change, and various change theories, the authors delve into the crucial aspects of managing change and its implications in educational settings.

Chapter 4, "The Impact of Distributed Leadership on Effective Professional Development via Organizational Innovativeness" by Ramazan Atasoy and Mehmet Yalçin, investigates the relationship between distributed leadership, organizational innovativeness, and effective professional development for teachers. Drawing from the TALIS 2018 survey, the authors discuss the significant influence of school principals' distributed leadership behaviors on the effectiveness of professional development activities.

xiii

In Chapter 5, "Walking a Mile in Their Shoes: Understanding Students in Poverty" by Queen Ogbomo, the focus shifts to the impact of a Poverty Simulation Project on preservice teachers' perceptions of students living in poverty. Ogbomo explores the experiential learning procedure and its effects on preservice teachers' biases and understanding of individuals in poverty.

Chapter 6, "Transforming School Organizational Culture Through a Contextually Relevant Change Leadership Approach Within a Pakistani Urban Private School" by Venesser Fernandes, explores the transformative journey of a K-12 Pakistani urban private school. The chapter highlights the shift from autocratic-charismatic leadership practices to distributed-strategic leadership practices, emphasizing sustained and continuous school improvement.

In Chapter 7, "Project for the Global Integration of Meaningful Learning of English in Early Childhood Education" by Antonio Juan Rubio, the focus is on the globalized teaching project aimed at achieving comprehensive training in English for Early Childhood Education pupils. Rubio discusses new methodologies, practical and interactive approaches, and the involvement of all stakeholders in the education process.

Chapter 8, "Adaptive Primary School Design: Post-Pandemic Reuse Projects for Adana Former Archeology Museum" by Orkan Güzelci, explores strategies for adapting existing buildings, specifically the Adana Former Archaeology Museum, for contemporary educational purposes post-pandemic. The chapter demonstrates the potential of adaptive reuse of heritage buildings for creating dynamic and adaptable learning environments.

Finally, Chapter 9, "Digitalization of Education in a School on the Basis Microsoft Teams Platform: Effectiveness of Synchronous and Asynchronous Learning" by Olena Hlazunova, Valentyna Korolchuk, and Tetiana Voloshyna, delves into the digitalization of education using the Microsoft Teams platform. The chapter presents modern approaches, methods, and models for organizing synchronous and asynchronous learning, evaluating their effectiveness in contemporary educational settings.

Together, these chapters offer a rich tapestry of insights, research findings, and practical applications that contribute to the overarching theme of leading and managing change for school improvement in the dynamic landscape of education. We hope that this edited reference book serves as a valuable resource for educators, administrators, and researchers navigating the challenges and opportunities of educational leadership.

Preface

IN SUMMARY

As editor of *Leading and Managing Change for School Improvement*, I take immense pride in presenting this meticulously curated collection of chapters that collectively form a comprehensive guide for educational leaders navigating the ever-evolving landscape of schools. The diverse perspectives offered by esteemed contributors contribute to a rich tapestry of insights, research findings, and practical applications, collectively addressing the multifaceted challenges and opportunities inherent in educational leadership and change management.

The chapters within this edited reference book encapsulate a broad spectrum of topics, ranging from effective leadership principles in K-12 school improvement to the transformative journey of school organizational culture in Pakistani urban private schools. They explore the impact of distributed leadership on professional development, the adaptation of existing buildings for post-pandemic educational reuse, and the digitalization of education using platforms like Microsoft Teams. Each chapter provides a unique lens through which readers can gain valuable insights and practical guidance.

Throughout this compilation, a common thread emerges—the recognition that effective leadership and adaptability are paramount in driving meaningful improvements in educational environments. The chapters not only synthesize theoretical perspectives from renowned authors but also present practical applications grounded in real-world challenges and experiences. From understanding the complexities of schools to embracing innovative teaching methodologies, from addressing the impact of poverty on students to adapting to the digital age, the contributors have provided a wealth of knowledge for educators, administrators, and researchers alike.

As I conclude this preface, we extend our gratitude to the insightful authors who have shared their expertise, making this edited reference book a valuable resource for those dedicated to enhancing educational leadership and fostering positive change in schools. I hope that the diverse range of topics covered in this book serves as a source of inspiration, sparking meaningful conversations, and contributing to the ongoing dialogue on effective leadership and school improvement.

May this collection empower and guide educational leaders, administrators, and researchers in their pursuit of excellence, ensuring that schools remain dynamic, adaptive, and responsive to the evolving needs of 21st-century education.

Warmest regards,

Nadire Gülçin Yildiz
Istanbul Medipol University, Turkey

Chapter 1
Leading Effectively for K–12 School Improvement

Raymond J. John Schmidt

(iD) https://orcid.org/0000-0003-4766-2303

Escuela Internacional Sampedrana, Honduras

ABSTRACT

This chapter explores six key principles essential for school leaders to effectively spearhead transformative initiatives. Central to this discourse is the understanding that successful change management necessitates collaborative efforts, stakeholder engagement, clear communication, and a focus on continuous professional development for educators. Moreover, fostering a culture of innovation, embracing evidence-based practices, and leveraging technology are imperative for addressing the multifaceted challenges faced by K-12 schools. Drawing upon seminal works by Darling-Hammond, Fullan, Kotter, and Senge, among others, this chapter elucidates a comprehensive framework for leading change that encompasses vision setting, capacity building, and sustainable implementation strategies. By synthesizing theoretical perspectives with practical insights, this chapter underscores the critical role of visionary leadership and effective management practices in driving meaningful improvements in K-12 educational environments.

INTRODUCTION

Navigating change within the K-12 educational landscape necessitates a nuanced understanding of leadership and management principles tailored to the unique complexities of school environments. As schools grapple with

DOI: 10.4018/978-1-7998-3940-8.ch001

Copyright © 2024, IGI Global. Copying or distributing in print or electronic forms without written permission of IGI Global is prohibited.

evolving societal demands, technological advancements, and pedagogical shifts, effective leadership emerges as a cornerstone for sustainable improvement. The interplay between leading and managing change is pivotal, with leadership setting the vision, fostering a culture of collaboration, and inspiring stakeholders, while management ensures the logistical, operational, and strategic facets align with the proposed changes (Fullan, 2007).

Consequently, it is imperative to recognize that the process of change in K-12 schools is multifaceted, demanding a blend of visionary leadership and pragmatic management. Leaders must cultivate a shared vision that resonates with diverse stakeholders, including educators, students, parents, and community members. This vision acts as a compass, guiding schools toward desired outcomes while fostering a collective sense of purpose and direction (Sergiovanni, 2001). Concurrently, effective management practices, such as strategic planning, resource allocation, and continuous monitoring, ensure that the envisioned changes are systematically implemented, evaluated, and refined to meet evolving needs (Kotter, 1996).

Furthermore, the role of leadership in facilitating change extends beyond mere administrative directives; it encompasses building capacity, nurturing a culture of innovation, and cultivating distributed leadership practices. Distributed leadership acknowledges that expertise and leadership potential exist at various levels within the school community, encouraging collaborative decision-making, shared responsibility, and collective efficacy (Spillane, 2006). By harnessing the collective intelligence and expertise of stakeholders, schools can leverage diverse perspectives, foster innovation, and cultivate a responsive learning environment attuned to the needs of 21st-century learners (DuFour & Marzano, 2011).

In today's rapidly evolving educational landscape, K-12 schools are continuously faced with the imperative to change, adapt, and innovate to meet the diverse needs of students, educators, and communities (Barron et al., 2020). Effective leadership and management of change are essential components in driving school improvement. This comprehensive discussion delves into the intricacies of leading and managing change within K-12 settings, drawing on scholarly research and best practices to illuminate strategies, challenges, and outcomes.

THE IMPERATIVE FOR CHANGE IN K-12 SCHOOLS

The necessity for change within K-12 schools stems from various factors, including shifting demographics, technological advancements, evolving pedagogical approaches, and changing societal expectations (Fullan, 2016). Moreover, the imperative to ensure equitable access to quality education for all students further underscores the need for continuous improvement efforts (Darling-Hammond, 2019). The K-12 educational system, which covers primary and secondary education, is a cornerstone of societal development. However, the traditional structures and methodologies of these schools are increasingly being viewed as outdated, necessitating comprehensive changes. This imperative for change arises from a myriad of reasons, ranging from technological advancements to evolving societal needs.

Technological Advancements

In recent decades, technological advancements have revolutionized various sectors, prompting a paradigm shift in how information is accessed, processed, and utilized (Prensky, 2001). The traditional chalk-and-talk methods, which dominated K-12 classrooms for centuries, are proving inadequate in preparing students for a digitally driven world. Today's students must be digitally literate to navigate an information-rich environment. Integrating technology into the curriculum not only enhances engagement but also equips students with essential skills for the 21st century (Matuchniak & Warschauer, 2010).

Diverse Learning Needs

The one-size-fits-all approach prevalent in many K-12 schools fails to accommodate diverse learning needs. Students possess varying strengths, weaknesses, interests, and learning styles that necessitate personalized learning experiences (Tomlinson, 2014). Adopting personalized learning models allows educators to tailor instruction to individual student needs, fostering academic growth and engagement (Baird et al., 2015).

Globalization and Cultural Competence

In an increasingly interconnected world, fostering cultural competence is paramount. K-12 schools must prepare students to thrive in diverse environments and appreciate global perspectives (Gay, 2010). Incorporating global education initiatives exposes students to different cultures, histories, and worldviews, cultivating empathy and intercultural understanding (Merryfield, 2002).

21st Century Skills

The demands of the modern workforce require more than academic proficiency; students must develop leadership, critical thinking, collaboration, problem-solving, and conflict-resolution skills (Fadel & Trilling, 2009). Transitioning from a knowledge-based to a skills-based curriculum empowers students to apply theoretical knowledge in practical Harris contexts, preparing them for real-world challenges (Partnership for 21st Century Learning, 2015).

Figure 1. 21st century skills

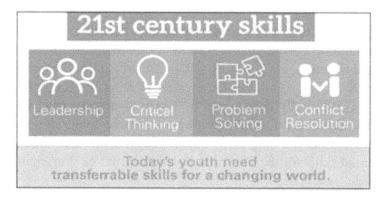

Social and Emotional Learning (SEL)

Recognizing the importance of holistic development, there is a growing emphasis on SEL in K-12 education. Addressing students' social and emotional needs fosters resilience, empathy, and emotional intelligence (Durlak et al., 2011). Incorporating SEL into the curriculum promotes positive behavior, reduces disciplinary issues, and enhances academic outcomes (Durlak et al., 2008).

Equity and Inclusion

Achieving educational equity and inclusion remains a significant challenge in many K-12 schools. Disparities in resources, opportunities, and outcomes persist among diverse student populations (Ladson-Billings, 2006). Implementing inclusive practices that address systemic inequities, promote diversity, and ensure access to quality education for all students is imperative (Santoro, 2017).

Summary

The imperative for change in K-12 schools is undeniable, driven by technological advancements, diverse learning needs, globalization, 21st-century skill demands, social and emotional learning, and equity considerations (Fullan, 2016). Embracing change is not merely an option but a necessity to cultivate future-ready learners equipped to navigate an ever-evolving world (Darling-Hammond, 2019).

THE ROLE OF LEADERSHIP IN DRIVING CHANGE IN K-12 SCHOOLS

Leadership plays a pivotal role in initiating, facilitating, and sustaining change within educational settings. According to Harris et al. (2008), effective school leaders exhibit transformational leadership qualities, inspiring stakeholders, fostering a shared vision, and cultivating a culture of collaboration and innovation. Leaders must communicate the rationale for change, engage stakeholders, and provide the necessary support and resources to facilitate implementation (Fullan & Hargreaves, 2012). In the realm of K-12 education, the dynamics of change are incessant, driven by evolving societal needs, technological advancements, and pedagogical innovations. At the forefront of such transformative journeys stands leadership. Leadership, in this context, is not merely administrative oversight but a visionary force that shapes the educational landscape, galvanizing stakeholders toward a shared mission of excellence and adaptability.

Visionary Leadership and Change

A foundational element of leadership in driving change is the articulation of a compelling vision. Fullan (2001) elucidates that successful leaders in education possess a keen ability to conceptualize and communicate a future state that is both aspirational and attainable. This vision serves as a North Star, guiding stakeholders through uncertainties and complexities inherent in change processes (Hargreaves, 2007). For instance, a school principal who envisions a technology-integrated curriculum can catalyze change by elucidating the benefits, outlining the implementation strategy, and aligning resources and professional development initiatives accordingly. Such clarity and direction mitigate resistance, foster collaboration, and cultivate a collective sense of purpose (Jantzi & Leithwood, 2005).

Fostering a Collaborative Culture

The centrality of collaboration in driving change cannot be overstated. Spillane (2006) posits that effective leadership transcends individual prowess, emphasizing collective capacity-building. Leaders adeptly leverage the expertise of teachers, administrators, parents, and community stakeholders, fostering a collaborative ecosystem where ideas are shared, refined, and implemented collaboratively.

In this context, distributed leadership emerges as a salient paradigm. Distributed leadership decentralizes decision-making, empowering educators at all levels to contribute to change initiatives (Harris, 2004). By cultivating a culture of trust, transparency, and inclusivity, leaders engender ownership, ensuring that change initiatives resonate with diverse stakeholder perspectives and needs.

Navigating Challenges and Resistance

Change, by its very nature, invites resistance. Leaders must, therefore, be adept navigators, skilled in mitigating challenges and cultivating a culture of resilience. Hallinger (2011) underscores the significance of adaptive leadership, wherein leaders demonstrate flexibility, responsiveness, and empathy. To navigate resistance, leaders must engage stakeholders proactively, soliciting feedback, addressing concerns, and co-constructing solutions collaboratively. By fostering open channels of communication, leaders mitigate misconceptions, build trust, and cultivate a shared commitment to change (Leithwood & Louis, 2011).

Professional Development and Capacity Building

A cornerstone of effective leadership lies in prioritizing professional development and capacity building. Reimer, Reiser, and Spillane (2002) highlight that leaders play a pivotal role in orchestrating learning opportunities that equip educators with the requisite skills, knowledge, and dispositions to navigate change adeptly. Leadership entails fostering a culture of continuous learning, where educators are empowered to innovate, reflect critically, and refine practices collaboratively (Andree et al., 2009). By aligning professional development initiatives with broader change objectives, leaders cultivate a skilled workforce adept at navigating complexities and driving sustained improvement.

Summary

Leadership stands as a linchpin in driving change in K-12 schools. Through visionary direction, collaborative ethos, adept navigation of challenges, and a steadfast commitment to professional development, leaders shape transformative journeys that resonate with the evolving needs of learners, educators, and communities alike (Fullan & Hargreaves, 2012). As educational landscapes continue to evolve, the imperatives of leadership in driving change remain paramount. By embracing the complexities, uncertainties, and opportunities inherent in change processes, leaders in K-12 schools cultivate environments characterized by innovation, excellence, and equity.

PRACTICAL CASE EXAMPLES FOR LEADING CHANGE IN K-12 SCHOOLS

Implementing change in K-12 schools requires strategic leadership and an understanding of the unique challenges and dynamics within the educational environment. Identifying practical case examples can highlight the importance of a strategic and collaborative leadership approach, as well as the need for ongoing professional development and community involvement in leading change within K-12 schools. Below are several relevant case examples of leading change in K-12 schools, along with correlating cited references.

Implementing Technology Integration in an Urban School District

In an effort to enhance teaching and learning experiences, a K-12 school district decided to implement technology integration across all grade levels (Fullan & Hargreaves, 2012). This involved introducing interactive whiteboards, digital learning platforms, and training teachers to effectively incorporate technology into their lesson plans (Fullan, 2017; Fullan & Hargreaves, 2012). Some effective leadership strategies include the following.

- Conducted a needs assessment to identify gaps in technology access and skills among teachers and students (Fullan, 2017).
- Established a technology integration task force comprising educators, administrators, and technology experts (Fullan, 2017).
- Provided ongoing professional development opportunities for teachers to build their technological proficiency (Fullan & Hargreaves, 2012).

- Fostered a culture of collaboration and shared best practices among educators (Fullan, 2017; Fullan & Hargreaves, 2012).

Implementing Technology Integration in a Rural School District

A rural K-12 school district faced the challenge of integrating technology into the curriculum to enhance student learning and prepare them for the digital age (Hall & Hord, 2015). The district leadership recognized the need to overcome resistance to change, limited resources, and the lack of teacher training in technology integration (Hall & Hord, 2015). The superintendent and school board initiated a comprehensive change management plan (Hall & Hord, 2015). They engaged teachers, parents, and the community in the decision-making process and communicated the benefits of technology integration for student success (Hall & Hord, 2015). Professional development programs were designed to empower teachers with the necessary skills and knowledge (Fullan, 2014). Additionally, the district formed partnerships with local businesses and organizations to secure funding for technology resources (Hall & Hord, 2015). Consequently, over a two-year period, the district saw a significant increase in technology usage in classrooms (Hall & Hord, 2015). Student engagement and achievement improved, and the school gained recognition for its innovative practices (Hall & Hord, 2015). The collaborative approach to change management contributed to the successful implementation of technology integration (Fullan, 2014).

Implementing a Project-Based Learning (PBL) Approach

A middle school decided to transition from traditional teaching methods to a project-based learning approach to engage students more deeply in their studies (Boss, & Krauss, 2017). This shift aimed to enhance critical thinking, problem-solving skills, and student motivation (Boss, & Krauss, 2017; Thomas, 2010). Some effective leadership strategies include the following.

- Provided professional development opportunities for teachers to understand and implement PBL methodologies effectively (Boss, & Krauss, 2017).
- Established a mentorship program where experienced PBL practitioners supported their peers in adopting the new approach (Boss, & Krauss, 2017).

Leading Effectively for K-12 School Improvement

- Involved parents and the community in the transition process, addressing any concerns and showcasing the benefits of PBL (Thomas, 2010).
- Regularly assessed and adjusted the implementation strategy based on feedback from teachers, students, and parents (Boss, & Krauss, 2017).

Creating a Culturally Responsive Curriculum in an Urban School District

An urban K-12 school district with a diverse student population recognized the need for a more culturally responsive curriculum (Ladson-Billings, 2004). The existing curriculum did not adequately reflect the backgrounds and experiences of all students, leading to disengagement and underperformance among certain student groups (Ladson-Billings, 2004; Gay, 2010). The district superintendent, in collaboration with a diverse team of educators, parents, and community members, initiated a curriculum redesign project (Ladson-Billings, 2004). They conducted cultural audits to identify gaps and biases in the existing curriculum and engaged in professional development focused on cultural competence (Ladson-Billings, 2004). The leadership team also worked to ensure representation in decision-making processes, including curriculum selection (Ladson-Billings, 2004; Gay, 2010). Consequently, the implementation of a culturally responsive curriculum resulted in increased student engagement, improved academic performance, and a more inclusive learning environment (Ladson-Billings, 2004). Students reported feeling more connected to their education, and teachers noted a positive impact on classroom dynamics (Ladson-Billings, 2004).

STRATEGIES FOR LEADING CHANGE IN K-12 SCHOOLS

Leading change in K-12 schools is a complex endeavor that requires a multifaceted approach, taking into consideration the unique needs of students, educators, parents, and the broader community. Effective leadership in this context demands visionary thinking, collaboration, communication, and a deep understanding of educational practices and policies (Bryk et al., 2015). The following delves into various strategies for leading change in K-12 schools, drawing on scholarly literature and research.

Visionary Leadership

Establishing a clear and compelling vision for school improvement is paramount. Leaders must articulate a shared vision that aligns with stakeholders' aspirations and values (Kotter, 2006). At the heart of any successful change initiative in K-12 schools is visionary leadership. Leaders must articulate a clear and compelling vision for change that resonates with stakeholders (Fullan, 2007). This vision serves as a roadmap, guiding the change process and inspiring commitment among teachers, students, and parents. A well-defined vision provides a sense of direction and purpose, helping to align efforts and resources toward achieving desired outcomes (Kotter, 2006).

Figure 2. Unleashing your visionary mindset

Collaborative Decision-Making

Engaging teachers, parents, students, and community members in the change process fosters ownership and commitment. Collaborative decision-making promotes inclusivity and leverages diverse perspectives to inform change initiatives (Bryk & Schneider, 2002). Effective change leadership in K-12 schools emphasizes collaborative decision-making processes that involve all stakeholders. Leaders should create opportunities for teachers, parents, students, and community members to participate in discussions, share perspectives, and contribute to decision-making (Bryk et al., 2015). By fostering a culture of collaboration and inclusivity, leaders can harness the collective wisdom and expertise of stakeholders, leading to more informed and sustainable change initiatives.

Professional Learning Communities

Professional learning communities (PLCs) play a crucial role in facilitating change and improvement in K-12 schools. PLCs are collaborative networks of educators who work together to analyze student learning data, share best practices, and develop innovative instructional strategies (DuFour & Eaker, 2008). Leaders should invest in building and sustaining PLCs, providing educators with the time, resources, and support needed to collaborate effectively and continuously improve their practice.

Data-Informed Decision Making

Establishing robust mechanisms for monitoring progress and evaluating outcomes is essential. Leaders must employ data-driven decision-making processes, assess the effectiveness of change initiatives, and make necessary adjustments based on feedback and evidence (Hallinger, 2011). Data-driven decision-making is essential for leading change in K-12 schools. Leaders should collect, analyze, and utilize a variety of data sources to assess student performance, identify areas for improvement, and monitor progress toward goals (Supovitz & Taylor, 2005). By making informed decisions based on reliable data, leaders can allocate resources more effectively, implement evidence-based practices, and measure the impact of change initiatives.

Stakeholder Engagement

Engaging stakeholders in the change process is critical for building buy-in and fostering a sense of ownership among teachers, parents, students, and community members. Leaders should communicate transparently, solicit feedback, and involve stakeholders in planning, implementing, and evaluating change initiatives (Bryk et al., 2015). By valuing and respecting the perspectives of all stakeholders, leaders can cultivate a shared commitment to continuous improvement and positive change.

Capacity Building

Investing in ongoing professional development ensures that educators possess the knowledge, skills, and dispositions required to implement change effectively. Professional learning communities, mentorship programs, and targeted training initiatives support capacity building and continuous improvement (DuFour & Eaker, 2008). Building the capacity of educators and school staff is essential for leading change in K-12 schools. Leaders should invest in professional development opportunities, mentorship programs, and collaborative learning experiences that empower educators to adapt to new instructional practices, technologies, and policies (Fullan & Hargreaves, 2012). By fostering a culture of lifelong learning and growth, leaders can equip educators with the knowledge, skills, and dispositions needed to meet the evolving needs of students and drive meaningful change.

Adaptive Leadership

Change is inevitable in K-12 schools, and leaders must be prepared to navigate uncertainty, complexity, and resistance. Adaptive leadership involves recognizing challenges, fostering resilience, and mobilizing resources to address emerging issues and opportunities (Heifetz & Linsky, 2004). Leaders should cultivate flexibility, creativity, and resilience, encouraging stakeholders to embrace change as a catalyst for growth and improvement.

Summary

Leading change in K-12 schools requires a strategic, collaborative, and adaptive approach that prioritizes visionary leadership, stakeholder engagement, data-informed decision-making, and capacity building (Bryk et al., 2015). By embracing these strategies and leveraging the collective expertise and commitment of stakeholders, leaders can create learning environments that foster innovation, excellence, and equity for all students.

MANAGING RESISTANCE TO CHANGE IN K-12 SCHOOLS

Resistance to change is a natural phenomenon that leaders must anticipate and address proactively. According to Fullan (2001), managing resistance requires empathy, transparency, communication, and collaboration. Leaders should acknowledge concerns, solicit feedback, address misconceptions, and involve stakeholders in the change process to mitigate resistance and build buy-in (Kotter & Schlesinger, 1979). Change is an inevitable facet of the modern educational landscape. From curriculum reforms to technological integration and pedagogical shifts, K-12 schools are constantly evolving to meet the demands of a dynamic society. However, these changes are often met with resistance from various stakeholders, including teachers, administrators,

Leading Effectively for K-12 School Improvement

parents, and students. Understanding and managing this resistance is crucial for the successful implementation of any change initiative in K-12 schools.

Understanding Resistance to Change

Resistance to change can be defined as the reluctance or opposition to alterations in the status quo (Carnall, 2007). In the context of K-12 schools, resistance may arise due to a variety of reasons, including fear of the unknown, perceived threats to autonomy, concerns about increased workload, or skepticism about the efficacy of proposed changes (Fullan, 2007). Additionally, cultural and organizational factors within schools can contribute to resistance, such as entrenched beliefs, traditions, and established routines (Hargreaves, 2007).

Causes of Resistance

- *Fear of the Unknown*: Change often introduces uncertainty, leading stakeholders to feel anxious about potential outcomes (Kotter & Schlesinger, 1979). In K-12 schools, teachers may fear that new initiatives will disrupt established practices, jeopardize student outcomes, or increase their workload (Louis & Miles, 1990).
- *Threats to Autonomy*: Teachers and administrators value their professional autonomy and may resist changes perceived as top-down mandates that undermine their expertise (Smylie, 1995).
- *Lack of Involvement*: When stakeholders are not involved in the change process, they may feel marginalized or disempowered, leading to resistance (Bryk & Schneider, 2002).
- *Resource Constraints*: Limited resources, including time, funding, and training opportunities, can hinder the successful implementation of change initiatives, leading to skepticism and resistance (Darling-Hammond, 2000).

Strategies for Managing Resistance

- *Communication and Transparency*: Open and transparent communication is essential for addressing concerns, dispelling rumors, and building trust among stakeholders (Fullan, 2007). Schools should involve all stakeholders in the change process, providing opportunities for feedback, collaboration, and shared decision-making (Bryk & Schneider, 2002).

- *Professional Development*: Providing teachers and administrators with the necessary knowledge, skills, and resources to implement change effectively can mitigate resistance (Darling-Hammond, 2000). Professional development opportunities should be tailored to address specific needs and concerns, ensuring that stakeholders feel supported throughout the change process (Louis & Miles, 1990).
- *Leadership and Vision*: Effective leadership is crucial for managing resistance to change (Kotter, 2006). School leaders should articulate a clear vision for change, inspire stakeholders through shared goals and values, and demonstrate commitment to the successful implementation of new initiatives (Hargreaves, 2007).
- *Incentives and Rewards*: Recognizing and rewarding stakeholders for their contributions to change initiatives can foster a positive culture and mitigate resistance (Carnall, 2007). Incentives may include professional growth opportunities, increased autonomy, or tangible rewards such as grants or recognition awards (Smylie, 1995).
- *Pilot Programs and Phased Implementation*: Implementing changes through pilot programs or phased approaches allows schools to test new initiatives on a smaller scale, gather feedback, and make necessary adjustments before full-scale implementation (Fullan, 2007). This incremental approach can reduce resistance by addressing concerns and building confidence among stakeholders (Bryk & Schneider, 2002).

Summary

Managing resistance to change in K-12 schools requires a multifaceted approach that addresses the underlying causes of resistance while fostering collaboration, communication, and shared ownership of change initiatives (Carnall, 2007). By understanding the concerns and perspectives of stakeholders, providing necessary support and resources, and demonstrating strong leadership and vision, schools can navigate the complexities of change and create learning environments that prepare students for success in a rapidly evolving world (Hargreaves, 2007).

BUILDING CAPACITY FOR CHANGE IN K-12 SCHOOLS

Building capacity for change entails cultivating a supportive organizational culture, fostering distributed leadership, and promoting professional learning communities. According to Spillane (2006), developing collective efficacy, promoting collaboration, and distributing leadership responsibilities across various stakeholders enhance the organization's capacity to navigate complex change processes effectively. In the rapidly evolving landscape of K-12 education, the imperative for change is more pressing than ever. However, implementing meaningful change requires not just vision but also the capacity to enact it. Building capacity for change in K-12 schools is a multifaceted endeavor that involves stakeholders at various levels, encompasses diverse strategies, and hinges on fostering a culture conducive to innovation and improvement.

Understanding Capacity for Change

Capacity for change refers to the collective ability of a school or district to successfully implement and sustain transformative initiatives (Fullan, 2007). This capacity is not merely about resources or infrastructure but involves human, social, and organizational elements. It encompasses the skills, knowledge, attitudes, and behaviors necessary to navigate the complexities of change effectively.

Engaging Stakeholders

One of the foundational elements in building capacity for change is engaging stakeholders – educators, administrators, students, parents, and the broader community. Fullan (2001) emphasized the importance of distributed leadership, where leadership responsibilities are shared among multiple stakeholders rather than centralized. By involving various stakeholders in the change process, schools can harness collective expertise, cultivate ownership, and foster a shared vision for improvement.

Professional Learning and Development

Building educators' capacity through targeted professional learning and development is paramount. Andree et al. (2009) underscored the significance of ongoing, job-embedded professional development that is aligned with instructional goals and student needs. Professional learning communities (PLCs), collaborative inquiry, mentorship programs, and reflective practices are instrumental in enhancing teachers' pedagogical knowledge, instructional strategies, and adaptive expertise.

Curriculum and Instructional Innovation

To build capacity for change, schools must prioritize curriculum and instructional innovation that is relevant, engaging, and aligned with 21st-century skills (Compton & Wagner, 2012). This involves integrating technology, promoting project-based learning, fostering critical thinking, and nurturing socio-emotional learning. By reimagining curriculum and instruction, schools can better prepare students for an ever-changing world while empowering educators to adopt innovative pedagogical approaches.

Data-Informed Decision Making

Data-driven decision-making is integral to building capacity for change. By utilizing formative and summative assessment data, schools can identify areas for improvement, monitor progress, and make informed instructional decisions (Reeves, 2008). Establishing a culture of continuous improvement, where data is systematically collected, analyzed, and utilized, enables schools to align resources, tailor interventions, and evaluate the effectiveness of initiatives.

Cultivating a Culture of Collaboration and Innovation

Building a culture of collaboration, innovation, and continuous improvement is central to fostering capacity for change (DuFour & Eaker, 2008). Schools must create environments where risk-taking is encouraged, failure is viewed as an opportunity for learning, and innovation is celebrated. By nurturing collaborative partnerships, fostering open communication, and recognizing diverse perspectives, schools can create conditions conducive to transformative change.

Resource Allocation and Sustainability

Building capacity for change necessitates strategic resource allocation and long-term sustainability planning (Hargreaves & Shirley, 2009). Schools must invest in human capital, infrastructure, technology, and community partnerships while aligning resources with strategic priorities. Additionally, fostering a culture of sustainability involves establishing structures, processes, and practices that ensure initiatives are scalable, replicable, and enduring.

Figure 3. Collaborative and innovative environment

Summary

Building capacity for change in K-12 schools is a complex, multifaceted endeavor that requires a concerted effort from educators, administrators, students, parents, and the broader community. By engaging stakeholders, prioritizing professional learning, fostering curriculum and instructional innovation, utilizing data-informed decision-making, cultivating a culture of collaboration and innovation, and strategically allocating resources, schools can navigate the complexities of change effectively (Compton & Wagner, 2012). As Fullan (2007) aptly stated, "Change is a journey, not a blueprint," emphasizing the importance of building capacity, fostering resilience, and embracing continuous improvement in the ever-evolving landscape of K-12 education.

SUSTAINING CHANGE AND CONTINUOUS IMPROVEMENT IN K-12 SCHOOLS

Sustaining change requires long-term commitment, ongoing reflection, and continuous improvement efforts. Leaders must cultivate a culture of innovation, resilience, and adaptability, fostering conditions that enable the organization to respond proactively to emerging challenges and opportunities (Senge, 2000). Moreover, fostering a growth mindset, celebrating successes, learning from failures, and promoting a culture of continuous learning and improvement are essential components of sustaining change (Dweck, 2006). Sustaining change and promoting continuous improvement in K-12 schools is pivotal for ensuring the delivery of quality education that meets the evolving needs of students, educators, and the broader community. In an era characterized by rapid technological advancements, diverse student populations, and shifting educational paradigms, schools must remain agile, adaptable, and forward-thinking. This necessitates a strategic approach to change management and a commitment to ongoing improvement efforts.

The Importance of Sustaining Change

Sustaining change in K-12 schools goes beyond merely implementing new initiatives or programs; it involves embedding these changes into the fabric of the school culture and ensuring their longevity. According to Fullan (2007), sustainable change occurs when educational innovations become part of the school's routine practices and are supported by ongoing professional development, leadership, and community engagement. Without sustainability, schools risk reverting to old practices, thereby undermining efforts to improve student outcomes and foster innovation. One key factor in sustaining change is building a shared vision among stakeholders, including administrators, teachers, students, and parents. As Senge (2000) posits in "The Fifth Discipline," creating a shared vision fosters commitment, collaboration, and a collective sense of purpose, which are essential for sustaining change initiatives. Moreover, effective communication, transparent decision-making processes, and a culture of trust and collaboration are critical components of sustaining change efforts in K-12 schools (Bryk & Schneider, 2002).

Continuous Improvement: A Framework for Excellence

Continuous improvement is another essential aspect of fostering excellence in K-12 schools. Rooted in quality management principles, continuous improvement emphasizes ongoing assessment, reflection, and adaptation to enhance teaching and learning outcomes (Deming, 1996). By adopting a systematic approach to improvement, schools can identify areas of strength and weakness, implement evidence-based practices, and monitor progress over time. The United States, Plan-Do-Study-Act (PDSA) cycle, a cornerstone of continuous improvement, provides a structured framework for schools to test new ideas, assess their impact, and make data-informed decisions (Langley et al., 2009). By engaging stakeholders in collaborative inquiry and utilizing data to drive improvement efforts, schools can create a responsive learning environment that meets the diverse needs of students and prepares them for success in the 21st century.

Strategies for Sustaining Change and Continuous Improvement

- *Leadership and Vision*: Effective leadership is paramount in driving change and promoting continuous improvement. School leaders must articulate a compelling vision, establish clear goals, and provide the necessary support and resources to facilitate change (Leithwood & Riehl, 2003). By fostering a culture of innovation and collaboration, leaders can empower educators, students, and parents to contribute to improvement efforts and embrace new challenges.
- *Professional Development*: Investing in professional development is essential for equipping educators with the knowledge, skills, and dispositions needed to implement change and improve instructional practices (Andree et al., 2009). By offering ongoing professional learning opportunities, schools can cultivate a growth mindset among staff and promote a culture of continuous improvement.
- *Data-Informed Decision-Making*: Utilizing data to inform decision-making is crucial for identifying areas of need, monitoring progress, and evaluating the effectiveness of change initiatives (Midgley et al., 2007). By collecting and analyzing various forms of data, including student achievement, attendance, and stakeholder feedback, schools can make informed decisions and allocate resources strategically to support improvement efforts.
- *Stakeholder Engagement*: Engaging stakeholders, including teachers, students, parents, and community members, is essential for fostering buy-in, building trust, and promoting collaboration (Allensworth et al., 2010). By involving stakeholders in the decision-making process and soliciting their input and feedback, schools can create shared ownership of change initiatives and leverage collective expertise to drive improvement.

Summary

Sustaining change and promoting continuous improvement in K-12 schools require a strategic, collaborative, and data-driven approach (Dweck, 2006). By fostering effective leadership, cultivating a shared vision, investing in professional development, utilizing data to inform decision-making, and engaging stakeholders, schools can create a responsive learning environment that meets the diverse needs of students and prepares them for success in an ever-changing world (Langley et al., 2009). While challenges may arise, by prioritizing sustainability and continuous improvement, K-12 schools can navigate complex educational landscapes, overcome barriers to change, and achieve excellence in teaching and learning (Allensworth et al., 2010).

CONCLUSION

Leading and managing change for K-12 school improvement is a multifaceted endeavor that requires visionary leadership, collaborative decision-making, capacity building, and sustained commitment. By embracing evidence-based strategies, addressing challenges proactively, and fostering a culture of continuous improvement, educational leaders can navigate complex change processes effectively, ensuring equitable access to quality education for all students.

Moreover, managing change within K-12 schools necessitates a systemic approach that prioritizes stakeholder engagement, data-informed decision-making, and iterative feedback loops. Effective change management strategies emphasize the importance of communication, transparency, and inclusivity, ensuring that all stakeholders have a voice in shaping the change process (Fullan, 2016). By fostering a culture of trust, collaboration, and shared accountability, schools can mitigate resistance, promote buy-in, and cultivate a collective commitment to continuous improvement (Leithwood & Riehl, 2003).

In closing, leading and managing change within K-12 schools for improvement requires a synergistic approach that integrates visionary leadership, strategic management, stakeholder engagement, and a relentless focus on student-centered outcomes. As schools navigate the complexities of educational reform, adaptive leadership practices, transformative pedagogies, and inclusive decision-making processes emerge as essential catalysts for fostering innovation, enhancing student engagement, and cultivating a culture of excellence (Hohepa et al., 2019). By embracing a holistic, collaborative, and evidence-based approach to change leadership and management, K-12 schools can navigate uncertainty, capitalize on emerging opportunities, and realize their full potential as vibrant learning communities committed to educational excellence.

REFERENCES

Allensworth, E., Bryk, A. S., Easton, J. Q., Luppescu, S., & Sebring, P. B. (2010). *Organizing schools for improvement: Lessons from Chicago.* University of Chicago Press.

Andree, A., Darling-Hammond, L., Orphanos, S., Richardson, N., & Wei, R. C. (2009). *Professional learning in the learning profession: A status report on teacher development in the United States and abroad.* National Staff Development Council.

Baird, M. D., Hamilton, L. S., Pane, J. F., & Steiner, E. D. (2015). *Continued progress: Promising evidence on personalized learning.* RAND Corporation.

Barron, B., Cook-Harvey, C., Darling-Hammond, L., Flook, L., & Osher, D. (2020). Implications for educational practice of the science of learning and development. *Applied Developmental Science, 24*(2), 97–140. doi:10.1080/10888691.2018.1537791

Boss, S., & Krauss, J. (2017). *Reinventing project-based learning: Your field guide to real-world projects in the digital age.* ISTE.

Bryk, A. S., Gomez, L. M., & Grunow, A. (2015). *Getting ideas into action: Building networked improvement communities in education.* Carnegie Foundation for the Advancement of Teaching.

Bryk, A. S., & Schneider, B. (2002). *Trust in schools: A core resource for improvement.* Russell Sage Foundation.

Carnall, C. A. (2007). *Managing change in organizations* (5th ed.). Prentice Hall.

Compton, R. A., & Wagner, T. (2012). *Creating innovators: The making of young people who will change the world.* Scribner.

Darling-Hammond, L. (2000). Teacher quality and student achievement: A review of state policy evidence. *Education Policy Analysis Archives, 8*(1), 1–44. doi:10.14507/epaa.v8n1.2000

Darling-Hammond, L. (2019). *A license to teach: Building a profession for 21st century schools.* Routledge. doi:10.4324/9780429039928

Deming, W. E. (1996). *Out of the crisis.* MIT Press.

DuFour, R., & Eaker, R. (2008). *Professional learning communities at work: Best practices for enhancing student achievement.* Solution Tree.

DuFour, R., & Marzano, R. J. (2011). *Leadership for differentiating schools & classrooms.* Solution Tree Press.

Durlak, J. A., Dymnicki, A. B., Pachan, M., Payton, J., Schellinger, K. B., Taylor, R. D., & Weissberg, R. P. (2008). *The positive impact of social and emotional learning for kindergarten to eighth-grade students: Findings from three scientific reviews. In Collaborative for Academic, Social, and Emotional Learning.* CASEL.

Durlak, J. A., Dymnicki, A. B., Schellinger, K. B., Taylor, R. D., & Weissberg, R. P. (2011). The impact of enhancing students' social and emotional learning: A meta-analysis of school-based universal interventions. *Child Development, 82*(1), 405–432. doi:10.1111/j.1467-8624.2010.01564.x PMID:21291449

Dweck, C. S. (2006). *Mindset: The new psychology of success.* Random House.

Fadel, C., & Trilling, B. (2009). *21st century skills: Learning for life in our times.* Jossey-Bass.

Fullan, M. (2001). *Leading in a culture of change.* Jossey-Bass.

Fullan, M. (2007). *The new meaning of educational change* (4th ed.). Teachers College Press.

Fullan, M. (2014). *Leading in a Culture of Change.* John Wiley & Sons.

Fullan, M. (2016). *Indelible leadership: Always leave them learning.* Corwin Press.

Fullan, M. (2016). *The new meaning of educational change* (5th ed.). Teachers College Press.

Fullan, M., & Hargreaves, A. (2012). *Professional capital: Transforming teaching in every school.* Teachers College Press.

Gay, G. (2010). *Culturally responsive teaching: Theory, research, and practice.* Teachers College Press.

Hall, G. E., & Hord, S. M. (2015). *Implementing Change: Patterns, Principles, and Potholes.* Pearson.

Hallinger, P. (2011). Leadership for learning: Lessons from 40 years of empirical research. *Journal of Educational Administration*, *49*(2), 125–142. doi:10.1108/09578231111116699

Hargreaves, A. (2007). *Teaching in the knowledge society: Education in the age of insecurity*. Teachers College Press.

Hargreaves, A., & Shirley, D. (2009). *The fourth way: The inspiring future for educational change*. Corwin Press. doi:10.4135/9781452219523

Harris, A. (2004). Distributed leadership and school improvement: Leading or misleading? *Educational Management Administration & Leadership*, *32*(1), 11–24. doi:10.1177/1741143204039297

Harris, A., Hopkins, D., & Leithwood, K. (2008). *Seven strong claims about successful school leadership*. National College for School Leadership.

Heifetz, R. A., & Linsky, M. (2004). A survival guide for leaders. *Harvard Business Review*, *82*(6), 65–74. PMID:12048995

Hohepa, M., Lloyd, C., & Robinson, V. M. (2019). *School leadership and student outcomes: Identifying what works and why*. Australian Council for Educational Research (ACER).

Jantzi, D., & Leithwood, K. (2005). A review of transformational school leadership research 1996–2005. *Leadership and Policy in Schools*, *4*(3), 177–199. doi:10.1080/15700760500244769

Kotter, J. P. (2006). *Leading change*. Harvard Business School Press.

Kotter, J. P., & Schlesinger, L. A. (1979). Choosing strategies for change. *Harvard Business Review*, *57*(2), 106–114. PMID:10240501

Ladson-Billings, G. (2004). The Dreamkeepers: Successful Teachers of African American Children. *The Journal of Negro Education*, *63*(4), 530–543.

Ladson-Billings, G. (2006). From the achievement gap to the education debt: Understanding achievement in U.S. schools. *Educational Researcher*, *35*(7), 3–12. doi:10.3102/0013189X035007003

Langley, G. J., Moen, R. D., Nolan, K. M., Nolan, T. W., Norman, C. L., & Provost, L. P. (2009). *The improvement guide: A practical approach to enhancing organizational performance* (2nd ed.). Jossey-Bass.

Leithwood, K., & Louis, K. S. (2011). *Learning from leadership: Investigating the links to improved student learning*. Center for Applied Research and Educational Improvement.

Leithwood, K., & Riehl, C. (2003). *What we know about successful school leadership*. Laboratory for Student Success, Temple University.

Louis, K. S., & Miles, M. B. (1990). *Improving the urban high school: What works and why*. Teachers College Press.

Matuchniak, T., & Warschauer, M. (2010). New technology and digital worlds: Analyzing evidence of equity in access, use, and outcomes. *Review of Research in Education, 34*(1), 179–225. doi:10.3102/0091732X09349791

Merryfield, M. M. (2002). *Teaching about international conflicts: Education, theory, and practice*. Peter Lang.

Midgley, S., Stringfield, S., & Wayman, J. C. (2007). *Leadership for data-based decision making: Collaborative educator teams*. Teachers College Press.

Partnership for 21st Century Learning. (2015). *P21 framework definitions*. Retrieved from https://www.p21.org/storage/documents/docs/P21_Framework_Definitions_New_Logo_2015.pdf

Prensky, M. (2001). Digital natives, digital immigrants part 1. *On the Horizon, 9*(5), 1–6. doi:10.1108/10748120110424816

Reeves, D. (2008). *Leading change in your school: How to conquer myths, build commitment, and get results*. ASCD.

Reimer, T., Reiser, B. J., & Spillane, J. P. (2002). Policy implementation and cognition: Reframing and refocusing implementation research. *Review of Educational Research, 72*(3), 387–431. doi:10.3102/00346543072003387

Santoro, N. (2017). *Challenging racial silences in Australian schools*. Springer.

Senge, P. M. (2000). *The fifth discipline: The art and practice of the learning organization*. Doubleday/Currency.

Sergiovanni, T. J. (2001). *The principalship: A reflective practice perspective*. Allyn & Bacon.

Smylie, M. A. (1995). Teacher learning in the workplace: Implications for school reform. In T. R. Guskey & M. Huberman (Eds.), *Professional development in education: New paradigms and practices* (pp. 199–218). Teachers College Press.

Leading Effectively for K-12 School Improvement

Spillane, J. P. (2006). *Distributed leadership*. Jossey-Bass.

Supovitz, J. A., & Taylor, B. Y. (2005). The search for productive professional development. *Phi Delta Kappan, 87*(3), 194–200.

Thomas, J. W. (2010). *A review of research on project-based learning*. Autodesk Foundation.

Tomlinson, C. A. (2014). *The differentiated classroom: Responding to the needs of all learners*. ASCD.

Chapter 2
Making Schools Effective:
21st Century School Leaders' Agenda

Reginah Ndlovu
University of Zimbabwe, Zimbabwe

ABSTRACT

The 21st century dispensation has brought a lot of challenges in developing countries such as Zimbabwe that have resulted in schools becoming ineffective. The study was prompted by the need for schools to prepare students to meet the demands of an emerging digital world. The change management theory was used with the aim to inform the changes which are taking place in 21st century schools. The corpus of the study has been published works for the years 2011 to 2014. The Nziramasanga Commission, which informs the basis of Zimbabwean education, was also studied.

INTRODUCTION

Globally the education sector has been affected by radical changes which have been brought about by the technological era. The 21st century twist has brought a new trend in education due to availability of powerful technologies which give way to critical thinking as well as problem solving in students. There is no country which can subsist in isolation in the face of a rapidly changing world. It is only those education systems which will transform their education systems which will remain relevant in the new technological dispensation. Given this, Zimbabwe's education system demands to be reviewed as well as transformed in the provision of quality education in order to remain abreast with the times. This calls for change in the system of governance in the whole

DOI: 10.4018/978-1-7998-3940-8.ch002

Copyright © 2024, IGI Global. Copying or distributing in print or electronic forms without written permission of IGI Global is prohibited.

Making Schools Effective

sector. There is need to redefine the roles and expectations of leadership in order to develop in students skills which are going to keep up with the 21st century. This study investigated works which have been published on Zimbabwean education through the lens of Kotter's change management theory. The review is made using the 21st century pillar of education called creativity. The study focused on the research question: How can schools be made effective in the 21st century? The study assumes that if school leaders are empowered with the necessary and sufficient competencies schools would be made effective in the 21st century. The characteristics of 21st century education would be discussed. Change management would also be defined.

BACKGROUND AND RATIONALE OF THE STUDY

This section gives the background of the study.

Article 26 of the United Nations Declaration of Human Rights recognises the right to education. Just because many countries are a signatory to the United Nations, this makes education compulsory in some countries. Subsequently UNESCO draws from this right to come up with four pillars of education on which education should be hinged. These are learning to know, learning to do, learning to live together and learning to be. (Oloniram, 2016). All these pillars are important in the 21st century learning as they make the student understand the world better and turn him into a responsible human being. Consequently Zimbabwe crafted its own education Act from these pillars. In order to understand the reforms which took place in Zimbabwean education there is need to understand its development from the colonial period. This is because some of the problems the system is facing now were inherited from the colonial era.

Zimbabwe has invested so much on education with the literacy rate reaching 91,4% (UNESCO, 2009). Between 1992 and 1999 the literacy rates of those who were between 15 and 24 years only went up to 98%. This came about as a result of the policy of Education For All which the government introduced soon after the country gained its Independence in 1980.(UNESCO,2009)This was meant to redress the inequalities which existed in colonial education where the British colonisers education system denied the Blacks opportunities to participate in education which was meant to make them economically sound. Foreign education had a hegemonic effect on the education system and was meant to dehumanise Africans. Local knowledge was devalued and deemed inferior. The education system either prepared indigenous Africans to take control of their social, cultural and economic lives but did more than corrupt

27

their thinking and sensibilities as Africans.(Shizha, 2005). For nearly a century when Zimbabwe was under colonial rule the majority of indigenous people had no say or influence on government policies and political decisions that affected the education system. (Zvobgo, 1996). This saw a dramatic increase in the number of learners enrolled in the education sector because primary education was declared free. As a result of this acceleration the government was faced with a situation whereby the demand for the construction of more schools, provision of books as well as the training of teachers rose rapidly. The rationale behind the Education For All policy was to tackle the quantity first which was later going to be followed by quality. Commenting on the access to education in Zimbabwe, the Transitional National Development Plan (1983,p.27) highlights that,

"Government recognises that education is a basic human right. It also recognises that education is an investment in human capital which sustains and accelerates the rate of economic growth and socioeconomic development. The challenge for Zimbabwe is not only one of redressing the educational qualitative and quantitative imbalances in the inherited system but also that of meeting the exceedingly large demands with limited resources."

The rapid expansion meant that the country became constraint in resources. It is against this backdrop that the Education For All policy was backtracked. After the rethinking of this socialist ideology tuition fees were introduced. This led to the birth of such policies as the Structural Adjustment Programme ESAP and Zimbabwe Programme for Economic and Social Transformation among others. (Shizha and Kariwo, 2011) Effective implementation of some of these policies was also hindered by lack of finances. As a result these challenges saw a decline in the education turnaround which was hailed by most countries and regarded as a miracle. The bold and aggressive move which was taken by the government is commendable.

These gains were later immensely affected by brain drain which resulted from massive teacher exodus due to poor salaries. Rodney (1982, p. 263) reports that,

Education is crucial in any type of society for the preservation of the lives of its members and the maintenance of the social structure...The most crucial aspect of pre-colonial African education was its relevance to Africans in sharp contrast with that which was later introduced (that is, under colonialism)... [T]he main purpose of colonial school system was to train Africans to participate in the domination of exploitation of the continent as a whole... Colonial education was education for subordination, exploitation, the creation of mental confusion and the development of underdevelopment.

Making Schools Effective

To this end there was need to redress the colonial imbalances which were at play during the colonial era. This is because the role of education is not to passively follow and react to trends. Education has to play a leading role in societal development. Accordingly, in January 1998 President Robert Mugabe appointed a 12 member committee which was led by Dr Caiaphas Nziramasanga to enquire on Zimbabwe's education system. According to the Term of Reference 2.1.2 of the enquiry the committee was mandated to "address more specifically areas in the education and training system requiring reform on short term, medium term and long term basis (Government of Zimbabwe, 1999). This led to the production of a 644 page report which was presented to the President in August 1999.This report contained the committee's findings on educational matters as well as the challenges which were hindering progress in the education system. Recommendations which were meant to be a guide for the education system were elaborately spelled out. These were meant to be a guide into the New Millenium.Term of Reference 1.2 mandated the committee to enquire and make some recommendations on "the basic principles and philosophy of Zimbabwe's educational and training needs and aspirations on the eve of the 21st century and having regard to the challenges of a competitive global environment in the information age. (Government of Zimbabwe, 1999).

This study reviews the following chapters of this report: Chapter 2 of the Nziramasanga Report which is entitled "Education for the 21st century"(Chapter 2 Pages 21-32), Chapter 3 entitled "Provision of Education (Chapter 3, Pages 34-59), Chapter 12 entitled "Curriculum and structure" (Chapter 12 Page 232-259), Chapter14 entitled "Primary Education"(Chapter 14 Pages 287-296).Recommendations which were made by this commission are reviewed in order to see whether they have been implemented or not.What prompted this study is the observation that recommendations which were made by past commissions in the colonial era such as Lewis commission, Judges commission, Fox commission as well as Kerr commission were only partly implemented by the British coloniser.(Government of Zimbabwe, 1999). This concern was raised by the Lewis Taylor committee (p.3),

"are all aware that in respect of any report prepared by an independent body on behalf of a government- however acceptable the report may be in principle- only some recommendations be immediately implementable and some for good reasons of which the recommenders were not cognisant, are not relevant or cannot be implemented.

In light of the above, the study is organised around investigating the implementation of the recommendations which were made in the studies which have been carried out in education. The successes and challenges which have been faced in the implementation of the recommendations would be illustrated. More specifically, recommendations which were made in other works which have been published in Zimbabwean education system would also be explored in line with the Nziramasanga Report. This study was also prompted by the relevance and the quality of the education which is being offered by Zimbabwe in the 21st century. There is need not only to reform but to restructure the education as well as the training of teachers so that the country meets the challenges which are brought by the 21st century. Gladwell (2002, p.259) makes a case that, "We are powerfully influenced by our surroundings, our immediate context and the personalities of those around us." A lot of extensive studies have been carried out in the education system but the question is "Have the recommendations been implemented?" There are a plethora of challenges which are bedevilling the current education system and this gives the researcher another reason to analyse the recommendations which have been made by the previous studies to see if reference can be made to them or if they can be revisited with the application of proper change management theories.

In a bid to transform the current education system the Ministry of Primary and Secondary education developed a curriculum framework which goes from 2015 through to 2022.It is a plan for the transformation of education system. This came as a response to the Nziramasanga commission recommendations which were made in 1999.The curriculum framework requires students to be exposed to life skills which are going to make them relevant in the world. This is a shift from the academically oriented curriculum to a technologically and vocationally based curriculum. It advocates that theory knowledge would not be enough, there is need to develop critical and higher order thinking skills. However innovations which take place in the education sector are imperative and will only be effective if they are based on research and also imbued with a 21st century discourse of education.

LITERATURE REVIEW

This section explores literature on the studies which have been conducted in Zimbabwean education. Extensive studies have been carried out in Zimbabwean education sector.

Making Schools Effective

Nyagura et al (1993) carried out a study on quantitative development in Zimbabwean education and access to quality education. In this study he points out that although quantity has been achieved those communities which are poor continue to struggle in terms of the quality of teachers they receive, materials and facilities. Rural community primary schools have more dropouts, oldest pupils, poor teacher accommodation, high teacher-pupil ratios, heavy teaching loads and poorly educated parents in communities where the schools are situated. Nyagura (1996b). The same study provides evidence that schools run by female heads tend to be more effective than schools headed by males. It laments that the sector has failed to keep its qualified personnel due to poor salaries as well as conditions of service. This has led to a decline in the quality of education in Zimbabwe.

Another study which has been conducted on Zimbabwean education was done by Ncube (2004) on the efficiency of rural day secondary schools. It set out to look into the efficiency of rural schools. It cites the factors which lead to dropout rates and low pass rates. Findings of this study indicate that there is low efficiency in rural schools. The percentage of dropouts is higher from Form one to Form four. Pass rate at O level is also very low owing to lack of resources as well as non payment of fees. BSPZ was cited as the most effective programme which was introduced to improve the results. The study goes on to recommend more funding which should be channelled towards rural schools. This could assist in building laboratories and libraries. He calls upon re engineering of the curriculum so that it may suit the rural child.

Another study which was carried out was conducted by Zanamwe (2013) on the use of social networks in developing Zimbabwe. The study indicates that most learners use Facebook and My space. These are used for educative purposes mainly to conduct group work. The study indicates that these social skills enhance education by helping them to communicate in different ways with other people across the world. He points out that there is heated debate on whether these should be used for educative purposes.

Colcough et al (1990) also conducted a study on localisation of the curriculum. If minority languages are left out this could make the progress slow in advancing towards globalisation. Colcough et al (1990, p.66)

It is necessary to recruit more teacher trainees from minority tribes if curriculum relevance and localisation of the curriculum is going to have any meaning at all in these areas. These students would then be used as resource persons in the curriculum design and materials development that incorporate their local languages and cultures.

These sentiments are valid to facilitate the smooth cascade of the curriculum into all the corners of the country. There is need to involve all stakeholders in designing of a new curriculum. Policy change should look into this.

This section explores some of the literature which has been carried out on Zimbabwe's education system. Previous studies have been mainly focused on how Zimbabwe's education has progressed from the colonial era while the proposed chapter looks at Zimbabwe's education system from a change management perspective. This study seeks to contribute to the existing body of knowledge. To the researcher's knowledge there is no study which has been carried out to investigate change management in the education system of Zimbabwe. The study therefore fills the gap. The study differs from the studies which have been carried out so far by its aim to interrogate and unveil the proper implementation of change theories in the changes which have been made in Zimbabwe's education system. It sought to understand how education is affected by changes as well as determining the impact of the changes which have been made. The study sought to study the trends which occur in the previous researches. The assumption is that these would reflect how Zimbabweans embrace change in order to face the challenges of the 21st century. It adds to the existing body of knowledge as well as informing the Zimbabweans, Parliamentarians, heads of schools, teachers, policy makers and the whole body of leaders in the education sector. From the researcher's knowledge there is very little literature on change management in Zimbabwe's education system This is the lacuna which the study fills.

CHANGE MANAGEMENT

In order to bring about positive change leaders should devise ways of implementing as well as promoting change in schools.De Jager (2001, p.24) states that,

Change is a simple process. At least, it's simple to describe. It occurs whenever we replace the old with the new. Change is about travelling from the old to the new leaving yesterday behind in exchange for the new tomorrow. But implementing change is incredibly difficult so people are reluctant to leave the familiar behind. We are all suspicious about the unfamiliar, we are naturally concerned about how we get from the old to the new, especially if it involves learning something new and risking failure.

Making Schools Effective

This view implies that a whole range of people's competencies and abilities are affected by change and this is what makes people feel insecure about adopting change. In order for schools to thrive in the 21st century leaders ought to know how to lead and manage change (Small-business.chron.com, 2017). Change does not happen by accident but it is planned. The most important aspect in change management is the focus which it gives to people. This is so because whenever change is implemented people are the ones who are responsible for the initiation of positive change.

Change makes people accept new values as well as processes and technologies. With the new inventions in the world, technology is the powerful force which shapes the future. Change can be prompted by some external factors such as the political, social economic or technological factor. These factors will dictate the pace at which change takes place. Some of the factors which can influence change are internal and these are policies and systems. As such people who are involved in the change process should all understand the roles which they play. In the education system the President of any country has a critical role as the custodian of the constitution. It is the constitution which will be interpreted and give birth to the Education Act. Members of Parliament are lobbyists who lobby for changes in the Education Act. The cabinet ministers are policy makers. A board of management depending on whether the school is a Trust school, government school or local authority runs the schools and has a role to play on the procurement of resources. School heads or Principals are the key players who are at the core of the change process. When the goals have been set, it is the school head who directs the achievement of these goals.

Union leaders can be effective in reforms being made in education. In order for the implementations to be done smoothly there is need for the involvement of Unions at all important decision making stages. If the Unions are involved they encourage their members to support the change initiative because the integration of technologies greatly affects the traditional roles as well as the responsibilities of teachers who can end up resisting the changes. Since they are the catalysts of change, unions can adopt a position of encouraging them all the way in the integration of technology into the curriculum. The Curriculum Development Unit (CDU) is responsible for designing the curriculum. The parents as well as the learners should be involved because they are the ones who are going to be impacted by the change. It is important that they understand the change initiative as it will directly affect them. The business community needs to understand the change initiative as well because the learners who are going to be produced are going to be absorbed by this sector. Their input on the kind of workers they expect to employ in the 21st century is very important. These roles and expectations should be made aware to every stakeholder for the smooth transition of change management. Whether these changes affect them at a personal or professional capacity, all these stakeholders need to give their voice in the change initiative so that there could be no stage which is going to face some form of resistance. The recipients of change who are the teachers should not be left out. Lowendahl and Revange (1998, p.755) asserts that,

In this context [change agents] need to go beyond the theoretical lenses and paradigms they have been trained in to explore the implications of these changes at a more fundamental level....[change agents] need to refocus attention on the underlying assumptions in order to explore their areas of applicability and the limits to the relevance.

Just because the changes do not impact them on their personal lives but have a bearing on their work, they have to fully understand the nature of the change. The education system should take a holistic approach. Contributions of students should be invited to allow for the fulfillment of UNESCO's mission as the 21st century is drawing to an end. Given this, it is the responsibility of all these leaders to strive towards a shared vision and support it. Educational planning should not come in as a way of resolving an imminent crisis but the planning should be systematically done as a way of projecting into the future which is not so remote. Reflections on the current and the future generation should provide the changes which are to be made in the education system.

21st CENTURY AGENDA

There is need to define what an agenda is. An agenda is a list of items which are to be dealt with in a meeting. The 21st century agenda is a plan for action on how a country can implement some changes in order to meet the challenges of the New Millennium. In this study published works will be explored to come up with the themes which are going to serve to inform the leaders on the way forward. These themes would develop a 21st century vision and would thus be defined as the agenda for the 21st century.

The 20th century education was teacher centered. The teacher was the sole provider of knowledge. The learning process was passive and the methods used were drills, memorisation, rote learning. The 21st century is an era of transformations as well as changes in the world. It is said to have "begun on

Making Schools Effective

January 1 2001 and will end on December 31, 2100"(United states Naval Observatory) link

The emergence of the new technologies has led to innovations as well as creativity in the world. Drucker (2001, p. 95) describes the transition which is taking place as " Profound Transition- and the changes are more radical perhaps than even those that ushered in the "Second Industrial Revolution" of the middle of the 19th century. Agreeably Martin (2006) describes the 21st century as the era which has changed everything we do. The period is termed the information age because of the technological revolution which revolves around the rise in the use of computers and communication technologies. In order to prepare students for the 21st century education there is need to develop skills which are necessary. 21st century students should be critical thinkers and also be problem solving. This is so because the world is ever changing and problems are ever arising. Workforce (2007,p.17) maintains that, "Our core problem is that our education training systems were built for another era, an era in which most workers needed only a rudimentary education." As such complex problems we have never conceived will arise in future. Students need to be equipped with ability to take risks in order to be able to navigate through the terrains of the 21st century. .

Creativity is another 21st century skill which needs to be developed in students. Students need to be empowered to think creatively in order to be able to express themselves in a unique way. They should be able to face some challenges and figure out on their own how to solve them. This makes the students discover their unique capabilities. This is the skill which informs this research. Analytic thinking is another 21st century skill which needs to be developed in students. They should be able to see from different perspectives and from different angles. These skills are going to help students even when they leave school to be able to make effective decisions. Collaboration is another critical skill. Digital students are social and they mingle a lot. They are well connected to the world. Communication so the ability to communicate in all forms of communication modes. They need this skill in order to be able to build relationships. These skills are very important for the students future successes.

CORPUS

The corpus of the study is made up of published works in Zimbabwean education between 2000 and 2019.This period was chosen because it is the 21st century era. The period is a fertile ground for such a study as the recommendations made are within the 21st century. The researcher investigates the reviews using Kotter's change management theory.

The published works used in this study are shown in the table below;

Table 1. Literature

2011	Teacher Competence in ICT: Implications for Computer Education in Zimbabwean Secondary Schools	Mubika and Bukaliya
2013	Barriers to effective integration of information and communication technology in Harare secondary schools.	Nyaruwata et al
2014	Challenges facing University education in Zimbabwe.	Majoni, C.
2014	Zimbabwe Two pathway education curriculum.	Pedzisai et al
1999	Nziramasanga Report	Nziramasanga, C et al

OBJECTIVES

The study is guided by the following objectives:

To examine challenges faced by school leaders during educational change.
To investigate the role and competencies of a school leader to cope with change.
To explain ways in which leaders can be empowered to meet the educational challenges of the 21stcentury.
Schools can be made effective in the 21st century by empowering the leaders.

QUESTIONS

In its analysis of making schools effective in the 21st century the study focuses on the following research questions:

What are the challenges faced by school leaders during educational change?
What are the competencies required for a school leader to cope with change?
How can leaders be empowered to meet the educational challenges of the 21st century?
How can schools be made effective in the 21st century?

Making Schools Effective

THEORETICAL FRAMEWORK

The study uses Kotter's eight step change model to analyse the published works.Dr John Paul Kotter in his book Leading change explains the eight important steps which need to be followed when transforming an organisation. In this model Kotters emphasis is on leading rather than managing change. Kotter (1996) suggested sequences of actions that organisations can adopt (Pettigrew and Whip, 1993).

The first step is to establish a sense of urgency. Change begins with employees when after evaluating the competitive situation from their competitors they begin to see the need for change. Kotter (1995, p.430) posits that "Bold or risky actions normally associated with good leadership are generally required for creating a strong sense of urgency." The recipients of change must first understand the need for change for them to effectively implement the change. The first is considered as the most critical step which should be handled aggressively. A lot of measures can be employed to put the message across clearly to the recipients of change. Kotter (1996, p.44) also recommends the use of consultants as a tactic for creating a sense of urgency and challenge the status quo in order to make it possible for the recipients of change to see the need for change, Newspapers, radios and televisions can be used to put the message across.

The urgency put across to the employee should be that if the change does not take place they stand to perish. This does not only prepare the employee for the imminent change but it makes him see the difference between the current situation and the envisioned one. If different messages are used to persuade the employee the message is not only communicated but the employee would be committed to the change. Apathy is conveyed if there is little interaction regarding change thus deeming it unimportant. Jansen (2004). Most importantly is the need to have expectations when one approaches the employees in order to convince them that change is possible. If the employees are made to see the attractiveness of the change a positive attitude would be created in them. However at this stage the leader should not underestimate the fear and the anger which exists because it can be difficult to drive people out of their comfort zones. Risk taking can be paralysing.

Step 2: Create a Guiding Coalition

If only one person tries to push the initiative change may not be successful. Kotter (1996, p.52) states that, "No one person is capable of single handily leading and managing the change process in an organisation." There is need to build a team by bringing together people and assigning them roles and responsibilities which they have to report on. Putting together the right guiding coalition of people to lead a change initiative is critical to its success. These people have to be people with positions of authority and enough expertise. They should be respected by the other workers and should have leadership qualities. Kotter (1996, p.58) maintains that, "Guiding coalition with good managers and poor leaders will not succeed."However there are some opposing views which say that just because the model is sequentially ordered it makes it daunting for all the steps to be followed. Kotters (1996, p.26) Others say that there is need to build multiple coalitions in order to deal with different phases of the change process. The researcher argues that careful following of these steps is a systematic way of implementing change so every step needs to be closely followed.

Step 3: Develop a Vision and Strategy

It is the vision which steers people into the right direction. The vision should not be complicated but should give a clear picture of the future. Creating a clearly defined vision makes it easy for the workers to not only understand but to also act on the vision. Kotter (1996, p.68). An effective vision is essential in breaking the status quo and looking beyond the immediate goals of the organisation. A clear vision will make the workers see beyond the current situation and to address long term issues in the present. Kotter (1996, p.67) states that, "The vision should therefore be desirable so that it appeals to the long term interest of employees, customers, shareholders and others who have a stake in the enterprise."

Step 4: Communicate the Change

This seeks to address anxieties as well as confusion, anger and remove distrust. Communication should not only be simple but should be heartfelt. There is need to contently communicate the new vision to both the workers and the stakeholders especially those who will be impacted by the vision. It is not enough to communicate the vision but it is also important to listen to them as well. This is a very crucial step because if communication is inadequate it may be impossible for the employees to get to see some opportunities. If the leader discusses changes which are taking place with the workers as the vision unfolds this involvement would remove frustrations and make them feel that they are a part of the vision. Kotter (1996, p.90) asserts that "Two way communication is always more powerful than one way communication."

Step 5: Empower Broad-Based Action

There is need to give the employees opportunities to try out some new ideas as well as approaches. Obstacles which may lie on the way have to be removed. Creating team ownership and a bottom up or empowered employee base is important to help an organisation transform successfully (Paper etal, 2001) If the workers are given an opportunity for empowerment it can give them a sense of control over the change process and help move the change effort along (Kappelman et al, 1993).

Step 6: Generate Short-Term Wins

In order for workers not to be discouraged the leader has to recognise those employees who achieve periodic wins. These small victories are the ones which create self confidence and belief that bigger successes are possible and this builds up the momentum towards the longer term goals (Peters, 2002). These small victories should thus be celebrated and rewarded in order to provide direction that the vision is on the right direction. Kotter (1996, p.122) states that, "Short term wins demonstrate that the change is paying off. The leader should model the behaviour which the employees should emulate."

Step 7: Consolidate Gains and Produce More Change

Victory should not be declared prematurely because the vision has to be pushed until it is fulfilled. The reputation of short term should be used to continue bringing about changes. The unnecessary previous steps that are no longer necessary should be eliminated. In ridding oneself of the tasks that wear you down the leader can delegate some duties.

Step 8: Making Change Stick

A new and supportive organisational culture should be created in order for the change to remain. A supportive culture will provide new shared values as well as social norms. If the new behaviours are not consolidated they are likely to vanish.

This has been universally adopted as a change model. Opposing views say that the model is prescriptive because of the sequential order in the steps to be followed. Again they say it cannot be applied in all the transformations. The researcher argues that the steps are clear and easy to follow hence it is a working model.

The theory is relevant for this study because it spells out explicitly the steps which need to be followed for changes to be successful. Most organisations fail to implement changes because of wrong approaches. The theory helps the researcher to analyse the themes in order to come up with a clear agenda on how schools can be made effective in the 21st century.

ANALYSING PUBLISHED WORKS ON CHANGE MANAGEMENT IN ZIMBABWEAN EDUCATION

This section focuses on analysis of the recommendations which were made by some scholars on Zimbabwean education.The analysis answers the questions which guide this research. The published works are analysed using Kotter's change management theory. The analysis is done using themes which are emerging in the published works. The review is founded on creativity as a pillar of 21st century education. It is noted that most researches which are done end up facing stillbirth. The analysis unveils how much has been done as far as the implementation of the concerned recommendations has been done. The researcher adopts an interpretive approach in order to fully understand and comprehend implementation of change management in Zimbabwean education. Creasy (2007,p.2) asserts that, "Change itself is a reaction to an opportunity, challenge or an event that sets in motion the path for change." Kanter,Stem and Jick() defines change as " …. the shift in behaviour of the whole organisation." The study investigates whether the changes which have taken place in Zimbabwean education are bound to produce a shift in behaviour.

Curriculum

This section explores Kotter's change management theory on the way changes have been made in the Zimbabwean curriculum. Since the attainment of Independence Zimbabwe has made some changes in the curriculum. The Nziramasanga commission observed that Zimbabwean education was based on the academic and did not prepare the student for the global world. Recommendations were made that; Nziramasanga Article 1.1 " The twenty first century education and training policy makers should bear in mind the future will be dominated by globalisation and that Zimbabwe will be part of a global community….Therefore we must prepare well for the world

Making Schools Effective

that we, and especially our children are going to live in."In light of this the commission recommended a skills based curriculum which would move from the academic to include the 21st century as well as vocational skills. With the 21st century in mind it also recommended that the rural schools be electrified on the eve of the 21st century. The researcher notes that these recommendations are prevalent in the other published works which call for a skills based curriculum to prepare for the 21st century.

All this is an effort to advance changes in light of the 21st century. Although these other researches echo the same sentiments, of interest is the Nziramasanga report. According to Kotter after these recommendations were made a sense of urgency was to be created where people should have been informed about the urgent need for change in the curriculum on the 21st century eve to produce students who are going to be creative and empowered with skills that would make them effective and digitally proficient. There was no state of urgency which was created towards the change of the curriculum. The commission also recommended an establishment of a body that would look into th implementation of the recommendations made by the commision. According to Kotter's change management theory, the commission was advocating for a guiding coalition which was going to be made up of people with expertise. Sadly this was not put in place. The changes from this commission were only implemented fifteen years later when the New curriculum was introduced. Due to financial constraint the rural schools could not be electrified. Years after these recommendations the curriculum remained unchanged and the findings suffered a stillbirth. Coltart (2012,p.2)states that, " One of the key concerns about our education system has been the bias for academic subjects and the resultant failure of our education system to prepare students adequately for Zimbabwe's economy. The researcher notes that other factors which could impede implementation are the parents who opt for an academic curriculum. The education sector has thus been preoccupied with an examination oriented curriculum. The researcher further argues that what makes parents opt for an academic curriculum is the omission of some of the change management stages. Lack of adequate information will not make them see the need as well as the urgency for change. This bears testimony to the theory. The 21st century vision broadly lies with policy makers. Parents are stakeholders who impacted by the change so their acceptance will depend on how much they know about the desired change.

Some scholars cite a number of factors Bennie and New stead (2001,p.1) states that " They include issues of time, parental expectations, public examinations, unavailability of required materials, lack of clarity about curriculum reform, teachers' lack of skills and knowledge and the limited mismatch between the teacher's residual ideologies and the principles underlying the curriculum innovation." Through the lens of this theory the researcher argues that if the steps in change management are followed even the parents will leave their comfort zones. Despite the recommendations which emerge in all these reviews the past fifteen years seem to have witnessed slow progress in attempts by policymakers to implement change. However at the implementation of the curriculum some of the tenets of the theory are at play as public consultations were made and these involved stakeholders who were afforded an opportunity to contribute towards the curriculum. These consultations were held in all the provinces. At this stage a guiding coalition was created and the vision was cascaded to all the social facets. This is the position which should have been taken when the recommendations were made. A close look at the tenets of this theory shows that although extensive consultations were made and the change was communicated certain crucial steps of change management were omitted. People were not empowered. As such there are no textbooks and the resources are limiting and slowing down the progress of the curriculum. Rural schools which do not have electricity and textbooks are having a difficult time. This has resulted in pressure in learners, students, teachers as well as parents. It is the process of implementation which has lasting consequences. If the plan is correctly implemented, that is, following the change tenets then it becomes easy for the goals to be fulfilled in no time.

Lack of Infrastructure

Another emerging theme is lack of infrastructure. This section presents an agenda for leaders on how to make the school environments effective for the 21st century.

The most important asset for any community are the buildings. The challenge for the 21st century is not to make stimulating but rewarding environments as well. The theme which runs across is that most schools lack enabling environments to intergrate the creativity which is required in students. This has an impact on the students and limits the ambitions of the students. Buildings are not only difficult to build but they are also expensive to maintain. Erecting new classrooms can take several years and can be expensive. Most of the classrooms which are found in schools were built for the traditional curriculum which was characterised by teachercenterd lessons and the teaching space was dedicated.Just because the teacher was the sole provider of knowledge, the teaching space was also specialised. The equipment and facilities were fixed as they were meant to serve a defined curriculum.

Making Schools Effective

With the advent of the 21ˢᵗ century through bringing technology into the classroom as well as online learning opportunities which enhance education in the 21ˢᵗ century most schools do not seem to have adequate infrastructure which is needed to support digital education. Each school has got budgetary demands. Just because building can be expensive, there is no need to build new schools but those which are in existence need to be made to adapt to the demands of the 21ˢᵗ century and embrace 21ˢᵗ century pedagogies. The technologically savvy generation of students is expectant and buildings have a great impact on how they learn. The old buildings can thus be fixed to create dynamic learning environments that prepare children for creativity and innovation. Schools should provide a future workforce which is creative and highly collaborative in its thinking skills. These are qualities which are difficult to find in a traditional classroom. For the schools which are being built during this technological era, the above should be taken into consideration. The theme which runs across in lack of infrastructure suggests the country can have the best education system but if its support infrastructural needs are not in place this would impede progress into the 21ˢᵗ century. With the explosion of new technologies, leaders have to rethink the design of school buildings which continue to be a hindrance into the future as they do not conform to the 21ˢᵗ century standards. For example the flexibility which is required on a day to day basis can be limited by the area of a classroom. This can hinder the variety of activities which can be done. If the furniture inside the classrooms is fixed to suit the traditional pedagogies this may reduce the flexibility and creativity of 21ˢᵗ century students. Poor ventilation as well as the lighting systems have an effect on the attainment of the 21ˢᵗ century skills. 21ˢᵗ century students learn in groups, are highly mobile and they need enough space for groups. The researcher notes that even the teaching styles can be affected. Common themes which are emerging from these works suggest that schools should not only adapt to short term but also to long term learning methods. Buildings should foster creativity at the same time cultivating a learning culture. A wide range of activities as well as experiences should be accommodated so that the diversity in learners is supported.

There is need to rethink the design of buildings in the 21ˢᵗ century. The researcher argues that leaders as well as stakeholders have got a fixed perception of what schools are, not only that but what also should be done by schools as well what their roles need to be. The parents as well as the planning committees are biased towards the traditional models of schools with the assumption that teachers are the sole providers of knowledge yet the 21ˢᵗ century sets out to mould creativity and problem solving in students. Designing buildings for a future which is uncertain can be a tough challenge.

This is why most planning committees in schools still remain conservative in nature. The wider community should be made aware of the urgent need for change. A guiding coalition of people who have a greater understanding what makes a 21st century infrastructure to be formed in all schools. The right attitudes can even source funding to not only fix the old buildings but to erect examples of 21st century classrooms. If it is the aspiration of the Ministry to create 21st century schools it should make people aware of the urgent need in the design of classrooms.

Lack of Resources

This section deals with another theme which runs across the published works which is lack of resources. In Zimbabwe the national ICT policy was developed in 2005.This followed the recommendations on the use of computers in the teaching and learning by the Nziramasanga commission. The policy which was adopted in 2005 promotes the use of ICTs in all educational institutions (Isaac, 2007). Just because of this policy even the higher learning institutions have integrated the use of computers thereby exposing the students to advanced ways of learning. However most schools do not have adequate facilities to run effective e-learning classes. At its inception, the President's office embarked on a campaign to donate computers to schools. The government should be commended for this because it is through this campaign that some schools benefitted and were thus enabled to make use of these computers in teaching as well as learning. Not all schools benefitted from the programme. The only computers which have been availed to schools are limited compared to the number of students. Students end up sharing. As much as this informed the basis of the integration of the ICT into the curriculum doing this in partnership with other leaders or stakeholders could have delivered a teamwork, sharing of responsibilities and building of relationships among leaders which could have resulted in greater provision.

Another dimension is the zoning of schools which makes the distribution of resources inequitable. To complicate matters government schools were further split into Group A,B and C (Atkinson, 1982; Dorsey, 1989) Group A schools which are high fee paying and former white student schools are superior when it comes to availability of resources. Group B schools which are low fee paying usually fall under government schools and resources are usually substandard when compared to Group A schools. Group C are usually found in the rural areas where resources are scarce and infrastructure is poor. (Atkinson, 1982) .Group A schools are well equipped, have better facilities and attract highly qualified teachers because the parents have a high socio

Making Schools Effective

economic status (Zindi, 1996). The researcher feels that these imbalances have created a digital divide in the information technology. However, the researcher acknowledges that society will always be stratified and social classes will always exist. A call is being made upon the donor and government to look upon the Group B and C respectively in terms of resource allocation.

The paper argues that while a lot of evidence points that wide consultations were made in the implementation of the curriculum the fifth tenet which calls for empowerment before any process of change can take place was not adequately addressed. In contrast the paper states that while the government should be hailed for bringing transition into the 21st century the country is not prepared for the transformation in terms of resources. The vision is great but again the implementation part is challenged by lack of resources. Some leaders are faced with challenges of being in possession of not only poor technological but outdated resources. They could be old and slow. Some computers are not only inadequate but they are also fragile. This brings in the aspect of lack of technical assistance in the malfunctioning of computers. Teachers lose time fixing the problems encountered with hardware and software. Becta (2004, p.1) states that, "If there is a lack of technical support available in schools then it is likely that technical maintenance will not be carried to regularly resulting in higher risk of technical breakdown." Continued breakdowns will give rise to expenses incurred. In some schools computers there is one computer which has to be booked in advance and shared by teachers. Reflections indicate that lack of resources is a serious impediment making schools effective in the 21st century.

It will be argued that in the consultative meetings the government should have taken on board all the stakeholders and it should have informed them of its position in terms of resources. If people arc included in the change process they can contribute not only their views but also the resources needed. The business community could have been persuaded to contribute in their communities. This is because change creates a great demand on society and it cannot be held single handedly, but it requires contributions from more people through collaborative working. This does not only remove barriers but it also removes disengagement of some stakeholders. The researcher argues that if all leaders are fully engaged they can share resources. In some areas there is no need to build individual libraries and ICT resource centres. These can be community shared. Tailoring the ICT into the curriculum calls for robust procedures in recognising every step in change management models. The researcher feels while information was given, creating a supportive environment is a dimension of change which was skipped.

The researcher develops the argument further by suggesting that network providers should have been roped in as stakeholders because they have a crucial role to play in the provision of network. Although internet facilities may be available in some schools, access to internet may be restricted. This may result in slow speed in downloading which may end up wasting time and slowing down syllabus coverage. This could destroy the enthusiasm of a technologically savvy generation. To increase effectiveness there is need not to skip the crucial step of empowerment. While a lot of evidence points to lack of resources there is another aspect which needs to be considered. Challenges which are being faced in resources are a result of omission of some steps in implementing change. The conclusion which is arrived at indicates the need for considering change management theories in implementing changes.

Lack of Skills

Another theme which emerges in all the reviews and is closely related to the above is lack of skills.

Recommendations cited draw evidence to lack of computer skills among teachers. The previous section talks of lack of resources. In some cases the resources would be there but school heads and teachers lack the necessary skills on how to utilise and to manage the resources and this becomes a barrier. The heads of schools should be proficient in technology because they are held accountable for their schools performance in technology. There is need to also train the teachers as well as school heads who are the key players in rolling out the ICT programmes in schools. The previous section cited lack of computers as an impediment to the adoption of ICT.There has not been adequate training opportunities for teachers in the use of ICT. Change management theories say that human resource is the root of any effective change. They emphasise that whenever change takes place it is not the organisation which changes but it is the employees. Kotter (1999, p.166) echoes the same sentiments when he says "Without sufficient empowerment, critical information about quality sits unused in workers' minds and energy to implement change lies dormant." Kotter's theory of management change states that a sense of urgency should be created first in change management. This is the preparatory stage where employers are motivated to break down their old habits and move towards the desired change. Workers are most willing and supportive of the change process if they feel they are a part of it. They should be included in decision-making so that they can also share their concerns because they are the ones who would be implementing the change at the grassroots. Some scholars in change management say people will not change because they are asked to but they need reason to change (C.C. Ganiere, personal communication, August 22, 2012). Some proponents of change management theories who echo these sentiments are Kurt Lewin in his unfreezing stage and Adkar. This signifies the importance of this stage which can make the whole process slow or difficult. The government should be hailed for introducing ICT to schools. To ensure that this move would be effective there was need for the involvement of teachers. They could have been able to raise some of the challenges which are being faced today. Proper training and continued professional development should have been done to empower both the heads and the teachers. Newhouse (2002, p.45) postulates that, "Teachers need to not only be computer literate but they also need to develop skills in integrating computer use into their teaching and learning programmes." Lack of skills leads to teachers being unenthusiastic in integrating the skills into their teaching. There is fear among teachers that they may end up exposing their ignorance and embarrassing themselves before the technologically proficient students. For teachers to effectively teach the digital generation they have to be knowledgeable. 21st century students breathe technology. To them technology is oxygen and that is what they expect from the adult world.

The world is fast becoming a global village due to globalisation and teachers should be able to connect their learners to ever-changing social and cultural networks. They should expose them to various ways of acquiring knowledge and of communicating because cultural barriers have been broken and learners across the world have been brought together. Bolman and Deal, (2008, p. 28) points that,

We are not sure what the problem is. We are not sure what is really happening. We are not sure what we want. We do not have the resources we need. We are not sure how to get what we want. We are not sure to determine whether we have succeeded.

The above ambiguous sentiments seek to try to understand the perceptions of technology leaders in the 21st century. They echo the leaders dilemma which is prevalent in the 21st century leader who is baffled by the demands and expectations of 21st century leadership and management for which he is not adequately trained. If these leaders do not receive adequate training their attitudes will remain lagging behind.

Failure to implement changes by and large means the country could repeat traditional education flaws which would jeopardise the current education's reputation as a contributor to the effectiveness of 21st century schools.

RECOMMENDATIONS

The findings of this research indicate that policies are made, clear visions are created but when it comes to implementation of the policies, this is where the focus is missed. Recommendations are hereby made that whenever changes are made in the education system the changes should be guided by change management theories. More importantly evidence examined points that all the stages of the change management theories are not properly followed. The wealth of the intellectual viewpoints and recommendations made in the reviews under study were not made full use of. Recommendations which have been made by other scholars to be analysed and effected.

CONCLUSION

The study sought to explore how change management is implemented in Zimbabwe's education. It looked at the published works from 2000 to 2019. The research interrogated the recommendations which were made in these studies to see if they have been implemented and if the tenets of change management theories were followed in their implementation. Firstly the research establishes that changes which were recommended by the Nziramasanga commission were not implemented. They were only implemented years later yet they sought to prepare the students for the 21st century. The researcher notes that if these recommendations had been implemented, the country would be in a better position to meet the 21st century challenges. Some of the recommendations which were made by scholars under study were also partly implemented. The study reveals that over the years the curriculum has been biased towards academic subjects neglecting the urgent need of preparing students for the vocational and 21st century skills. The analysis concludes that lack of infrastructure and human and material resources has been a major an impediment on the implementation of the 21st century pedagogies. The researcher notes the country's ill preparedness to create effective schools in the 21st century. There is need to train both school heads and teachers on the pedagogical skills in ICT as they are the key actors in the implementation process.

The researcher notes that given the proper skills and knowledge teachers are innovative and can easily spearhead the effectiveness of making 21st century schools effective because they have a clear view of what is going on in their classrooms. The study opted for a bottom up approach to change management in order to suggest the need for policies to start from the bottom to the top with the involvement of teachers. The study concludes that if changes are made in the education sector, there is no proper indication of the use of the management change models.The researcher notes that the policies would be comprehensive and clear but they end up failing because of improper implementation. In some cases the stages are partly followed. A systematic approach has to be followed This paper calls upon policy makers to make changes which are informed by change management theories and to adhere to all the stages in order for the implementation process to succeed. Omission of any part of the theories can create a fatal flaw in the implementation process. They should foster acceptance by creating a supportive environment. The study calls upon all countries which are undergoing transformation in preparation for 21st century to check their state of preparedness in every area and apply change management theories in order to make schools effective in the 21st century.

REFERENCES

Atkinson, N. D. (1972). *Teaching Rhodesian: A history of educational policy in Rhodesia*. Longman.

Bennie, K., & Newstead, K. (1999). *Obstacles to implementing a new curriculum*. In M.J. Smit, & A.S. Jordaan (Eds.), *Proceedings of the National Subject Didactics Symposium* (pp.150-157). Stellenbosch: University of Stellenbosch.

Coltart, D. (2012). Education for employment,developing skills for vocation. Speech at the African Innovation Summit, Cape Town, South Africa.

Creasy, T. (2007) *Defining management*. https://www.pro-sci.com/change-management/thught-leadership-library/change-management-definition

De Jager, P. (2001, May- June). Resistance to change: A new view of an old problem. *The Futurist*, *53*(3), 24–27.

Drucker, P. F. (2001) *Management Challenges for the 21st Century*. Harper Business.

Fullan, M. (2007). *Leading in a culture of change* (revised edition). Jossey-Bass.

Isaac, S. (2007). *Survey of ICT and education in Africa: Zimbabwe country report*. Retrieved from http/:www.infodev.org

Kotter, J. P. (1995, Mar.). Leading change: why transformation efforts fail. Harvard Business Review, 59-67.

Kotter, J. P. (1996). Leading change. Harvard Business School Press.

Majoni, C. (2014). *Challenges facing university education in Zimbabwe.* Academic Press.

Mubika, K., & Bukaliya, R. (2011). Teacher competence in ICT: Implications for Computer Education in Zimbabwean secondary schools. *International Journal of Social Sciences and Education, 1.*

Nyagura, L. M. (1991b). *Multilevel Investigations of Effects of schools, Classrooms and Student Characteristics on Academic Achievements in Zimbabwe Primary Schools.* Human Resources Research Center: University of Zimbabwe.

Nyaruwata, L. T., Thomas, K. A., & Ndawi, V. E. (2013). Barriers to effective intergration of information and communication technology in Harare secondary schools. *International Journal of Science and Research, 2.* www.ijsr.net

Nziramasanga, C. T. (1999). *Report of the Presidential commission of inquiry into education and training.* Government Printers.

Oloniram, S. O. (2016). *Revisiting UNESCO Four pillars of education and its implications for the 21st century teaching and learning.* http:www.UNESCO. org/delors/fourpil.htm

Pedzisai, C., Tsvere, M., & Nkhonde, M. (2014). The Zimbabwe Two Pathway Education Curriculum: Insights into policy implementation challenges and opportunities. *International Journal of Advanced Research in Management and Social Science, 3*(5).

Zindi, F. (1997). *Special education in Africa.* Tasalls.

Zvobgo, R. J. (1996). *Transforming Education the Zimbabwean experiences.* Bulawayo.

Chapter 3
Organizational Change in Educational Organizations

Özcan Doğan
https://orcid.org/0000-0003-1950-7090
Eskişehir Osmangazi University, Turkey

Damla Ayduğ
İstanbul Gedik University, Turkey

ABSTRACT

Change is an inevitable fact of life from birth to death, affecting cultures, countries, and societies. Especially today, change is happening faster than in the past, and this causes societies and organizations to face much more change that they need to keep up with. Organizations can only survive if they change themselves by adapting to these rapid changes. In this study, definitions of organizational change were given, and the factors that cause organizational change were described. Then, the theories of change were mentioned depending on the reason for the change and the changes it brings about in the organization. Then, resistance to change, management of organizational change, and organizational change in educational organizations were examined.

INTRODUCTION

Change is the differences that occur in the structure, quality and status of an organization over a long period of time. The change is defined in the dictionary of the Turkish Language Association (2022) as "the totality of changes within

DOI: 10.4018/978-1-7998-3940-8.ch003

Copyright © 2024, IGI Global. Copying or distributing in print or electronic forms without written permission of IGI Global is prohibited.

a period of time, alteration". Change is determined by measuring the difference between the initial structure and the final structure of the organization. There are planned, unplanned, incremental, rapid, repetitive and unpredictable types of change (Poole, 2004).

Change is an inevitable fact of life from birth to death, affecting cultures, countries and societies. Especially today, change is happening faster than in the past and this causes societies and organizations to face much more change that they need to keep up with. Organizations can only survive if they change themselves by adapting to these rapid changes (Erdoğan, 2012). Change involves recognizing the current situation, determining the desired results, initiating an action plan and implementing the plan in line with a purpose (Calabrese & Shoho, 2000).

Change means to make different. It is aimed to transform an object from its current state into a different state. Those affected by change can both initiate change and be affected by change beyond their control. However, in the end, the changed individual or organization is not the same as its initial state (Calabrese & Shoho, 2000). The concept of change also includes development.

Organizational change describes the act of moving an organization from its current state to another desired state in order to increase its effectiveness. The reasons for organizational change include competitive forces, economic forces, political and global forces, social-demographic forces and ethical forces (George & Gareth, 2002). The simplest definition of organizational development is to change the organization in order to achieve its objectives because competitive conditions require organizations to protect themselves and survive under these conditions. Organizational development affects change through learning processes. In the learning process, new ideas and attitudes emerge that change the behavior and culture of the organization (Ellis & Dick, 2003). Organizational change is the process and art of deliberately and intentionally changing an organization in order to improve its performance. Organizational change is the work of putting ideas into action. Organizational change aims at organizational development, in other words, increasing effectiveness of the organization by increasing the capacity and competencies (Floyd, 2002).

Organizations change cautiously, deliberately and continuously to bring themselves into strategic alignment by influencing or choosing their environment (Demers, 2007). Organizational change should not be considered in isolation from the history of the organization and other factors that bring about change. Instead, organizational change should be carried out continuously, taking into account the historical, cultural and political context in which the organization exists. Change involves a cyclical process of generating new knowledge and putting that knowledge into practice. Change is a priority for organizational development (Choi & Wendy, 2011).

According to Demers (2007), changes introduced and developed by leaders are considered as "top-down" change. On the contrary, the change that starts from the lower parts of the organization and increases towards the top management is considered as "upward change". The so-called planned change can be called "top-down" change because it is carried out by top management.

Planned change is a deliberate effort by leaders to change the functions of employees, teams, departments or the entire organization. One of the planned change approaches is the economic approach. The aim of the economic approach is to increase profits. The economic approach, which has a top-down hierarchical management approach, focuses on structure and strategy. Employees are motivated by incentives to increase performance. The second approach is the organizational development approach. The aim of this approach is to develop the capacities of employees. Participatory leadership characteristics are commonly seen in this approach, which emphasizes organizational culture (Hellriegel & Slocum, 2011).

Change is a central issue for leaders because change is imperative and organizations often have difficulties adapting to their environment. Forces driving organizations to change include globalization, technology, social networks and generational differences (Hellriegel & Slocum, 2011). According to some researchers, change can start due to many different factors such as economic, environmental, technological factors etc. When a problem arising from these factors occurs, change is initiated to solve this problem and to provide a balance (Leonard, 2013).

Organizational change has an impact that reaches all units of the entire organization. Among the causes of organizational change, two types of factors, internal and external, can be mentioned. While the internal factors include human resources problems, managerial behaviors and decisions, and obsolescence in the organizational structure, the external factors include globalization and competition, socio-cultural trends, economic conditions, government laws and regulations, and technology (Yılmaz et al., 2014).

Reasons for Change in Organizations in Terms of System Approach

Since the 1960s, organizational change has been explained by systems theory. This approach, which sees organizations as organisms that strive to adapt to the changing environment, relates organizational research to the external environment rather than the internal structure (Şimşek & Louis, 1994). According to the general system theory, the normal state of organizational systems is a state of dynamic equilibrium. In this state of equilibrium, a balance is established between the forces that oppose change and the forces that want change. According to Lewin (1958), it would be an effective approach to use an incremental model and realize change by creating a careful balance with the forces that oppose change.

All human systems strive to create equilibrium and sustain their existence in relation to their environment. However, as environmental conditions are constantly changing, there is a constant imbalance between systems and the environment. For change to occur, there must first be an inequality strong enough to mobilize the organization (Schein, 2010). Individuals, groups and social systems are constantly seeking a balance. The overall goal of management implementing organizational change is to maintain social balance and personal arrangements (Johns, 1973).

According to the open systems approach, organizations should not be seen as structures separate from the world. Organizations react to changes coming from internal and external environment. This approach sees organizations as a whole and this is reflected in the change approach (Ellis & Dick, 2003). In a changing world, internal and external incompatibilities create dilemmas. Changes in the environment cause organizations to experience adaptation problems and decreases in performance. Organizations need to be flexible enough and adapt to their new environment in order to fill the gaps with the environment and regain their performance (Hakonsson et al., 2012). Today, change has generally accelerated with technology and there has been a rapid production of information in all kinds of fields. Obtaining better quality products and services causes organizations to change and adapt to the conditions. Educational organizations also need to change themselves according to the expectations of their environment (Özdemir & Cemaloğlu, 1999).

As in all organizations, organizational change occurs in educational organizations as a result of changes in environmental conditions. Therefore, change is an inevitable phenomenon because educational institutions are both affected by the environment and have the capacity to affect the environment. The school has an environment that affects it, on which it is dependent and with which it interacts and communicates. It is impossible for the school to survive without communicating with this environment. Perceiving the school as a system helps to understand that it interacts with and is affected by other systems around it. The school, which interacts with the other systems around it, cannot draw clear boundaries around its environment. As an open system,

Reasons for Change in Organizations in Terms of Environmental Conditions

the school is both affected by the changes in its environment and has the ability to affect its environment (Gül, 2006).

Reasons for Change in Organizations in Terms of Environmental Conditions

Understanding and managing change involves complex challenges. Organizations today must have very strong capacities to adapt to the rapidly changing environment. If adaptation to changes in the environment is not fast enough, organizations are likely to fail. Therefore, leaders and employees need to understand the causes and nature of change (Hellriegel & Slocum, 2011).

Globalization: It has developed as a result of multinational corporations spreading across the world and seeing the whole world as a market, both to serve this market and to feed from this market. Just as global companies need to adapt to local markets, organizations in local markets need to innovate in order to compete against global forces. Coping with global competition requires "flexibility" that many organizations lack (Hellriegel & Slocum, 2011).

Globalization causes multinational companies to be affected by changes occurring at national, regional and global levels. The concept of globalization is perceived as both an opportunity and a threat because the complexity associated with globalization makes it difficult to understand and predict globalization trends and drivers. Organizations' responses to these trends and their ability to change are factors that determine their future success (Floyd, 2002).

Technology and social networks: Another factor that enables organizations to achieve flexibility is technology. Information technologies enable changes in the structure, products and markets of organizations. Information technologies increase the value of other assets in the organization. It helps employees to work more flexibly (Hellriegel and Slocum, 2011).

The pace of technology development and adaptation in recent years has been breathtaking. Technology and its applications act as a catalyst for improved organizational performance. The appropriate use of technology has led to very positive results in performance levels and productivity (Floyd, 2002). Another reason for change is social networks. Social networks in the organization enable solutions to be offered by going beyond the existing chain of command in the organization. Different generations working together in organizations cause leaders to develop new management approaches (Hellriegel & Slocum, 2011).

ORGANIZATIONAL CHANGE THEORIES AND MODELS

Theories of Organizational Change

Life cycle theory, teleological theory, dialectical theory and evolutionary theory, which are the most commonly used theories to explain organizational change, are given in the Table 1. According to these theories, the reasons for change, the process of change, the outputs obtained as a result of change and the benefits of change to the organization are indicated.

Table 1. Theories of organizational change

	Life cycle Theory	Teleological Theory	Dialectical Theory	Evolutionary Theory
Reasons for Change	Leaders' Guidance for Individual Developmnet	Leaders, Internal Environment	Dialectical Tension of Values, Norms, Goals, and Forces	External Environment
Process of change	Naturally progressive, cumulative, predetermined, sequential stages	Rational, linear, purposeful, iterative	Second-order changes follow first-order changes, iterative discrete succession, negotiations and power	Adaptive to the environment, slowly recurring, gradual, cumulative, not purposeful or constrained
Outputs of change	New organizational identity	New structure and organizing principles	New organizational ideology	New structure and processes
Keywords	Organizational development	Purposeful collaboration	Opposition, conflict	Surviving the competition
Key metaphor	Teacher or counselor	Change expert	Social movement	Self-producing organism
Example	Development models, organizational decline, social psychology of change	Organizational development, strategic planning, restructuring, TQM	Empowerment, bargaining, influence and power, social movement	Resource dependence, strategic choice, population ecology
Benefits of change	Stages associated with change, focusing on the individual in the organization	The importance of change agents, management techniques and strategies	Determinism, lack of environmental concerns, little guidance for leaders	Emphasis on the environment, systems approach
Criticisms	Lack of empirical evidence, deterministic nature	Too rational and linear, insufficient to explain second-order changes, excessive individuality	The fact that change is not always progressive, irrationality, the role of power	Lack of emphasis on the human, deterministic nature

Organizational Change in Educational Organizations

Reference: Van de Ven, A. H., & Poole, M. S. (1995). Explaining development and change in organizations. *Academy of Management Review, 20*(3), p.514.

Life Cycle Theory

This model likens the lives of organizations to the lives of individuals. In this model, change is seen as a stage. Change implies development and is also rational. Organizations are born, grow, mature, accelerate and ultimately collapse. Since change occurs naturally, it cannot be stopped or directed (Ellis & Dick, 2003; Kezar, 2001; Leonard, 2013). According to this theory, organizations necessarily pass through predetermined stages and change can occur at any time (Yılmaz et al., 2014). The theory focuses on predicting development or death and making necessary arrangements accordingly (Leonard, 2013). This model is similar to the evolutionary model in terms of adaptation and systems approach. The life cycle model emphasizes systematic individual change. It is not possible to plan change because change is a natural process that cannot be changed or stopped. According to this theory, the environment is full of uncertainties and dangerous. A new organizational identity is formed as a result of change.

This model emphasizes that all individuals in organizations have an important role in the change process because if all individuals are not prepared for change, change cannot be successful. For this reason, actions that emphasize individual development, overcoming the fear of change, education and learning are included in the change process. The task of leaders is to analyze the necessary training, evaluate the organizational culture and observe the environment and life cycle. Since each organization goes through certain stages, its needs are different at each stage. For example, a young organization needs creativity and entrepreneurial spirit, while organizations focus on their internal processes and practices as they move into the development stage. As time passes, leaders find ways to better examine their environment and seize opportunities (Kezar, 2001).

Teleological Theory

A popular model, it encompasses a cycle of *goal setting, implementation, evaluation and action or goal realignment.* It is based on what the organization or social system has learned or intended (Leonard, 2013). Change is the result of purposeful and adaptive actions. Change occurs to realize a goal (Yılmaz et al., 2014). Teleological model has different names such as planned change, scientific management and rational model. Strategic planning, organizational development, learning adaptation approaches can be grouped under this model. These theories started to emerge at the same time as the evolutionary theory. According to this theory, organizations act for a purpose and organizations have the capacity to adapt to their environment. Change happens because leaders and change agents want it to happen. Change is straightforward and rational as in evolutionary theories. Change is used as a tool by leaders. In this theory, the leader is central. Change results in a new organizational structure or principles. Teleological model aims at organizational learning (Kezar, 2001).

Dialectical Theory

This theory is based on the Hegelian model of change, which argues that a synthesis emerges as a result of conflicts between organizations and social systems. According to this model, conflicts will generate the energy necessary for change and development (Leonard, 2013). The world is a field of contention between opposing, competitive groups. The change that occurs as a result of collisions and confrontations in these areas is explained by the dialectical model. Change is a process of creating a balance of power and is far from rational. It may not always lead to a positive outcome (Yılmaz et al., 2014). Organizations go through a long period of evolutionary change and a short period of revolutionary change. Opposing belief systems of the organization collide and change takes place. The resulting change is the organization's modified ideology or identity. Development and rationality are not a product of this model. Change does not always produce a better organization. In this model, social interaction is more important than environmental scanning and planning (Kezar, 2001).

According to dialectical theory, not everyone is interested in the process of change. The process of change varies according to the availability and distribution of resources. If there are too many resources, few people are interested in change and conflict arises, but if there are few resources, individuals act to make more use of them. In this model, social interaction is more important than studying the environment, planning or assessing the life cycle of the organization. The metaphor used in the theory is social mobility (Kezar, 2001).

Evolutionary Theory

This model builds on Darwinian constructs such as natural diversity and selection of the most capable species. This process is governed by the drive

Organizational Change in Educational Organizations

to compete and survive using scarce resources (Leonard, 2013). Organizations are not static. They are constantly evolving. According to this theory, change is constantly repeated. Organizations change to adapt to environmental factors. Since environmental conditions cannot always be predicted in advance, change is unplanned and reactive (Yılmaz et al., 2014). According to evolutionary theory, organizational change depends on situations, situational variables and the environment. Change takes place because the environment demands it. The main concepts are systems, organization-environment relationship, openness, internal equilibrium and evolution (Kezar, 2001).

There are two types of evolutionary theory. These are the social evolution model and the biological model. Many models have developed from models of adaptation, resource dependence, self-management, probability and systems theory, strategic choice, equilibrium, and population ecology. The theory was initially developed under the influence of biology and was defined as gradually changing to adapt to the environment. Later it influenced theories in the social sciences and politics. In general, this theory attributes the realization of change to environmental conditions because social systems depend on their environment and naturally evolve over time. According to this theory, individuals cannot influence their environment but they are influenced by it. The basic concepts of the theory are system, interaction of organizations with their environment, openness, internal balance and evolution. The term "system" indicates that there are independent parts of the organization and that a change at any point will affect other areas. Interaction means that the structures in organizations must be in relationship with each other in order for change to take place. Change is a process that the whole organization will create together. Openness refers to the relationship between an organization's environment and its internal transformation. Internal balance means establishing a balance between the internal structure of an organization and its environment (Kezar, 2001).

Kezar's Models of Organizational Change

In addition to the life cycle, teleological, evolutionary and dialectical models, Kezar's (2001) organizational change models include the cultural model, chaos model, organizational development model and total quality model.

Cultural model: According to this model, change occurs naturally in response to changes in the environment and cultures are constantly changing. The process of change is long and slow. Change in an organization occurs by changing values, beliefs, myths and rituals. Change is not linear. It is constantly evolving and dynamic.

Chaos model: Planned change is indifferent to environmental variables and is not conducive to change. Organizations react organically to demands from the environment. This model involves observation of the environment, analysis of the organizational system and the creation of new structures to respond to the environment.

Organizational development model: According to this model, change is driven by internal characteristics and decisions. The external environment has little influence. Organizations are purposeful and adaptable structures. Change is necessary because leaders, change agents and others see that change is necessary.

Total quality management model: According to this model, organizations aim to achieve quality. However, they do not examine the barriers to change necessary for quality, such as culture and acquired values. In order to achieve a quality culture, the leader should (1) emphasize vision, mission and organizational products, (2) demonstrate creative and supportive leadership, (3) give importance to personal development, (4) make decisions based on data, (5) support collaboration, (6) delegate authority in decision making, (7) plan change in a prudent manner (Kezar, 2001).

Demers' Models of Organizational Change

Demers' (2007) models of organizational change include the rational adaptation approach, the organic adaptation approach, the life cycle approach and the selection and simulation approach.

Rational adaptation approach: According to this approach, the reason for change is the disruption of balance in the organization due to changes in the environment. In the process of change, the organization seeks to adapt in order to achieve balance. The task of the change agent is to make the necessary adjustments in the organization to ensure that the organization can adapt. According to the rational adaptation approach, organizations should combine their structural networks to achieve change. According to *the contingency theory* within this approach, organizations are open systems and interact with their environment. Organizational change is developed by managers according to environmental conditions. According to *the purposeful action approach*, there is a mutual interaction between the environment and the organization to change each other. This approach is divided into strategic choice and resource dependency approaches. *Strategic choice approach* requires taking actions that will affect the environment. *The resource dependency approach* argues that organizations need to obtain resources from the environment in order to survive.

Organizational Change in Educational Organizations

The organic adaptation approach: In this approach, change occurs as organizations adapt, but change is not always rational. The organization is not a place where the manager can manage as she/he wants because there are various political and interest groups within the organization.

Life cycle approach: The life cycle approach argues that organizations go through certain phases just like living organisms. These stages go from birth to death. It is normal to have some pauses and accelerations during the life of the organization.

Selection and simulation approach: According to the selection and simulation approach, organizations resemble their competitors over time and struggle for survival through adaptation. There are two types of this approach. These are population ecology and new institutionalization. *Population ecology* views organizations as living beings. Change is explained by concepts from biology such as natural selection and evolution. Organizations are also seen as open systems as they are affected by the environment. According to this approach, organizations that cannot adapt to innovations perish. In addition, as a resistance to change in organizations, there is an "inertia" structure within the organization. As organizations grow, this structure grows with them and the resistance to change increases. According to *the new institutionalism approach,* the reason why organizations change is to gain legitimacy. Organizations are connected to each other in a social network. This network creates an organizational field. Organizations in this field gradually resemble each other. This is called organizational isomorphism. There are three types of isomorphism. *Coercive isomorphism* refers to the ability of strong organizations to influence and change weak ones. *Analogical isomorphism* arises from the idea that some organizations are better and other organizations imitate these successful organizations. *Normative isomorphism* refers to the similarity of organizations with educational and professional network connections (Demers, 2007).

Lewin's Model of Organizational Change

The organizational change model created by Lewin (1958) includes the stages of "unfreezing", "change" and "refreezing". The unfreezing phase is the realization of the need for change in the organization, making the necessary preparations and the beginning phase. It is the end of the stagnation period in the organization and the completion of preparations for action. The stage of change is the stage of taking action and sustaining it. The important point at this stage is timing. Mistakes made by the manager in timing can lead to problems. When the intended change is achieved, the organization is refrozen.

Leaders as change agents should make change a culture in the organization (Örücü, 2013).

RESISTANCE TO CHANGE

The main strategy of change is to overcome the resistance to change. It is very difficult to anticipate all problems in the process of organizational change. Using both reward and punishment methods together in the change process will be very effective (Johns, 1973). There is always an obstacle to change and these obstacles consist of various elements. For example, the tension between "doing business as usual" and "creating the future and change" is one of the first tensions (Floyd, 2002).

There is always a barrier to change and these barriers are composed of various elements. For example, the tension between "doing work as usual" and "creating the future and change" is one of the first tensions encountered (Floyd, 2002). Reactions to change in organizations can occur at any stage of the change process, including planning, initiation and implementation. The sources of reactions to change in organizations can be very different. If the change affects the status of individuals and is imposed from the top management, and if there is a lack of information and skills, more resistance is encountered (Willower, 1963).

Since change involves many unknowns about the future, individuals may resist change because they are afraid of losing things such as their position and salary at the end of the change. Individual resistance to change can be caused by differences in personal perceptions, personality traits, habits, threats to power and influence, and fear of the unknown (Hellriegel & Slocum, 2011). Individuals are generally against change for fear of losing their current status and power. If the organizational management has a hierarchical structure, change will be more difficult in this organization than in a horizontally structured organization. In addition, if the existing rules and values in the organization will be affected by change, this situation also makes change difficult (George & Gareth, 2002).

It has been stated by many researchers that there is a connection between the organization and its environment. Organizations resist change because they have technical and institutional connections with their environment. The internal and external environment of the organization expects the organization to work efficiently at a certain standard. If an organization fulfills what is expected of it and achieves certain standards in its activities, the need for change may not be felt because it is thought that internal routines and external

Organizational Change in Educational Organizations

connections may be damaged by change (Amburgey et al., 1993). When the reasons why individuals resist change are understood, it becomes easier for change to occur. The reasons why individuals resist change are as follows (Ellis & Dick, 2003):

- Loss of control: Change is acceptable for the individual bringing about the change, but not for others.
- Uncertainty: Any change involves uncertainty and this causes individuals to be hesitant.
- Surprise: It is normal for individuals to resist a new situation.
- Future anxiety: Individuals have many concerns about the new situations that will arise with changes.
- Chain effect: The change may cause a chain reaction by affecting other areas.
- More workload: Change involves more time, effort and energy.
- The threat is real: The threat perceived by individuals is real because change often creates two groups, winners and losers.

An important reason why individuals resist change is related to their status. Experienced individuals who have spent many years in their jobs have been found to resist change more than younger ones (Willower, 1963). Individuals show more resistance when they see change as a threat to themselves (Johns, 1973). Resistance to organizational change arises because individuals are satisfied with the status quo and fear of losing their position (Floyd, 2002).

The sense of competition between the units in an organization may cause resistance to change because some units are likely to gain superiority over others in change situations. If the change that will occur will benefit certain departments in an organization more than others, other departments may react against the change (Willower, 1963).

Another reason for resistance is uncertainty. Change is both imposed by external factors and voluntary when individuals are uncomfortable with the status quo. In both cases, the situation faced with change is full of uncertainties. These uncertainties sometimes cause individuals to experience fear (Ellis & Dick, 2003; Fullan, 2006).

MANAGING ORGANIZATIONAL CHANGE

Organizational change is a difficult process for managers to implement because there will be a lot of resistance to change from inside and outside the organization. Managers who want to manage change effectively and create a culture of change within the organization should ensure change by creating a collaborative culture and mutual understanding. The reason for this situation is that among the reasons for the resistance to change is the criticism that other individuals in the organization are not sufficiently involved in the process, are not represented or consulted (Floyd, 2002).

One of the most important skills of a leader is to make the organization accept change with the least resistance. Even if the organization is instinctively opposed to change, it must react to the actions of its social and economic environment in order to exist (Johns, 1973). For change to be successful, the management team and employees need to cooperate. Training, performance and organizational development are effective in the success of change. Change is both inevitable and permanent. Successful organizations not only respond to change, but also drive it (Lee & Krayer, 2004). Change practices take a long time and when the change process is completed, the factors that initiated this process may have changed. For this reason, it is necessary to initiate a change initiative again (Johns, 1973).

Today, change can start with unfreezing the organization. The second phase occurs when it is understood that the change will benefit the employees and the organization. In the third phase, the culture in the organization becomes dynamic and employees wait for the next change. For this reason, in today's conditions, it is never possible to go to the stage of refreezing the organization (Ellis & Dick, 2003). In order to carry out an effective change program, it is important that all organizational members support and are willing to change. Some characteristics of successful change processes are as follows (Hellriegel & Slocum, 2011):

1. Overcome resistance to change and motivate leaders and employees to be ready for change.
2. Create a shared vision for the desired future state of the organization.
3. Develop political support for needed changes.
4. Manage the transition from the current state to the expected state.
5. Change should be at a certain pace.

In addition, there are three important strategies to ensure effective change in organizations. These are creating structures to create new synergies, opening borders to create strategic partnerships, and creating new structures to support innovation and entrepreneurship (Ellis & Dick, 2003). According to Dent and Goldberg (1999), classical change management techniques are not sufficient because change is happening very fast today. In today's conditions, it is necessary to catch the speed of change and react to change as soon as possible. The ultimate goal of change is for organizations to become learning organizations. What needs to be done to be a learning organization as follows (Calabrese & Shoho, 2000):

1. Organizational employees need to feel threat-free in order to sustain change because individuals who feel threatened immediately become defensive.
2. The organizational structure must support change.
3. Members must work together to perceive reality.
4. Real change occurs and develops simultaneously at different levels. Organizational change occurs at the conscious, subconscious and behavioural levels of members.
5. Awareness of the current situation is key feature of change. Effective change occurs when individuals are aware of the current situation and the consequences.
6. Dialogue is necessary to develop a sense of responsibility. Dialogue is fundamental in learning organizations as it fosters honesty, trust and perception.
7. Need or hunger is necessary for change. Individuals must be hungry for learning. Hunger occurs when there is a realization of the need for change.

According to the change model proposed by Kotter (1996), change involves an eight-stage plan. This plan is seen as a more comprehensive approach than Lewin's model. The plan is based on the mistakes made by leaders during change initiatives. The stages of Kotter's (1996) change plan include the following: 1. Create a sense of urgency, 2. Build a coalition to guide change, 3. Develop a vision and strategy, 4. Communicate about the vision for change, 5. Strengthen broad-based actions, 6. Create short-term gains, 7. Reinforce gains and bring about more change, 8. Embed new approaches into the culture.

ORGANIZATIONAL CHANGE IN EDUCATIONAL ORGANIZATIONS

Change can occur in nature and at every stage of human life. It is not possible to escape this natural change. Similarly, organizations also need to go through a certain change. Natural change is a phenomenon that cannot be prevented, but organizational change is planned by managers for the development of organizations (Argon & Özçelik, 2008). Organizations that cannot keep up with the changes occurring in their environment first become ordinary and then disappear (Açıkalın, 1998). It is quite natural for schools to be affected by the need for change because schools, which are open systems, cannot remain unresponsive to change in their environment (Beycioğlu & Aslan, 2010). Change in education involves change in practices. For this reason, the changes that will occur will be in dimensions such as teachers, administrators, schools, school districts and families. During the planning of a possible change, it is necessary to anticipate what the possible changes in new materials, new methods and beliefs will be (Fullan, 2007).

The ability of schools to adapt to changes in their environment depends on their capacity. School capacity means all staff working together to improve student achievement. The five interrelated elements of school capacity are: Teachers' knowledge, skills and character, professional community, program coherence, technical resources, and administrative leadership (Fullan, 2007). Since schools are institutions that are quickly affected by social, cultural, political and technological changes in society, they have to change in order to keep up with these changes (Argon & Özçelik, 2008). When school change is mentioned, it is generally meant the steps taken for the improvement of the school. Change in educational organizations should be continuous because educational institutions have a duty to prepare the future of the country. The changes that may occur while creating the future should be seen in advance and change needs should be identified (Beycioğlu & Aslan, 2010). Fullan and Hargreaves (1998) explained the forces shaping change in schools under the following headings:

1. Schools cannot close their doors and separate themselves from the outside world.
2. More diversity demands more flexibility.
3. Technology is breaking down the walls of schools.
4. Schools are the last hope for renewing and saving society.
5. Teachers can do more with more help.
6. Education is fundamental to democracy.
7. The phenomenon of competition in the education market, parental preferences and the individual's desire for self-governance require schools to engage with the wider environment.
8. Schools need to be more and more similar to the life that awaits students.
9. The pressure today's complex environment on schools is increasing.
10. Schools have turned into tired institutions with their present structures.

Organizational Change in Educational Organizations

It can be seen that schools should not be seen as a system separate from their environment. The most important pressures for school change come from technology, competition, family preferences and school-environment relations. The current structure of schools is another factor indicating the need for change because schools have become tired institutions that cannot compete with the important developments taking place in the world. In order to realize a successful change in educational administration, the following points should be considered (Fullan, 2007):

1. The change you think should happen may not be the same as the change that needs to be implemented or can be realized.
2. A significant innovation, if it is to result in change, requires individual practitioners to make their own meaning. Specific changes involve a noticeable degree of uncertainty and ambivalence about the meaning of the change.
3. Conflict and disagreement are inevitable and essential for successful change. Because individuals have very different realities, a change that involves everyone brings conflict.
4. Individuals need some pressure in change situations, even if they themselves want it. However, this pressure will only be effective if they are able to react, formulate their own position, interact with other practitioners and receive help to build capacity.
5. Effective change takes time. It is a process of development. Unrealistic or undetermined timelines prevent the understanding that practices evolve.
6. Deficiencies in practice should not be perceived as a reaction to the values that come with change.
7. Most individuals or groups do not change. Development occurs step by step. As a result, the number of people involved and affected increases.
8. A plan is needed that builds on the above assumptions and emphasizes the factors that will influence implementation. Evolutionary models of planning, which are based on knowledge of the process of change, and problem solving models are very important.
9. It is not entirely clear how much information is needed for which action. Action decisions are a mix of valid information, political considerations, snap judgments and intuition.
10. The main agenda in organizational change is not to implement single innovations but to change the culture of the organization.

The Roles of School Principals as Change Agents in Educational Organizations

The change process in schools takes place under the management of the school principal. However, each school has its own unique needs and the need for change varies according to the environmental conditions. In the researches conducted, important issues such as the social and physical structure of schools, increasing teacher qualifications, financial resources and the quality of parents have emerged among the elements that need to change in schools. School administrators state that teachers have difficulty in using technology. However, since younger teachers are better at using technology than more senior teachers, the problem of change in technology is only experienced by more senior teachers. School principals stated that they tried to find financial support from the environment and received help from other senior administrators, such as the governor, in preparing the staff in their schools for change. In order to overcome the difficulties encountered in the change process, it has been observed that school principals motivate teachers by making various assignments, organizing social activities, and providing educational equipments to teachers. It is seen that resistance to change usually emerges as a result of teachers' refusal to keep up with the times, in other words, in terms of using technology (Altunay et al., 2012).

Change is one of the most important issues on the agenda of managers and it is often a very challenging issue for managers. Especially when it is challenging for the manager, it is difficult for managers to work effectively. Another factor that complicates the work of managers is the fact that the manager is in the middle of the relations between the external environment and the school. Successful school managers not only demonstrate effective management, but also have structures that include everyone in the processes and make things easier. In addition, successful managers try to institutionalize the emphasis on student achievement. They can also create an environment of change by combining pressure and support. In short, these leaders are relationship-centered, value professional standards, seek ideas and relationships across the country, and monitor school performance (Fullan, 2007).

School managers who will realize change in schools should be leaders who have developed themselves. In addition to these, school administrators should follow the current information about their field. They should know the reasons and time of change and possible resistance mechanisms (Bennett et al., 1992). Some of the competencies that the manager who will ensure change should have are as follows (Gökçe, 2004): 1. Know how to motivate. 2. Know the structure and culture of the organization where the change will take place. 3. Know the environment of the organization. 4. Have knowledge about change techniques and processes. Changes that occur under the leadership of leaders who create the necessary conditions for organizational efficiency are more successful.

The Role of Teachers as Change Agents in Educational Organizations

Another important actor for change at the school level is the teacher. In the process of change, the task of the school principal as an educational leader is to convince teachers, parents and other employees to change (Taş, 2009). This is because the human factor is perhaps the most important factor in responding to change today. In order for the change to be fast and effective, it is necessary to get the contributions of the human resources in the organization during the preparation and implementation of the change. There will be less resistance to a change planned together. In addition, the motivation and effort of the personnel for change has an accelerating effect on change (Argon & Özçelik, 2008).

The most important actors of change in schools are managers and teachers. For this reason, the opinions of people in both groups should be taken for a successful change management (Beycioğlu & Aslan, 2010). One of the things to be done to determine the need for change in schools is to bring together teachers and managers to discuss what needs to be done in the current situation. In this way, both organizational participation will be ensured and those who are likely to resist change can be convinced from the very beginning (Argon & Özçelik, 2008). Since teachers are one of the most important actors of change in the education system, the success of change depends on what teachers do and think. If the quality of teachers is improved and their working environment is organized in a way that encourages them, schools and students will be more successful (Fullan, 2007).

Barriers to Organizational Change in Educational Organizations

Some of the obstacles to change in educational organizations, or more narrowly in schools, are resource inadequacies, teacher qualifications, crowded classrooms, infrastructure inadequacies, and transition problems between school levels (Karip, 2005). Change is not a necessity for people who do not have a concern for development in organizations and who only seem to be doing their jobs. For these people, change is perceived as a problem (Ceyan

& Summak, 1999). One of the reasons for teachers' negative beliefs about change is that they are worried about economic and social loss (Töremen, 2002). School principals may be reluctant to take risks and transfer authority in the change process because they think that they will be affected by the negative situations that may occur due to the fact that all the responsibility lies with them (Taş, 2009).

CONCLUSION

Organizations affect other organizations around them and cause change on them, and at the same time, they are affected by the changes that occur in their environment. Organizational change is necessary for organizations to develop and keep pace with changing conditions. Today, change continues at a dizzying pace. The information produced and the news received by individuals are consumed in a very short period of time. It is difficult for individuals and organizations to keep up with this speed. Hovewer, catching up with change is one of the most important requirements of today. Some factors that cause change are globalization, gaining competitive power, survival, etc.

Change is a necessity, but individuals do not favor change when they are not complaining about the current situation. For change to occur, there must be a disturbing situation or a problem in the environment. Effective change must solve a problem. In cases where individuals do not see a problem in the environment, resistance to change emerges. In fact, the reasons for resistance to change include individuals' desire to maintain their current situation, the idea that change will bring uncertainty and concerns about the new situation that will arise as a result of change.

The success of the changes to be realized at the school level mostly depends on the success of the leaders. For this reason, school principals should assume a leadership role. School principals can effectively manage change by giving importance to communication with teachers, creating a collaborative culture and making themselves a part of the change (Taş, 2009). Leaders as organizational change agents should create a sustainable culture of change. In order to achieve change at today's pace, leaders need to constantly examine their environment, make change plans and guide individuals. If there is a culture of consensus, tolerance and trust in the organization and the need for change is felt by all employees, resistance to change will be low.

Unfortunately, change is not sufficiently effective in education and educational policies, the main purpose of which is to bring about positive changes in the behavior of individuals. Educational institutions are both affected

Organizational Change in Educational Organizations

by the environment and affect their environment through the individuals they raise. Therefore, changes in educational institutions will affect the whole country and shape everyone's future. While planning change to solve the problems that arise in educational institutions and education policies, focusing only on the problem and ignoring the social and cultural dynamics of the country will solve the problem for a short time and will not bring a permanent solution. Since the change models or solutions proposed or put into practice are models based on data obtained in other countries, especially in western countries, they do not fit the conditions of Turkey. As a result, while trying to solve one problem, other problems arise. Therefore, Turkey-specific models need to be developed to solve the problems of education in Turkey. Social and cultural characteristics should be taken into account when defining and solving educational problems.

The most important priorities should be to identify the attitudes of teachers and managers, who are among the most important actors in the Turkish education system, towards change and resistance to change, as well as to investigate why they react to change and to include them in change processes. If teachers are not happy in their jobs, they will reflect this unhappiness to their students and an efficient educational environment will not be created. Since teachers who are happy in their job will devote theirself more to their job, equip theirself with new knowledge and raise happier and more successful students, change in the Turkish education system should start with solutions that will make teachers happy.

REFERENCES

Açıkalın, A. (1998). Üç rakamlı yıldönümlerine doğru. *Kuram ve Uygulamada Eğitim Yönetimi, 16*(16), 387–393.

Altunay, E., Arlı, D., & Yalçınkaya, M. (2012). İlköğretim okullarında değişim yönetimine ilişkin nitel bir çalışma. *Kuram ve Uygulamada Eğitim Bilimleri, 12*(2), 713–730.

Amburgey, T. L., Dawn, K., & Barnett, W. P. (1993). The dynamics of organizational change and failure. *Administrative Science Quarterly, 38*(1), 51–73. doi:10.2307/2393254

Argon, T., & Özçelik, N. (2008). İlköğretim okulu yöneticilerinin değişimi yönetme yeterlikleri. *Mehmet Akif Ersoy Üniversitesi Eğitim Fakültesi Dergisi, 8*(16), 70–89.

Bennett, N., Crawford, M., & Riches, C. (Eds.). (1992). *Managing change in education: individual and organizational perspectives.* Sage.

Beycioğlu, K., & Aslan, M. (2010). Okul gelişiminde temel dinamik olarak değişim ve yenileşme: Okul yöneticileri ve öğretmenlerin rolleri. *Yüzüncü Yıl Üniversitesi Eğitim Fakültesi Dergisi, 7*(1), 153–173.

Calabrese, R. L., & Shoho, A. (2000). Recating educational administration programs as learning organizations. *The Journal of Educational Management, 14*(5), 210–218.

Cameron, E., & Green, M. (2004). *Making sense of change management.* Kogan Page.

Ceyhan, E., & Summak, M. S. (1999). Haşlanmış kurbağa ve değişim yönetimi. *Kuram ve Uygulamada Eğitim Yönetimi, 20,* 521–544.

Choi, M., & Wendy, E. A. (2011). Individual readiness for organizational change and its implications for human resource and organization development. *Human Resource Development Review, 10*(1), 46–73. doi:10.1177/1534484310384957

Demers, C. (2007). *Organizational change theories: A synthesis.* Sage.

Dent, E. B., & Goldberg, S. G. (1999). Challenging "resistance to change". *The Journal of Applied Behavioral Science, 35*(1), 25–41. doi:10.1177/0021886399351003

Ellis, S. & Dick, P. (2003). Introduction to organizational behaviour. London: Mc Graw Hill.

Erdoğan, İ. (2012). Eğitimde değişim yönetimi (3rd ed.). Ankara: Pegem Akademi.

Floyd, P. (2002). *Organizational change.* Capstone.

Fullan, M. (2006). *Change theory: A force for school improvement.* Centre for Strategic Education.

Fullan, M. (2007). *The new meaning of educational change.* Teachers College Press.

Fullan, M., & Hargreaves, A. (1998). *What's worth fighting for out there?* Teachers College Press.

George, J. M., & Gareth, R. (2002). *Understanding and managing organizational behaviour.* Pearson.

Gökçe, F. (2004). Okulda değişmenin yönetimi. *Eğitim Fakültesi Dergisi,* *17*(2), 211–226.

Gül, H. (2006). Çevresel baskı gruplarının okulun genel işleyişine etkileri (Kocaeli-İzmit örneği). *Kocaeli Üniversitesi Sosyal Bilimler Enstitüsü Dergisi,* *11*(1), 71–84.

Hakonsson, D. D., Klaas, P., & Carrol, T. N. (2012). The structural properties of sustainable, continuous change: Achieving reliability through flexibility. *The Journal of Applied Behavioral Science, 49*(2), 179–205. doi:10.1177/0021886312464520

Hellriegel, D., & Slocum, J. W. Jr. (2011). *Organizational behaviour.* Cengage Learning.

Johns, E. A. (1973). *The sociology of organizational change.* Pergamon.

Karip, E. (2005). Daha bir eğitimde değişim tartışmaları. *Kuram ve Uygulamada Eğitim Yönetimi, 42,* 149–150.

Kezar, A. J. (2001). *Understanding and facilitating organizational change in the 21st century: Recent research and conceptualizations. ASHE-ERIC Hiigher Education Reports, 28(4).*

Kotter, J. P. (1996). *Leading change.* Harvard Business School Press.

Lee, W., & Krayer, K. J. (2004). An integrated model for organizational change. *Performance Improvement, 43*(7), 22–26. doi:10.1002/pfi.4140430708

Leonard, H. S. (2013). The history and current status of organizational and systems change. In The Wiley-Blackwell handbook of the psychology of leadership, change, and organizational development (pp. 239-366). Oxford: John Wiley ve Sons, Ltd.

Lewin, K. (1958). Group decisions and social change. In E. E. Maccobby, T.M. Newcomb, & E. L. Hartley (Eds.), Readings in Social Psychology (pp. 330-344). New York: Holt, Rinehart &Winston.

Örücü, D. (2013). Örgütsel değişimin yönetimi. In S. Özdemir (Ed.), Eğitim yönetiminde kuram ve uygulama (pp. 445-479). Ankara: Pegem Akademi.

Owens, R. G. (2004). *Organizational behavior in education: Adaptive leadership and school reform.* Pearson.

Özdemir, S., & Cemaloğlu, N. (1999). Eğitimde değişimi uygulama modelleri. *Kuram ve Uygulamada Eğitim Yönetimi, 17*(17), 91–103.

Özmen, F., & Sönmez, Y. (2007). Değişim sürecinde eğitim örgütlerinde değişim ajanlarının rolleri. *Fırat Üniversitesi Sosyal Bilimler Dergisi, 17*(2), 177–198.

Poole, M. S. (2004). Central issues in the study of change and innovation. In M. S. Poole, & A. H. Van de Ven (Eds.), Handbook of organizational change and innovation (pp. 3-31). New York: Oxford University Press.

Schein, E. H. (2010). *Organizational culture and leadership.* Jossey-Bass.

Şimşek, H., & Louis, K. S. (1994). Organizational change paadigm shift: An analysis of the change process in a large, puplic university. *The Journal of Higher Education, 65*(6), 670–695.

Taş, A. (2009). Ortaöğretim okulu müdürlerinin değişimi yönetme davranışlarına ilişkin öğretmen algılarının değerlendirilmesi. *İnönü Üniversitesi Eğitim Fakültesi Dergisi, 10*(2), 1-18.

Töremen, F. (2002). Eğitim örgütlerinde değişimin engel ve nedenleri. *Fırat Üniversitesi Sosyal Bilimler Dergisi, 12*(1), 185–202.

Türk Dil Kurumu. (2022). *Değişim.* https://sozluk.gov.tr/

Van de Ven, A. H., & Poole, M. S. (1995). Explaining development and change in organizations. *Academy of Management Review, 20*(3), 510–540. doi:10.2307/258786

Willower, D. J. (1963). Barriers to change in educational organizations. *Theory into Practice, 2*(5), 257–263. doi:10.1080/00405846309541873

Yılmaz, D., Kılıçoğlu, G., & Turan, S. (2014). Örgütsel değişim. In S. Turan (Ed.), Eğitim yönetimi: Teori, araştırma ve uygulama (pp. 253-292). Ankara: Pegem Akademi.

Chapter 4

The Impact of Distributed Leadership on Effective Professional Development via Organizational Innovativeness

Ramazan Atasoy
https://orcid.org/0000-0002-9198-074X
Harran University, Turkey

Mehmet Tufan Yalçın
Çankırı Karatekin University, Turkey

ABSTRACT

This chapter aims to explore to what extent distributed leadership affects effective professional development of teachers mediating organizational innovativeness in the sample of the countries participating in the TALIS 2018 survey. Accordingly, the sample consisted of 15,980 schools and 261,429 teachers from 48 countries participating in TALIS 2018. The study found that teachers' gender, education level, and experience have a significant, albeit low, effect on their thoughts on the effectiveness of professional development activities. Another important research finding has shown that school principals' distributed leadership behaviors contribute to the effectiveness of professional development activities by promoting organizational innovativeness. Based on the findings of this study, the identified variables should be considered in the development of policies and practices for teacher learning. Future research could explore multilevel models that would examine the potential impacts of various leadership styles and teacher attributes on teacher learning.

DOI: 10.4018/978-1-7998-3940-8.ch004

Copyright © 2024, IGI Global. Copying or distributing in print or electronic forms without written permission of IGI Global is prohibited.

INTRODUCTION

Contemporary educational research focusing on educational administration and policies shows that teacher quality has a significant impact on school outcomes (Buske, 2018; Darling-Hammond et al., 2017; Hattie, 2009). For this reason, studies to determine the characteristics of effective professional development activities that improve the quality of teachers' knowledge and skills remain a priority for practitioners, researchers, and policymakers (Ainley & Carstens, 2018; Bates & Morgan, 2018; Desimone, 2009). Therefore, despite the gap between theory and practice in teacher professional development, the linkage f the relationship between them should be taken into account (Day, 1997; EL-Deghaidy et al., 2015; Mansour et al., 2014). Enhancing teacher attributes and learning is the main focus of most education reforms to improve student learning outcomes. Remarkably, several studies highlight that teacher professional development is equivalent to educational reforms (Desimone, 2009; Sykes, 1996). Along with these efforts, it is seen that there is a need for empirical studies using advanced statistics to discover the characteristics of activities that increase the quality of teachers and to determine the school and individual level variables that affect teacher learning (Ainley & Carstens, 2018, p. 49; Darling-Hammond et al., 2017; Desimone, 2009). When these studies are scrutinized, the school principal's leadership behaviors and the school's innovative structure come to the fore as variables emerge as characteristics that can affect teachers' professional development studies at school level.

Leadership is essential for organizational innovativeness and effective school improvement efforts. The study of hierarchies dominated organizational theory for most of the last century, but now researchers are more interested in peer-based dynamics, interactions and distributed leadership (Heckscher, 2007). This shift is evident in both the academic and the practical literature on management, especially in the growing fields of complexity science and network theory. According to a complexity view, formal leaders focus on "managing interdependencies" and care more about fostering rich relational networks than "controlling processes or outcomes" (Leithwood et al., 2009). This circumstance has been one of the key forces that highlight distributed leadership in the context of altering contemporary school management approaches as well as effective school and organizational innovativeness activities.

Many studies have explored the organizational structures, leadership roles, and school conditions that foster innovation (Blase & Blase, 1999; Hallinger & Heck, 1996). For decades, theoretical perspectives on management and leadership have traditionally been viewed as individual activities, i.e., something that a leader does or is supposed to do. However, this paradigmatic assumption has been questioned and criticized as a "romance of leadership" or "heroic leadership." Moreover, alternative perspectives such as distributed leadership (DL) characterized as the sharing of generic leadership tasks to affect resource availability, decision making, and goal setting within an organizational perspective have recently emerged in the field of management and leadership research (Jønsson et al., 2016). Researchers have reported that successful leadership can generate the effective professional development conditions in which followers can maximize their efficacy (Hallinger, 2011; Harris, 2004; Harris & Muijs, 2004; Wallace, 2002). However, there still seems to be a lack of empirical studies that demonstrate how successful the school principals of the participating countries are in improving the conditions of their teachers' professional development.

School leadership is more than just an individual activity or an organizational role. It involves multiple actors and interactions that shape how a school organization is led (Gronn, 2002). To understand this complexity, management and leadership researchers need to examine the mechanisms of alternative leadership that enable organizational adaptation to complex tasks and demands. DL is consistent with other traditional bureaucratic management systems in this regard. Some researchers have shown how principals can foster and maintain effective forms of shared decision-making at the school level (Blase & Blase, 1999). Higher degrees of DL behavior may lead to successful organizational change and better outcomes for student learning and professional development in schools (Blase & Blase, 1999; Harris, 2008, 2009, 2013). However, this theoretical perspective requires more serious empirical support (Bolden, 2011).

The literature suggests that distributed leadership can have a positive impact on organizational change (Graetz, 2000; Iandoli & Zollo, 2008). Organizational change is an expression of organizational innovation and school improvement efforts (Bangs & Frost, 2012). In this context, building and sharing leadership capacity within the school is crucial for organizational innovativeness and school improvement. Moreover, research shows that effective school leaders who have shared visions and norms focused on a sense of collective responsibility for school development, collaboration, and students' academic success create expectations, motivation and opportunities for effective teachers' professional development (Newmann & Wehlage, 1995).

Literature strengthened that DL can improve schools and enhance teachers' professional capacity for development. However, it does not specify how this distributed leadership should operate in school settings. Bennett and friends (2003) point out that there is a lack of empirical studies on how distributed leadership works in practice. Therefore, it is hard to find examples and images of distributed leadership in action (Hopkins & Jackson, 2002). While empirical studies on DL are still scarce, it may be worthwhile to lead some research on distributed leadership using various related variables of effective school improvement. In this context, the study is unique, remarkable, and distinctive in that the distributed leadership behaviors of school principals selected from all participating countries in the Teaching and Learning International Survey (TALIS) 2018 could provide extensive data-based information on organizational innovativeness and effective professional development of teachers. This study is also very important in terms of identifying individual and organizational level characteristics that affect teacher education and providing evidence-based insights for policy development processes.

THE PURPOSE OF THE STUDY: LITERATURE REVIEW

This book chapter explores the impact of distributed leadership on organizational innovativeness and effectiveness of professional development evidence base, highlighting both the possibilities and the limitations as a force for positive change and improvement in schools. In this section, first of all, the definition, conceptual framework and importance of the concepts of distributed leadership, organizational innovativeness and effectiveness of professional development have been mentioned. In the second part, we aimed to explore to what extent distributed leadership affect effective professional development of teachers mediating organizational innovativeness in the sample of the countries participating in the TALIS 2018 survey.

Effective Professional Development

Teacher professional development refers to the ongoing improvement of teachers' qualifications and their active engagement in addressing educational and training challenges. Teachers' professional development affects their pedagogical expertise and classroom performance, which in turn impacts the academic achievement of their students (Bates & Morgan, 2018; Desimone, 2009). Teacher feedback and development are crucial areas of interest for education systems globally from policymakers to practitioners, as they aim to provide teachers with the necessary competencies to equip students with the skills required for the 21st century (Ainley & Carstens, 2018, p. 47; Hattie, 2009). In this context, the gap between theory and practice in teachers' professional development is a well-known challenge, but scholars have emphasized the importance of examining how they are connected (Day, 1997; EL-Deghaidy et al., 2015; Mansour et al., 2014). The views and needs of teachers should be respected and addressed in the design of professional development programs. Otherwise, it has been noted that teachers may feel dissatisfied with the quality and relevance of the learning opportunities they are offered. The following are the findings of several research that have identified the features of effective professional development programs in the literature. One of these studies is the report on Effective Teacher Professional Development by the Learning Policy Institute research team, which reviewed a substantial amount of literature that demonstrated a relationship between teachers' professional development practices and positive student learning outcomes (Darling-Hammond et al., 2017). Based on their meta-analysis of 35 studies, the research team identified seven design elements that enhance the quality and impact of professional development.

Focus on Content: A key principle of professional development is to focus on instructional methods and current information that are relevant to a specific curriculum setting. Effective professional development also involves incorporating and addressing different ways of teaching content to diverse student groups. For instance, science teachers read articles to keep abreast of current trends in their discipline, to deepen their understanding, and to engage students' interest in science teaching and learning.

Active Learning: This strategy seeks to shift teachers away from traditional learning methods and environments that are lecture-based and have no direct relationship to their classrooms or students. According to the approach, teachers are directly involved in the design and implementation of teaching strategies to provide professional learning, giving them the opportunity to learn how to design a similar teaching model for their students. This principle involves enhancing teachers' abilities to evaluate student work and use resources effectively by engaging in or leading the model lesson. These experiences enable teachers to address the difficulties they may face in practice and to question and reflect on them (Bates & Morgan, 2018).

Support for Collaboration: This approach proposes that teachers can enhance their collective expertise by exchanging ideas and working together for effective professional development. Moreover, teachers can collaborate to create communities that positively influence the culture and instruction of their classroom, school and district. Highly collaborative teachers establish a trusting relationship so they can take risks to address practice issues related to students' learning.

Models of Effective Practice: High-quality professional learning encourages teachers to share effective curriculum models and courses. These resources, which comprise sample lesson plans, unit plans, student activities, peer observations, and video or written teaching cases, should offer teachers concrete examples of what best practices look like.

Coaching and Expert Support: This element involves providing teachers with teaching coaches, teaching leaders, university scholars, and experts who can cater to their specific needs. The main goal of these studies is to support teachers in their classrooms and to give them customized feedback based on their needs and strengths. This is because, according to this perspective, there is no universal professional development approach.

Feedback and Reflection: Feedback and reflection are distinct but interrelated processes in professional development. This approach proposes that teachers should have adequate time to reflect and receive feedback, examine outcomes, and modify their practice.

Sustained Duration: The final element concerns the duration of effective professional development. Therefore, no matter how engaging and successful professional development is, it cannot be achieved in a single session. In other words, quality professional development should be spread over time and its duration should be measured in weeks, months, and years.

All of these elements, outlined by Darling Hammond and colleagues (2017) are gears for effective professional development. All components need to work together. In this way, it can ensure that planning and decisions about professional development are not haphazard (Bates & Morgan, 2018). In another important study in the literature describing the features of activities that improve teachers' knowledge, skills and attitudes, Desimone (2009) identified five essential features of effective professional development. These features are described below:

Content Focus: This principle highlights the importance of developing teacher content knowledge for effective professional development. Therefore, it suggests that content-specific teacher education be implemented to ensure quality professional development.

Active Learning: Providing teachers opportunities to engage in active learning is also related to both their own learning development and the effectiveness of applied professional development from experts on how to implement active learning for students.

Coherence: The literature highlights two important aspects of the concept. First, the concept refers to how much teacher learning matches teachers' knowledge and beliefs. Second, it is described as the coherence of school, district and state reforms and policies with what is taught in professional development.

Duration: It entails devoting enough time to activities that will result in intellectual and pedagogical transformation in teachers. Although research does not specify a time frame, it does demonstrate that activities lasting a term and comprising 20 hours or more result in more effective teacher learning.

Collective Participation: Collective participation, the final critical element, suggests that teacher learning activities involving teachers from the same school, grade, or department are more effective.

It is clear that studies on effective teacher professional development and teacher learning stress common features (Darling-Hammond et al., 2017; Desimone, 2009; Hattie, 2009). Research over the last decade has shown that more empirically valid methods are needed to examine how teachers' professional development is effective in their teaching practices (Desimone, 2009). TALIS 2013 provided information on how feedback and professional development relate to teachers' working lives, but TALIS 2018 aimed to explore the relationships in depth. In this context, TALIS 2018 aims to provide data that will help us better understand the professional development activities that teachers find useful, as well as the characteristics of these activities (Ainley & Carstens, 2018, p. 49). In this book chapter, we have sought to reveal the personal, professional, institutional, and wider policy contexts that influence the conditions or factors related to teacher learning and professional development in education systems. In other words, this research examines the critical features of effective professional development, which are evidently active components of teacher interaction that are intended to guide professionals in the design, implementation and evaluation of professional development programs.

Distributed Leadership

DL is currently a hot topic, vogue, dynamic, relational, inclusive, collaborative, contextually, and fluid phenomenon in the field of school leadership. It has generated a great deal of curiosity, widespread interest, debate, and "unbridled enthusiasm" with researchers, policy makers, educational reformers in the field. Everyone seems to have an opinion on distributed leadership, whether they support it or not. What is undeniable is that distributed leadership has become the most popular leadership concept of the present time. This heightened interest can be linked to a shift away from theorizing and empirical research that focuses on a single leader and structural changes within schools and across school systems (Harris, 2009). So, what precisely does DL imply? Despite increasing interest in the concept, there are competing and sometimes contradictory interpretations.

Distributed leaders have to create a common culture of expectations and foster a creative school culture that uses individual skills and abilities maximizing the human capacity within the organization. This can also be seen as an approach that relies on flexible and expert power of control and coordination mechanisms in distributed leadership. A common culture that aligns with organizational goals and is embraced by all followers also provides the basis for how to improve teaching and share leadership (Elmore, 2000).

Some educators have chosen to articulate a broad spectrum of ambiguous definitions of DL, extending from "additive to holistic or person-plus" (Gronn, 2000; Spillane, 2006; Spillane et al., 2004), from the normative to the theoretical and, by implication (Harris, 2008), ranging from seeing a cure-all recipe for whatever afflicts schools to describing it as "a set of vague notions flying in loose formation." It is obvious that similar notions in the present literature outlining the distributed leadership strategy generally coincide with the concepts of shared, collaborative, democratic, and participative leadership. According to Day and friends (2010), successful school principals have several characteristics that align with the distributed leadership perspective. These include enhancing the conditions for teaching and learning, developing and diversifying the curriculum, reorganizing the school structure, raising teacher quality, building connections with external stakeholders, and fostering relationships within the school community. Therefore, DL can be characterized as the sharing of generic leadership tasks to affect resource availability, decision making, and goal setting within an organizational perspective, according to Gronn (2000) and Jønsson and friends (2016) agency model. We are interested in Spillane's (2006) holistic or "person-plus" labels for distributed leadership, which emphasize the deliberate and synergistic interactions among various leadership resources in the organization. This view of DL considers the whole of the leaders' work, not just the individual parts. It also recognizes the high interdependence and complexity of the collective social processes that lead to learning for both the individuals and the organizations involved in leadership. It incorporates the assumptions that underlie it (Pearce & Conger, 2003).

Distributed leadership implies that the leader-plus aspect is an important element in school improvement and organizational change (Harris, 2004; Wallace, 2002). It is based on the idea that people at all levels can engage in direction-setting and influence practices, rather than having these practices confined to top-level administrators with certain personal traits and attributes (Fletcher & Kaufer, 2003). Because all leadership entails influencing, coordinating, and controlling the organization, leadership is always distributed to some extent within the organization. This does not, however, imply that under DL theory everyone within the organization would lead at the same time. DL theory perspective recognizes that followers rather than a fixed phenomenon have the ability to lead inside the organization, but the secret to success will be how administration is facilitated, regulated, and fostered (Harris, 2008; Leithwood et al., 2007). This perspective on leadership does not focus on the actions and beliefs of a single leader, but rather sees leadership as a dynamic and fluid organizational process.

The key concept in the basis of distributed leadership is interaction in the execution of particular leadership tasks. According to Spillane and friends (2004), and Heckscher (2007), DL emerges from the interaction of leaders, teachers, and orchestrating contextual instructional situations. It is a kind of horizontal leadership where the leadership practice (empowering others to lead) is divided among organizational members. In this case, organizational impact and decision-making processes depend on the interaction of leaders, followers, and their situation within the school rather than solely a single leader's ability, skill, charisma, and/or cognition. DL also involves developing the leadership abilities of others and overseeing their leadership work, giving them constructive feedback on their performance.

Distributed leadership is a useful analytical tool to examine how organizational development and learning occur. Gronn (2000) states that social influence is a key feature of leadership. He also suggests that leadership can be more or less distributed in school organizations, where coordinated actions and leadership of these actions are essential for all members of the organization. These actions can arise from a situation as spontaneous collaboration, they can be based on intuitive working relationships that rely on mutual understanding and knowledge, or they can be formalized as formal or informal practices. According to Harris and Muijs (2004), school organizations have a suitable context for distributed leadership. They argue that leadership capability and capacity are not fixed, but can be extended. This means that different people in schools can assume or be assigned leadership roles, creating a dynamic pattern of distributed leadership. This new leadership approach requires flexible, creative, and fluent leadership resources to meet the changing leadership needs of the organization. It also makes the school organization more responsive to organizational change and innovation.

Research findings provide important clues about how the teacher element can create a driving force in differentiating effective schools from others. Çoban and Atasoy (2020) found a relationship between distributed leadership and organizational innovativeness. Similarly, the research evidence also showed a positive link between distributed leadership, organizational improvement, and student achievement (Blase & Blase, 1999; Harris, 2008; Heck &

Hallinger, 2010; Iandoli & Zollo, 2008). Leithwood and friends (2009) found that leadership distribution that was planned had a more positive effect on school development and change. According to Leithwood and Jantzi (2000), teacher effectiveness can be improved by sharing more leadership roles with teachers. Leithwood, and Jantzi (2000) explored that a higher proportion of leadership activity distributed to teachers had a positive influence on school outcomes. Therefore, the performance of a school depends on how leadership practice is distributed among its members, according to Leithwood and friends (2007). They also found that the effect of distributed leadership on school outcomes differed based on the distribution pattern of leadership. They pointed out two key conditions for effective leadership distribution. First, those who are assigned leadership roles should possess or acquire the relevant knowledge and abilities. Second, there should be a planned way of coordinating distributed leadership (Leithwood et al., 2007).

Organizational Innovativeness (OI)

Today, innovativeness is considered as a necessary characteristic for almost every organization and institution, including educational organizations, to inevitably adapt to change and ensure its sustainability. Organizational innovativeness is a concept based on the change management approach. It refers to the ability of an organization to create a learning culture that can adopt and respond to innovative processes and approaches quickly (Gopalakrishnan & Damanpour, 1997; Subramanian & Nilakanta, 1996). Organizational innovativeness can be defined as the effort spent to become more advantageous compared to its competitors by producing new products and services or by discovering different usage areas of existing products and services by using new ideas, strategies, policies, inputs, programs, techniques (Ni et al., 2021). According to Lumpkin and Dess (1996) organizational innovation is defined as the organizational capacity that triggers creative processes, experiences, ideas, new approaches and techniques to produce new products and services. From another point of view, organizational innovation can also be considered as the compulsory but dynamic capability of the organization that reveals an innovation for industries or stakeholders and enables these innovative approaches to be used in products (Gabler et al., 2015). In this book chapter, we use the TALIS 2018 definition of organizational innovativeness, which measures teachers' willingness to develop new ideas, their openness to change, their problem-solving skills and their collaborative environment where they exchange practices with each other.

Thurlings and friends (2015) describe the three basic elements for the realization of innovation in educational organizations. These are individuals who adapt quickly to society, the need for innovation and professional guidance to educational institutions. In educational institutions in order to increase organizational innovation, all members of the organization, including students, should be willing to adapt to innovation. In this context, the interaction of teachers with school leaders and students will facilitate the instructional management based on innovation (Nurutdinova et al., 2016).

A distributed leadership that reduces instructional barriers (OECD, 2015) plays an important role in establishing and maintaining an innovation culture in educational organizations. In addition, teachers who are open to innovation, support innovation, use technology, cooperate and communicate efficiently are another important pillar for the sustainability of innovation and school outcomes (Lee et al., 2016). Organizational innovation contributes to increasing the success and satisfaction of students by providing equal opportunities in education and providing students with the skills they will need in the future (Lee et al., 2016). Blomeke and friends (2021) found out that schools with a greater focus on innovation tend to have more positive results when it comes to teacher collaboration and knowledge sharing, job satisfaction, cognitive engagement of students, and innovative teaching methods.

To create an innovative and sustainable organizational improvement in educational settings, one needs to work continuously, maintain innovation with intrinsic motivation, willingness, and embrace change at all levels of the organization. Nevertheless, researchers have long argued that Technology-Enhanced Learning innovations have great potential and demand, but they also face significant challenges that often lead to disappointing outcomes (Coburn, 2003; Niederhauser et al., 2018). Undoubtedly, it is necessary to explore the background of this negative feedback received in technology-supported school structures, which is reflected in the research. Otherwise, individual and organizational resistance may develop against innovative initiatives. Organizational innovativeness can face many obstacles, such as lack of funds, insufficient national policies, or teacher reluctance. However, some studies suggest solutions to this problem (Fullan, 2001; Rodríguez-Triana et al., 2020) such as developing collaborative cultures at schools and involving teachers in co-designing innovative methods and co-creating effective professional development practices. At this point, it would be beneficial to create an innovative school climate and focus on the professional development of all human resources of the school organization. To create an effective innovative learning environment, Trask and friends (2023) highlights the importance of considering and regulating multiple factors, including curriculum, social relations, individual needs, and spatial characteristics, as these are constantly evolving. In summary, innovative learning environments must be adaptable to changing dynamics and address multiple factors that impact the learning experience.

Organizational Innovativeness and Education

Organizational innovativeness approaches, which are a powerful tool in strengthening school improvement practices in line with 21st century skills, are important topics of leadership and Educational Management research. Each member of a school organization must recognize and lead innovation, which can be affected by school improvements and organizational changes.

In education, organizational innovativeness means that schools can adapt to new ways of teaching and learning. In other words, organizations that have more organizational innovative tend to introduce or adopt more innovations (Hurley et al., 2005). For this to happen, school principals need to act as distributed leaders and create a shared vision for their schools. Teachers can develop innovative ideas more effectively when they have access to quality professional development and opportunities to collaborate with their peers. School principals can foster a culture of organizational innovation in their schools by encouraging and supporting teachers to work together and learn from each other.

Scholars have explored how school leadership factors shape the structure, processes and outcomes of schools. They have also sought to identify the types of distributed leadership roles and practices that foster school improvement (Bangs & Frost, 2012). School improvement can benefit from educational innovations, but this depends on whether school principals value innovative practices and teachers adopt new teaching and learning practices that foster analytical, creative and inquiry-based learning (Webb & Cox, 2004). Huberman (1998) has revealed that teachers may lose faith in the positive potential of change initiatives if they have experienced mismanaged approaches concerning school improvement and organizational change. The way a reform is introduced can greatly affect teachers' willingness to implement it. Therefore, it is important that school principals, as distributive leaders, support teachers' professional development and sustain organizational innovation and school development. This can enhance the impact of educational reforms. It is also crucial that distributed leaders support teachers' involvement in decision-making. Moreover, organizational innovation in school organizations should aim at creating a learning culture for both students and teachers and developing a pedagogy that enables learning organizations. This perspective

The Impact of Distributed Leadership

implies a new understanding of the school, but it also demands a significant change in the school administrator, the teacher's role, the student's role and the support they need.

School organizations can use organizational innovativeness to improve their performance and innovative capacity. A collaborative approach is in line with House and Senge (2010) idea that learning organizations have a shared vision of organizational aims, and that open-mindedness accommodates diverse viewpoints, experimenting, questioning existing assumptions, and shared beliefs to promote continuous innovation. This means that they work in teams to find, create, and apply new knowledge from various sources. They also communicate and act on the new ideas they receive for school improvement (Hansen & Birkinshaw, 2007). School systems can learn how to create innovative and adaptive learning organizations by looking at innovativeness, which is a cultural factor and a social resource that supports innovative behavior. A culture of organizational innovation has some individual and group-level traits that show idea generation, learning, creativity, and change at both levels. While innovative ideas come from individual insight, learning in social and dynamic systems like educational organizations only happens when ideas are shared, action is taken, and common meaning is created at the group and organizational level (Hurley et al., 2005). At this point, distributed leadership can be helpful in building an innovative culture in schools.

METHODOLOGY

Our research method is based on a literature review. We conducted a secondary data analysis using The Teaching and Learning International Survey (TALIS) 2018 data. TALIS 2018 data provides researchers with robust international indicators from a large-scale and ongoing survey. TALIS collects data from teachers, school leaders and their learning settings as well as contextual information for schools. It focuses on lower secondary schools (ISCED 2), with the option to include primary (ISCED 1) and upper secondary (ISCED 3) schools using clustered sampling. The TALIS 2018 investigates how effective instructional and institutional conditions might improve student learning. It also explores how these conditions differ within and between countries, as well as through time.

This research used the data set collected from school leaders and teachers in their schools by TALIS. The sample consisted of 15,980 schools, 261,429 teachers from 48 countries participating in TALIS 2018. This chapter presents the results of the two level structural equational model using these data. It also reviews the related literature and provide various suggestions based on the purpose of this chapter. The school principals who participated in the research had the following characteristics: 45.5% (7,269) were female, 50.9% (8,137) were male, and 3.6% (574) had missing data on gender. Regarding education, 3.4% (541) had associate degrees or lower, 35.9% (5,737) had undergraduate degrees, 48% (7,675) had master degrees and 3.8% (601) had doctorate degrees, and 8.9% (1,421) had missing data on highest level of formal educational completed. On average, these principals had 8.76 years of managerial experience. The teachers who participated in the research had the following characteristics: 68.8% (179,731) were female, 31.2% (81,686) were male, and 0,003% (9) had missing data on gender. Regarding education, 6.2% (16,383) had associate degrees or lower, 51.5% (134,693) had undergraduate degrees, 35.1% (91,821) had master degrees and 1.1% (2,747) had doctorate degrees, and 6.0% (15,782) had missing data on highest level of formal educational completed. On average, these teachers had 16.20 years of experiences as a teacher in total.

DATA ANALYSIS

The TALIS 2018 study utilized a "complex survey design" methodology. This involved the random selection of approximately 200 schools in each participating country. From these schools, a two-step cluster sampling method was used to sample 20 teachers (OECD, 2019, p. 114). The analytical aim of this study is to mitigate errors through the utilization of a model-based technique that effectively addresses the issue of non-independence among observations. In order to implement this methodology, variables are defined at each hierarchical level and subsequently used to construct multilevel analysis models. Applying sampling weights to data analysis is crucial due to the variability in sampling probability and response rates among schools. The sampling weights used in this study to represent teachers were derived from the TCHWGT variable, which was rescaled by the OECD through a series of steps to account for variations in selection probability, response rates, and other relevant factors. This measure was implemented to guarantee that every sample had an equitable influence on the estimation of the parameter. The data analysis employed IBM SPSS 25 software for conducting basic statistical analyses and examining correlations. Additionally, Mplus 8.3 software was utilized for investigating latent variable structures and performing structural equation modelling.

The Impact of Distributed Leadership

VARIABLES

The study considers various contextual variables at the teacher and school levels. The teacher level variable is the effective professional development (T3EFFPD) variable, which contains items on the characteristics of professional development activities that have had the greatest positive impact on teachers' profession over the past 12 months. This scale consists of 4 items to measure the characteristics of professional development activities that improve teachers' teaching skills. The answers range from "Yes" (1), "No" (2). However, these items are reverse coded. Example item can be given as "It built on my prior knowledge-TT3G26A". In addition, the scale also had acceptable levels of reliability coefficients, model fit and measurement invariance at all ISCED levels (OECD, 2019, p. 267).

The school-level independent variables were the scores of the principals on distributed leadership (DL) and organizational innovativeness (T3PORGIN). DL and T3PORGIN were considered as a one-dimensional structure. The items belonging to these variables were taken from the TALIS 2018 research. In the DL variable section, school principals were asked to report how often they performed 3 different activities related to these variables in the last 12 months using a 4-point Likert scale (1 = Strongly disagree, 4 = Strongly agree). We can say that the internal consistency values of DL (Cronbach's alpha, α= 0.758) are reasonably reliable (Can, 2018, p. 351; George & Mallery, 2003). T3PORGIN variable section, principals were asked to agree with four statements about innovation using a 4-point Likert scale (1= Strongly disagree, 4= Agree). The reliability coefficient of T3PORGIN is strong for most populations, except for three cases. It is only acceptable for Slovenia ISCED level 2 and Viet Nam ISCED level 3, and it is weak for Viet Nam ISCED level 2 (OECD, 2019, p. 414). The control variables were the teacher's gender (1= Female, 0= Male), education level and total years of work experience as a teacher.

This study calculated ICC1 (inter-country variability) as .415 and ICC2 (inter-country reliability) as .920 for the T3EFFPD variable. It was found that the ICC1 value exceeded the threshold of .05, while the ICC2 value exceeded the threshold of .70 (Bliese, 2000). The results indicate that the data structure and reliability are appropriate for conducting multilevel analysis.

Figure 1. Conceptual model

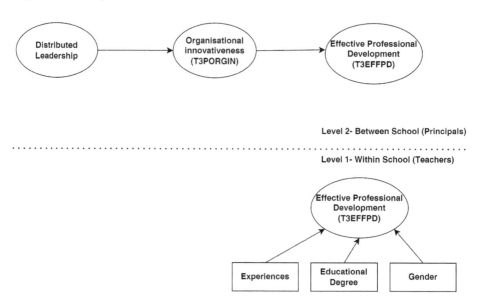

RESULTS

Preliminary Analyses

This study examined the impact of school principals' behaviors on teachers' perceptions of effective professional development in the TALIS 2018 survey. A Pearson correlation analysis was conducted as the final preliminary analysis to examine the relationships between the variables in the study. Table 1 presents the average values and Pearson correlation coefficients for the variables.

Table 1 displays the mean value of the dependent variable, T3EFFPD, as 12.44. The T3EFFPD variable exhibits a weak correlation with other control variables at the teacher level. There exists a weak yet statistically significant correlation between the T3EFFPD variable and school-level variables. In the second phase of the study, we utilized MSEM to assess the contextual model and investigate the direct impacts on effective professional development. The model fit statistics suggest a strong fit. The findings indicate a strong alignment with the data: RMSEA = .020; CFI = .934; TLI = .893; $SRMR_{Within}$ = .000; $SRMR_{Between}$ = .035. Table 2 shows the outcomes of the multilevel model.

The Impact of Distributed Leadership

Table 1. Descriptive statistics and correlations among variables

Variable	Mean	1	2	3	4
Teacher level (n=187.509)					
1. T3EFFPD	12.44	1	-.019**	-.056**	.031**
2. Gender	-		1	-.041**	-.020**
3. Educational Degree	5.30			1	.027**
4. Experiences	16.20				1
School level (n=15.980)					
1. T3EFFPD	12.42	1	.068**	.049**	-
2. DL	11.24		1	.230**	-
3. T3PORGIN	12.45			1	-

Note(s): T3EFFPD = Effective Professional Development, DL = Distributed Leadership, T3PORGIN= Organizational Innovativeness, ** p <. 01. Gender (reference group is female)

Table 2. The standardized model results

Construct	Coefficient		95% Confidence Interval		*p*
	Estimate	SE	Lower Bound	Upper Bound	
Direct effects *(School level)*					
T3PORGIN → T3EFFPD	.037	.010	.018	.056	.000**
DL → T3PORGIN	.389	.011	.367	.410	.000**
Direct effects *(Teacher level)*					
GENDER→ T3EFFPD	.015	.003	.010	.021	.000**
EDUCATIONAL DEGREE → T3EFFPD	-.014	.003	-.020	-.008	.000**
EXPERIENCES → T3EFFPD	.027	.003	.022	.032	.000**
Total indirect effects					
DL → T3PORGIN→ T3EFFPD	.014	.004	.007	.022	.000**

Note(s): T3EFFPD = Effective Professional Development, DL = Distributed Leadership, T3PORGIN= Organizational Innovativeness, ** p <. 01. Gender (reference group is female)

Table 2 shows that "T3PORGIN" is lower level significantly positively affects teachers' effective professional development ($\beta = .037$, p < 0.01) at the school level. Furthermore, the study reveals that the school principal's DL behaviors have a medium positive impact on organizational innovativeness at the school level ($\beta = .39$, p < 0.01). At the teacher level, the gender ($\beta = .015$, p < 0.01), experiences ($\beta = .027$, p < 0.01), and educational degree ($\beta = -.014$, p < 0.01) of the school teachers have a low but notable effect on thinking of the professional development activity. The study concluded that distributed leadership has a significant total effect on organizational innovativeness. Additionally, distributed leadership was found to have a significant indirect effect on teachers' perceptions of effective professional development through organizational innovativeness ($\beta = .014$, p < 0.01).

CONCLUSION

This study investigates the outcomes of a model that shows the effects of distributed leadership and organizational innovativeness (school level) and gender, education level and experience (individual level) variables on teachers' views on their effective professional development. According to the results obtained using TALIS 2018 research data, it is revealed that teachers' gender, education level and experience have a significant effect, albeit at a low level, on their thoughts on the effectiveness of professional development activities. When these results are analyzed in depth, it can be stated that female teachers have a more positive attitude to teacher learning activities than males. Moreover, as teachers' working time in their field increases, they consider professional development activities as more useful. On the other hand, as teachers' education levels increase, they perceive the effectiveness of professional development activities as inadequate. This result suggests that the activities undertaken do not adequately address personal requirements. This implies that the global practices of professional development do not align with the criteria of enhancing teacher content knowledge (Content focus) and respecting teachers' existing knowledge and beliefs (Coherence) (Darling-Hammond et al., 2017; Desimone, 2009). Therefore, it is advisable that policy-makers and practitioners design activities for teacher learning that cater to their interests, needs and expectations.

Another result of the study was that distributed leadership had a medium significant effect on organizational innovativeness directly. This result is consistent with other studies conducted in the educational setting (Birasnav et al., 2022; Buyukgoze et al., 2022; Çoban & Atasoy, 2020). In this instance, activities and practices should be designed to improve school principals' distributed leadership skills in order to accomplish the required education reforms.

Another significant research finding has revealed that school principals' distributed leadership behaviors indirectly foster effective teacher learning by enhancing organizational innovativeness. That is, school principals can establish an innovative and trust-based school culture in their schools by exhibiting distributed leadership behaviors, and thereby, they can reinforce and strengthen teachers' positive attitudes towards professional development activities. Therefore, it can be recommended that teachers' gender, experience and education levels should be considered in the policies and practices to be developed on teacher education. Moreover, a positive perception can be fostered in schools for teacher learning by developing the leadership skills of school principals. Future research may explore multilevel models that will uncover the potential effects of different leadership approaches and different teacher characteristics on teacher learning.

REFERENCES

Ainley, J., & Carstens, R. (2018). *Teaching and learning international survey (TALIS) 2018 conceptual framework.* OECD. doi:10.1787/799337c2-

Bangs, J., & Frost, D. (2012). *Teacher self-efficacy, voice and leadership: Towards a policy framework for educational international: A report on an international survey of the views of teachers and teacher union officials.* Education International Research Institute.

Bates, C. C., & Morgan, D. N. (2018). Seven elements of effective professional development. *The Reading Teacher*, *71*(5), 623–626. doi:10.1002/trtr.1674

Bennett, N., Harvey, J. A., Wise, C., & Woods, P. A. (2003). *Distributed Leadership: A Desk Study.* www.ncsl.org.uk/literaturereviews

Birasnav, M., Gantasala, S. B., Gantasala, V. P., & Singh, A. (2022). Total quality leadership and organizational innovativeness: The role of social capital development in American schools. *Benchmarking: An International Journal.* doi:10.1108/BIJ-08-2021-0470

Blase, J., & Blase, J. (1999). Implementation of shared governance for instructional improvement: Principals' perspectives. *Journal of Educational Administration*, *37*(5), 476–500. doi:10.1108/09578239910288450

Bliese, P. D. (2000). Within-group agreement, non-independence, and reliability: Implications for data aggregation and analysis. In *Multilevel theory, research, and methods in organizations: Foundations, extensions, and new directions* (pp. 349–381). Jossey-Bass/Wiley.

Blomeke, S., Nilsen, T., & Scherer, R. (2021). School innovativeness is associated with enhanced teacher collaboration, innovative classroom practices, and job satisfaction. *Journal of Educational Psychology, 113*(8), 1645-1667. doi:10.1037/edu0000668

Bolden, R. (2011). Distributed leadership in organizations: A review of theory and research. *International Journal of Management Reviews, 13*(3), 251–269. doi:10.1111/j.1468-2370.2011.00306.x

Buske, R. (2018). The principal as a key actor in promoting teachers' innovativeness–analyzing the innovativeness of teaching staff with variance-based partial least square modeling. *School Effectiveness and School Improvement, 29*(2), 262–284. doi:10.1080/09243453.2018.1427606

Buyukgoze, H., Caliskan, O., & Gümüş, S. (2022). Linking distributed leadership with collective teacher innovativeness: The mediating roles of job satisfaction and professional collaboration. *Educational Management Administration & Leadership*. doi:10.1177/17411432221130879

Can, A. (2018). *SPSS ile bilimsel araştırma sürecinde nicel veri analizi*. Pegem.

Çoban, Ö., & Atasoy, R. (2020). Relationship between distributed leadership, teacher collaboration and organizational innovativeness. *International Journal of Evaluation and Research in Education, 9*(4), 903-911. doi:10.11591/ijere. v9i4.20679

Coburn, C. E. (2003). Rethinking scale: Moving beyond numbers to deep and lasting change. *Educational Researcher, 32*(6), 3–12. doi:10.3102/0013189X032006003

Darling-Hammond, L., Hyler, M. E., & Gardner, M. (2017). Effective teacher professional development. Learning Policy Enstitute. http://creativecommons. org/licenses/by-nc/4.0/ doi:10.54300/122.311

Day, C., Sammons, P., Hopkins, D., Harris, A., Leithwood, K., Gu, Q., & Brown, F. (2010). *10 Strong claims about successful school leadership*. https://assets.publishing.service.gov.uk/government/uploads/system/uploads/ attachment_data/ file/327938/10-strong-claims-about-successful-school-leadership.pdf

Desimone, L. M. (2009). Improving impact studies of teachers' professional development: Toward better conceptualizations and measures. *Educational Researcher, 38*(3), 181–199. doi:10.3102/0013189X08331140

Elmore, R. (2000). *Building a New Structure for School Leadership*. Albert Shanker Institute.

Fletcher, J. K., & Kaufer, K. (2003). Shared leadership: Paradox and possibility. In C. J. Pearce & C. Conger (Eds.), Shared leadership: Reframing the how and whys of leadership (pp. 21–47). Sage.

Fullan, M. (2001). *New meaning of educational change* (3rd ed.). Teachers College Press. doi:10.4324/9780203986561

Gabler, C. B., Richey, R. G. Jr, & Rapp, A. (2015). Developing an eco-capability through environmental orientation and organizational innovativeness. *Industrial Marketing Management, 45*, 151–161. doi:10.1016/j.indmarman.2015.02.014

George, D., & Mallery, M. (2003). *Using SPSS for Windows step by step: A simple guide and reference*. Allyn & Bacon.

Gopalakrishnan, S., & Damanpour, F. (1997). A review of innovation research in economics, sociology and technology management. *Omega, 25*(1), 15-28. doi:10.1016/S0305-0483(96)00043-6

Graetz, F. (2000). Strategic change leadership. *Management Decision, 38*(8), 550–562. doi:10.1108/00251740010378282

Gronn, P. (2000). Distributed Properties: A New Architecture for Leadership. *Educational Management & Administration, 28*(3), 317–338. doi:10.1177/0263211X000283006

Hallinger, P. (2011). Leadership for learning: Lessons from 40 years of empirical research. *Journal of Educational Administration, 49*(2), 25-142. doi:10.1108/09578231111116699

Hallinger, P., & Heck, R. H. (1996). Reassessing the principal's role in school effectiveness: A review of empirical research, 1980-1995. *Educational Administration Quarterly, 32*(1), 5-44. doi:10.1177/0013161X96032001002

Hansen, M. T., & Birkinshaw, J. (2007). The innovation value chain. *Harvard Business Review, 85*(6), 121-130. PMID:17580654

Harris, A. (2004). Distributed leadership and school improvement: Leading or misleading? *Educational Management Administration & Leadership, 32*(1), 11–24. doi:10.1177/1741143204039297

Harris, A. (2008). Distributed leadership: According to the evidence. *Journal of Educational Administration, 46*(2), 172–188. doi:10.1108/09578230810863253

Harris, A. (2009). Distributed leadership, studies in educational leadership. Springer.

Harris, A. (2013). *Distributed leadership matters: Perspectives, practicalities, and potential.* Corwin Press. doi:10.4324/9780203607909

Harris, A., & Muijs, D. (2004). *Improving schools through teacher leadership.* Open University Press.

Hattie, J. (2009). *A synthesis of over 800 meta-analyses relating to achievement.* Routledge., doi:10.4324/9780203887332

Heck, R. H., & Hallinger, P. (2010). Testing a longitudinal model of distributed leadership effects on school improvement. *The Leadership Quarterly, 21*(5), 867-885. doi:10.1016/j.leaqua.2010.07.013

Heckscher, C. (2007). *The collaborative enterprise: Managing speed and complexity in knowledge-based businesses.* Yale Books.

Hopkins, D., & Jackson, D. (2002). Building the capacity for leading and learning. In A. Harris, C. Day, D. Hadfield, D. Hopkins, A. Hargreaves, & C. Chapman (Eds.), *Effective Leadership for school improvement* (pp. 84–105). Routledge.

Senge, P. M. (2010). *The fifth discipline: The art and practice of the learning organization.* Crown Publishing Group.

Huberman, M. (1998). Teacher careers and school improvement. *Journal of Curriculum Studies, 20*(2), 119–132. doi:10.1080/00220272.1988.11070783

Hurley, R. F., Hult, G. T. M., & Knight, G. A. (2005). Innovativeness and capacity to innovate in a complexity of firm-level relationships: A response to Woodside (2004). *Industrial Marketing Management, 34*(3), 281–283. doi:10.1016/j.indmarman.2004.07.006

Iandoli, L., & Zollo, G. (2008). *Organisational Cognition and Learning: Building Systems for the Learning Organization.* Idea Group Incorporated.

Jønsson, T., Unterrainer, C., Jeppesen, H. J., & Jain, A. K. (2016). Measuring distributed leadership agency in a hospital context: Development and validation of a new scale. *Journal of Health Organization and Management, 30*(6), 908–926. doi:10.1108/JHOM-05-2015-0068 PMID:27681024

Lee, P. C., Lin, C. T., & Kang, H. H. (2016). The influence of open innovative teaching approach toward student satisfaction: A case of Si-Men Primary School. *Quality & Quantity, 50*(2), 491–507. doi:10.1007/s11135-015-0160-x

Leithwood, K., & Jantzi, D. (2000). The effects of different sources of leadership on student engagement in school. In K. Riley & K. Louis (Eds.), *Leadership for Change and School Reform* (pp. 50–66). Routledge.

Leithwood, K., Mascall, B., & Strauss, T. (2009). *Distributed leadership according to the evidence.* Routledge. doi:10.4324/9780203868539

Leithwood, K., Mascall, B., Strauss, T., Sacks, R., Memon, N., & Yashkina, A. (2007). Distributing Leadership to Make Schools Smarter: Taking the Ego Out of the System. *Leadership and Policy in Schools, 6*(1), 37–67. doi:10.1080/15700760601091267

Lumpkin, G. T., & Dess, G. G. (1996). Clarifying the entrepreneurial orientation construct and linking it to performance. *Academy of Management Review, 21*(1), 135–172. doi:10.2307/258632

Newmann, F. M., & Wehlage, G. G. (1995). *Successful School Restructuring: A Report to the Public and Educators.* American Federation of Teachers. https://eric.ed.gov/?id=ED387925

Ni, G., Xu, H., Cui, Q., Qiao, Y., Zhang, Z., Li, H., & Hickey, P. J. (2021). Influence mechanism of organizational flexibility on enterprise competitiveness: The mediating role of organizational innovation. *Sustainability (Basel), 13*(1), 1-23. doi:10.3390/su13010176

Niederhauser, D. S., Howard, S. K., Voogt, J., Agyei, D. D., Laferriere, T., Tondeur, J., & Cox, M. J. (2018). Sustainability and scalability in educational technology initiatives: Research-informed practice. *Technology. Knowledge and Learning, 23*(3), 507–523. doi:10.1007/s10758-018-9382-z

Nurutdinova, A. R., Perchatkina, V. G., Zubkova, G. I., & Galeeva, F. T. (2016). Innovative teaching practice: Traditional and alternative methods (Challenges and Implications). *Science Education, 11*(10), 3807–3819.

OECD. (2015). *Schools for 21st-century learners: Strong leaders, confident teachers, innovative approaches.* Organisation for Economic Co-operation and Development. https://www.oecd-ilibrary.org/education/schools-for-21st-century-learners_9789264231191-en

OECD. (2019). *TALIS 2018 technical report* [Research Report]. https://www.oecd.org/education/talis/TALIS_2018_Technical_Report.pdf

Pearce, C. J., & Conger, C. (2003). *Shared leadership: Reframing the hows and whys of leadership.* Sage. doi:10.4135/9781452229539

Rodríguez-Triana, M. J., Prieto, L. P., Ley, T., de Jong, T., & Gillet, D. (2020). Social practices in teacher knowledge creation and innovation adoption: A large-scale study in an online instructional design community for inquiry learning. *International Journal of Computer-Supported Collaborative Learning, 15*(4), 445–467. doi:10.1007/s11412-020-09331-5

Spillane, J. P. (2006). *Distributed leadership.* Jossey-Bass.

Spillane, J. P., Halverson, R., & Diamond, J. B. (2004). Towards a theory of leadership practice: A distributed perspective. *Journal of Curriculum Studies, 36*(1), 3–34. doi:10.1080/0022027032000106726

Subramanian, A., & Nilakanta, S. (1996). Organizational innovativeness: Exploring the relationship between organizational determinants of innovation, types of innovations, and measures of organizational performance. *Omega, 24*(6), 631-647. doi:10.1016/S0305-0483(96)00031-X

Sykes, G. (1996). Reform of and as professional development. *Phi Delta Kappan, 77*(7), 464- 489.

Thurlings, M., Evers, A. T., & Vermeulen, M. (2015). Toward a model of explaining teachers' innovative behavior: A literature review. *Review of Educational Research, 85*(3), 430–471. doi:10.3102/0034654314557949

Trask, S., Charteris, J., Edwards, F., Cowie, B., & Anderson, J. (2023). Innovative learning environments and student orientation to learning: A kaleidoscopic framework. *Learning Environments Research, 26*(3), 727– 741. doi:10.1007/s10984-022-09449-3

Wallace, M. (2002). Modelling distributed leadership and management effectiveness: Primary school senior management teams in England and Wales. *School Effectiveness and School Improvement, 13*(2), 163–186. doi:10.1076/sesi.13.2.163.3433

Webb, M., & Cox, M. (2004). A review of pedagogy related to information and communications technology. *Technology, Pedagogy and Education, 13*(3), 235–286. doi:10.1080/14759390400200183

Chapter 5

Walking a Mile in Their Shoes:
Understanding Students in Poverty

Queen Ogbomo
Tennessee Tech University, USA

ABSTRACT

This study examined the impact of a poverty simulation project, an experiential learning procedure on preservice teachers' perception of elementary students living in poverty. Thirty undergraduate preservice teachers from two cohorts in a public university in the southern part of the United States were asked to participate in a poverty simulation activity to expose them to the lived experiences of people living in poverty. An early analysis of the debriefing session after the simulation project showed that students viewed this simulation project as an engaging learning experience. Means and standard deviations of scores in relation to pre-test and post-test personal bias toward poverty, understanding individuals in poverty, effort in teaching students living in poverty, and responsibility for students living in poverty were obtained. While there was no significant difference from the paired sample t-tests, there was a slight difference in three of the four areas measured.

In assessing what it means to live in poverty, it was of paramount importance for me to look at the personal experiences of families and other people in the community in which I grew up. Poverty in Nigeria, where I am originally from, means not having access to basic human needs such as food, clothing, medical facilities, quality education, and government assistance. For my experience I will go with Alexander, et al., (2020) definition of poverty. These authors suggest poverty is characterized by living with restricted

DOI: 10.4018/978-1-7998-3940-8.ch005

Copyright © 2024, IGI Global. Copying or distributing in print or electronic forms without written permission of IGI Global is prohibited.

economic resources and includes various income thresholds that vary based on geographical location. This is the situation in Nigeria.

However, according to the United States Census Bureau, the poverty threshold is based on related income given the number of people in the household. The poverty threshold was $13, 300 for a one-person household with an individual who is under the age of 65. Their threshold for a four-person household with householders and two children under the age of 18 is $26, 370. Thus, to be considered poor, the family income must be at or below $26, 370 (United States Census Bureau, 2020). In examining my own experience growing up and looking back at the lives of children I went to elementary school with, I would conclude I came from a somewhat middle-class family because my parents could afford to send me to a boarding school. I had friends who did not have that luxury because their parents did not have enough money to send then to secondary school (high school).

I would therefore not say I know what it really means to be poor. Having lived both in Nigeria and the United states, I would say the term living in poverty is different in these two countries. This is because the needs of the people are different, and so are the available resources. In the United States the poverty threshold for a family of 4 is around 26,370 dollars a year (United States Census Bureau, 2020), but in Nigeria, people living below the poverty line earn about the equivalent of $1.90 a day in U.S. dollars (Poverty and Shared Prosperity 2022 Correcting Course, 2023). In Nigeria, if you are poor, you are on your own, as there are no government services or assistance programs compared to individuals living in the United States. Having not experienced poverty, my views about poverty were very different when I first started teaching in the United States. My first teaching job was in a suburban school district with mostly middle-class families who one would perceive as caring about what their kids were learning in school. These families were very willing to come to the classroom to volunteer any time they were needed. The situation was, however, different at the second school I taught at because it was more populated with students from low income families. The perspective here was different as parents were preconceived as not caring about their child's education. This is because these families sometimes would not show up for parent/teacher conferences or to pick up their child's report card. This is supported in the literature by Smith-Carrier, T., et, al. (2019) who stated, that "students and practitioners from privileged socio-economic backgrounds may thus have little understanding about the root causes, effects and experiences associated with poverty" (p. 3). Through continued research on poverty and academic success, I have come to conclude that these families/ guardians could not afford to come to their child's parent/teacher conference because they had to work two to three jobs to put food on the table for their children.

After taking several parent involvement classes in graduate school, I made it my mission to create an environment where all kids and families/guardians would be valued members of my classroom. In an attempt to individualize my instruction, I always started the year by inviting parents/guardians to tell me about their child through writing. The parents who could not complete the writing were invited to have a face-to-face conversation with me about their child. I continued to do this because parents were very receptive to the idea. This involved them telling me the strengths and areas for improvement of their children and what they thought their children needed from me to succeed in my classroom.

I tried to implement a similar activity in a new school district located in the Midwestern region of the United States where, according to the National Center for Education Statistics (NCES; n.d.), out of the 289 students in the 2018–2019 school year, 270 of the school population participated in the federal free and reduced lunch program. Much to my surprise, I did not get the same response from most of the parents at that school as my previous school. *Why was I surprised you may ask? Was it because of my lack of experience working with a diverse students' population?* In reflecting on my stance at that time, I would say yes. I was faced with parents who I assumed did not come to school events or pick up their children's school report cards. Based on this experience, I, too, contemplated what Gorski (2008) referred to as myths about poverty including, "Poor people are unmotivated and have weak work ethics" and "Poor parents are uninvolved in their children's learning" (p. 2).

Grounded on this belief, I decided to do all I could to "save the children." In retrospect, I now believe that I was working from the assumption of what Yasso (2005) described as "the assumption in structuring ways to help disadvantaged students whose race and background has left them lacking necessary knowledge, social skills and abilities" (p.70). In reconsideration, I would say this was in line with what I learned from the culture of poverty as preached by Ruby Penne in many of her professional development seminars paid for by the school district. Recent research from scholars such as Gorski (2008) have suggested Penne's ideas are based on stereotypes about people living in poverty. For example, I would bring snacks to school and try to make sure all their assignments were completed in class. This had an unintended, negative consequence, as the children saw what I was trying to do in a different light. Some thought I was trying to "look down" on them because of their socio-economic status (SES), which of course was not my intention. In one instance, a female student said that I was trying to fix the way she and her peers talked because I insisted that they use the formal English register in the classroom. Since reading about the Critical Race Theory (CRT), I wonder if they thought I was trying to erase their culture and identity as pointed out by Yosso (2005). I wish now that I had reassured the students that making them use standard English in the classroom was an attempt to give them the opportunity to learn and be successful in the real world. I should have clearly explained to them or helped them to recognize that the more language you have, the more opportunities you have to navigate a dominant space, as suggested by Yosso (2005).

Today, as I reflect on my experiences in that Midwestern elementary school, I realize that I did not know the burdens or barriers the children came to school with or what their parents had to do to survive. I should not have made the assumption that parents did not care about the success of their children because they did not have time to come to school like some of my middle-class families. Additionally, I could have increased my communication with parents through phone calls or house visits as I later did. I also could have built more trust with my students by being clear of my intentions to make sure that they had everything they needed to succeed in school. I should have facilitated meaningful learning through utilizing community and cultural assets in addition to eliciting and harnessing students' life experiences more in my teaching. I hope takeaways from my mistakes provide a lesson all teachers can learn from. In my teacher education program, I wish I had been given the opportunity to "challenge preconceived notions about the root causes of poverty" (Smith-Carrier, et al., 2019, p.3) and was more exposed more to students and families experiencing poverty.

As a teacher educator now, I often ponder about how to provide opportunities for preservice teachers (PSTs) to become self-aware of their own biases or preconceived notions they may have about students from low SES backgrounds. It is my belief that PSTs have limited understanding of how to effectively engage with, plan for, and teach students living in poverty, and I hope to share the lessons I have learned with them. Some studies have found that many educators are often unaware of the challenges that students living in poverty face and are therefore unable to adequately plan for them (Wright et al., 2019). For example, Howard and Rodriguez-Scheel (2016) suggest that many educators are not well prepared to react to the effect of poverty on children. Cochran-Smith and Villegas (2016) also posited that PSTs find it difficult to design instruction that builds on students' knowledge and experiences because most PSTs live in economically isolated communities which offer limited opportunities to interact with people from lower SES.

Research continues to indicate that child poverty has a detrimental impact on academic outcomes and a child's ability to learn (The Anne. E Casey Foundation, 2023). Ongoing studies underscore the significance of socio-economic status (SES) in influencing children's educational and learning outcomes (Broer et al., 2019). A 2021 US Census Bureau revealed that 38.1million people in the United States live in poverty and of that number, one-third of them are children under 18 years of age (McFarland et al., 2019). Research from the NCES (2015; 2017) further suggests that living in poverty during the early educational years is associated with lower-than-average academic performance in elementary through high school. Hair et al. (2015) further stated that the longer children stay in poverty, the greater their academic shortfalls. Prior research (NCES, 2015) also revealed a correlation between family risk factors such as low SES and poor educational outcomes, including low achievement scores, grade retention, and an elevated high school dropout rate. In support of this argument, O'Connell (2019) noted that student backgrounds have great influence on their academic achievement.

With a lack of education on how poverty affects the academic outcome of students, PSTs may harbor low expectations for students in poverty. These views include but not limited to the belief that poor people are lazy, feel entitled, or have parents who do not care about the education of their children. A poverty simulation activity is one way to educate and challenge the perceptions of PSTs about students living in poverty. It is imperative for PSTs and in-service teachers alike be exposed to situations that allow them to comprehend and address the needs of all their students, particularly those living in poverty. With this understanding, I conceived the idea of having my PSTs participate in a poverty simulation activity.

I wish someone had made me aware of the life experiences of students from low SES backgrounds earlier in my career. I would have understood what their parents go through every day, or how many hours they have to work to keep a roof over their heads. Would this have made a difference in the way I taught my lessons? Definitely. I would have found more opportunities to make what I was teaching more relevant to their everyday life experiences and culture. Yosso (2005) defined culture as "behaviors and values that are learned, shared, and exhibited by a group of people" (p. 75). I know that through making connections to my students' cultures and lives, their attitudes might change towards what we were learning. For example, in my last year of teaching 5th grade, the students and I embarked on a book project where they were given the option of writing what was happening in their neighborhoods. I could see how happy they were to be writing about what they knew and experienced every day. With this mindset, a plan emerged that would allow

PSTs to gain a critical understanding of how to effectively engage with, plan for, and teach students living in poverty.

THE POVERTY SIMULATION PROJECT

The poverty simulation project is the brainchild of the Missouri Association for Community Action Network (Missouri Community Action Network, 2018). This poverty simulation is an engaging experiential activity that allows participants to step into or assume the role of families facing poverty. It can also be seen as a learning tool to increase the awareness of what people living in poverty go through every day. The goal of this simulation project is to provide opportunities for pre-service teachers to challenge any misconceptions or erroneous thoughts that they may have about people living in poverty. It is also to explore whether participating in the simulation activity would change PSTs instructional plans to meet the needs of students living in poverty as they embark on their teaching practical journey.

Some critics have questioned the validity and effectiveness of the use of simulations in the classroom and wondered if simulations as a learning tool enhance students learning (Gosen & Washburn, 2004; Shellman & Turan, 2006). For example, Shellman and Turan (2006) suggested that "there is little evidence that active learning exercises facilitate learning" (p.2). Gosen and Washbush (2004) asserted that only tentative conclusions can be drawn regarding simulations as valid learning techniques. They further propose that simulations require more testing and evaluation of techniques to show their effectiveness. However, proponents of simulations see its potential as a well-established learning tool in many disciplines. Kaufman and Ireland (2016) posited that "simulations can strengthen critical aspects of teacher preparation as programs look for ways to better equip their graduates for future challenges" (p. 260). Furthermore, simulations afford students with real life opportunities to reduce multifaceted situations and provide environments to practice intricate skills (Chernikova et al., 2020). Simulation is a great learning experience that provide PSTs, the opportunity to be actively engage and encounter real-world, problem-based situations and learn to come up with solutions for these problems.

Before going on with the description of the simulation, it is important to take a look at the history of the Missouri CAN. Since 1964, when President Lyndon B. Johnson declared war on poverty and signed the Economic Opportunity Act into law, many community action agencies have continued to provide services to low income families around the U.S. (Missouri CAN,

2018). The Missouri Community Action Network is one of such agencies, whose goals include educating communities about the realities of poverty.

I first learned about this specific simulation from a National Social Studies conference and a nursing school simulation I attended, which led to my participation in their training. To afford the cost of the training, I wrote a Quality Enhancement Plan (QEP) Curriculum Development grant, which enabled me to incorporate inquiry-based pedagogy in my social studies methods course. After obtaining the grant, I travelled to Kansas City, Missouri for the training and bought the simulation project kit. The experience was so profound because it enabled the participants to interact with people from the community who had benefited from the Missouri Community Action network. To hear them talk about their experiences and how difficult it is to navigate the system and obtain government services to survive everyday was very moving. In hindsight, I would have appreciated participating in this kind of activity instead of some of the in-service professional development activities which my school district required. Such an activity would have addressed the misconceptions I had about people living in poverty in my early experience as a teacher. The impact of engaging in such an activity would have been insightful if I had participated in it as a PST, as it would have afforded me an opportunity to examine my own biases and experiences and to really understand what it means to be poor in America.

Based on my own previous experiences as discussed in the earlier part of this chapter, as well as the lessons I have learned, I wanted to afford my PSTs an opportunity to walk a mile in the shoes of students living in poverty, just like I did in Kansas City. Two or three years into my career as a teacher educator, I started to embark on projects that would get PSTs out of their comfort zones and into the communities in which they will someday be teaching. The purpose was to have them learn and appreciate where their students would be coming from and the challenges people from these communities face every day. During the end of project reflections, students would share about the experiences they encountered with members of these communities. Through the discussions, I learned that the PSTs needed more engaging experiences other than the traditional way of teaching to help them examine their own misconceptions about students living in poverty and students with cultural experiences different from theirs. To understand the rationale, one must understand where some of my students come from demographically. Their experiences range from middle class families to those who have had their share of struggles. This really lends itself to having rich discussions on how all our experiences are different. The objective of doing this poverty simulation project with PSTs, therefore, was to evaluate the effect of a poverty simulation activity on their attitude and understanding toward students living in poverty and what they can do to engage, motivate, and find opportunities for success in regard to students in their future classrooms.

Situating Teaching PSTs About Poverty in the Evidence

Through the poverty simulation, I wanted preservice students to appreciate the challenges that people in poverty face daily. Though much has been written on the effect of simulations in the field of nursing (Dalinger et al., 2020; Patterson & Hulton, 2012), very little writing exists about using simulations in the field of elementary education. There are different definitions of simulation; for the purpose of this chapter, I used the definition by Prescott and Garside (2009) cited by Patterson and Hulton (2012), which states, "Simulation is the promotion of understanding through doing" (p. 144). Though more research is needed to establish the impact of using simulation to effect change or promote learning in the classroom, many studies have shown that it is an effective teaching strategy. In examining using simulations in political science education, Asal and Blake (2007) found that they "provide students with the opportunity to develop their communication, negotiation, and critical thinking skills and in many cases, improve their teamwork skills" (p. 2). If we see teacher education as a way to inform, heighten student awareness and to apply theory learned in class to real life situations, then simulations in this instance could be a useful tool to meet that goal. In 2006, Shellman and Turan's empirical evaluation on an international relations simulation found that simulations "can immerse students into the environment and involve them with course materials that traditional techniques like reading and lecturing cannot" (p. 1). Frederking (2005) posited that experimental evidence exists that shows students benefitting significantly in American government courses when they participate in simulations. Also, in support of the benefits and the impact of simulations on learning outcomes are, Smith-Carrier, et al., 2019 and Sanko, et al., 2021.

Although the use of simulations is nothing new in the fields of medicine or business, not much has been written on the use of simulations in the field of teacher education (Azer et al., 2013; Bennet, 2008; Boet et al., 2014; Noone et al., 2012). The use of simulations in teacher education could provide PSTs with the opportunity to work together cooperatively to solve real-world problems. Simulation, according to Azer et al. (2013, Sanko et al., 2021), fosters a learner-centered approach to learning where students take the lead to demonstrate profound understanding of concepts learned and an opportunity to apply skills and knowledge acquired. Sottile Jr. and

Brozik (2004) suggest that simulation "allows for role playing and hands-on-learning" (p. 1). Simulations also allow for experiential learning, which gives a welcoming break from the traditional delivery of lessons and exposes students to real-life situations that permit them to apply theoretical knowledge learned in the classroom. It is noteworthy, however, that for simulations to be effective, they must be rigorous and taken seriously by students (Goshen & Washbush, 2004, Sanko, et al., 2021). Additionally, the instructor must make time for reflections, debriefing, and for students to repeat the simulation.

Study Purpose

Based on current literature, I concluded that a simulation project, when implemented correctly, is a reasonable way for PSTs to develop critical thinking skills, immerse themselves in an environment similar to what their future students might come from, and inform the way they plan to engage their future students.

I explored two research questions:

1) What are PSTs' perceptions of children living in poverty?
2) How will participation in a poverty simulation activity influence how PSTs perceive students living in poverty?

METHODS

Approach to Teaching PSTs About Poverty

Thirty undergraduate PSTs from a public university in the southern part of the United States were asked to participate in the poverty simulation activity as part of an elementary social studies methods course. The PSTs were from two different cohorts. In their field experience placements, PSTs are usually confronted with the challenge of dealing with children who come to school with many economic and emotional issues that make it difficult for them to learn. Through this poverty simulation, a creative inquiry-based approach, students worked collaboratively to examine the complexities of poverty, grapple with critical questions related to poverty, assess resources found to mitigate negative influences of poverty, and engage in critical dialogue with their peers and the instructor.

The Activity

In our discussion about teaching for social justice, the question of inequity, particularly poverty in our society, came up. This led me to ask students to write narratives of their own experience with poverty or what they knew about poverty. Based on their reflections, the students and I then had an interesting discussion of what it means to be poor. After the discussion, the students were informed that they were going to participate in a simulation activity which involved experiencing what people living in poverty go through every day. In other words, these students would walk a mile in the shoes of someone considered to be poor. The poverty simulation activity took place in a 3-hour elementary social studies methods class where participants were allotted roles of low-income families, businesses, and community organizations that a family member must interact with (Missouri CAN, 2018; Strasser et al., 2013). Before the activity, students were assigned roles of families living at the poverty level; families ranged from elderly people living alone to multigenerational families of three to four people including children, single parents with school age children, families living with an unwedded teen with a child, families with children who had no car and lived on food stamps. Using the information from the Missouri CAN (2018) manual, the different roles were clearly explained to the PSTs.

For the simulation, 30 students participated in the activity during the course two semesters. Each cohort comprised of 15 students each. 4 faculty members who were my colleagues and 5 students from other classes were recruited and trained to assist with the simulation activity. Faculty members and students recruited, posed as service providers from different governmental agencies where participants would go to request for varied social services. These volunteers were asked to either assist or hinder participants from getting the service they needed. The simulation occurred in a large room on campus where tables had been arranged. Each table represented different services such as a pawn shop, employment agency, a school, child protection service, police station and food bank. Each simulation started with me acting as a facilitator and giving participants, who by this time had been placed in different family situation an introduction on what they were to do and how long each segment would last.

I stated that the objective for each simulated family was to try to survive 1 month making sure to get food, shelter, and pay bills. For the class period, 1 hour represented 1 month. One week was represented by each 15-minute period. During this 3-hour period, PSTs were to interact with community agencies such as schools, as well as other businesses such as banks, social services, the

Walking a Mile in Their Shoes

police, utility agencies, job centers, and pawn shops to obtain resources and services. Provided with written instructions and materials, faculty members acted as staff of these agencies. Students were given cards with different scenarios and were charged to prioritized necessities and make decisions to survive a month with very little as would be experienced by people living in poverty. Before each simulated week, they were asked to review their family situation, consult with each other to learn about their weekly budget, income, expenses, and their roles. These roles included going to pay bills, going to work, school, going to find employment and to access community services depending on their age. Each family had different challenges to contend with, including but not limited to not having enough money to pay for utilities, not being able to pay for a field trip for a school age child, and not being able to provide enough food for the family. Since I had fewer students participating in the simulation from each cohort, not all the family situations provided in the Missouri CAN kit (2018) were represented. The most important part of the simulation was at the end of each simulation, would gather students and led them in a debriefing session where I would encourage them to share their experiences with the group. In the next Social Studies methods class, students and I would discuss what they would do if they had a student in their classroom going through what they had experienced from the simulation. We would then brainstorm where they could find the necessary resources to help students and their families in their various communities.

Analysis of Poverty Survey Items: Pre- and Post-Data

To evaluate the perceptions of PSTs toward students living with poverty relative to the simulation activity, an 11-question survey (see Figure 4.1) instrument was developed along with two open-ended interview questions: 1) What did you learn from this poverty simulation experience? and, 2) How has this activity encouraged you to make changes in both the academic and non-academic needs of your students?

For purposes of analysis, all subgroupings of survey items relating to specific criteria of perceived personal bias, understanding, effort in teaching, and responsibility were grouped together. Constructed categorization by item are reported in Table 1 above. Means and standard deviations of scores in relation to pre-test and post-test personal bias toward poverty, understanding individuals in poverty, effort in teaching students living in poverty, and responsibility for students living in poverty concepts by category are reported in Figure 1.

Walking a Mile in Their Shoes

Table 1. Poverty simulation activity survey

	Strongly disagree	Disagree	Neutral	Agree	Strongly Agree
I have biases about teaching children from low socio-economic levels.					
I understand the challenges low income families face.					
Most poor people are unwashed/dirty.					
Poor people think they deserve to be supported.					
Unemployed poor people could find jobs if they tried harder.					
Poor people are discriminated against.					
Children raised on welfare will never amount to anything.					
Poverty impedes the education of children.					
Poverty takes an emotional toll on children.					
It is harder to teach poor children.					
It is my responsibility as a teacher to meet the non-educational needs of my students.					

Pre-test and post-test personal bias, understanding, effort in teaching, and responsibility scores were analyzed using paired samples t-tests. The analyses were performed on the subjects' perceptions and attitudes before and after participating in the poverty simulation activity. There was a significant difference in PST's understanding between the pre- and post-test for (M=-0.04, SD=1.09, $t(26)$=0.18, p=0.01).While there was no significant difference from the paired sample t-tests, there was a slight difference in three of the four areas measured. It is worthy of note that the decrease in "responsibility" (that teachers have the responsibility to work with students living in poverty) from the pre to the post-test may be because of the 3 students who were absent from class the day the post test was administered.

Figure 1. Pre-test and post-test means

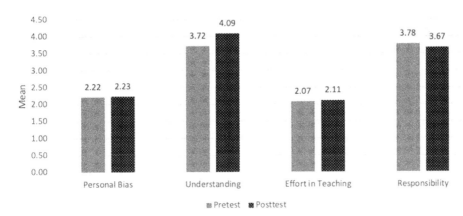

RESULTS FROM QUALITATIVE ANALYSES

Discussion

Alone, the survey data did not yield significant information, however, when considered in tandem with the pre-service teachers' open-ended interview responses, a discrepancy with respect to how PSTs' perceptions of people living in poverty were influenced emerged. For the first question, *"What did you learn from this poverty simulation experience?"* Twenty-four of the 27 PSTs indicated in their responses that they benefited from participation in the simulation. For example, one student wrote, "This was a great experience. I have never imagined how difficult it would be not to have services I need when I need them." Another said, "I truly did not think poverty would be something I might have to deal with in my classroom." An additional student said, "I am glad I did this activity; it helped me look at poverty in a different light."

In response to the second open-ended question, *"Has/How has this activity encouraged you to make changes in both the academic and non-academic needs of your students?"* 21 students acknowledged a change in their thinking regarding how they might work to meet the needs of students living in poverty. Some examples of their responses include: "In my future classroom, I will make sure I know both the academic and non-academic needs of all my students"; "I definitely want to learn more of how to help students who might be from such homes"; and "This was an eye opener for sure. I have always focused on only the academic needs of children."

After the simulation activity, there was a difference in how the PSTs responded in class on issues of diversity. For example, they more frequently made connections from their learning in the simulation to their readings and assignments. This was particularly evident in the heritage assignment, where students had to go in the community to experience another culture other than their own by going to a different grocery store or restaurant, they had never been to before and trying to interact with the people from that community. Before the simulation, students would talk about their fear of going into a community of people not from their culture or neighborhood; after the simulation, they were more open to the experience. As one student put it, if not for this assignment, "I would have never thought of going there," or "I now know the importance of knowing where your students come from and incorporating that into your lesson."

USING SIMULATIONS: IMPLICATIONS FOR TEACHERS

Though not much has been written in the literature about the effective use of simulations in teacher education, using this poverty simulation activity was an effective way for my PSTs to work to find solutions to authentic problems involving poverty. They also learned how and where to find community resources that would be helpful to students and their families living in poverty. As Ben Ouahi et al. (2022) suggested, the use of simulations in the classroom can enhance instructional effectiveness and build students' conceptual knowledge. Other studies have shown that participating in a simulation such as the Poverty Simulation was an effective way to educate practicing teachers and teacher candidates about the challenges students living in poverty face every day (Miller & Vick, 2022; Northrup et al., 2020). Through simulators such as the one in this study, PSTs can become more sensitive to the needs of their students and have a more positive attitude, which in turn can lead to higher expectations for their students from low SES backgrounds. Through lessons learned in this study, there are some tips that would make for a successful simulation in the field of teacher education. These tips aim to enhance the deep learning which will occur when using simulations as a learning tool or strategy. As the use of simulations continue to grow in educational practices,

Walking a Mile in Their Shoes

it is crucial to look at four main dimensions that contribute to a successful simulation experience and include pre-briefing, the actual activity, debriefing, and assessment.

Tip #1: Importance of Pre-Briefing

According to Tyerman et al. (2016), not much is written about the importance of pre-briefing. The authors describe pre-briefing as an information session that should be held before the simulation experience. This should include but not be limited to pre-reading about the topic, the main objective and expectations of the activity, and the roles each participant will play during the simulation. This, they conclude, will foster learner engagement and simulation experience. A few days before the actual activity, we discussed what my PSTs knew about students living in poverty and where they could find resources in the community to help students be successful in the classroom. This was followed by an explanation of all the materials needed, the reason we were engaging in the activity, and how long each section would take. On the day of the simulation, knowing what to expect made it run smoothly.

Tip #2: Anticipate Logistical Challenges

Despite the benefits associated with simulations, there are a number of challenges. A range of logistical issues arise when putting any simulation together. In the case of the poverty simulation carried out in this study, some of the issues occurred at the initial stage of putting everything together, including not having enough faculty or people to play the parts of families, businesses, and other social services. Some students may not show up on the day of the simulation, which may create a disruption. This challenge can be mitigated if the facilitator creates groups with varying numbers that can be adapted during the simulation. In the case of not having enough faulty members or volunteers in the business roles, students can assume the roles of businesses or other social services.

Tip #3: Debriefing/Self-Reflection Time

An important component of a simulation activity is the debriefing process and giving students time to reflect. To enhance the learning process, it is imperative to employ the metacognitive process of self-reflection. Students need time to evaluate the values and benefits of skills presented through the simulation. A successful debriefing involves allowing each student to express their views of the experience. Give students or participants opportunities to communicate change in attitude or even challenges encountered without interruption (Boet et al., 2014; Lindquist & Reeves, 2007; Missouri CAN, 2018). At the end of the activity, students had time to discuss with their peers what they learned. For a more detailed reflection, there was a written portion that gave students an opportunity and privacy to share their thoughts with me. Giving students the chance to privately share their thoughts proved to be more rewarding for me as they shared more without fear of being criticized by their peers.

Tip #4: Assessment

It is equally important to conduct an evaluation of the simulation activity aimed at finding out if the intended goal or objective of the activity was achieved, and if not, what can be changed next time. Boet et al. (2014) advise that it is meaningful to consider both qualitative and quantitative forms of assessments. Qualitative assessments would be beneficial for collecting a detailed description of how students' attitudes changed through the course of the simulation experience. On the other hand, including a quantitative assessment portion can provide statistical evidence of what was learned. For the purpose of this paper, I used both quantitative and qualitative assessments. However, for the course, I relied more on the qualitative written reflections to determine the success or lack thereof of the simulation activity. Students were candid in explaining what they learned or gave suggestions of what could be done differently within their qualitative responses. For an easy-to-read version, please see Table 2.

CONCLUSION

I believe that the simulation activity has the potential to influence the development of PSTs in all four areas measured (personal bias, understanding, effort in teaching, and responsibility) based on their reference to their simulation experience in their class readings and assignments. However, a more comprehensive examination of poverty is still warranted, one that requires collaboration with members of the community with lived experiences of poverty. Living without knowing where the next meal will come from, being homeless, and not being able to afford to go to the doctor are just a few examples of life in poverty. Inviting community members into this simulation may provide a more realistic and comprehensive exploration of changes in personal bias, beliefs, perspectives, and attitudes.

Walking a Mile in Their Shoes

Table 2. Results from qualitative analyses

Poverty Simulation Experience
Question 1: "What did you learn from this poverty simulation experience?" 24 out of 27 PSTs indicated benefiting from the simulation, gaining insights into the challenges of poverty, and expressing changed perspectives. Examples include increased awareness of difficulties without necessary services and a different understanding of poverty's potential impact in the classroom.
Question 2: "Has/How has this activity encouraged you to make changes in both academic and non-academic needs of your students?" 21 students acknowledged a change in their thinking and expressed a commitment to understanding and addressing both academic and non-academic needs of students in poverty.
Impact on Class Discussions
Post-simulation, PSTs showed increased engagement in class discussions related to diversity, making connections between simulation experiences, readings, and assignments. This was evident in the heritage assignment, where students became more open to experiencing different cultures after the simulation.
Using Simulations: Implications for Teachers
The poverty simulation was an effective tool for PSTs to address authentic problems involving poverty and to learn about community resources. Literature suggests simulations enhance instructional effectiveness and build conceptual knowledge. Tips for successful simulations include pre-briefing, anticipating logistical challenges, debriefing/self-reflection time, and assessment.
Tips for Successful Simulations in Teacher Education
Tip #1: Importance of Pre-Briefing Pre-briefing, including pre-reading about the topic, clarifying objectives, and explaining participant roles, enhances learner engagement and simulation experience. Discussion days before the activity helped students know what to expect, making the simulation smoother.
Tip #2: Anticipate Logistical Challenges Despite the benefits, logistical issues may arise. Anticipating challenges, such as faculty shortages and student absences, is crucial. Adaptations, like students assuming roles, can address such challenges.
Tip #3: Debriefing/Self-Reflection Time Debriefing is essential for reflection and metacognition. Giving students time to evaluate and express their views without interruption enhances the learning process. A written reflection component allowed students privacy to share thoughts.
Tip #4: Assessment Evaluating the simulation's success is crucial. A mix of qualitative and quantitative assessments provides a detailed description of attitude changes and evidence of learning. Qualitative written reflections were relied upon in this study.

Getting community members who are actually going through some of the challenges depicted in the simulation kit make it real for students. These members of the community get a chance to educate PSTs about their situation and in turn create a partnership of people working together to help students succeed in the classroom no matter their circumstances. For the PSTs, they are able to see what they are learning in class come to life as they place themselves in these situations. The activity becomes more meaningful for PSTs when directly working with the people who have these life experiences to share.

It is also the expectation that PSTs would continue to learn from my experience as mentioned at the beginning of this chapter and continue to have high expectations for all students no matter their circumstances. Critics of simulations might worry about long-term reflection after the simulation. How will we know if this experience will translate to effective teaching of students living in poverty? It should be noted that this experience should not be a one-time activity, but that instructors should continue to do follow up activities to reinforce high expectations for all students that are not based on pity but empathy, which is the ability to understand other people's feelings and share in their experiences. Also necessary are follow up classroom observations during practicum to see how this experience translates to how PSTs continue to value what students bring with them to the classroom, or what Yosso (2005) described as "the cultural and community wealth or assets with an array of knowledge, skills, and abilities" (p.77). Worth also noting are the quantitative survey results (see Table 4.2), as there were no significant differences in the pre- and post-surveys regarding efforts in teaching and responsibility scores. This may imply that PSTs already believed that it is the responsibility of the teacher to teach all students, and that teachers should make the effort to meet all academic and nonacademic needs of students to assure their success in the classroom. I hope that simulations continue to be considered as necessary tools to enhance PST's experiences in teacher preparation programs.

REFERENCES

Alexander, K., Clary-Muronda, V., Smith, J. M., & Ward, J. (2020). The relationship between past experience, empathy, and attitudes toward poverty. *The Journal of Nursing Education*, 59(3), 158–162. doi:10.3928/01484834-20200220-07 PMID:32130418

Anne E. Casey Foundation. (2023). *Child poverty.* Retrieved from https://www.aecf.org/topics/child-poverty

Asal, V., & Blake, E. L. (2006). Creating simulations for political science education. *Journal of Political Science Education*, 2(1), 1–18. doi:10.1080/15512160500484119

Azer, S. A., Guerrero, A. P., & Walsh, A. (2013). Enhancing learning approaches: Practical tips for students and teachers. *Medical Teacher*, 35(6), 433–443. doi:10.3109/0142159X.2013.775413 PMID:23496121

Ben Ouahi, M., Lamri, D., Hassouni, T., Ibrahmi, A., & Mehdi, E. (2022). Science teachers' views on the use and effectiveness of interactive simulations in science teaching and learning. *International Journal of Instruction, 15*(1), 277–292. doi:10.29333/iji.2022.15116a

Boet, S., Bould, M. D., Layat Burn, C., & Reeves, S. (2014). Twelve tips for a successful interprofessional team-based high-fidelity simulation education session. *Medical Teacher, 36*(10), 853–857. doi:10.3109/014215 9X.2014.923558 PMID:25023765

Broer, M., Bai, Y., & Fonseca, F. (2019). A Review of the Literature on Socioeconomic Status and Educational Achievement. In *Socioeconomic Inequality and Educational Outcomes. IEA Research for Education* (Vol. 5). Springer. doi:10.1007/978-3-030-11991-1_2

Chernikova, O., Heitzmann, N., Stadler, M., Holzberger, D., Seidel, T., & Fischer, F. (2020, August). Simulation-based learning in higher education: A meta-analysis. *Review of Educational Research, 90*(4), 499–541. doi:10.3102/0034654320933544

Cochran-Smith, M., & Villegas, A. M. (2016). Preparing teachers for diversity and high-poverty schools: A research-based perspective. In Lampert & Burnett (Eds.), Teacher Educa tion for high poverty schools (pp. 9-31). Springer International Publishing. doi:10.1007/978-3-319-22059-8_2

Creamer, J., Shrider, E. A., Burns, K., & Chen, F. (2021). U.S. Census Bureau, Current Population Reports, P60-277, Poverty in the United States. U.S. Government Publishing Office.

Dalinger, T., Thomas, K., Stansberry, S., & Xiu, Y. (2019). A mixed reality simulation offers strategic practice for pre-service teachers. *Computers & Education, 144*. Doi-10.1016/j.compedu.2019.103696.

Fontenot, K., Semega, J., & Kollar, M. (2018). *Income and poverty in the United States: 2017.* U.S. Census Bureau, 60–263. Retrieved from https://www.census.gov/content/dam/Census/library/publications/2018/demo/p60-263.pdf

Frederking, B. (2005). Simulations and student learning. *Journal of Political Science Education, 1*(3), 385–93. doi:10.1080/15512160500261236

Gordon, D. (2005). Indicators of poverty & hunger. *Expert Group meeting on youth development indicators, 1*(1), 12–14. https://www.un.org/esa/socdev/unyin/documents/ydiDavidGordon_poverty.pdf

Gorski, P. C. (2008a). The myth of the 'culture of poverty.' *Educational Leadership*, *65*(7), 32. https://www.researchgate.net/publication/228620924

Gorski, P. C. (2008b). Peddling poverty for profit: Elements of oppression in Ruby Payne's framework. *Equity & Excellence in Education*, *41*(1), 130–148. doi:10.1080/10665680701761854

Gosen, J., & Washbush, J. (2004). A review of scholarship on assessing experiential learning effectiveness. *Simulation & Gaming*, *35*(2), 270–293. doi:10.1177/1046878104263544

Hair, N. L., Hanson, J. L., Wolfe, B. L., & Pollak, S. D. (2015). Association of child poverty, brain development, and academic achievement. *JAMA Pediatrics*, *169*(9), 822–829. doi:10.1001/jamapediatrics.2015.1475 PMID:26192216

Howard, T. C., & Rodriguez-Scheel, A. (2016). Difficult dialogues about race and poverty in teacher preparation. In Lampert & Burnett (Eds.), Teacher Education for High Schools (pp. 53–72). Springer. doi:10.1007/978-3-319-22059-8_4

Kaufman, D., & Ireland, A. (2016). Enhancing teacher education with simulations. *TechTrends*, *60*(3), 260–267. doi:10.1007/s11528-016-0049-0

Lindqvist, S. M., & Reeves, S. (2007). Facilitators' perceptions of delivering interprofessional education: A qualitative study. *Medical Teacher*, *29*(4), 403–405. doi:10.1080/01421590701509662 PMID:17786761

McFarland, J., Hussar, B., Zhang, J., Wang, X., Wang, K., Hein, S., Diliberti, M., Forrest Cataldi, E., Bullock Mann, F., & Barmer, A. (2019). *The Condition of Education 2019 (NCES 2019-144)*. U.S. Department of Education. Retrieved from https://nces.ed.gov/pubsearch/pubsinfo.asp?pubid=2019144

Miller, J., & Vick, C. (2022). An examination of the community action poverty simulation in rural education. *Alabama Journal of Educational Leadership, 9,* 133–141. https://eric.ed.gov/?id=EJ1362044

Missouri Association for Community Action Network (CAN). (2018). *Community Action Poverty Simulation*. Retrieved from https://www.communityaction.org/povertysimulations/

National Center for Education Statistics (NCES). (2015). *U.S. Department of Education report on the "condition of education 2015."* NCES. Retrieved from https://nces.ed.gov/programs/coe/pdf/Indicator_CCE/coe_cce_2015_05.pdf

National Center for Education Statistics (NCES). (2017). U.*S. Department of Education report on the "condition of education 2017."* NCES. Retrieved from https://nces.ed.gov/pubs2017/2017144.pdf

Noone, J., Sideras, S., Gubrud-Howe, P., Voss, H., & Mathews, L. R. (2012). Influence of a poverty simulation on nursing student attitudes toward poverty. *The Journal of Nursing Education, 51*(11), 616–622. doi:10.3928/01484834-20120914-01 PMID:22978272

Northrup, A., Berro, E., Spang, C., & Brown, M. (2020). Teaching poverty: Evaluation of two simulated poverty teaching interventions with undergraduate nursing students. *The Journal of Nursing Education, 59*(2), 83–87. doi:10.3928/01484834-20200122-05 PMID:32003847

O'Connell, M. (2019). Is the impact of SES on educational performance overestimated? Evidence from the PISA survey. *Intelligence, 75,* 41–47. doi:10.1016/j.intell.2019.04.005

Patterson, N., & Hulton, L. J. (2012). Enhancing nursing students' understanding of poverty through simulation. *Public Health Nursing (Boston, Mass.), 29*(2), 143–151. doi:10.1111/j.1525-1446.2011.00999.x PMID:22372451

Poverty in USA. (n.d.). *The Population of Poverty USA.* Poverty in USA. Retrieved from https://www.povertyusa.org/facts

Sanko, J., Matsuda, Y., Salani, D., Tran, L., Reaves, R., & Gerber, K. (2021). A comparison of learning outcomes from two poverty simulation experiences. *Public Health Nursing (Boston, Mass.), 38*(1), 427–438. Advance online publication. doi:10.1111/phn.12853 PMID:33410560

Shellman, S. M., & Turan, K. (2006). Do simulations enhance student learning? An empirical evaluation of an IR simulation. *Journal of Political Science Education, 2*(1), 19–32. doi:10.1080/15512160500484168

Smith-Carrier, T., Leacy, K., Bouck, M. S., Justrabo, J., & Decker Pierce, B. (2019). Living with poverty: A simulation. *Journal of Social Work, 19*(5), 642–663. doi:10.1177/1468017318766429

Sottile, J., & Brozik, D. (2004). *The use of simulations in a teacher education program: The impact on student development* [A critical review]. Paper presented at the 2004 Hawaii International Conference on Education (HICE). Honolulu, HI. https://files.eric.ed.gov/fulltext/ED490383.pdf

Strasser, S., Smith, M. O., Pendrick Denney, D., Jackson, M. C., & Buckmaster, P. (2013). A poverty simulation to inform public health practice. *American Journal of Health Education*, *44*(5), 259–264. doi:10.1080/19325037.2013.811366

The World Bank. (2023). *Poverty and Shared Prosperity 2022 Correcting Course.* The World Bank. Retrieved from https://www.worldbank.org/en/publication/poverty-and-shared-prosperity

The World Bank. (n.d.). *Poverty.* The World Bank. Retrieved from https://www.worldbank.org/en/topic/poverty/overview

Tyerman, J., Luctkar-Flude, M., Graham, L., Coffey, S., & Olsen-Lynch, E. (2016). Pre-simulation preparation and briefing practices for healthcare professionals and students: A systematic review protocol. *JBI Database of Systematic Reviews and Implementation Reports*, *14*(8), 80–89. doi:10.11124/JBISRIR-2016-003055 PMID:27635748

United States Census Bureau. (2020). *Poverty thresholds by size of family and number of children.* Census.gov/data/tables/time-series/demo/income-poverty/historical-poverty-thresholds.html

Wright, T., Nankin, I., Boonstra, K., & Blair, E. (2019). Changing through relationships and reflection: An exploratory investigation of pre-service teachers' perceptions of young children experiencing homelessness. *Early Childhood Education Journal*, *47*(3), 297–308. doi:10.1007/s10643-018-0921-y

Yosso, T. J. (2005). Whose culture has capital? A critical race theory discussion of community cultural wealth. *Race, Ethnicity and Education*, *8*(1), 69–91. doi:10.1080/1361332052000341006

Chapter 6

Transforming School Organisational Culture Through a Contextually Relevant Change Leadership Approach Within a Pakistani Urban Private School

Venesser Fernandes
iD https://orcid.org/0000-0003-3907-7673
Monash University, Australia

ABSTRACT

This chapter focuses on the transformative journey of a K-12 Pakistani urban private school in moving from autocratic-charismatic leadership practices to distributed-strategic leadership practices through the use of a total quality management change leadership approach integrated over two years. This study found that distributed educational leadership practices are developed at the school level through contextually relevant change leadership approaches that focus on sustained and continuous school improvement. The chapter provides insights into possibilities for further developing school organisational culture through emphasis given to collaborative and strategic decision-making practices amongst senior-level, middle-level, and teacher-level leaders in urban private schools in Pakistan.

DOI: 10.4018/978-1-7998-3940-8.ch006

Copyright © 2024, IGI Global. Copying or distributing in print or electronic forms without written permission of IGI Global is prohibited.

INTRODUCTION

Within Pakistan, research indicates that a majority of school leaders demonstrate an autocratic, predominantly bureaucratic approach to leadership with the principal positioned as the main decision-maker within the school (Ahmad & Dilshad, 2016; Salfi et al., 2014; Simkins et al., 2003). This practice is largely prevalent in public schools (Jehan, 2015; Rizvi, 2008), where school principals follow the directives of their respective superiors and have limited freedom to utilise transformative educational change leadership approaches for school improvement. This constraint has negatively impacted student achievement outcomes (Jehan, 2015) and might be one of the main reasons for high student dropout rates in public schools across Pakistan and rising enrolments in private schools (Fernandes, 2019a).

In contrast, examples of distributed leadership approaches are found within the private sector, especially in community-based private schools (Salim, 2016; Shah, 2018). Private schools now constitute one-third of the schools within Pakistan (ISAPS, 2010). Unlike the public sector, the absence of a central regulating system offers private schools greater freedom to construct their educational philosophy independently (Raza et al., 2021) using transformative leadership approaches (Burns, 1978; van Oord, 2013). This educational philosophy reinforces the curriculum choice, pedagogical practices, and operational strategies, which make up their school's organisational culture. In fact, due to this autonomous nature of private schools (Nadeem et al., 2019), private school principals are able to use a distributive-strategic leadership approach involving others, such as teachers and school personnel, in engaging in transformative school improvement (Salfi et al., 2014) and participative decision-making models (Fernandes, 2019a).

This chapter focuses on the transformative journey of a K-12 private urban school in Pakistan, moving from an autocratic-charismatic leadership to a distributed-strategic leadership approach adopted through use of a total quality management (TQM) change leadership approach (Fernandes, 2019c). The main research question that forms the basis of this chapter is,

"How do Pakistani private schools use contextually-relevant change leadership approaches to transform their organisational culture"?

Transforming School Organisational Culture

LITERATURE REVIEW

Schools as Complex Adaptive Educational Systems

Schools are recognised as complex adaptive systems (CAS) where change is emergent (Grobman, 2005), continuous (Keshavarz et al., 2010) and recursive (Koh & Askell-Williams, 2021). Schools as natural complex systems are subject to uncertainty and constantly changing organisational environments (Daft, 2016; Fidan & Balci, 2017) where adaptation is continuous and predictable (Holland, 1998). Schools have become more complex over time becoming more open and nested than before (Fernandes, 2019c). As open systems, they are always interacting with their environments and are structured to deal with forces within these environments. CAS have distributed control (Kurtz & Snowden, 2003) and are highly context-dependent. Schools as CAS are open social systems with fuzzy boundaries so that when planning, implementing or even evaluating initiatives, they consider how contextually-relevant these change initiatives will be (Holland, 1998; Rosas, 2017).

CAS literature has focused on theoretical similarities between actual organisations and complex adaptive systems using a complexity perspective (Keshavarz et al., 2010). This is the right time to focus on studying strategy-focused studies in schools on complexity management (Fidan & Balci, 2017). Further, empirical research will identify the influences of CAS strategies on schools and CAS interrelationships amongst school stakeholders. A research gap existent in CAS studies on schools is, "in our understanding of the real-world conditions essential for sustaining improvement initiatives in schools" (Koh & Askell-Williams, 2021, p.310). They suggest identifying which components of sustainability should be a part of the CAS within a school; how these components interact with each other; combinations of components that are most effective together; and, the importance of certain components over others across various times and contexts.

This organisational case study identifies CAS components responsible for sustaining transformative organisational culture within schools operating as open systems. It looks at combinations of contextual components considered at this particular school, how these components interact together and whether certain combinations need to be considered at any given time within the school, to sustain transformative organisational culture change within this case-study school.

Pivoting the Organisational Culture of Schools Towards Transformative Contextually Relevant Change Leadership Approaches

Organisational culture has been defined as the accumulated shared learning within a group representing the organisation (Schein & Schein, 2016). A school as an organisation uses this learning to solve complex problems arising from external adaptation or internal integration. This shared learning allows current and new members to know how to perceive, think, feel and behave while dealing with complex problems. Organisational culture is defined more broadly as "a pattern or system of beliefs, values, and behavioural norms that come to be taken for granted as basic assumptions [for the organisation]" (Schein & Schein, 2016, p.21).

Braun et al. (2011, p. 588) identified four sets of interconnected contexts in relation to school leadership: "situated-contexts', "professional-contexts', "material-contexts' and "external-contexts'. "Situated-contexts' are aspects linked through historical and locational links to the school, such as a school's setting, history and intakes (Braun et al., 2011, p. 588). 'Professional-contexts' focus on value systems, teacher commitments and experiences, and school policy management and enactment processes (Braun et al., 2011, p. 591). 'Material-contexts,' refer to administrative processes dealing with school budgets, ongoing staffing requirements, physical buildings, information and communication technology and other school infrastructure (Braun et al., 2011, p. 592). 'External-contexts' connects with influences of local and national policies and their pressures and expectations imposed on schools (Braun et al., 2011, p. 592). These may include school improvement and accountability processes, legal responsibilities and obligations, and local authority supports such as Ministries or Departments of Education, school linkages and partnerships or associations with other schools or organisations. School leaders use contextual intelligence to better understand and practice educational leadership within their diverse contexts (Clarke & O'Donoghue, 2017). Likewise, contextual intelligence requires school leaders to have an intuitive grasp of relevant past events, awareness of existing contextual variables, and understandings of a preferred future so they can make good decisions and exert leadership influence within their school community (Kutz, 2008, p.18). School improvement, school leadership theory and school context are all interconnected.

According to Marishane (2020, p.11),

Intelligent school leaders are first and foremost situated in a given context – a school organisational context – of which they are aware and how they relate to and connect with this context depends on the knowledge they possess, the image they project, the relationship they establish, how they conduct themselves, the work they do, how they perform their work, the choices they make and actions they take, as informed by [their] practical intelligence.

In increasingly complex environments, school leaders need to be contextually intelligent, where their core knowledge about schooling becomes more context-dependent whether concerning curriculum, school organisation, management, school improvement or societal changes (Brauckmann et al., 2020). The current study adopted a contextually-relevant position, designed in keeping with the South Asian urban cultural context. The findings from this study contribute to a limited body of literature on contextually relevant school leadership in South Asia.

In contextually-sensitive cultural studies conducted in Pakistan, findings suggest that private sector principals have greater power and authority and exercise more leadership independence than their public counterparts (Simkins et al., 2003; Simkins et al., 1998). Research indicates that top-down, autocratic leadership approaches are exercised in public Pakistani schools (Jehan, 2015; Rizvi, 2008) where the Ministry of Education and various Departments of Education give directives to school principals who have limited power and authority within their leadership roles as compared to their private counterparts who exercise a transformational leadership style (Salfi et al., 2014). According to transformational leadership theory (Bass, 1998), a transformational school leader understands the organisational culture of their school, enabling them to realign the school and its organisation by providing it with a vision and revising its collectively shared assumptions, norms and values. When exercising transformational school leadership, principals exercise reciprocity in their culturally intelligent leadership style and the context within their school (Marishane, 2020). They do this by responding to the contextual demands of their school environment and through tactical and strategic thinking and acting while pursuing organisational goals (Bass & Avolio, 1993) to maintain organisational effectiveness.

In another small-scale empirical study conducted on a low-cost private community school in Pakistan, a distributed leadership model was studied through teachers' roles in shared decision-making practices within that school (Salim, 2016). Culturally, whether in public (Rizvi, 2008) or private schools (Shah, 2018), research in Pakistani schools suggests that the level of involvement of teachers in school leadership and decision-making depends on school principals providing opportunities for teachers to become involved. Findings from this study (Shah, 2018) suggested that teachers were positively inclined towards shared decision-making, preferring it over traditional decision-making models. However, while they believed decision-making processes at their school were collaborative, more than half the teachers did not feel empowered to make decisions because their input, though sought out by management, was not incorporated into final decisions. The findings further identified intrinsic and extrinsic factors within and outside the school that impacted the willingness and agency of these Pakistani community school teachers to participate in shared decision-making processes. While these teachers felt ready to assume shared decision-making responsibilities, they needed relevant knowledge and skills developed within themselves to meaningfully participate in the process and take charge of their professional landscape. These findings were relevant to the current case study school as both schools were low-cost private schools in urban settings and a major part of this study involved teacher leaders and middle-level school leaders in participative decision-making processes. Likewise, in another study conducted with three Pakistani private schools, the role of the principal in developing participative decision-making processes was highlighted. As Retallick (Retallick, 2005, p. 40) discussed,

In all cases, the principal delegated significant responsibility to others in the school ... and ensured that accountability accompanied the delegation of responsibility. This produced a sense of shared responsibility... by empowering others to make decisions and take appropriate actions, though always within a framework or a set of guidelines provided by the principal.

Niesche (2016) maintains that school leaders should fundamentally address concerns for social justice and fairness where leadership in schools should not be limited to procedures, models, standards, and effectiveness. They should provide safe nurturing learning environments, inculcating an organisational culture of shared decision-making, continual learning and professional development of school teachers and school leaders. Nasreen and Odhiambo (Nasreen & Odhiambo, 2018, p. 247) suggest that, "[Pakistani] school principals must prioritise their own professional development as highly important ...to perform their complex roles". Nasreen and Odhiambo (2018) found that Pakistani school leaders described their training programmes as being focused on content knowledge in specific subject areas and on teaching strategies and school discipline, while there was an absence of leadership development in curriculum planning, technology, classroom management and

Transforming School Organisational Culture

discipline, assessment techniques, research work and communication skills, all of which are crucial for principals to function as effective school leaders. It is increasingly important to build the knowledge and skills of principals, teachers and administrative staff to deal with complexity (Schleicher, 2016) by developing schools as strategically-oriented learning organisations (Fernandes, 2019a). Schools using Strategic TQM (Fernandes, 2019c) have a transformative framework with an improvement philosophy, tools and processes to make cultural changes and to sustain continuous improvement approaches. As discussed elsewhere, through Strategic TQM, schools engage in five critical transformations: structural, cultural, organisational, processual and environmental defined as the SCOPE improvement cycle. They make use of a progressive-reflective organisational change leadership approach (Fernandes, 2019c). This cycle equips schools to culturally engage with complex changes taking place internally and externally in their environment using quality assurance and quality enhancement practices. However, this organisational leadership practice takes time and requires supportive school leaders because it requires the deployment of time, resources and commitment (Sallis, 1993).

Successful Pakistani school leaders work on culturally developing their teaching staff through distributive leadership responsibilities used while building school vision (Nawab & Asad, 2020; Salfi, 2011). Private school principals have greater autonomy in their leadership practices making it more likely to adopt distributed leadership practices with their teachers (Nadeem et al., 2019). They support the professional development of their teachers and engage their teaching staff in collaborative decision-making processes for school improvement. This type of proactive leadership found in community-based schools in Pakistan has multiple stakeholders involved in school leadership practices such as individual teachers, teaching staff teams, parents, administrative staff, students, middle-level leaders and vice principals as well as the principal or headteacher (Tajik & Wali, 2020). These leadership practices (Spillane, 2015) are sustained and institutionalised over time within these private schools where school stakeholders are engaged in complex adaptive work while working on transforming their organisational culture.

THE IMPACT OF NATIONAL CULTURE ON THE EDUCATIONAL CONTEXT IN PAKISTAN

As a nation, present-day Pakistan is an Islamic country with a strong traditional, conservative culture. This national culture has a deep influence on the education system of Pakistan. As a conservative, traditional, collectivist society, Pakistan holds its patriarchal values strongly and there is an adherence to systems and structures that are already set in place with those in authority respected for their positional power and authority (Fernandes et al., 2019). Within Pakistani society, a school principal as the positional head of the school has both legitimate and expert power bases within their school community. A number of studies confirm that Pakistani principals are mostly authoritative and bureaucratic (Ahmad & Dilshad, 2016; Salfi et al., 2014) and mostly sole decision-makers within their schools (Mansoor, 2015) exercising an autocratic leadership style (Simkins et al., 2003) amongst their teaching staff. A growing shift towards more transformative ways of school leadership and collaborative ways of school improvement remains scattered across the nation in small pockets of school improvement with the autocratic approach still being undertaken by numerous school leaders in Pakistani schools (Ahmad & Dilshad, 2016; Salfi et al., 2014; Simkins et al., 2003).

RESEARCH METHODS

Design of the Study

An instrumental organisational single case (Baxter & Jack, 2008; Stake, 1995) was used for this small-scale research study. Crowe and colleagues (Crowe et al., 2011) suggest that by using case study approaches researchers actively engage in multi-faceted explorations of complex issues within real-life settings. The phenomenon being investigated through this study was understanding how Strategic TQM (Fernandes, 2019c) was used as an organisational change leadership approach to transform autocratic-charismatic leadership and management behaviours into distributed-strategic leadership and management behaviours within this urban private school in Pakistan. The researcher worked closely with the senior and middle levels of school leadership over two years to assist them in embedding this organisational change approach within their school. The role of the researcher was that of a participant-observer working as an educational consultant at the school while helping the school to transform and redefine a new organisational culture for itself. The researcher observed how three tiers of school leadership: senior-level leadership, middle-level leadership and teacher-level leadership were activated (Fernandes, 2019b) through this transformative organisational change approach undertaken at this case-study school.

Study Site

This small-sized single-sited school is located in the suburban part of the city of Karachi, Pakistan. The school has been in place since the 1990s. The school is an English medium, medium fee-paying school making it a preferred option amongst local public schools and other lower fee-paying schools in its vicinity. The school has three sections: a three-year Pre-Primary section (two-year Montessori + one-year transition), a five-year Primary section and a five-year secondary section. The school has eighteen classrooms, two Secondary Science laboratories, a Computer laboratory, a Library, an Administrative Office, a Reception, Senior Management offices, a Staff room and a School Hall. The school is co-educational, with enrolments averaging between 400 to 450 students and having a spread of 51% male and 49% female students. It has 40 personnel on staff as given in Table 1. This includes 3 Senior Leadership members, 3 Middle-level leaders, 25 Teaching staff, 2 Part-time Teaching staff, 2 Administrative staff and 5 Maintenance staff members. The school staff consists of 10 men and 30 women, thus having a majority of female staff working at the school.

Table 1. Organisational structure of school personnel

School personnel	Gender	Age	Years of Experience	Years at Current School
Senior Leadership				
Director	Male	55 – 60	22 years	22 years
Administrator	Male	50 – 55	14 years	3 years
Principal	Female	55 – 60	25 years	2 years
Middle Leadership				
Pre-Primary Senior Mistress	Female	40 – 45	18 years	10 years
Primary Senior Mistress	Female	50 – 55	27 years	8 years
Secondary Senior Mistress	Female	40 – 45	20 years	6 years

continues on following page

Transforming School Organisational Culture

Table 1. Continued

School personnel	Gender	Age	Years of Experience	Years at Current School
Teaching Staff				
Pre-Primary Teachers				
1. 3-Year-Old Kindergarten Teacher	Female	30 – 35	10 years	7 years
2. 4-Year-Old Kindergarten Teacher	Female	35 – 40	11 years	1 year
3. Transition Teacher	Female	40 – 45	12 years	12 years
Primary Teachers				
1. Grade One Teacher	Female	20 – 25	3 years	3 years
2. Grade Two Teacher	Female	20 – 25	4 years	1 year
3. Grade Three Teacher	Female	20 – 25	4 years	2 years
4. Grade Four Teacher	Female	25 – 30	6 years	4 years
5. Grade Five Teacher	Female	30 – 35	9 years	2 years
6. Primary Art Teacher	Female	20 – 25	4 years	4 years
7. Primary Sports Teacher	Female	25 – 30	8 years	5 years
8. Primary ICT Teacher	Female	25 – 30	7 years	1 year
9. Primary Urdu Language Teacher	Female	30 – 35	9 years	2 years
10. Primary Islamiyat Teacher	Female	30 – 35	9 years	4 years
Secondary Teachers				
1. Secondary English Language Teacher	Female	30 – 35	11 years	11 years
2. Secondary Urdu Language Teacher	Female	40 – 45	13 years	8 years
3. Secondary Geography Teacher	Female	40 – 45	12 years	12 years
4. Secondary History Teacher	Female	40 – 45	13 years	3 years
5. Secondary Science Teacher* (Later became Vice-Principal)	Female	40 – 45	18 years	12 years
6. Secondary General Mathematics Teacher	Male	30 – 35	11 years	1 year
7. Secondary Physics/Advanced Mathematics Teacher	Male	30 – 35	9 years	4 years
8. Secondary Chemistry/Biology Teacher	Female	30 – 35	8 years	4 years
9. Secondary Art Teacher	Female	30 – 35	9 years	3 years
10. Secondary Sports Teacher	Male	30 – 35	8 years	5 years
11. Secondary ICT Teacher	Female	25 – 30	6 years	2 years
12. Secondary Islamiyat Teacher	Female	40– 45	16 years	1 year
Part-time Teaching Staff				
1. Primary Sindhi Language Teacher	Male	30 – 35	11 years	8 years
2. Secondary Sindhi Language Teacher	Male	40 – 45	14 years	7 years
Administrative Staff				
1. Receptionist	Female	20 – 25	3 years	1 year
2. School Finance Officer	Male	30 – 35	7 years	6 years
School Maintenance Staff				
1. School Groundskeeper	Male	30 – 35	8 years	7 years
2. Pre-Primary Maintenance Staff (Junior)	Female	20 – 25	4 years	3 years
3. Primary Maintenance Staff (Primary)	Female	30 – 35	7 years	6 years
4. Secondary Maintenance Staff (Secondary)	Female	30 – 35	8 years	8 years
5. School Security Attendant	Male	30 – 35	8 years	6 years

FINDINGS

Using a Contextually-Relevant Organisational Change Leadership Approach

Navaratnam's (Navaratnam, 1997) model for organisational change was used for data analysis because of its cultural relevance to the context. It consists of a *quality journey plan* for an educational organisation such as a school to engage in while changing organisational culture through an integrated, people-centric approach with the commitment of senior-level leaders, middle-level leaders, teachers, administrative staff, parents and students. The school improves itself through cyclical continuous improvement strategies based on an interdependent systems of planning, implementing, evaluating, and decision-making. This Strategic TQM model places emphasis on incremental and continuous quality improvement. The model consists of six interdependent core improvement phases, focused on contextual organisational culture transformations. The six phases of the quality journey plan are outlined in Figure 1.

Figure 1. Six phases of the quality journey plan

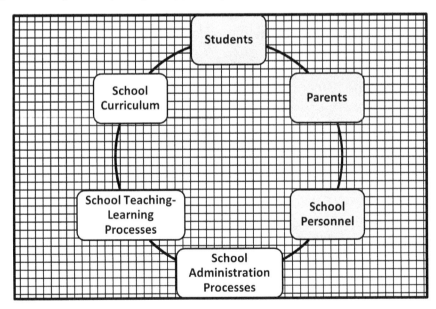

Senior leaders were concerned with an increasing number of private schools in their neighbourhood and their own dwindling student numbers over three years. The previous principal retired five years earlier, having served more than fifteen years. The ex-principal was a strong educational and relational school leader. After their departure, staff morale had lowered and a series of new school leaders brought in quick episodic, insufficiently planned changes that left parents concerned with decreasing student learning outcomes. At the time of the study, approximately 50 students had exited causing significant concern. A new female principal was appointed. The school leadership team consisted of the principal, other senior leaders, including the director-owner and the school administrator, who had a previous military background. The three senior leadership members felt strongly that developing a new identity for the school through a contextually-relevant organisational change leadership approach would assist in re-building school culture. The principal and senior mistresses felt a relational approach to organisational change leadership allowed them to work with staff in identifying existing issues, build up new organisational processes and focus on continued leadership capacity-building across three leadership levels: Top, Middle and Teacher-levels (Fernandes, 2019b). The principal felt by making use of a Strategic TQM change leadership approach, the school would essentially develop both distributed and strategic organisational leadership capabilities within their school organisational processes and improve its educational delivery.

In her words,

Our staff morale is quite low, a number of experienced teachers have left, and our results are decreasing with each passing year. Teachers feel like their efforts are wasted and their voice is not heard. . . . We have become very autocratic with them.

Navaratnam's (Navaratnam, 1997) change leadership model uses improvement cycles within a six-stage quality journey plan. This model was contextually-relevant, involving a whole staff approach to identifying contextual issues within the school. In the absence of sustained external support from the government or other regulatory bodies, such as the private educational institutions' regulatory authority, the school leaders felt they had to proactively develop internal accountability and improvement. During its organisational change leadership process, the school worked across six interactive cyclic improvement processes to build a distributed leadership approach amongst the teaching and administrative staff and a strategic leadership approach amongst senior and middle-level leaders.

Stage One: Awareness and Self-Assessment

This stage involved getting initial agreement and confirmation from senior and middle-level leaders for the commencement of this organisational change approach. It involved helping them understand Strategic TQM philosophy (Fernandes, 2019c) and organisational cultural change methodology (Navaratnam, 1997). The researcher worked with senior-level leaders, middle-level leaders, teachers and administrative staff members to help build an understanding of how this change model would help in identifying current challenges experienced by the school. There were concerns amongst the senior mistresses on understanding their leadership practice within this model. As the primary senior mistress discussed, "I'm really happy to see us once again thinking about the quality of education for students and that concerns of teachers are being heard. Will we, however be given authority to deal with teacher concerns?" The secondary senior mistress questioned whether her authority as a school leader would be extended by stating, "If we are to use this change approach, then we will need to be more directly involved in school decision-making. At the moment, we are expected to do what is directed and get our staff to do the same". The Montessori senior mistress raised her concerns, "Will we be able to run our school as a learning institution and not as a profit-generating business if we follow this change model?"

Stage Two: Training and Team-Building

As Pakistan identifies as a strong patriarchal society (Fernandes et al., 2019), even though the school principal and senior mistresses were female, the administrator had a strong autocratic view of school improvement (Ahmad & Dilshad, 2016; Salfi et al., 2014). As a key gatekeeper, it was imperative for him to see the importance of collective visioning taking place through workshops with all staff. These initial workshops and consultations with leadership, teaching and administrative staff allowed the researcher to work at building their teamwork, collaborative decision-making and problem-solving skills (Retallick, 2005; Shah, 2018). Moving a school from an autocratic-charismatic top-down approach to a bottom-up, distributed-strategic approach requires efforts at removing mistrust and fear. School personnel worked collaboratively and engaged in adaptive work, developing a mission statement while collectively identifying six areas of improvement to focus upon (See Figure Two); they were beginning to understand the cultural difference this change approach would make to their working environment.

Figure 2. Six areas of quality improvement

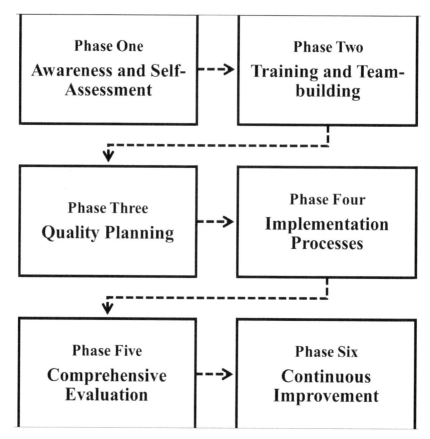

The second series of workshops provided opportunities for more adaptive work by school personnel in the development of the three-year strategic plan for the school, known as its school development plan. Six quality improvement teams investigated and identified strategies and activities within their respective areas of improvement over a three-year period. As one of the administrative staff members stated, "I feel like the TQM approach used by the six quality improvement teams belongs to us because we are defining it for our school".

There were concerns amongst few teachers on the increase in administrative workload on staff. Likewise, the administrator resigned and the director decided that with the new philosophical emphasis of this process, the school was best served if there was a vice-principal appointed from within the teaching staff who focused mostly on school curriculum and the teaching-learning process; supported by the senior mistresses. The principal would focus on school administrative processes and external networking. This leadership direction was welcomed amongst the teaching staff with the appointment of the new vice principal. Senior leaders were working in line with the mission statement and providing support to their staff as they engaged in this adaptive work. As one secondary school teacher discussed,

I was initially quite confused about the whole change approach as I haven't seen something like this happen before. However, as we spend more time and are given time to work on this process, I believe we are making good changes.

Deliberate changes in the school timetable provided teachers with allocated time to work within their improvement teams. This cultural change was symbolic and appreciated by everyone.

Stage Three: Quality Planning

A Strategic TQM change approach requires that quality assurance and quality enhancement processes are operating in order to sustain the adaptive work required in building up continuous school improvement processes. While developing the school strategic plan, senior school leaders decided that all school policies needed revision and realignment with the new school mission. Hence, the middle-level leaders worked closely with senior leaders in aligning these policies with institutional planning processes focusing on teaching-learning processes and administrative processes. Building this new strategic intent helped strengthen the school purpose - providing better quality education than their competitors. The Director noted,

These workshops have shown us many new ways in which to think through the problems we face in our school. I am encouraged by the work done by our quality improvement teams in developing good educational strategies changing how we educate students and encouraging a positive work culture.

Each team prepared its own set of recommendations within its individual area of improvement. Six sets of recommendations were drafted after each team had investigated the issues through the use of relevant quality tools, gathered the evidence and analysed it through a consultative process with relevant stakeholders; before identifying possible avenues for improvement. These recommendations were first shortlisted; then approved and included in the school development plan. Each year, these teams would work at developing plans for one additional year within the school development plan while working on the short-term action plan for the current year. This progressive-reflective model of continuous school improvement (Fernandes, 2019c) allowed the school to be able to connect future improvement work across its six areas of improvement through the continued work of the quality improvement teams while working each year on short-term action plans across these six areas. This strategic leadership approach allowed staff to work with school leaders through allocated budgeted improvement strategies that were future-focused and planned in advance.

Stage Four: Implementation

The fourth interactive cycle of implementation involved school personnel using a team approach towards identifying school problems and reaching amicable solutions. This distributive leadership approach developed a collegiate management style across the school teams. The recommendations given by each quality improvement team in effect influenced school personnel and had an impact on the school policy review and strategic planning processes being developed across the school. The building up of a strong team approach now involved all school personnel in an extensive problem-solving exercise over two years through interactive cycles of continuous improvement. As the Vice-Principal stated, "I am really pleased to see how the focus has shifted from blaming each other to actually working towards solving the problem. I hope we can continue to work in this way in the future as well". Likewise, this team approach provided the basis for transformational work as it allowed the school to establish and strengthen its existent communication processes which had broken down due to the autocratic leadership approach taken by the administrator. The school principal observed, "I am pleased to see school leaders, teachers, and administrative staff, working together on finding better ways to work on our problems. We are changing our school culture". The cross-functional teams found that they shared a lot in common and that their diversity was harnessed as a strength. As one teacher suggested, "Working in my quality improvement team has given me an opportunity to listen to what others are saying and also to give my own suggestions".

As the school started identifying better ways of working, it began focusing on developing a strong client service approach with those working in the school reception office. The school receptionist discussed, "Since I developed this task checklist and am using it regularly, my work is done on time, with fewer errors. I now have more time to work on updating my information boards in the school reception". Likewise, the school started looking closely at school finances and putting in control charts to monitor expenses. The head of the pre-primary section discussed, "With this new revised form of budgeting, I

Transforming School Organisational Culture

am more accountable of the expenses within my section. We are developing resource lists each term and seeing where our major expenses are located and if that fits our school development plan".

Creating a staff development plan allowed identification of specific areas for professional development of school leaders, teachers, administrative staff and support staff. This staff development plan was connected with the short-term one-year school action plan and long-term three-year school development plan. The school principal discussed that this plan was, "a good way for moving forward with the direction mapped out for us; helping us to focus on where to upskill our staff".

The school developed its own school quality plan. This plan provided the school with school policies closely aligned with school processes and linked the various planning documents with policies and processes. This physical operational manual symbolically represented the transformation in administrative processes taking place. As the director discussed,

The school quality manual has brought together all our planning, policies and practices into one space. I have placed a copy of it in the staffroom and at the reception so everyone can access it as often as they want.

This manual would be revised after every three-year cycle of school improvement by the principal and a cross-functional quality improvement team.

Stage Five: Comprehensive Evaluation

Built within the structure of the organisational change leadership approach, the interactive cycles of evaluation focused on specific school monitoring mechanisms. These included setting up an annual auditing system at the school; evaluation of current school policies and setting up of procedures for regular revision of school policies; evaluation of school procedures and setting up regular revisions of school procedures within the school quality manual; setting up staff appraisal processes as well as staff development plans; and, setting up regular quality improvement teams. It was decided that school evaluation would now be a regular part of the school's own internal accountability and improvement.

Stage Six: Continuous Improvement

The school developed its own system of continuous improvement through its short-term and long-term planning tools. It had begun to identify its contextual barriers and enablers being faced by school leaders and the teaching and administrative staff. As a primary teacher discussed, "working together with everyone to understand and solve the problems that our school faces is productive. Instead of being blamed we now feel we are part of the solution". Developing a strong professional development plan and staff appraisal processes, assisted the school in transforming itself into a strategically-oriented learning organisation. The principal discussed how, "developing my school personnel is very important to me. I like to see my staff empowered to be strong professionals demonstrating their talents and capabilities as we improve this school." The role of middle-level leaders such as the senior mistresses (Fernandes, 2019b) was envisaged as leaders who would create spaces for interactive dialogue and sensemaking developing this school into a strategically-oriented learning organisation.

DISCUSSION

Visible Transformative Change Needs to be Driven by Senior-Level Leaders

Successful organisational change needs the support of senior-level leaders in schools (Raza et al., 2021). As found in this study, the transformative change being envisioned needed to be first realised and then directed by senior-level school leaders as the mission statement was developed prior to it being translated into planned actions and strategies across the six quality improvement teams with complex adaptive work being done by senior-level, middle-level and teacher-level leaders (Fernandes, 2019b). The findings indicate how Pakistani private schools as open complex organisations need to work through old culture, learn and transform through new cultural values and beliefs and then embed new organisational cultural practices, demonstrated through new skills learnt and put into practice through innovative, operational procedures and school strategic plans (Schein & Schein, 2016). Within a Pakistani culture, it is imperative that senior-level school leaders are at the front leading this change and mandating and validating the small organisational changes that are taking place. This adaptive zone of productive disequilibrium requires all staff to work together at removing beliefs and processes that have been detrimental and develop new ways of sense-making that transform their contextually-relevant beliefs, practices and action through situated cognition and practice.

Sustaining Continuous School Improvement Through a Proactive Team-Based Approach

Similar to most schools today, the findings from this study suggested that this case-study school was subject to the complexities (Daft, 2016; Fidan & Balci, 2017) arising from the uncertainty of enrolments being lost and constantly changing organisational environments such as a rising number of competitive schools and frequent staff attrition both at leadership and teaching levels (See Table 1). In this study, it was found that through a strong team-based approach, focusing on both quality enhancement and quality assurance processes; collaboration and communication processes were improved within this school (Fernandes, 2019c). The school developed leadership at all levels (Tajik & Wali, 2020) by using a proactive team-based approach across six interactive stages utilising participative decision-making and problem-solving while working on alignment of school policies, procedures and planning. The findings suggest that the school used a cross-functional team-based approach while working on changing its organisational culture (Retallick, 2005; Shah, 2018). In this change process, school administrative processes and school educational processes were integrated with the school mission statement so that both short and long-term plans were developed by working together with a common and shared purpose. The findings indicate how the school had begun to operate as a complex, adaptive, open social system. The school had made use of contextually-relevant change initiatives (Holland, 1998; Rosas, 2017) by deeply investigating the condition and impact of its surrounding environments on the school and then using collaborative and participative decision-making approaches within the planning stages, implementing and even evaluating of its organisational initiatives. It was foreseen that if the school sustained the continuous school improvement processes that had been put in place, the new transformative organisational culture now operating within this school would continue to strengthen and sustain itself over time.

Developing a Strategically-Oriented Learning Organisation Approach

The findings indicate that after working at the whole school level to reset the school vision and planning, senior-level and middle-level school leaders found that the active involvement of the six quality improvement teams made a huge difference on how the school was now operating. These teams had effectively worked together in identifying what their external adaptation needed to be, as well as what the internal integration issues currently being faced were

(Schein & Schein, 2016). Through the support of the school leaders, these six quality improvement teams used four interconnected contexts within which the school was nested as an open system: situated-contexts, professional-contexts, material-contexts and external-contexts to problem-solve relevant school issues (Braun et al., 2011) using real-world conditions while identifying and sustaining improvement initiatives for their school (Koh & Askell-Williams, 2021). They srecognised that the contextually-relevant transformation of their school into a strategically-oriented learning organisation (Fernandes, 2019c) required upskilling their teachers in pedagogical practices as well as actively involving them in complex adaptive work being done through this change process. By developing staff appraisal processes, a staff professional development plan, a school quality plan and a school quality manual, the leaders transformed their school into a learning organisation using continuous school improvement strategies closely aligned with the school mission statement.

CONCLUSION

Distributed educational leadership practices (Nawab & Asad, 2020) are best developed at the individual school level through a proactive Strategic TQM approach (Fernandes, 2019c) focusing on sustained and continuous school improvement using clear communication and open collaboration in building up positive relationships across the school. The findings in this chapter, provide insight into understanding the symbiotic relationship between pedagogical practices and administrative processes in schools. In using a complex adaptive system approach, it was found recognition of the importance that both these aspects of school organisational culture must work together in tandem (Spillane, 2015) when transformatively leading urban, private schools in Pakistan as strategically-oriented learning organisations.

This chapter suggests further research on school leadership development undertaken with special emphasis on the development of organisational change leadership approaches that make use of shared decision-making processes (Salim, 2016) and distributed educational leadership practices (Shah, 2018) amongst senior-level, middle-level and teacher-level leaders (Fernandes, 2019a) in Pakistani private schools.

REFERENCES

Ahmad, M., & Dilshad, M. (2016). Leadership styles of public schools' heads in Punjab: A teachers' perspective. *Pakistan Journal of Social Sciences*, *36*(2), 907–916.

Bass, B. M. (1998). The ethics of transformational leadership. In J. B. Ciulla (Ed.), *Ethics: The heart of leadership* (pp. 169–192). Praeger.

Bass, B. M., & Avolio, B. J. (1993). Transformational Leadership: A response to critiques. In M. M. Chemers & R. Ayman (Eds.), *Leadership theory and research: Perspectives and directions*. Academic Press Inc.

Baxter, P., & Jack, S. (2008). Qualitative case study methodology: Study design and implementation for novice researchers. *Qualitative Report*, *13*(4), 544–559.

Brauckmann, S., Pashiardis, P., & Ärlestig, H. (2020). Bringing context and educational leadership together: fostering the professional development of school principals. *Professional Development in Education*.

Burns, J. M. (1978). *Leadership*. Harper & Row.

Clarke, S., & O'Donoghue, T. (2017). Educational Leadership and Context: A Rendering of an Inseparable Relationship. *British Journal of Educational Studies*, *65*(2), 167–182. doi:10.1080/00071005.2016.1199772

Crowe, S., Cresswell, K., Robertson, A., Huby, G., Avery, A., & Sheikh, A. (2011). The case study approach. *BMC Medical Research Methodology*, *11*(1), 100. doi:10.1186/1471-2288-11-100 PMID:21707982

Daft, R. L. (2016). Organisational theory and design (12th ed.). South-Western Cengage Learning.

Deniz, U., & Demirkasimoğlu, N. (2022). The cultural dimensions of Pakistani teachers' zone of acceptance regarding school principals' authority. *International Journal of Leadership in Education*, 1–30. doi:10.1080/1360 3124.2022.2076288

Fernandes, V. (2019a). Disrupting the norm: implementing educational business improvement models in Pakistani public-private school partnerships. In V. Fernandes, & P. W. K. Chan (Eds.), Asia Pacific Education: Leadership, Governance and Administration (1st ed., pp. 187-204). Information Age Publishing.

Fernandes, V. (2019b). From the middle out: empowering transformational leadership capability of middle-level school leaders. In R. Chowdhury (Ed.), *Transformation and Empowerment through Education: Reconstructing our Relationship with Education* (1st ed., pp. 195–213). Routledge.

Fernandes, V. (2019c). The Case for Effectively Using Existing Business Improvement Models in Australian Schools. In A. Normore, L. Long, & M. Javidi (Eds.), *Handbook of Research on Effective Communication, Leadership, and Conflict Resolution* (2nd ed., pp. 98–124). Information Science.

Fernandes, V., Khan, F., Raj, L., & Thenabadu, S. (2019). Persistent inequality in female education within South Asia: comparing Bangladesh, India, Pakistan and Sri Lanka. In R. Chowdhury & L. K. Yazdanpanah (Eds.), *Identity, Equity and Social Justice in Asia Pacific Education* (1st ed., pp. 44–65). Monash University Publishing.

Fidan, T., & Balci, A. (2017). Managing schools as complex adaptive systems: A strategic perspective. *International Electronic Journal of Elementary Education, 10*(1), 11–26. doi:10.26822/iejee.2017131883

Grobman, G. M. (2005). Complexity Theory: A New Way to Look at Organisational Change. *Public Administration Quarterly, 29*(3/4), 350–382.

Holland, J. H. (1998). *Emergence: From chaos to order.* Oxford University Press. doi:10.1093/oso/9780198504092.001.0001

Institute of Social and Policy Sciences (ISAPS). (2010). *Private Sector Education in Pakistan – Mapping and Musing.* ISAPS.

Jehan, M. (2015). *High school principals' ethical decisions: A comparative analysis of sociocultural and structural contexts in Pakistan and United States* (Doctoral dissertation).

Keshavarz, N., Nutbeam, D., Rowling, R., & Khavarpour, F. (2010). Schools as social complex adaptive systems: A new way to understand the challenges of introducing the health promoting schools concept. *Social Science & Medicine, 70*(10), 1467–1474. doi:10.1016/j.socscimed.2010.01.034 PMID:20207059

Koh, G. A., & Askell-Williams, H. (2021). Sustainable school-improvement in complex adaptive systems: A scoping review. *Review of Education, 9*(1), 281–314. doi:10.1002/rev3.3246

Kurtz, C. F., & Snowden, D. J. (2003). The new dynamics of strategy: Sense-making in a complex and complicated world. *IBM Systems Journal*, *42*(3), 462–483. doi:10.1147/sj.423.0462

Kutz, M. (2008). Toward a conceptual model of contextual intelligence. *Kravis Leadership Institute Leadership Review*, *8*(8), 1–31.

Mansoor, Z. (2015). The paradigm shift: Leadership challenges in the public sector schools in Pakistan. *Journal of Education and Practice*, *6*(19), 203–211.

Marishane, R. N. (2020). *Contextual intelligence in school leadership: Responding to the dynamics of change.* Brill Sense. doi:10.1163/9789004431263

Nadeem, M., Arif, S., & Asghar, M. Z. (2019). Effectiveness of the teacher appraisal system in public higher secondary schools of Punjab (Pakistan). *Global Regional Review*, *4*(1), 194–208. doi:10.31703/grr.2019(IV-I).22

Nasreen, A., & Odhiambo, G. (2018). The Continuous Professional Development of School Principals: Current Practices in Pakistan. *Bulletin of Education and Research*, *40*(1), 259–280.

Navaratnam, K. K. (1997). Quality management in education must be a never-ending journey. In K. Watson, C. Modgil & S. Modgil (Eds.), Educational Dilemmas: Debate and Diversity, Vol. VI: Quality in Education. Cassell.

Nawab, A., & Asad, M. M. (2020). Leadership practices of school principal through a distributed leadership lens: A case study of a secondary school in urban Pakistan. *International Journal of Public Leadership*, *16*(4), 411–422. doi:10.1108/IJPL-08-2020-0081

Niesche, R. (2016). Perpetuating Inequality in Education: Valuing Purpose over Process in Educational Leadership. The Dark Side of Leadership: Identifying and Overcoming Unethical Practice in Organisations. *Advances in Educational Administration*, *26*, 235–252. doi:10.1108/S1479-366020160000026013

Preiser, R., Struthers, P., Suraya, M., Cameron, N., & Lawrence, E. (2014). External stakeholders and health promoting schools: Complexity and practice in South Africa. *Health Education*, *114*(4), 260–270. doi:10.1108/HE-07-2013-0031

Raza, M., Gilani, N., & Waheed, S. A. (2021). School Leaders' Perspectives on Successful Leadership: A Mixed Methods Case Study of a Private School Network in Pakistan. *Frontiers in Education*, *6*, 656491. doi:10.3389/feduc.2021.656491

Retallick, J. (2005). Managing school success: A case study from Pakistan. *Leading & Managing, 11*, 32–42.

Rizvi, M. (2008). The role of school principals in enhancing teacher professionalism: Lessons from Pakistan. *Educational Management Administration & Leadership, 36*(1), 85–100. doi:10.1177/1741143207084062

Rosas, S. R. (2017). Systems thinking and complexity: Considerations for health promoting schools. *Health Promotion International, 32*, 301–311. PMID:26620709

Salfi, N. A. (2011). Successful leadership practices of head teachers for school improvement: Some evidence from Pakistan. *Journal of Educational Administration, 49*(4), 414–432. doi:10.1108/09578231111146489

Salfi, N. A., Virk, N., & Hussain, A. (2014). Analysis of leadership styles of head teachers at secondary school level in Pakistan: Locale and gender comparison. *International Journal of Gender and Women's Studies, 2*(2), 341–356.

Salim, Z. (2016). *Teachers' Roles in Shared Decision-Making in a Pakistani Community School* (Unpublished Thesis) George Mason University.

Sallis, E. (1993). *Total Quality Management in Education*. Kogan Page.

Schein, E. H., & Schein, P. A. (2016). Organisational Culture and Leadership (5th ed.). John Wiley and Sons, Inc.

Schleicher, A. (2016). *Teaching excellence through professional learning and policy reform: Lessons from around the world. International Summit on the Teaching Profession.* OECD Publishing. doi:10.1787/9789264252059-en

Shah, S. (2018). *An Analysis of the Interaction of the Gender of Head teachers with their Leadership Styles in Secondary Schools in Pakistan: A Pragmatist Perspective* (Unpublished Thesis). University of Cambridge.

Simkins, T., Garrett, V., Memon, M., & Ali, R. N. (1998). The role perceptions of government and non-government head teachers in Pakistan. *Educational Management and Administration, 26*(2), 131–146. doi:10.1177/0263211X98262003

Simkins, T., Sisum, C., & Memon, M. (2003). School leadership in Pakistan: Exploring the headteacher's role. *School Effectiveness and School Improvement, 14*(3), 275–291. doi:10.1076/sesi.14.3.275.15841

Spillane, J. (2015). Leadership and Learning: Conceptualising Relations between School Administrative Practice and Instructional Practice. *Societies (Basel, Switzerland)*, *5*(2), 277–294. doi:10.3390/soc5020277

Stake, R. E. (1995). The art of case study research. *Sage (Atlanta, Ga.)*.

Tajik, M. A., & Wali, A. (2020). Principals' strategies for increasing students' participation in school leadership in a rural, mountainous region in Pakistan. *Improving Schools*, *23*(3), 245–263. doi:10.1177/1365480220923413

Uhl-Bien, M., Marion, R., & McKelvey, B. (2007). Complexity leadership theory: Shifting leadership from the industrial age to the knowledge era. *The Leadership Quarterly*, *18*(4), 298–318. doi:10.1016/j.leaqua.2007.04.002

van Oord, L. (2013). Towards transformative leadership in education. *International Journal of Leadership in Education*, *16*(4), 419–434. doi:10.1080/13603124.2013.776116

Chapter 7
Project for the Global Integration of Meaningful Learning of English in Early Childhood Education

Antonio Daniel Juan Rubio

https://orcid.org/0000-0003-3416-0021
Universidad de Granada, Spain

ABSTRACT

This study is based on the premise that learning English has become a necessity in an increasingly globalised world, and that its teaching is simpler and more effective from an early age, offering better results. Based on studies related to the subject, this project has been conducted on various aspects such as current teaching in so-called "bilingual schools" or the influence of the family and new technologies on the use of routines in the teaching of pupils in the early childhood education stage. This chapter defends the application of a leading project based on new methodologies that share an eminently practical and interactive approach and that manage to involve all the agents related to the education of pupils, incorporating the necessary resources to facilitate linguistic immersion. All of this is aimed at achieving an improvement in the results of language teaching. The general objective of this chapter is to present a globalised teaching project that generates significant learning capable of achieving comprehensive training in English in early childhood education pupils.

DOI: 10.4018/978-1-7998-3940-8.ch007

Copyright © 2024, IGI Global. Copying or distributing in print or electronic forms without written permission of IGI Global is prohibited.

Project for the Global Integration of Meaningful Learning of English

INTRODUCTION

This chapter responds to the need to ensure that students are able and competent to cope in an increasingly global, plural, and changing world. Languages are becoming increasingly relevant in aspects such as employment, where in many fields English has taken on a decisive role, becoming a fundamental requirement for access to certain jobs. For this reason, there has been growing concern in recent years, and it is clear that the demand for English language learning in schools in Spain has soared (García, 2021).

There has been a large-scale conversion to bilingualism in schools. The first bilingual programmes in public schools appeared in 1996 thanks to an agreement between the Ministry of Education and the British Council, establishing an integrated Spanish-British curriculum for children from 3 to 16 years of age. But, given the lack of uniformity in the implementation of bilingualism in schools, the number of hours to be taught, the qualifications and/or knowledge of teachers, etc., it is difficult to comment on the situation of bilingualism in a generalised way. In broad terms, at the Early Childhood Education stage, it is usually treated as a first approach to the language according to López and Rodriguez (2019). However, this proposal aims to highlight the importance of starting the teaching of English from an early age.

The main aim of the project is to turn the language into an instrument that is given greater practical applicability. The aim is to reduce the use of textbooks as the only resource in the teaching of English, encouraging the use of language to achieve a greater fixation in the mental scheme of the pupils, extrapolating it to their daily reality. We also propose to include Information and Communication Technologies (ICT) as they provide very useful and motivating resources. Language training is included for all teachers, not only specialists, as well as for families, to improve their competences, the achievement of objectives and motivation.

The innovative proposal of this project seeks to promote meaningful learning and is born out of a double need: to acquire the vocabulary and structures of the language while integrating routines through activities carried out in daily practice, which fosters confidence in the students. The use of English in the child's everyday tasks becomes an effective tool for language fixation, and once they have acquired sufficient security and confidence, the pupils will move on to a second phase of oral production.

The general objective of this chapter is to present a globalised teaching project that generates significant learning capable of achieving comprehensive training in English in Early Childhood Education pupils. The specific objectives are the following:

1. To identify the most relevant aspects that influence the learning of a language for Early Childhood Education pupils.
2. To investigate the use of Information and Communication Technologies (ICT) as a resource in language teaching.
3. To analyse the participation and integration of the family in school education.
4. To describe the most appropriate methodology for language teaching.

This project complies with the legislative references of Royal Decree 95/2022, of February 1, 2022, which establishes the minimum teaching for the second cycle of Early Childhood Education. In this Decree, as an objective of the area of languages: communication and representation, we can read: "To initiate the oral use of a foreign language to communicate in activities within the classroom, and to show interest and enjoyment by participating in these communicative exchanges" (p. 481)

THEORETICAL FRAMEWORK

Theoretical Bases on Language Learning

This section aims to provide a brief theoretical contextualisation of the numerous contributions that can be found on this subject. The most relevant ones for our study have therefore been selected since it was not possible to cover so many perspectives and authors in this approach. It should be noted that, in this theoretical review, no attempt has been made to diminish the great relevance and importance of the other theories not mentioned in the chapter.

In the light of Piaget's theory of cognitive development (1983), we must emphasise the role of action in the child's learning process since this learning will be actively constructed. According to Pakpahan and Saragih (2022), knowledge is not a copy of reality, so if we want to know something, we have to do more than just look at it: we have to act on it.

For Vygotsky (1987), language and social interaction play an important role in the child's development, as the child is very much influenced by the environment in which he lives, by his culture, etc. Vygotsky considered that we should focus on what the child is able to do with the help of an adult or an advanced peer, thus coining the term "zone of proximal development" (ZPD) to refer to the gap or difference that exists between the skills that the child already possesses and those that can be acquired thanks to the support that can be provided by another more competent agent. It is about differentiating between the actual level of development and the level of development they can achieve in order to reach their potential level of development (Silalahi, 2019). However, it has to be borne in mind that the reaction of learners to support may be different even though they are at the same point of development.

Bruner (1984) develops some of Piaget's and especially Vygotsky's ideas about the importance of interactive and cultural aspects in the development of language and thinking. According to Bruner, the most important factor in cognitive development is language. The central idea of his instructional model is "scaffolding", a term he uses to refer to the help of an adult or a peer to facilitate the child's language learning. The aim of the process is to promote the independence and autonomy of the learner. In Bruner's "discovery learning theory", children construct knowledge through guided discovery, but being the protagonists of their own learning and motivated by their own curiosity (Cahyani & Yulindaria, 2018).

But if there is one author who stands out as a potential inspiration for this project it is Ausubel with his "meaningful learning theory" (1968), which is defined as the process through which new information interacts with a previous cognitive structure of the individual and gives rise to a new structure of knowledge, leading to its assimilation. It is necessary to start with the most basic concepts and integrate the concepts that will appear later. Based on Ausubel's theories of discovery learning, we must affirm, according to Bryce and Blown (2023), that the linguistic exponents of a communicative function can be heard, understood, and used meaningfully, provided that the appropriate prior knowledge exists in the subject's cognitive structure.

Álvarez and Grande (2023) point out the importance of applying "learning in/through experience", "learning in action" or "learning by doing", which could be framed as active learning that favours a more autonomous learner. According to them, the school should facilitate contextualised activities and experiences, building on prior knowledge to create meaningful environments for students to be more participative and involved. The role of the teacher will be that of a facilitator of learning and not a mere transmitter of knowledge.

According to the "critical period hypothesis", postulated by Lenneberg (1967), children learn a second language better before reaching puberty, since the brain loses its plasticity, experiencing the specialisation of the two hemispheres (lateralisation). Lenneberg went so far as to specify that, to learn a language through mere exposure, one should start from the age of 2, as the child has not previously developed the necessary skills to assimilate and produce it. Subsequently, the existence of multiple critical periods for language acquisition has been proposed. This theory has also been justified because children can use the learning mechanisms of their mother tongue.

Although it is true that the starting age for language learning has generated a great deal of controversy, most studies conclude that the earlier we start, the better we will learn, since in the early years they build their own mental schema and resources to be able to communicate and learn the language (Siahaan, 2022; Azieh, 2021).

Mur (2018) offers us a series of characteristics of children in the Early Childhood Education stage which will help them to learn the language and which we should take advantage of, such as the ability to grasp the meaning of messages without the need to understand each word. Intonation, gestures, facial expressions, and actions help them to deduce it. It also highlights the innate ability to relate to others, which is an advantage for language classes. As López and Rodríguez (2019) corroborate, the child's imitative capacity and desire to communicate facilitate the acquisition of the foreign language.

However, although children generally have a natural tendency to be uninhibited and spontaneous in their communication, they may also feel shy and teachers must respect the period of silence or pre-production period, during which there is no oral production in the foreign language by these pupils. There is no fixed duration for this period, depending on the individual learner (Graciela, 2020). In fact, there will be times characterised by non-verbal communication or even the use of the mother tongue. Teachers should not force learners to communicate if they do not feel confident to do so yet, as this may demoralise them.

To keep this stage as short as possible, teachers should develop motivating activities, but, above all, show support and affection to the learner to increase their confidence. Rodriguez stresses the importance of affective and motivational factors when designing activities in the language classroom for Early Childhood Education learners. A suitable environment must be created in which the learner's interest is aroused so that he/she is motivated and participates. To this end, certain resources can be used, including "experiences, routines, images, fictional characters from cartoons or stories, songs, symbols and the use of information and communication technologies" (2014, p. 158).

Teacher Training in Language and New Technologies

The acquisition of the first language and the acquisition of a foreign language are different processes which take place under different conditions, but it is important for the teacher to be familiar with the process of acquisition of the mother tongue and of those sounds or structures which the learner is not able to produce in his/her mother tongue. The important thing is not so much to speak without making mistakes, but to treat it as a process of discovery

Project for the Global Integration of Meaningful Learning of English

to be used as a means of communication to interact in the classroom and in extra-linguistic activities in coordination with the tutors. Moya and Albentosa (2023) argue that the tutor should also be a specialist in English, thus fulfilling two essential requirements: knowledge of the world of children and of the language to be taught, and they call this figure: "specialist in foreign language in Early Childhood Education" (2023, p. 33).

In this line, Violante (2018) stresses the importance of the teacher being aware of what the child is able or not to do and what they are learning every day in their curriculum with their classroom teacher. In turn, Castro (2020) states that the fact that the class teacher is also an English specialist facilitates the work of programming the different areas of the curriculum.

García et al. (2019) defend the selection of a linguistic input that has to be related to the games and routines that children from 3 to 5 years old usually develop in the classroom, as well as those topics related to their physical and social environment, body, physical needs, etc., promoting transversality in the integral formation of the individual.

León et al. (2022) corroborate the idea that language is a learning tool applicable to the different curricular areas. They state that language must be experienced and act as a means of communication and interaction. At school it would mean "learning to know, to do, to be". These ideas defend the approach on which this project is based.

In addition to the purely linguistic aspects, it is important for teachers to have technical and pedagogical training in the latest educational technologies, to know how to apply technology to learning. The possibilities they offer are endless, putting a large number of resources at the service of teachers. Murado (2020) talks about the great influence of technological advances in the evolution of schools in recent years. He stresses the usefulness of new technologies in the teaching of English because of the motivation it provokes in students, especially the use of computers and, above all, the Internet.

Rodrigo and Gómez state that language teaching and learning has experienced an increase in quality and effectiveness thanks to ICT: "First and foremost, ICT - and the Internet in particular - offer language learners the opportunity to use a language meaningfully in authentic contexts" (2023, p. 85). These authors underline the motivating effect of the Internet, which offers quick and easy access to a multitude of current materials. This variety makes them adaptable to different learning styles and thus to different learning needs.

As mentioned above, it is important to provide pedagogical training for teachers. Ciriza et al. (2023) argue that knowledge of models and practices used in foreign language teaching will encourage teachers to reflect on which technologies to use or not and how to use them, depending on the context of their classroom and curriculum. It should also be borne in mind that not all resources are equally efficient, and it is important to make a good selection. Fleta (2019) points out that the school should have certain objectives in this respect to develop habits and procedures for searching, selecting, and classifying information, through the development of procedures for handling information on the Internet to educate to form conscious audiences who know how to decide freely what content is relevant and appropriate.

Matas (2019) states that technologies can be an element that provides great opportunities in the learning of English as long as a responsible use of the resources they offer us is conducted, pointing out the large number of resources available in the area of English. He adds the importance of the motivating and interactive nature of media such as the computer. It is worth noting the objectives that Matas believes teachers must carry out with respect to technologies: "to recognize English as a means of global communication and as an essential tool for access to sources of information" (2019, p. 65).

In addition, it is necessary for teachers to have technical training, and the most appropriate way to know their needs is to consult them directly. By knowing their perception, it is possible to plan both initial and continuous training given the rapid evolution of technologies. If we make the best of technologies available to teachers without adequate training in their use, it will not only mean an economic loss and underuse of resources, but teachers will continue to apply the traditional methodology.

In general, teachers refuse to accept that the teaching process should be enjoyable and prefer to use a traditional methodology rather than trying to speak the same language that their students speak. This causes students to become demotivated, as they have to go back to the past, which is the opposite of their natural tendency. It is necessary to try to ensure that digital immigrants evolve and are trained in technology, reconsidering the methodologies they use. Teachers must be able to communicate with the language of the "natives", combining inherited content such as writing or mathematics with those provided by the digital age. According to Huerta et al., "it is a matter of adapting the materials to the language of the natives" (2020, p. 269).

Inclusion of the Family in School Education

The family is the first nucleus of socialization, especially in the first years of a child's life. Therefore, they are primarily responsible for educating in values, norms, attitudes, and they constitute the role model for minors. The importance of this educational agent makes the family-school relationship essential.

Project for the Global Integration of Meaningful Learning of English

Vila (2018) argues that a good relationship between educational agents helps the education of students, as well as a lack of knowledge between family and school will reduce the quality of education in both areas. It is necessary to have coordination and feedback on the activities and routines that are developed in both contexts. In family-school relations, it is necessary for teachers to be on an equal footing with respect to the educational knowledge of families, as well as to provide mutual trust.

The proposal to involve parents in their children's school life is evident in the ideas defended by authors such as Solé (2016), who understands collaboration between parents and teachers as a task to be shared, rather than mere information about homework. If both factors come together to form a work team, each assuming their role, extraordinary results are achieved. As she states, "it is difficult to think of a successful school education without a clear participation of families" (2016, p. 11).

Zhang (2023) supports that the family should be informed and at the same time participate in their children's school life whenever possible. To this end, she proposes regular communication through letters, meetings, or circulars. Also, through direct participation in the centre on special days or situations, with the aim of improving relationships, sharing experiences, and improving mutual coexistence.

With regard to Early Childhood Education, Matsumoto et al. (2023) state that informal contacts occur almost daily since most families take their children or pick them up from school. At the same time, formal contact is greater than in stages such as Primary Education, with families of socio-cultural level being the ones who least attend these meetings, intensifying even more if they are immigrants or those living under marginalization or poverty. They defend them by stating that, despite showing interest in their children's teachers, they have low self-esteem and do not feel capable of contributing anything to their children's education, and therefore do not usually attend meetings.

Otero et al. (2022) set out the actions that the centre can propose in the face of difficulties or deficiencies in the family:

- Provide documentation on the subject to be discussed in order to clarify certain aspects and facilitate the family's action.
- Plan meetings to clarify any doubts or problems and delve into the topic at hand.
- Conduct training courses aimed at families to expand their knowledge on different topics.

- Establish parent schools. These are groups of parents who meet on certain days to exchange knowledge and concerns about their children¡s development.

On the other hand, an aspect to be addressed given the importance of this project is Information and Communication Technologies in the field of the home, since they are a tool for leisure, but also for learning. It is not a question of refusing to use ICTs for fear of the problems generated by their misuse. It is necessary to make parents and guardians aware of the educational tools and to make known the opportunities offered in the teaching of languages by these electronic media that are part of their children's lives.

Technologies are changing the way we communicate and relate in the family environment at breakneck speed. Their different ways of understanding and points of view are often at odds because of the lack of mastery and control in the use of ICTs by families. The generation gap between children and their parents or guardians must be considered.

Despite what it might seem, according to the studies carried out by Ballesta and Guardiola (2021), families manifested a positive attitude towards the media in the education and training of their children. However, a more critical and reflective minority of parents, who coincide with those with a higher level of education, point out certain dangers of these media, although they also recognize the benefits of their integration into the classroom.

Technologies will be a support in the project, helping families to lose the fears they may have, since they are undoubtedly beneficial for supporting learning. At home, children are in contact with computers, smartphones, tablets, game consoles, etc. Therefore, our goal is to make the most of the technologies available to families, helping parents to select and critically analyse what they offer.

In the work of Moya and Albentosa (2023), we can find some advantages that the use of the computer brings with it: it is an instrument that favours interaction and demands attention, it is stimulating and motivating, it personalizes learning allowing work according to the pace and level, it is a complement to what has been worked on during the class, it promotes autonomy and self-esteem when used freely, and it allows them to discover, imagine, and create.

Towards a Natural Methodology

The Natural Approach of Krashen and Terrel (1983) forms our methodological basis for the project since it deals with language teaching from a communicative approach in favour of a passive study of grammar and is considered to be the most appropriate method for the Early Childhood Education stage. Its fundamental hypothesis is the so-called "acquisition-learning hypothesis" that proposes the learning of a language from real communicative situations, unconsciously and naturally, just as it occurs in the mother tongue and not by explicitly studying its grammar. You learn by listening to and being exposed to the language.

Considering the research conducted by Rodríguez on the techniques used in Early Childhood Education for the teaching of English: "The learning of this second language focuses on oral comprehension and expression, which constitute the starting point for the teaching of a foreign language. The progression that is followed in the teaching-learning process tends to imitate the natural process that children follow when they learn their mother tongue" (2014, p. 159).

In the studies of Krashen and Terrel (1983), it is highlighted that in the first years of language learning an infinite number of expressions or formulas are used, which they also call routines and patterns to be able to communicate. These routines and patterns are used by children as tools to cope with their linguistic deficiencies and, as their language expands, the use of these expressions decreases, including in their vocabulary a greater variety and richness of structures in their expressions.

Considering these aspects, it is worth talking about the "input hypothesis" on which Krashen's natural approach (1985) is based, which highlights the importance of approaching the student through an understandable language, focused on their interests, and that their degree of difficulty, without being too simple, can be understood and not demotivated. Hajimia et al. (2020) establish a series of strategies that teachers use to make themselves understood among their students:

- Speak more slowly
- Take breaks when it comes to a foreign language and especially with those of beginner students to facilitate comprehension.
- Change pronunciation to be clearer, less reduced and contracted.
- Simplify vocabulary and grammar.
- Modify the discourse.

Based on the previously presented ideas of creating an environment that provides security to students, we find Krashen's hypothesis of the "affective filter" monitoring theory. This author considers that the key to facilitating or inhibiting the acquisition of a foreign language lies in affective variables. A lack of motivation, self-confidence, or anxiety will hinder the process (Liu, 2023). Hence, the project is based on the routines, habits, and social skills that are worked on in their mother tongue and that are given continuously over time, to provide security and confidence in the students.

Asher, author of the "Total Physical Response" (TPR) methodology, also argues for a natural approach to second language teaching against traditional systems of learning through grammar and writing (1968). It is based on communication through instructions given by the teacher in which students react with body movements. Students only have to concentrate on listening to the instructions and are not forced to speak, so they are easier to accept the new structures. This characteristic makes it deviate from the objective of the project since it seeks not only understanding but also production. In addition, other disadvantages of this method can be added, cited by Rambe (2019):

- It is not a suitable method for shy children.
- It is suitable only for beginner levels.
- It is not flexible to use in all cases and can be repetitive. It would be appropriate in combination with other methods and techniques
- It is not suitable for explaining abstract vocabulary and should therefore be supported by other resources (picture cards) and also for teaching narrative forms, descriptions, or a conversation as such.

In conclusion, despite being a very practical method for Early Childhood Education students, it is not able to achieve all our expectations, although its use as a basis for certain initial activities in the classroom is not excluded.

METHODOLOGY

The objective is to conduct a practical methodology, since we need to prepare students for the Early Childhood Education stage, focused mainly on the second cycle, since according to Lenneberg's theories, it is from the age of two when they begin to develop the necessary skills to assimilate the language and produce it.

It is about extrapolating to their lives and making use of what they learn in a real context, contributing to their integral development. At the same time, without really being aware of the steps they are taking, or questioning what they are doing, we will be able to make them experiment and enjoy learning. It is not a question of approaching language as an end in itself but as a communication tool to relate to the environment.

Project for the Global Integration of Meaningful Learning of English

Under these premises, teachers seek to work with a motivating language and activities, adapted to the needs of the classroom, working at different rhythms if necessary. At the same time, they conduct routine activities to increase their safety and be able to increase their level of difficulty with new elements or new activities that can complement the first ones to deepen their learning. The aforementioned period of silence must be considered, not forcing its production until it is safe enough as we can cause the opposite effect to the desired one. In addition, it must be considered that since it is not their language of reference, they are under the temptation to use their mother tongue, so we will have to be flexible, as will happen with pronunciation or grammatical structures.

The project approach will be totally communicative, focusing on oral expression and considering the significant nature of the learning. Initially, we will focus on receptive versus production skills in the foreign language, just as it is done in the mother tongue. The students will answer in Spanish for as long as they need, but little by little they will change the language effortlessly and without being conscious, since they use it in a natural environment. Patience and repetition are the basis that will underpin the performance with the students.

Routines are very important in Early Childhood Education, and learning a second language is no exception. That is why the activities to get started in learning the language will be directed in this direction. Through these activities, their security and confidence will increase, as well as their self-esteem.

But it's not just about motivating them towards the language but also towards their culture. The activities will progressively increase their level of difficulty, integrating different contents and reinforcing those already learned. Also, the difficulty will increase at the linguistic level, as students acquire a greater vocabulary and handling of grammatical structures.

We will work from a playful side that captures their attention and encourages them to participate. We will use practical and motivating activities such as songs, rhymes, games, puppets, interactive resources, etc. Participation in the class should be varied: in groups, pairs or individually, etc. We should consider it as a preparation for future studies.

The project is designed for the class-group, and we must consider those students with special educational needs. To this end, activities have been designed to be able to work in cooperative groups so that they can support their colleagues. However, the teacher must always remain attentive to any problems that may arise to design the necessary adaptations. If necessary, collateral activities adapted to the difficulties in each case will be provided, to stimulate them so that they can approach the work of the group, always adapted to their pace. Likewise, the characteristics of the context in which the school, the classroom, the individual students, etc., are framed must be considered to adapt this Project according to the needs.

FINDINGS: EDUCATIONAL PROJECT

Project Objectives

The final objective of the project is to develop students' comprehension and oral production capacity in a language other than their mother tongue through the use of routines, habits and social skills that are developed in daily reality. To this end, the following sub-objectives must be achieved:

1. Establish routine and monitoring mechanisms that stimulate students' ability to be more autonomous and responsible by being protagonists of their learning.
2. Design activities to promote social skills, while at the same time making known how to behave correctly.
3. Promote motivating strategies to promote the development of active and understanding listening, feeding, and encouraging their curiosity to discover.
4. Develop an action plan that contributes to increasing the safety and confidence of students so that they can be able to express themselves in a language other than their mother tongue.
5. Integrate Information and Communication Technologies (ICT) into the teaching-learning process, providing students with active roles in their learning.
6. Establish training courses in educational technologies and languages, both for teachers and families, promoting their active participation.

Participants

The main agents that make the implementation of the project possible are the teachers and families involved in an Early Childhood Education state school in Spain. While it is true that material resources are of great importance, such as the new technologies, it is considered that a comparison with human resources is not feasible. The latter are the ones who come to give life to the project and, in turn, the knowledge they have about technologies is what will determine the potential that can be obtained from these technological resources in teaching:

- Lectures on the importance of language and the resources they can use: cartoons, movies, internet games, etc.
- Creation of a blog where the activities and resources that are developed in class are posted so that they can continue practicing at home. To do this, recordings of songs and stories, interactive resources, etc., will be made.
- English courses for parents so that they become familiar with the language their children are learning and can understand or even help them.

Materials

As it is a learning based on the oral methodology, hardly any material is necessary. Classes will almost always take place in the school's classrooms. However, some of the material resources available are the following:

- School supplies
- Computer resources
- Tablets/pc, computer, and projector
- Cards and poster boards
- Puppets and dolls
- Cultural festivals. Families will be asked to contribute material, as they participate directly in it and feel involved in the project.
- New technologies: tablet-PCs. Finally, the one that would mean the greatest economic cost, if it were not available, would be the implementation of new technologies.

Timing

This project is designed to be developed during an academic year, starting in October, since the month of September is considered to be one of adaptation and change, until June. The activities in class with the students will be developed daily and the time dedicated to language teaching will also be progressively increased.

With the aim of clarifying the different proposals worked on, a table has been designed in which two areas of action are distinguished: the school, in which the activities of the students and teachers would be included and, on the other hand, the family, which would be the activities specifically designed for them.

a)   Initial Phase:

The first steps will be towards a natural use of the foreign language in the daily class routines.

- *Analysis of initial knowledge.* To obtain information about the group, a study of the students' knowledge of English is conducted. The proposal is established to work in a generalized way with groups of the Early Childhood Education stage, but we must not forget the particular aspects of each group of students in general and of each student in particular, context, situation, etc. Therefore, it is recommended that these tasks be developed for at least a week to get to know the group and be able to establish the starting point.
- *Daily Assembly.* For an approach to English that motivates the little ones, it has been decided to use a mascot in the form of a puppet, Sam, a dinosaur that speaks to the students in English. With it, they will practice daily greetings and introductions, as well as other aspects that are considered basic in learning a language and that will be progressively included during the course as the teacher notices progress in the students. The songs of the different activities should be worked with images and body gestures for a better association of meanings. There will be a student in charge of assisting the teacher, who will rotate each week according to the class list.
- *Greeting.* By introducing the class with a song, we seek to achieve a double main objective: motivate the students to encourage their attention and interest for the following activities and, on the other hand, increase their confidence because once they learn the song, they will feel that they can participate, reducing the role of the teacher.
- *Roll call.* The attendees will count, saying the numbers in English and will make a subtraction of those who should be and those who are. The person in charge will take the photographs of the missing students and stick them on the little house placed on the wall of the classroom.
- *Date.* A song will be used to teach students the following numbers: ordinal numbers, days of the week and months of the year. In turn, they will have to identify them as they will indicate what day of the month, day of the week and month they are on. At the end of the song, they will have to put it all together and learn the structure. To be able to

identify the day they are on, they will have at their disposal a calendar, as well as cards with the days in numbers, and the days of the week and months in print that the person in charge will change and paste next to the calendar, as appropriate.

- *Weather, seasons, and clothing*. They will begin by singing the song of the weather with which they will learn the different weather times and the associated garments. When they finish singing the song, the attendant will stick the weather card that corresponds to that day next to the calendar. Finally, the teacher will have the dinosaur's clothes prepared so that he can dress him according to the weather. In order for the students to acquire the vocabulary, the teacher will name the clothes one by one, and ask them if they should wear that garment or not.

b)   Social skills

They will be gradually incorporated according to their degree of complexity. Since they are developed in their daily lives in the mother tongue, they will serve as a support to reinforce behaviour and be understood more easily. They will be worked on largely through observation and modelling.

It will be tried as far as possible, as it is defended in the proposal, that it is the teachers-tutors of the Early Childhood Education classroom who put into practice the teaching of these skills in English, since it is very positive that they practice them on a regular basis to become effectively familiar with the vocabulary and structures.

- *Basic Social Skills*. The following are some of the basic social skills to work on: say thank you and please; ask permission (to go to the bathroom, to talk, to go out, to go to the yard, to drink water, etc.); ask for help; distribute class materials; commands (turn lights off and on, stand in line, get up, sit down, be quiet, go somewhere, put coats on hangers, pick up, etc.).
- *Advanced Social Skills*. Once a greater command of the language is acquired, other social skills that require an advanced command of the language will be included, as well as knowledge about socially accepted behaviours. It is proposed to introduce some of these social skills through the following actions, either alone or in combination: the student speaks in his/her mother tongue and the teacher is a constant guide who acts by repeating in English what the student says, but in the form of a question; role-playing activities to help the student about

the steps to follow; through the class mascot, Sam, to be motivating given the complexity that these language levels require. Some of these advanced social skills can be: expressing moods (happy, sad, angry), opinions, complaints, decision-making, conflict resolution, etc.

(c) Integration activities

Although without forgetting the activities of the initial phase, the level of difficulty will be progressively increased and activities that involve a higher level of knowledge of the language will be included. Let's take a look at some of them:

- *Birthday*. Say when my birthday is and ask my classmates when theirs is. Make a mural for class with our birthdays and sing the song "happy birthday".
- *Food*. It is a job that we do in collaboration with the parents, we try that whenever they can, they look for the name of the menu in English that they have prepared for that day. The next day, the children are asked what they have eaten, whether they like it or not, and the colours of that food. Everyone is always asked to repeat the name of the food and is shown a picture on the screen. It is practiced daily, even if not all students are asked.
- *Parts of the house*: From different images on the net or cards. They are asked a battery of questions about the elements that are in the picture or what they can do in each part of the house, so that the children say whether or not they are done there. A drawing is made on the blackboard, and a story is built with our pet that goes through the rooms of the house and develops activities. Also, the children participate to direct Sam according to the instructions given by the teacher.
- *Bathing (body parts)*. Sam goes to take a bath, and we tell him which part of his body he needs to wash. At the same time, they point out where that part is in our body.
- *Clothing & Colours*. They will indicate what clothes they are wearing and what colour they are.
- *Family*. Cards are made that represent the different members of the family (grandparents, aunts, uncles, parents, siblings, cousin, etc.). They will be asked the names of each member of the family, and they will say: My grandfather's name..., my mother's name....
- *Classroom Material*. The teacher will give instructions about the material they will have to use to make a drawing. At the same time,

Project for the Global Integration of Meaningful Learning of English

it will help them practice actions (drawing a dog, cat, tree, etc.) and vocabulary (pink paint, scissors, glue).

- *Hours.* The times of classroom changes, recess, end of class... in English so that they can begin to get acquainted.
- *How we get around.* It is about getting to know the means of transport, practical activities will be developed to find out how they go to school, what transport they have used to travel, description, type (air, land), etc.
- *Games for the psychomotor skills class in English*: Example: Food. Two groups are made in class and given a list of foods. There has to be one member of each team with each food. Each team sits at one end of the class and one member of each team sits in the middle. The teacher names a food item, and they have to go out, touch their partner's hand and go back to their team. He will give them directions in English (walking, running, going with one leg alone, crawling...).

d)   Introduction to the Anglophone culture

As mentioned above, our proposal is not only in line with a knowledge of the language, but also of its culture and for this reason, thematic activities have been proposed that will be developed throughout the course and in which any member of the educational community can participate. Ideal opportunity to meet families in a relaxed and playful atmosphere:

- Halloween in October
- Thanksgiving in November
- Christmas in December
- St. Valentine's Day in February
- St. Patrick's Day in March
- Easter

e)   We extrapolate our knowledge outside the classroom

Given the importance we have given to practical applicability, we could not miss the opportunity to include English in other environments that surround the child in the centre, and thus account for meaningful learning. Based on coordination through meetings with different agents of the educational community, the following activities will be developed:

- *Recess*: Communicating with teachers in English (e.g., asking for help opening the snack)
- *Dining room*: This activity has been developed for the school as a whole and not only for the Early Childhood Education classrooms. The menus will be written in both languages: Spanish and English. The specialist language teachers will be in charge of the translations and will rotate so that each day, at least one of them is in the dining room. The idea is that the child communicates with them in English to practice vocabulary, to maintain good table manners, and habits.
- *Departures*: A visit to the zoo is planned, which will be conducted partially in English and Spanish. Then, once in class, parallel activities will be developed.
- *Performance*: Perform in our end-of-year school theatre, the songs, and rhymes that we have learned during the course.

(f) New technologies

An attempt will be made to provide technological resources for each classroom, if they are not available, through public or private investment. The idea is to have four tablet-pcs with which to work on activities and resources, in our case a wiki, adapted to the knowledge of each level. It can even be made more flexible and adapted to the learning rhythms of each student, as their initial levels will be considered through tests that will be linked to different activities. By having at least four tablet-pcs per classroom, it could be practiced in corners. In addition, the results are recorded so that the teacher can know first-hand the knowledge and progress of each student.

For their learning outside the classroom, they will have a blog where teachers will post the resources that are practiced in class, even recordings will be made that will serve as support and motivation, so that they can continue practicing.

Evaluation

The evaluation is formative since it will be continuous in order to serve as a corrector and improvement from several perspectives: as an instrument of improvement for teaching and training practice, in the improvement of the teaching-learning process of the students, as well as in the development and achievement of the objectives previously set for the project, serving as a basis to establish our evaluation criteria which will be the following:

Project for the Global Integration of Meaningful Learning of English

1. Develop students' comprehension and oral production capacity in a language other than their mother tongue through the use of routines, habits and social skills that are developed in daily reality.
2. Establish routine and monitoring mechanisms that stimulate students' ability to be more autonomous and responsible by being protagonists of their learning.
3. Apply different situations based on real contexts to facilitate learning and achieve fixation in the mental scheme of the students to integrate vocabulary and expressions in the foreign language to use and apply them when the situation requires it.
4. Design activities to promote respect for socially established norms and guidelines, thus making known how to behave correctly.
5. Encourage motivating strategies to promote the development of active and understanding listening, feeding, and encouraging their curiosity to discover.
6. Develop an action plan that contributes to increasing the security and confidence of students so that they are able to express in a language other than their mother tongue.
7. Integrate Information and Communication Technologies (ICT) into the teaching-learning process, providing students with active roles in their learning.
8. Promote the participation of families in the development and implementation of strategies by extrapolating their use in real contexts other than the school one, which facilitate a greater integration of the language.

An evaluation will be conducted through direct observation, since in the activities they will be accompanied at all times by the teacher. Therefore, it becomes a dynamic process in which, thanks to continuous reflection, modifications and readjustments are possible to adapt it to the reality of the classroom during its development. Detecting difficulties on the part of two or three students will involve different measures than if it is the whole class but taking them in time so as not to aggravate the problems they may have in the future, becomes an essential objective.

Given the fundamentally oral approach of our project and the spontaneity in the use of the language, the evaluation must be directed in the same direction, this means that the evaluation will be conducted both on those actions most planned by the teacher and on those that arise from the spontaneity in the use of English by the children when interacting. At the same time, the evaluation will be both individual and group depending on the activities to be developed.

Informal observation is a basic element in qualitative evaluation. This information will determine the degree of compliance with the established evaluation criteria and will take the necessary actions in this regard. The instruments used for the collection of information will be the following:

- *Teacher's diary*: in which information will be collected throughout the course of the project on the following issues: how it has been conducted, achievement of objectives, motivation and interest or laziness, complications, possible improvements, time spent, class environment, use of language, attitude, interaction, participation, attitude, level of understanding or production, and degree of sequencing.
- *Video recordings*: These recordings, which were commented on in a blog, have a double purpose. Regular recordings can be very valuable, as it is difficult to capture the attention of 30 students and can make us reflect on our own practice.
- *Student evaluation reports*: Observation scales will be drawn up with a series of criteria for observing and evaluating students. Aspects such as the degree of comprehension of the expressions of greetings and farewells, degree of production with respect to the previous ones, degree of comprehension of orders, degree of autonomy, capacity for initiative, degree of relationship of contents with those previously seen, comprehension of instructions to develop the activities, following songs and their comprehension, etc. will be considered.

It is worth mentioning the families given the important role they play in the project, and it is necessary to involve them in the evaluation process as well. In this case, information will be collected in written form through a series of surveys and questionnaires to evaluate the results observed in their children, the work that the students do at home through the activities that are implemented in the courses and workshops, their participation in the centre, the motivation, the use of the resource bank deposited in the blogs and its functionality, as well as having a general opinion about the degree of satisfaction with the project and the points of improvement that could be highlighted. In this way, it is intended to take the opinion from a different point of view.

Project for the Global Integration of Meaningful Learning of English

CONCLUSION

The main purpose of this chapter was to design a teaching-learning project of English for students in the Early Childhood Education stage based on a natural and meaningful approach. To this end, a review of the main existing studies on the subject has been conducted to base our project on an adequate theoretical basis.

Considering the theoretical review conducted, it should be noted that the learning of a language is influenced by various aspects, to which the different theories presented, with their different approaches, give different prominence. Piaget considers the role of action to be of vital importance, yet Vygotsky emphasizes social interaction. Bruner, on the other hand, comes to fundamentally develop and complete Vygotsky's ideas and, Ausubel, with his theory on the importance of creating meaningful learning, provides the title to the chapter. In short, all these theories are not exclusive but offer different perspectives and points of view, and all, to a greater or lesser extent, have enriched the project presented.

On the other hand, focusing on the educational stage analysed, it is important to consider the advantages of starting to teach a language at these ages for various reasons, such as: the brain plasticity of the students, the use of the learning resources of the mother tongue, the disinhibition, and the desire to communicate, the curiosity typical of these ages, etc. However, the period of silence should not be forgotten, so as not to demoralize the student.

The idea of working with motivating, repetitive activities to increase children's safety, and showing affection to achieve better performance in language learning has been defended. On the other hand, digital technology has meant a great advance in society as a whole and the education sector was not going to be an exception. Its application in language teaching has a very positive impact on students, such as the motivation and interest they arouse given their interactive nature. In addition, they allow us to personalize teaching, adapting it to the particular needs of each student. The problem is that not all teachers know how to use these tools properly, so an investment in technological resources without sufficient training does not make much sense.

The use of ICTs is defended, always from an approach of respect and care, selecting the resources they offer, without leaving them in the hands of children without any type of control. In order for this selection to be made in the most effective way possible, the offer of training for both teachers and families is defended. This is due to the fact that students are not only in contact with technologies at school, but also in the student's home. It is also important that families have access to adequate training in this field, so that

167

they do not simply prohibit their use out of fear or ignorance, nor, on the contrary, give them inappropriate use.

At the same time, the aim is for families to participate in classroom activities so that children feel supported and their introduction to a new language is facilitated in the most contextualized and global way possible. It is of vital importance that the most influential educational agents in the education of the student can get to know each other better to achieve better results in the quality of the child's education.

With regard to the training of teachers who are part of a bilingual school, they must have a didactic training typical of the Early Childhood Education stage combined with knowledge of the language of study. In this way, an effective linguistic immersion can be achieved, working on the language at a global and interdisciplinary level within the curriculum of the educational stage. Seeking to provide meaning and contextualize communication, negotiating meanings and learning from a "Natural Approach".

Based on the ideas defended by Krashen and Terrell, based on communication in real and meaningful contexts, we decided that the students start in oral comprehension and finally move on to production, without forcing them to abandon their mother tongue. We work on the basis of routines, social skills and patterns used in the daily life of the students to achieve safety.

As an important limitation, the project may be too ambitious given the current situation in most schools. The teaching of English in Early Childhood Education in Spain usually consists only of a vague approximation to the language, when it really should be the most important stage, given the excellent results obtained when starting with the teaching of the language at an early age. We are confident that in the not-too-distant future this evidence will prevail, and that language learning will be given greater relevance from the earliest years.

In this sense, we believe that a very interesting future line of research may be based on the study of the introduction of the modifications that the school has to develop to achieve a significant learning of the language with greater load and value from the first school years in a generalized way. It would be a matter of identifying the steps to follow, as well as the evolution of the process that would lead to achieving the desired goals demanded by our times.

REFERENCES

Álvarez Vega, E., & Grande de Prado, M. (2023). Early Childhood Care in Spain before the lockdown. *Encyclopedia*, *3*(4), 1306–1319. doi:10.3390/encyclopedia3040093

Asher, J. J. (1968). The Total Physical Response Method for Second Language Learning. *The Clearing House: A Journal of Educational Strategies, Issues and Ideas.*

Ausubel, D., Novak, J. D., & Hanesian, H. (1968). *Psicología educativa, un punto de vista cognoscitivo* [Educational psychology, a cognitive point of view]. Trillas.

Azieh, S. (2021). The Critical Period Hypothesis in Second Language Acquisition: A Review of the Literature. *International Journal of Research in Humanities and Social Studies*, *8*(4), 20–26. doi:10.22259/2694-629.0804001

Ballesta, J., & Guardiola, P. (2021). *Escuela, familia y medios de comunicación* [School, family, and mass media means]. CCS.

Bruner, J. (1984). *Acción, pensamiento y lenguaje* [Action, thought, and language]. Alianza Psicología.

Bryce, T. G., & Blown, E. J. (2023). Ausubel's meaningful learning re-visited. *Current Psychology (New Brunswick, N.J.)*, 1–21. doi:10.1007/s12144-023-04440-4 PMID:37359615

Cahyani, I., & Yulindaria, L. (2018). The effectiveness of Discovery learning model in improving students' fiction writing. *Indonesian Journal of Learning and Instruction*, *1*(1), 37–45. doi:10.25134/ijli.v1i1.1281

Castro Zubizarreta, A. (2020). La participación de los niños en el marco de la educación infantil: algunas coordenadas para su práctica efectiva. [Children's participation in Early Childhood Education: some coordinates for its effective practice]. *Dossier Revista del IICE*, *49*, 43–58. doi:10.34096/iice.n48

Ciriza Mendivil, C.D., Mendioroz, A., Hernández de la Cruz, J.M. & Rivero, P. (2023). Cultural Heritage in Early Childhood Education: An analysis of the perception of future teachers. *Social and Education History*, 1-18. https://doi.org/ doi:10.17583/hse.120525

Fleta, T. (2019). *From research on child L2 acquisition of English to classroom practice*. De Gruyter.

García Grau, P., Martínez Rico, G., McWilliam, R., & Grau, D. (2019). Early Intervention and Family-Centeredness in Spain: Description and Profile of Professional Practices. *Topics in Early Childhood Special Education, 41*(2), 160–172. doi:10.1177/0271121419846332

García Mayo, M. P. (2021). Research on EFL learning by young children in Spain. *Language Teaching for Young Learners, 3*(2), 181–188. doi:10.1075/ltyl.00022.edi

Graciela Torcomian, C. (2020). Infancia y aprendizaje: Experiencias de niña en la escuela pública [Childhood and Learning: Girl's experiences in a public school]. *Acta Académica, 66,* 67–90.

Hajimia, H., Sarjit Singh, M. K., & Mariandavan Chethiyar, S. D. (2020). Second Language Acquisition: Krashen's Monitor Model and the Natural Approach. *People International Journal of Social Science, 6*(3), 87–99. doi:10.20319/pijss.2020.63.8799

Huerta Guerra, M. C., Cárdenas González, V. G., & León, D. (2020). Practices to foster learning to learn in Early Childhood Education. *Aula Abierta, 49*(3), 261–278. doi:10.17811/rifie.49.3.2020.261-278

Krashen, S. (1985). *The input hypothesis: issues and implications.* Longman.

Krashen, S. D., & Terrel, T. D. (1983). *The Natural Approach. Language acquisition in the classroom.* Pergamon.

Lenneberg, E. H. (1967). *Fundamentos biológicos del lenguaje* [Biological foundations of language]. Alianza Editorial.

León, M., Palomene, D., Ibañez, Z., Martínez Virto, L., & Gabaldón Estevan, D. (2022). Between equal opportunities and work-life balance: Balancing institutional design in early years education in Spain. *Papers. Revista de Psicología, 107*(3), 1–22.

Liu, X. (2023). The effect of affective filter hypothesis on college students' English writing teaching and its enlightment. *OAlib, 10*(9), 1–9. doi:10.4236/oalib1110671

López, G., & Rodríguez, M. T. (2019). *Reflexiones y propuestas para trabajar la lengua inglesa en Educación Infantil* [Reflections and proposal for working on the English language in Early Childhood Education]. Servicio de Publicaciones de la Universidad de Oviedo.

Matas, A. (2019). El inglés y las nuevas tecnologías: motivar el alumnado con destrezas que conoce [English and new technologies: motivating students with skills they know]. *Cuadernos de Educación y desarrollo, 1*(7), 1-5.

Matsumoto, M., Mendoza, K., Gómez-Estern, B. M., & Poveda, D. (2023). Early Childhood Education and Care in Spain: A model to understand diverse conditions in the current system. *C&E, Cultura y Educación*, *35*(1), 588–621. doi:10.1080/11356405.2023.2200593

Moya, A. J., & Albentosa, J. I. (2023). *La enseñanza de la lengua extranjera en la Educación Infantil* [Foreign Language Teaching in Early Childhood Education]. Servicio de Publicaciones de la Universidad de Castilla-La Mancha.

Mur, O. (2018). *Cómo introducir el inglés en Educación Infantil* [How to introduce English in Early Childhood Education]. Editorial Escuela Española.

Murado, J. L. (2020). *Didáctica del Inglés en Educación Infantil. Métodos para la enseñanza y el aprendizaje de la lengua inglesa* [Didactics of English in Early Childhood Education: Methods for Teaching and Learning the English Language]. Ideaspropias.

Otero Mayer, A., González Benito, A., & Gutiérrez de Roza, B. (2022). Implicaciones emocionales en maestros de Educación Infantil y las familias en pandemia en España. [Emotional implications for Early Childhood Education Teachers and Families during the pandemic in Spain]. *Mendive. Review of Education*, *20*(1), 255–269.

Pakpahan, F. H., & Saragih, M. (2022). Theory of Cognitive Development by Jean Piaget. *Journal of Applied Linguistics*, *2*(2), 55–60. doi:10.52622/joal.v2i2.79

Piaget, J. (1983). Piaget's Theory. In P. Mussen (Ed.), *Handbook of Child Psychology*. Wiley & Sons.

Rambe, S. (2019). Total Physical Response. *English Education Journal for Teaching and Learning*, *7*(1), 45–58. doi:10.24952/ee.v7i01.1652

Rodrigo Monche, M., & Gómez Redondo, C. (2023). El material no estructurado en la práctica educativa dentro de Educación Infantil [Unstructured material in educational practice within Early Childhood Education]. *Pulso. Review of Education*, *46*, 76–101. doi:10.58265/pulso.5884

Rodríguez, B. (2014). Técnicas metodológicas empleadas en la enseñanza del inglés en Educación Infantil: Estudio de caso. Didáctica [Methodological Techniques used in the teaching of English in Early Childhood Education: A case study]. *Lengua y Literatura*, *16*, 145–161.

Royal Decree 95/2022, of February 1, 2022, establishing the minimum teaching for the second cycle of Early Childhood Education. Official State Gazette, 28, 2022.

Siahaan, F. (2022). The Critical Period Hypothesis of SLA Eric Lenneberg's. *Journal of Applied Linguistics*, *2*(2), 40–45. doi:10.52622/joal.v2i2.77

Silalahi, R. M. (2019). Understanding Vygotsky's Zone of Proximal Development for Learning. *Polyglot Jurnal Ilmiah*, *15*(2), 169–186. doi:10.19166/pji.v15i2.1544

Solé, I. (2016). Las relaciones entre familia y escuela [Relationships between family and school]. *C&E, Cultura y Educación*, *8*(4), 11–17. doi:10.1174/11356409660561241

Vila, I. (2018). *Familia, escuela y comunidad* [Family, school, and community]. Horsori.

Violante, R. (2018). Didáctica de la Educación Infantil: Reflexiones y Propuestas [Didactics of Early Childhood Education: Reflections and Proposals]. *Revista Senderos Pedagógicos*, *9*(9), 131–150. doi:10.53995/sp.v9i9.961

Vygotsky, L. (1987). *Pensamiento y Lenguaje* [Thought and Language]. La Pléyade.

Zhang, R. (2023). The characteristics of Early Childhood Education in Spain. *Journal of Education and Educational Research*, *6*(1), 8–10. doi:10.54097/jeer.v6i1.14124

Chapter 8

Adaptive Primary School Design:
Post-Pandemic Reuse Projects for Adana Former Archeology Museum

Orkan Zeynel Güzelci

ⓘ https://orcid.org/0000-0002-5771-4069
Istanbul Technical University, Turkey

ABSTRACT

This chapter explores the strategies for adapting existing buildings in a way that respects both cultural and environmental sustainability. It specifically focuses on the adaptive reuse of the Adana Former Archaeology Museum, exploring its transformation into a primary school in response to post-pandemic needs. The primary goal is to demonstrate the potential of adaptive reuse of heritage buildings for contemporary educational purposes while preserving their cultural essence. The methodology involves a teaching experiment (case study) with undergraduate interior design students, who develop various scenarios and spatial designs for the museum's transformation. This case study offers practical insights into the challenges and opportunities of adaptive reuse in architecture and interior design. The chapter highlights adaptive reuse's major implications for educational leaders, emphasizing the importance of creating dynamic, flexible, and adaptable learning environments.

DOI: 10.4018/978-1-7998-3940-8.ch008

Copyright © 2024, IGI Global. Copying or distributing in print or electronic forms without written permission of IGI Global is prohibited.

INTRODUCTION

The current global pandemic has impacted the functionality of numerous building types. While there have been substantial efforts to adapt existing buildings to this new and unexpected situation, flexibility has become a main concept in the design and development phases of architectural and interior design projects. Compared to certain building typologies that fulfill basic public needs, such as hospitals, supermarkets, banks, and other public service facilities, the adaptation of educational buildings to the pandemic situation has been relatively slower.

In the context of Turkey, when adapting educational facilities to pandemic conditions, certain factors presented more significant challenges for adaptation. These included the number of teachers, the student population, the overall count of educational buildings, and the physical sizes of these buildings. The rapid growth in student numbers at primary and middle school levels was not matched by an equivalent increase in the availability of teachers and school infrastructures. The physical limitations of the buildings, influenced by aspects such as land area, courtyard boundaries, and the high population density of their surrounding neighborhoods, made them particularly challenging to modify (Güzelci et al., 2020).

Confronted with such challenges, recent research, including those by the author and colleagues has discussed the adaptation of educational buildings to post-pandemic reuse (Al-Delfi & Salman, 2022; Güzelci et al., 2020; Güzelci et al., 2021; İsmailoğlu & Kulak Torun, 2022; Putra, 2021; Yatmo & Atmodiwirjo, 2022). These studies primarily examine a range of educational facilities, including primary schools, secondary schools, and universities, which continue to function as educational spaces. Unlike existing studies, this chapter focuses on the adaptation and adaptive reuse of a building that has lost its original function.

Within the scope of this chapter, the Adana Former Archaeology Museum, a registered building currently functioning as a marriage registry office, was chosen as the site. The design brief involved the adaptive reuse of the museum building for its transformation into a primary school. This design brief was assigned to interior architecture students in an undergraduate-level design studio. The design process, which was conducted in the recent past under pandemic conditions, primarily utilized remote education as the mode of communication (Figure 1).

This chapter is structured as follows: it begins by providing a background on key concepts, such as adaptive reuse, post-pandemic reuse, flexibility, and adaptability. Following this, the chapter presents and discusses the four experimental steps conducted in the interior architecture design studio: site analysis, theme analysis, scenario development, and project development. Lastly, the concluding section summarizes the main findings and their implications.

Figure 1. Poster of the Interior Architecture Design Studio III-IV by Aycan Kızılkaya

BACKGROUND

Adaptive reuse involves the transformation of an existing building or site while retaining its historical character and essence. This approach to sustainable development aids in preserving cultural heritage, minimizing waste, and fostering urban regeneration. In the fields of architecture and urban planning, adaptive reuse has gained widespread acceptance as a cost-effective alternative to new construction, as evidenced by various studies (Bassett, 1997; Lo Faro & Miceli, 2019; Vardopoulos, 2023; Wong, 2016). Additionally, adaptive reuse entails the repurposing of historical buildings for uses different from their original purposes. This practice can range from transforming a factory into a loft apartment complex to converting a sport complex into a hotel (Lanz & Pendlebury, 2022; Patil et al., 2021).

Under the umbrella term of adaptive reuse, environmental sustainability is significantly advanced. Adaptive reuse conserves valuable resources and decreases the burden on landfills by limiting demolition and its associated resource extraction and waste generation (Bullen & Love, 2010; Bullen & Love, 2011). It represents a key step towards a more closed-loop, circular economy in a society struggling with resource scarcity and climate change. Furthermore, reusing existing structures, which have already had energy invested in them, significantly saves energy usage compared to new construction. This approach aligns with global efforts to reduce carbon footprints and transition to a low-carbon future (Lanz & Pendlebury, 2022; Li et al., 2021).

Adaptive reuse is critical for preserving social and cultural aspects. It protects historical buildings and landmarks, thus preserving physical links to the past and strengthening the cultural foundations of communities. Adaptive reuse promotes a sense of place and identity, contributing to the social well-being of communities. Furthermore, effective adaptive reuse initiatives can serve as catalysts for urban renewal, injecting dynamism and economic activity into previously neglected areas (Hasnain & Mohseni, 2018; Vafaie et al., 2023). Economic feasibility adds a new dimension to adaptive reuse. Compared to the costs of new construction, transforming existing structures can be far more cost-effective (Ijla & Broström, 2015). This is particularly true for projects that utilize pre-existing infrastructure and foundations, resulting in shorter construction periods and potentially lower costs (Highfield & Gorse, 2009).

Buildings must adapt to the new realities and challenges related to a post-pandemic world, such as health and safety issues, social distancing needs, and evolving user demands. In this context, adaptive reuse emerges as a critical strategy for post-pandemic building use. The process of reusing existing structures to fit the evolving needs of a world altered by the pandemic is known as the post-pandemic reuse of buildings. The adaptation of existing buildings for post-pandemic reuse is a key research topic in architecture. Developing a systematic method to address building adaptation challenges for post-pandemic reuse creates a new conceptual framework in these disciplines (Han et al., 2022; Spennemann, 2021).

Flexibility in architecture is defined as the capacity of a space to adapt to changing demands without necessitating substantial physical modifications. This concept emphasizes the ease with which a space can be modified or rearranged without significant physical intervention. During the pandemic, many buildings have been challenged to demonstrate flexibility. For instance, hospitals expanded their capacity by using modular units, tents, or repurposing other spaces; schools shifted to hybrid or online learning models using digital platforms, flexible furniture, or outdoor classrooms; offices adopted remote work policies utilizing cloud-based services, or collaborative tools; and restaurants adapted to delivery services through online ordering, or outdoor dining areas (De Paris et al., 2022; Güzelci et al., 2021; Owojori et al., 2021).

Adaptability in architecture refers to the ability to perform physical, spatial, or organizational adjustments to meet new requirements, often necessitating structural changes. It encompasses a building's capacity for modification or reconfiguration to accommodate new uses or needs. This concept includes design strategies that anticipate future demands, easily accessible building systems for maintenance, structural features that support reconfiguration, and the adaptive reuse of existing structures. For example, school buildings need to be flexible and adaptable to address evolving educational needs, instructional methods, technological advancements, and unexpected challenges. Making early design decisions is crucial for ensuring a building's potential for flexibility and adaptation, thereby reducing the need for costly post-occupancy modifications. Understanding the intricate interplay between function and form, activities and space, as well as user needs and spatial affordances, is considered fundamental in designing spaces that are truly flexible and adaptive (Güzelci et al., 2021; Heidrich et al., 2017; Pinder et al., 2017; Spennemann, 2021).

CASE STUDY

In this section, the 'Setup' subsection details the selected site and building designated for the design of an adaptive primary school, along with the design brief provided to the students. Subsequently, the 'Analysis' subsection presents a sequential overview of the results, encompassing site analyses, theme analyses, scenario development, and project development stages conducted by the students. The results obtained from these phases, coupled with the conducted analyses, are integrated into this discussion.

Setup

Site

The Adana Former Archaeology Museum, opened to the public in 1972, is a notable landmark in the city, evoking memories for both tourists and locals. Over time, the size of the museum's land has been reduced due to various interventions, such as the construction of roads, bridges, and surrounding buildings. Notably, authorities including the municipality and the governorship have proposed demolishing the building more than once to make space for development in Adana (Mimarlar Odası Adana Şubesi, 2019).

Despite serious demolition attempts, the Adana Branch of the Chamber of Architects was actively involved in the process and successfully prevented the building's demolition. The DOCOMOMO Turkey working group began conservation and registration efforts for the museum building in 2006, followed by the Adana Branch of the Chamber of Architects in 2017. However, these attempts faced rejection, as authorities deemed the project 'typical,' claiming it was similar to existing museum buildings. The Adana Branch of the Chamber of Architects systematically documented museum buildings, noting that the Adana Archaeology Museum building featured distinctive elements setting it apart from others. This substantial evidence led to the initiation of the building's registration process in 2018. Subsequently, the museum building has been transformed and currently serves as the Adana Metropolitan Municipality's 'marriage registry office.' Looking to the future, the Adana Branch of the Chamber of Architects envisions the former Archaeology Museum building becoming the 'Adana Architecture Center.' The proposed adaptive reuse of the building as an architecture center aims to respect its historical significance and contribute to Adana's architectural discourse and heritage (Mimarlar Odası Adana Şubesi, 2019).

Brief

The design brief provided to the students for the adaptation and reuse of the Adana Former Archaeology Museum as a primary school is divided into four distinct phases. Each phase has specific expectations, which are detailed in the following part:

- **Phase I - Site Analysis:** Students collaborated in groups to analyze the surroundings and the building of the Adana Former Archaeology Museum. They aimed to understand the urban fabric, considering social,

Adaptive Primary School Design

cultural, psychological, and economic aspects. They also examined the architectural character of the museum, including its relationship with climatic, microclimatic, and environmental factors. The groups presented their analyses using various mediums, such as 2D-3D-4D representations, incorporating sketches, mappings, collages, diagrams, videos, and animations.

- **Phase II - Theme Analysis:** Students worked individually to conduct in-depth studies on school designs, exploring both traditional and contemporary learning/teaching approaches. This phase resulted in a presentation of selected school examples and themes, providing the foundation for subsequent design and project development phases.
- **Phase III - Design Development:** This phase focused on scenario development and functions for the architectural program. Students emphasized exploring the conceptual and spatial requirements of their scenarios, presenting their studies in various forms, including texts, diagrams, collages, sketches, drawings, and 3D models.
- **Phase IV - Project Development:** The final phase required students to convert their abstract design ideas into concrete design outcomes. This involved preparing technical drawings and 3D visuals, focusing on the detailed design of the school. Submissions included 1/50 scale interior space plans and sections, and 1/20 scale representations of unique project components, furniture, and details.

Analysis

Phase I - Site Analysis

The surroundings of the Adana Former Archaeology Museum reveal a blend of historical and contemporary elements. Notable buildings, some with significant historical importance, contribute to the area's cultural richness. The coexistence of these elements forms a distinctive narrative, illustrating Adana's architectural evolution. Conducting a year-by-year development analysis reveals valuable insights into the changing natural and manmade landscape surrounding the museum.

Demographic trends, closely linked with factors such as educational levels and the prevalence of schools, help us understand the intellectual level of the community. This analysis plays a crucial role in comprehending the community's needs and anticipating potential future developments.

Conducting an in-depth analysis, which takes into account various factors such as temperature, wind, sunlight, sound, traffic, and people density, provides valuable insights. In the city of Adana, characterized by a hot and arid climate, an analysis of the wind has been conducted, which can effectively mitigate the impact of high temperatures. The intensity of sound, influenced by factors like road types, serves as a reflection of the urban rhythm. Traffic density at different times of the day contributes to the overall soundscape (Figure 2).

Figure 2. Analysis of the site by student groups: a. Sacide Akkoyun & Elif Çay, b. Betül Ünlü & Ömer Muttaki Karataş, c. Zeynep Yıldız & Eda Hatip, d. Berfin Güner & İlknur Sena Özer, e. Fatma Betül Kavurmacı & Esra Aksu

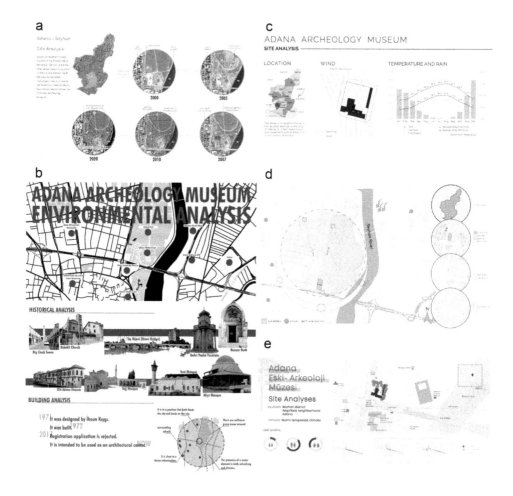

The building has an identifiable architectural character, consisting of three distinct geometric masses connected by a transparent entrance space. The analysis emphasizes how the geometry and transparency of the facade

Adaptive Primary School Design

contribute to climate adaptability and visual aesthetics. The solid-void ratio of building facades is linked with these criteria. Sophisticated elements, such as motifs, reliefs, and band windows, improve the architectural quality of the building. Furthermore, the architectural reaction to wind and traffic patterns is critical (Figure 3).

Figure 3. Analysis of the building by student groups: a. Berfin Güner & İlknur Sena Özer, b. Sacide Akkoyun & Elif Çay, c. Fatma Betül Kavurmacı & Esra Aksu, d. Dilan Pakkan & Nur Sarıaltın

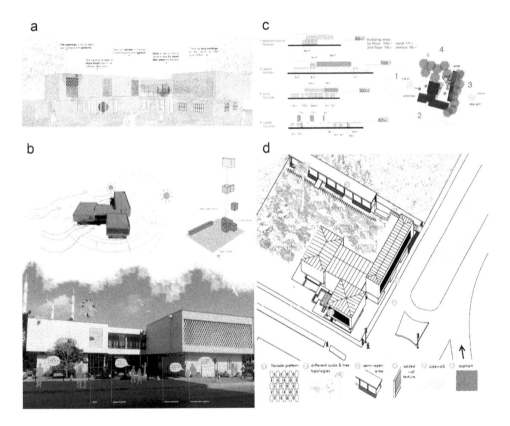

In summary, this holistic analytical approach fosters a deeper understanding of the site, the building, and its potential for future reuse and/or transformation. Specifically, focusing on the principles and details of the building lays a foundation for a design that sensitively responds to the building and existing environment.

Phase II - Theme Analysis

During the thematic analysis stage, students presented various pedagogical approaches, including outside lessons, class circles, collaborative and collective work, learning by doing, empathy, social and emotional development, and observation. The range of pedagogical concepts presented embraces a holistic perspective on learning, providing a diverse set of strategies to enhance the educational experience. From the perspective of well-being and sustainability, themes of organic and local foods in the schoolyard, permaculture, and zero waste stand out. In the context of a flexible design perspective, the following concepts were introduced: multipurpose spaces, open plans, need-based design, suitability for different age groups, tiered seating areas, alternative seating options, learning streets, indoor-outdoor space connectivity, playgrounds, exhibition spaces, and a design approach that eliminates physical walls.

Outdoor lessons, which expand learning beyond the traditional classroom boundaries, engage students in experiential learning and build a strong connection with the natural world. With its collaborative and inclusive seating arrangement, the class circle promotes a sense of community and fair involvement, encouraging open communication. Collaborative desks and shared walls physically remove typical classroom borders, enabling collaboration and shared learning experiences. The educational emphasis on learning by doing highlights the importance of hands-on experiences in improving understanding and knowledge transfer. Promoting teamwork and collaboration among students through collective work develops a sense of community and shared responsibility. Furthermore, an intentional focus on empathy and social-emotional development fosters an emotionally rich learning environment, preparing students for the complexities of social interactions. Using observation as an important approach enhances awareness for both students and educators, allowing teachers to adapt their teaching strategies to meet the varied needs of the students.

The integration of organic and local foods envisions the schoolyard as an extension of the learning environment, encouraging outdoor activities and an internal connection with nature. This concept not only promotes a healthier lifestyle but also incorporates organic, locally-sourced foods into the school's nutrition program, aligning daily practices with environmental consciousness. Complementing this, the adoption of permaculture and zero waste principles adds another dimension to the educational values by teaching fundamental environmental awareness. This approach goes beyond traditional teaching methods by actively involving students in sustainable practices and creating a sense of responsibility towards the environment. Together, these ideas create

Adaptive Primary School Design

an enhanced educational atmosphere that supports both the well-being of students and their ecological consciousness.

Designing flexible multipurpose spaces that can accommodate a variety of activities ensures optimal utilization of the school's infrastructure. The creation of learning street layouts fosters a sense of continuity and collaboration. Emphasizing need-based design prioritizes adaptability to evolving educational methodologies and ensures that spaces meet specific learner needs. Spaces designed to be suitable for different age groups encourage diversity by responding to the diverse requirements and developmental stages of students. Creating tiered seating arrangements and amphitheater-style spaces aims to provide dynamic and engaging settings for presentations and performances. The incorporation of alternative seating options and the maximization of natural light contribute to creating alternative seating areas that foster a comfortable and stimulating learning environment. Indoor-outdoor space connectivity blurs the boundaries between these areas, promoting a seamless connection with nature and enhancing openness and unity through a direct link between learning spaces and a courtyard. Integrating playful and dynamic elements, such as playgrounds, encourages physical activity and exploration within the school environment. Finally, the concept of no walls aims to remove physical barriers, encourage open communication, and provide dedicated spaces for exhibiting student work.

In conclusion, the school's thematic analysis reveals a diverse collection of strategies for learning, design elements, and sustainable practices that collectively create a holistic and contemporary educational setting. The schools exhibit an effort to enhance the educational experience through teaching methods such as outdoor lessons and collaborative work, as well as through flexible design elements like multifunctional spaces and open-plan layouts. The emphasis on well-being and sustainability, evident in themes like organic and local foods, permaculture, and zero waste, reflects a conscious effort to foster environmental awareness in students. Furthermore, incorporating these concepts not only regards the school as an extension of the learning environment but also actively engages students in sustainable decisions, promoting a sense of environmental responsibility. The focus on adaptation, inclusion, and a continuous connection with nature provides an enhanced educational environment that prioritizes both student well-being and ecological consciousness.

Phase III - Scenario Development

During the scenario development stage, ideas for schools to be designed were produced, including but not limited to Flipped School, Pellucid School, Conne-ou-in School, Happy Bee School, 3E School, TES School, Talent Love School, R&L School, Green+ Free School, School Plus+, Sunshine School, and Eco School. These scenarios provide the foundation for the project's development phase (Figure 4).

Flipped School is founded on the flipped classroom approach, which includes a model allowing students to work on schoolwork at home and complete homework in school. In response to this strategy, flexibility and transparency in classroom organization are emphasized, resulting in more participatory and group-based learning settings inside the school. Teachers can record in private rooms, and instead of lecturing at the board, they take on a more guiding and student-focused interactive role. The goal of this design is to create a student-centered, collaborative learning environment supported by technological tools.

Pellucid School presents an educational model based on ideas that integrate water into its essence. This unique school plan emphasizes direct interaction with water, celebrating its fluidity with elements like pipes in the interior, water elements integrated into both the slabs and inner walls, and a central pool in the garden.

Conne-ou-in School is an educational concept derived from the synthesis of the words connection, outside, and inside. This design aims to provide students with an experience that makes them feel like they are outside when inside the classroom and vice versa. The classroom atmosphere is designed to blur the boundaries between inside and outside.

Happy Bee School has a warm and inviting atmosphere, encouraging a sense of belonging by requiring students to remove their shoes upon entering. The school promotes a democratic climate by organizing class circles and meetings where every student's voice is heard. Communication is key to the school's philosophy, promoting open communication and collaboration.

The school introduces the 3E Model teaching method, aligning itself with the concepts of exploration, explanation, and extension. The model shows a dynamic learning ring representing the essence of active learning. Students are encouraged to engage in hands-on discoveries during the exploration phase, fostering curiosity and involvement. Collaboration and discussions improve understanding during the explanation phase, laying a solid foundation. The expansion phase emphasizes reinforcing and sustaining knowledge through practical application.

Adaptive Primary School Design

TES School, standing for technology, education, and sustainability, offers an educational model incorporating these three pillars. The school implements innovative strategies like green monitors, which encourage sustainability by managing energy consumption, and intelligent water meters that correspond with responsible resource use. Digital fabrication, utilizing technology, becomes a core component, encouraging students to engage in hands-on production using advanced tools. Lastly, coding supports the programming and robotic abilities of the students.

Talent Love School centers around the philosophy of self-discovery and fostering a love for individual talents. In Talent Love School, teachers play a crucial role as observers, dedicated to understanding and recognizing the individual talents and passions of each student. Through careful observation, educators aim to identify the strengths and interests that students bring to the learning environment. Recognizing that strengths often emerge in collaborative settings, the teachers arrange groups that support and encourage one another. Extracurricular activities are pivotal, providing diverse avenues for students to express and develop their talents.

R&L School (Reveal & Learn) is dedicated to encouraging a spirit of autonomy and freedom in children. Decisions are not only welcomed but encouraged here, allowing students to actively shape their educational experience. A distinguishing characteristic is the scheduling flexibility, which allows students of various grades to choose their weekly hours, creating a customized educational path. This perspective extends to time management, with students expected to take charge of their schedules.

Green+ Free School reflects the vision of creating a learning setting designed for a breath—a place where knowledge seeds are not just planted but carefully nurtured to grow. This concept combines the traditional academic environment with the inspiring experience of learning in nature, as well as a strong dedication to urban green initiatives, forming the very essence of this institution. Gardening successfully intertwines with the pleasure of leisure in this dynamic environment, providing students with an educational experience that is both playful and enriching. The inclusion of a seed bank and canteen adds to the dedication to sustainability and promoting a healthy lifestyle. The realization that nature provides limitless opportunities to enhance children's cognitive, physical, and emotional growth is central to this approach. It is a place where students can run free, take moderate risks, and actively engage with the natural surroundings around them.

School Plus+ is planned as a form of education based on David Kolb's concepts regarding experiential learning. The school's design emphasizes flexibility and fluid spaces to provide a dynamic and engaging learning environment.

Sunshine School's primary principle emphasizes each child's overall development through a unique teaching approach. The school focuses particularly on creating a strong sense of achievement in its students, encouraging them to advance at their own pace. Self-discipline is inevitably linked to the development of self-mastery in this supportive atmosphere. The use of multi-sensory materials is a crucial component of the program at Sunshine School, producing an immersive and robust learning experience that engages several senses. These materials support the educational experience by providing students with a rich and dynamic platform for exploration. Observational learning is another fundamental aspect of the school. Students at Sunshine School actively benefit from watching, interacting, and teaching one another.

Eco School embodies sustainability, zero waste, and permaculture. Its learning approach embraces the environment as the third teacher. Operating on a democratic model, students actively shape their educational experience. The compost kitchen transforms organic waste for soil improvement, complemented by edible gardens, and a cooperative structure. A quiet pool contributes to the school's appeal while also helping preserve water. Eco School seeks to promote an intense concern for the environment in its students, fostering a generation dedicated to a healthy and sustainable future.

The combination of several scenarios offered here demonstrates a shared vision for the future of education, emphasizing novel approaches, sustainability, and the development of well-rounded individuals. Collectively, these schools exceed old paradigms, embracing forward-thinking ideas that respond to the changing nature of education in contemporary society. The many educational models presented in these projects represent a departure from conventional approaches.

Whether it is the implementation of a flipped classroom model, the building of immersive spaces that blur indoor and outdoor borders, or the introduction of dynamic learning rings, each school project offers a unique lens through which education can be transformed. Sustainability emerges as a core value of these projects. From the integration of water elements to the pioneering practices of green monitors, intelligent water meters, and a commitment to zero waste and permaculture, these schools actively engage in practices that align with broader environmental goals.

Adaptive Primary School Design

Figure 4. Diagrams from the scenario development phase: a. Green+ Free School by Fatma Betül Kavurmacı, b. Eco School by Elif Çay, c. Conne-ou-in School by Gizem Sarbay, d. TES School by Dilan Pakkan, e. Sunshine School by Berfin Güner, f. Flipped School by İlknur Sena Özer

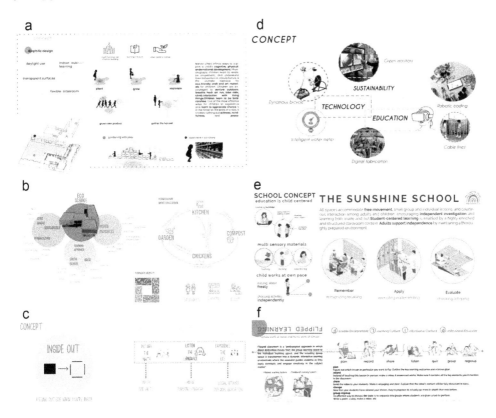

In brief, this collection of school proposals presents a clear image of a future-oriented education system—one that is adaptable, sustainable, and dedicated to developing students with the skills, values, and awareness required for success in the twenty-first century.

Phase IV - Project Development

In the concluding phase, students integrated their research, abstract ideas, and insights into interior and landscape designs (Figure 5).

In Flipped School Project, special rooms were designed for teachers, focusing on semi-open computer use and recording. Contrasting the logic of these rooms, classrooms were designed in a highly adaptable manner, featuring movable panel walls with large openings. This allowed students to

187

sit in different orientations in the classroom. The absence of a fixed teacher desk and whiteboard contributed to this flexibility within the space.

Pellucid School Project planned to incorporate the water element both physically and conceptually. Various functional pipes moved freely throughout the interior area, serving as fundamental components of the spatial designs. The water element was employed in a manner that allowed it to be touched, observed, and interacted with in both the courtyard and indoor areas, providing qualities that could be experienced by walking or sitting without being concealed.

In Happy Bee Project, significant open spaces were designated within the indoor areas. These spaces played a crucial role in accommodating gathering activities and events required for the project. Moreover, these areas could be divided to transform into spaces with different functions.

Within TES School Project, a substantial makerLAB had been established, featuring an exhibition space for exhibiting products created there. The architectural character included classrooms with LAB features, shared work tables, and walls equipped for hanging tools. The design incorporated raw wood materials for furniture and wall coverings, along with industrial flooring materials. Additionally, the courtyard incorporated technological elements like solar balls for energy harvesting.

In Talent Love Project, a circular space extending from the interior to the exterior was placed in the central area of the building. Multiple classrooms and workshops in smaller sizes were distributed around this circle. In this scenario where the corridor-based approach was eliminated, this central hall/square became a focal point for students from different units to gather.

The slab of the entrance space of R&L School Project was removed and transformed into a gallery. From the entrance space, all three blocks of the building could be seen. In this case, the level of illuminance was increased, and spaces looking at narrow corridors were avoided, but the spaces that the school needed were provided.

Green+ Free School Project had planting gardens and seed banks in the outdoor area, and a cafeteria and an open library in the semi-open area. The classes and dining hall also opened to this courtyard. Greenery walls were spaces with modular grids that could hold plants.

In School Plus+ Project, there were various puzzles in the outdoor and indoor areas of the building, on the floors and walls. The slide puzzle wall was achieved with colorful continuous tubes. These tubes served as puzzle underlays in some places.

Adaptive Primary School Design

The staircase design at Sunshine School Project served as a seamless connection between various levels, fostering interaction and visual engagement among students. The entrance seating element not only established a welcoming atmosphere but also encouraged social interaction beyond the confines of the classroom. Hallway sitting elements provided opportunities for observation, while the gallery space featured slender railings that maintained visual connectivity. The window nook design offered a unique space for children to sit, and observe outside activities.

Eco School Project featured a specially designed outdoor net element, providing both seating and a space for harvesting fruits. The interior spaces were arranged in a row, following the 'garden to table' approach. The design flowed from the courtyard to the kitchen, then to the dining area, and finally extended into the classrooms. The dining area was thoughtfully integrated with the library. The modular system designed for the kitchen and dining area extended seamlessly to the classrooms.

The various themes across these innovative school projects revolve around creating spaces that prioritize flexibility, interactivity, and integration of natural elements. This collective vision reflects a modern and forward-thinking approach to school design, emphasizing environments that go beyond traditional settings to foster engagement and facilitate dynamic learning experiences.

Flexibility is a key element in these designs, evident in the movable walls, adaptable seating arrangements, and the elimination of fixed elements like teacher desks. These features not only accommodates diverse teaching methods but also encourages students to actively participate in shaping their learning environments.

Interactivity is another central theme, highlighted through various features such as open spaces, collaborative work areas, and interactive elements like water installations, greenery walls, and puzzle structures. These design choices are intentional, aiming to promote hands-on learning experiences and meaningful interactions among students and educators.

Furthermore, the incorporation of natural elements, such as water features, planting gardens, and greenery walls, underscores a commitment to creating environments that connect students with nature (Figure 6). This approach aligns with contemporary educational philosophies that recognize the positive impact of natural elements on well-being and learning outcomes.

Adaptive Primary School Design

Figure 5. Interior design solutions from the project development phase: a. Green+ Free School by Fatma Betül Kavurmacı, b. Sunshine School by Berfin Güner, c. Eco School by Elif Çay, d. ACT School by Sacide Akkoyun, e. Molecule School by Esra Aksu, f. TES School by Dilan Pakkan

Figure 6. Open and semi-open space design solutions from the project development phase: a. Green+ Free School by Fatma Betül Kavurmacı, b. Moleculer School by Esra Aksu, c. Eco School by Elif Çay, d. Flipped School by İlknur Sena Özer

In brief, these projects collectively represent a departure from traditional educational settings, embracing a design philosophy that prioritizes flexibility, adaptability, interaction, and harmonious integration with the natural environment. By doing so, these schools not only provide functional spaces but also contribute to the creation of inspiring atmospheres conducive to holistic learning experiences.

CONCLUSION

This chapter presents the adaptive reuse of the Adana Former Archaeology Museum into a primary school. It highlights the significance of flexibility and adaptability in educational spaces and the role of physical space in teaching and learning. The presented projects embody a transformative approach to education, emphasizing the necessity to adapt to evolving methodologies, technologies, and student requirements.

However, it is crucial to acknowledge the study's limitations. The project studio's scope was limited to a specific building type within a particular geographic area. Students in the project studio, who had limited experience with educational strategies, necessitated a thematic analysis. Due to time constraints for each project phase, students faced challenges in their research. The initial perception of the original building's size as a drawback was overcome through decisions made by interior design students, including defining the school's scenario, utilization scenarios for educational spaces, and determining student numbers.

The existing two-story building, comprising closed, open, and semi-open spaces with sufficient natural light and regular geometries, facilitated both orthogonal and free-plan design solutions using curved forms within the space. Moreover, the ability to establish multiple interior-exterior spatial relationships enhanced circulation continuity in the projects. While these advantageous factors may not be universally present in every project, they show the need for specific analysis and customized development for each adaptive reuse project.

This chapter's content mostly concerns the project's design phases. However, the implementation phase may encounter challenges such as regulatory issues, financial constraints, and stakeholder decisions. Nevertheless, the sustainable approach of adaptive reuse, coupled with modern educational methods, is expected to make direct and indirect contributions to society, assisting in handling these challenges.

Given the challenging conditions faced by school leaders and administrators today, an agile response to the ever-changing educational landscape is necessary. This chapter emphasizes the necessity for spaces to evolve in parallel with changing teaching methodologies, technologies, and student needs to maintain relevance and effectiveness. The exploration of various teaching models highlights the significance of leaders embracing and implementing innovative educational strategies that support dynamic, interactive, and personalized learning experiences. The undergraduate-level design studio focused on the adaptive reuse of the Adana Former Archaeology Museum into a primary school, serving as an example of evolving demands in education and addressing crucial issues in contemporary educational leadership and management.

The projects highlight the critical role of physical space in learning and teaching, demonstrating how educational leaders can provide high-quality learning environments through adaptive reuse strategies. A detailed examination of spatial design and pedagogical approaches presents a forward-thinking and transformative approach to education. This discussion supports the essential need to recognize and embrace the dynamic nature of educational institutions to successfully guide them into the future.

ACKNOWLEDGMENT

The author extends sincere gratitude to research assistant Aycan Kızılkaya for her invaluable contribution to the project studio. Additionally, the author acknowledges the hard work and dedication of the students from the Interior Architecture Design Studio III-IV at the Interior Architecture Department of Istanbul Technical University during the 2020-2021 Spring Semester. Special thanks are given to the following students, listed in alphabetical order with their project names: Berfin Güner (Sunshine School), Betül Ünlü (Pellucid School), Dilan Pakkan (TES School), Eda Hatip (Happy Bee School), Elif Çay (Eco School), Esra Aksu (Molecule School), Fatma Betül Kavurmacı (Green+ Free School), Gizem Sarbay (Conne-ou-in School), İlayda Irmak Korkmaz (not specified), İlknur Sena Özer (Flipped School), İpek Bozkurt (3E Model), Kerem Ümitvar (R&L School), Muhammet Güner (Talent Love School), Nihat Yiğit Oktan (not specified), Nur Sarıaltın (School Plus+), Ömer Muttaki Karataş (Pattern of Shapes School), Sacide Akkoyun (ACT School), Vasıf Efe Tan (not specified).

REFERENCES

Al-Delfi, A. M. H., & Salman, A. S. (2022). Investigating the Impact of Educational Space Design in Fostering Social Distancing: A Case Study of the University of Technology Buildings, Iraq. *Journal of Sustainable Architecture and Civil Engineering*, *31*(2), 39–57. doi:10.5755/j01.sace.31.2.30746

Bassett, P. G. (1997). The theory and practice of adaptive reuse. In *Proceedings of the 1997 symposium on Software reusability* (pp. 2-9). 10.1145/258366.258371

Bullen, P., & Love, P. (2011). Factors influencing the adaptive re-use of buildings. *Journal of Engineering. Design and Technology*, *9*(1), 32–46. doi:10.1108/17260531111121459

Bullen, P. A., & Love, P. E. (2010). The rhetoric of adaptive reuse or reality of demolition: Views from the field. *Cities (London, England)*, *27*(4), 215–224. doi:10.1016/j.cities.2009.12.005

De Paris, S., Lacerda Lopes, C. N., & Neuenfeldt, A. Junior. (2022). The use of an analytic hierarchy process to evaluate the flexibility and adaptability in architecture. *Archnet-IJAR: International Journal of Architectural Research*, *16*(1), 26–45. doi:10.1108/ARCH-05-2021-0148

Güzelci, O. Z., Alaçam, S., Kocabay, S., & Akkuyu, E. (2020). Adaptability of primary and middle schools to post-pandemic reuse - a discussion in the context of flexibility. *Journal of Design Studio*, *2*(2), 5–22. doi:10.46474/jds.776665

Güzelci, O. Z., Şen Bayram, A. K., Alaçam, S., Güzelci, H., Akkuyu, E. I., & Şencan, İ. (2021). Design tactics for enhancing the adaptability of primary and middle schools to the new needs of postpandemic reuse. *Archnet-IJAR: International Journal of Architectural Research*, *15*(1), 148–166. doi:10.1108/ARCH-10-2020-0237

Han, P., Wang, L., Song, Y., & Zheng, X. (2022). Designing for the post-pandemic era: Trends, focuses, and strategies learned from architectural competitions based on a text analysis. *Frontiers in Public Health*, *10*, 1084562. doi:10.3389/fpubh.2022.1084562 PMID:36568743

Hasnain, H., & Mohseni, F. (2018, March). Creative ideation and adaptive reuse: A solution to sustainable urban heritage conservation. *IOP Conference Series. Earth and Environmental Science*, *126*(1), 012075. doi:10.1088/1755-1315/126/1/012075

Heidrich, O., Kamara, J., Maltese, S., Re Cecconi, F., & Dejaco, M. C. (2017). A critical review of the developments in building adaptability. *International Journal of Building Pathology and Adaptation*, *35*(4), 284–303. doi:10.1108/IJBPA-03-2017-0018

Highfield, D., & Gorse, C. (2009). *Refurbishment and upgrading of buildings*. Routledge. doi:10.4324/9780203879160

Ijla, A., & Broström, T. (2015). The sustainable viability of adaptive reuse of historic buildings: The experiences of two world heritage old cities; Bethlehem in Palestine and Visby in Sweden. *International Invention Journal of Arts and Social Sciences*, *2*(4), 52–66.

İsmailoğlu, S., & Kulak Torun, E. (2022). Spatial Organization of Interior Design Studios in the Normalization Process. *Turkish Online Journal of Design Art and Communication*, *12*(2), 497–514. doi:10.7456/11202100/019

Lanz, F., & Pendlebury, J. (2022). Adaptive reuse: A critical review. *Journal of Architecture (London)*, *27*(2-3), 441–462. doi:10.1080/13602365.2022.2105381

Li, Y., Zhao, L., Huang, J., & Law, A. (2021). Research frameworks, methodologies, and assessment methods concerning the adaptive reuse of architectural heritage: A review. *Built Heritage*, *5*(1), 1–19. doi:10.1186/s43238-021-00025-x

Lo Faro, A., & Miceli, A. (2019). Sustainable strategies for the adaptive reuse of religious heritage: A social opportunity. *Buildings*, *9*(10), 211. doi:10.3390/buildings9100211

Owojori, O. M., Okoro, C. S., & Chileshe, N. (2021). Current status and emerging trends on the adaptive reuse of buildings: A bibliometric analysis. *Sustainability (Basel)*, *13*(21), 11646. doi:10.3390/su132111646

Patil, D. T., Patil, A., & Patil, J. (2021). The Decision-Making Criteria for Adaptive Reuse for Sustainable Development. In *Advances in Geotechnics and Structural Engineering: Select Proceedings of TRACE 2020*, 599-607. doi:10.1007/978-981-33-6969-6_52

Pinder, J. A., Schmidt, R., Austin, S. A., Gibb, A., & Saker, J. (2017). What is meant by adaptability in buildings? *Facilities*, *35*(1/2), 2–20. doi:10.1108/F-07-2015-0053

Putra, I. N. G. M. (2021). Analysis of Proposed Adaptation of Fostered Environment and Evaluation of Built Environment in Bali in Facing Covid-19. *Architectural Research Journal*, *1*(1), 26–34. doi:10.22225/arj.1.1.3299.26-34

Spennemann, D. H. (2021). Residential Architecture in a post-pandemic world: Implications of COVID-19 for new construction and for adapting heritage buildings. *Journal of Green Building*, *16*(1), 199–215. doi:10.3992/jgb.16.1.199

Şubesi, M. O. A. (2019). Mutlu Haber: Eski Arkeoloji Müzesi Kültür Varlığı Olarak Tescillendi. *Mimarlık*, *408*, 10–12.

Vafaie, F., Remøy, H., & Gruis, V. (2023). Adaptive reuse of heritage buildings; a systematic literature review of success factors. *Habitat International*, *142*, 102926. doi:10.1016/j.habitatint.2023.102926

Vardopoulos, I. (2023). Adaptive Reuse for Sustainable Development and Land Use: A Multivariate Linear Regression Analysis Estimating Key Determinants of Public Perceptions. *Heritage, 6*(2), 809–828. doi:10.3390/heritage6020045

Wong, L. (2016). *Adaptive reuse: extending the lives of buildings.* Birkhäuser. doi:10.1515/9783038213130

Yatmo, Y. A., & Atmodiwirjo, P. (2022). Open Learning Spaces: Redefining School Design in a Post-Pandemic World. In Architectural Factors for Infection and Disease Control (pp. 245-257). Routledge.

ADDITIONAL READING

Douglas, J. (2006). *Building adaptation.* Routledge. doi:10.4324/9780080458519

Dovey, K., & Fisher, K. (2014). Designing for adaptation: The school as socio-spatial assemblage. *Journal of Architecture (London), 19*(1), 43–63. doi:10.1080/13602365.2014.882376

Dudek, M. (2000). *Architecture of Schools: The New Learning Environments.* Architectural Press.

Dudek, M. (2007). *A design manual schools and kindergartens.* Birkhäuser Verlag AG.

Grosvenor, I., & Burke, C. (2008). *School: Iconic Architecture.* Reaktion.

Plevoets, B., & Van Cleempoel, K. (2019). *Adaptive reuse of the built heritage: Concepts and cases of an emerging discipline.* Routledge. doi:10.4324/9781315161440

Pourebrahimi, M., Karimi Azeri, A. R., & Pour Ahmadi, M. (2023). A decision-making framework to prioritize existing buildings for adaptive reuse with a case study of school buildings in Guilan, Iran. *Architectural Science Review, 66*(3), 201–213. doi:10.1080/00038628.2023.2174067

Shabha, G. S. (1993). Flexibility and the design for change in school buildings. *Architectural Science Review, 36*(2), 87–96. doi:10.1080/00038628.1993.9696741

Woodman, K. (2016). Re-placing flexibility: Flexibility in learning spaces and learning. In K. Fisher (Ed.), *The Translational Design of Schools* (pp. 51–79). Sense Publishers. doi:10.1007/978-94-6300-364-3_3

Chapter 9

Digitalization of Education in a School on the Basis of Microsoft Teams Platform:
Effectiveness of Synchronous and Asynchronous Learning

Olena H. Hlazunova
National University of Life and Environmental Sciences of Ukraine, Ukraine

Valentyna I. Korolchuk
National University of Life and Environmental Sciences of Ukraine, Ukraine

Tetiana V. Voloshyna
National University of Life and Environmental Sciences of Ukraine, Ukraine

ABSTRACT

Educational institutions need a transformation in the methods and tools of organizing education. It is caused by technological evolution and external challenges, such as pandemics or wars. Effective organization of synchronous and asynchronous learning at school based on the Microsoft Teams platform is key to a successful transition to a distance (blended) format. The chapter presents modern approaches and methods of using Microsoft Teams to organize the learning process in synchronous and asynchronous modes. Models for the organization of synchronous and asynchronous interaction in schools are proposed. Criteria and indicators for evaluating the Microsoft Teams environment as a tool for synchronous and asynchronous interaction in modern conditions have been developed: functionality, reliability, effectiveness, interaction, availability, security and privacy, technical support, and assistance. The results of an experimental study evaluating the effectiveness of using Microsoft Teams for synchronous and asynchronous training are presented.

DOI: 10.4018/978-1-7998-3940-8.ch009

Copyright © 2024, IGI Global. Copying or distributing in print or electronic forms without written permission of IGI Global is prohibited.

THE DIGITAL EDUCATIONAL ENVIRONMENT ON THE MICROSOFT TEAMS-BASED PLATFORM

The onset of the pandemic has affected all spheres of life in the world, including education. Educational institutions have switched to distance and hybrid learning formats, and various activities have been conducted in synchronous and asynchronous modes using tools such as Zoom, Microsoft Teams, Skype, and Google Meet. Institutions were forced to switch from traditional face-to-face learning in the classroom to virtual learning using appropriate services and environments.

In today's environment, digital platforms of technology companies have become the main widespread option for organizing synchronous and asynchronous interaction between participants in the educational process during various types of learning activities, creating and delivering various types of content after the outbreak of the pandemic and the outbreak of war in Ukraine. During distance and hybrid learning, the teacher needs to conduct online classes in synchronous mode, according to the approved schedule, organize various types of learning activities using appropriate tools for video conferencing, etc. Microsoft Teams is a tool that allows you to schedule a meeting, conduct online classes, and provide access to various types of learning content. Gartner has recognized Microsoft Teams as a leader in unified communications as a service (UCaaS) and real-time meeting solutions (Herskowitz, 2021). This service offers a shared workspace for participants in the educational process, where they can schedule a meeting, establish communication and interaction, as well as collaborate on various types of educational content, and participate in various types of learning activities.

To support e-learning, a teacher needs to create an appropriate environment for the study group or flow of learners. Microsoft Teams has expanded the possibilities of distance learning, storing research data of teachers and learners, as well as providing access to the placement and use of various types of digital educational content.

Many researchers publish the results of their studies on the effectiveness of the use of Microsoft Teams in the educational process in such aspects:

- interaction and learning environment with using Microsoft Teams increases the motivation of learners to participate in online learning, as a result, it is easier for them to perceive educational material presented by a teacher (Rojabi, 2020);

- A. Sobaih6 et al. (2021) presented in their study the learning experience and feedback of learners on the use of Microsoft Teams as a single distance learning platform during COVID-19;
- D. Rizkana Hasanah and D. Novita Dewi (2022) stress the benefits of using Microsoft 365, as it ensures efficient work and increases productivity, which is undoubtedly very useful for teaching in conditions of remote tuition;
- the effectiveness of distance learning during the Covid-19 pandemic research by Mohammad Ali, Khan Mohammed Zaid, and Sudhir A. Shegunshi (2021) found that teachers and learners consider Zoom and Microsoft Teams effective tools for online learning;
- D. Karthikeyan (2020) analyzed Microsoft Teams from the perspective of undergraduate learners and showed that Microsoft Teams supports and easily fulfills the key aspects related to learning and acquiring knowledge from the perspective of learners, and also points to gray areas where user-friendliness can be improved when organizing different types of educational activities of participants in the educational process;
- the model of the business process of the project activity of education seekers using services for team management using the example of Microsoft Teams was created (Glazunova, Voloshyna, Gurzhii, Korolchuk, Parhomenko, Sayapina, Semyhinivska, 2020);
- the implementation of the Microsoft Teams service ensured the implementation of the concept of a single point of entry to the educational digital resources of the departments and interactive interaction of students with the teacher, monitoring of educational activity (Ivankova, Ryzhov, Androsov, 2020);
- features Microsoft Teams boost the platform's ability to assist English as a foreign language instructor in facilitating a better learning environment and engagement online. According to the findings of the survey, English teachers have very positive perceptions of the utilization of Microsoft Teams as a learning management system (Anh Thi Van Pham, 2023);
- Microsoft Teams supports synchronous and asynchronous communication which are essential for distance or remote learning (Poston, Apostel, Richardson, 2020);

- Zamora-Antuñano, et al. (2021) define Microsoft Teams as a communication platform accessed through an enterprise account with Microsoft 365 designed to improve communication and collaboration between work teams by creating custom spaces that include many different communication tools;
- use of Microsoft Teams enhance teaching and learning, teachers' ability to grade and monitor students' assignments, classroom organization, and teacher-student interaction (Alameri, Masadeh, Hamadallah, Ismail, Fakhouri, 2020);
- adoption of Microsoft Teams leads to smooth interaction between teacher and students and enhances effective classroom organization which consequently heightens the effectiveness of the teaching and learning process (Olugbade, Olurinola, 2021);
- students found Microsoft Teams to be extremely useful, and better than alternative platforms for key tasks including messaging, file sharing, and collaborative authoring (Buchal, Songsore, 2019);
- a strategy for the formation of digital competence was developed using a hybrid learning environment based on Microsoft 365 services (Hlazunova, Korolchuk, Voloshyna, 2022).

The digital environment of Microsoft Teams allows you to organize preparatory work and independent work, training, evaluation, and reflection of learners. In such an environment, teachers have the opportunity to plan learning activities, organize the selection of learning content in channels and tabs, organize learning activities of learners both independently and in teams, and learners can select and use digital learning content and use integrated digital tools for organization, planning and reflection training.

Teachers can organize a virtual learning environment by implementing specific strategies for each element of hybrid or distance learning according to Microsoft recommendations: learning environment, educational content, interactivity and interaction between participants in the educational process, assessment, and feedback (Figure 1).

The architecture of the digital educational environment for blended or distance learning based on Microsoft Teams in Figure 2 is presented. Microsoft Teams can be the basis for creating a digital learning environment. It allows the teacher to communicate with their learners during Teams calls, create and post educational content, and assignments, share resources, organize online classes, and promote effective interaction and collaboration.

Figure 1. Strategies for each element of hybrid (distance) learning

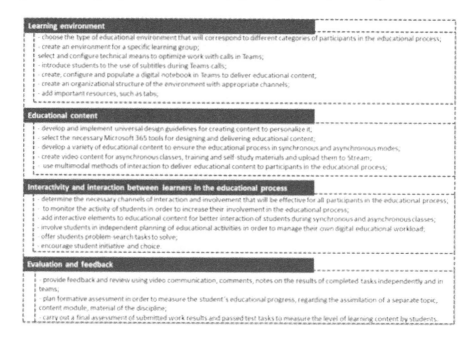

Figure 2. The architecture of the learning environment based on Microsoft Teams

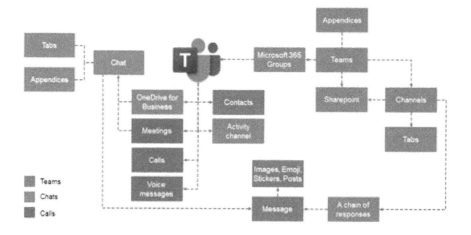

Teachers can create virtual classes for learners to work together. Also, teachers can join professional learning communities and communicate with colleagues, share experiences, and introduce new teaching technologies. Creating unified procedures for communication, creating and delivering

Digitalization of Education in a School on the Basis of Microsoft Teams

learning content, and organizing different types of learning activities in distance learning provides learners with a predictable structure of learning materials. This allows them to focus on learning rather than on selecting and learning new tools. To create such a digital environment for interaction between participants in the educational process, Teams offers to choose the type of teams that will cooperate in it at the stage of its creation. Teams in Teams are designed to bring together a group of people who collaborate to complete tasks. Teams can be created for a variety of learning purposes: to perform specific tasks (for example, implementing a team project), for discipline on an ongoing basis, to reflect all the learning material and tasks by the working curriculum, or for a specific structural unit to plan its activities. All presented types of teams allow to organization of a digital learning environment by educational goals.

1) "Staff"-type of team, which allows to create an environment for managing the organizational work of a school or its structural subdivision.
2) The "Professional Education Community" team type allows to creation of an environment for meeting a group of teachers to share experiences and collaborate, improving teaching skills and learner academic performance.
3) The "Class" team type is used for the management of educational activities, as it has a unique functionality for both teachers and learners. The use of this type of team allows teachers to organize an electronic course within the framework of studying a discipline or a separate educational module. It is possible to place educational content, to assign tasks to be performed and evaluate them, to plan and conduct online classes in the form of a meeting, organize group work of learners.
4) The "Other" team type is used for organizing a digital environment for study groups or small group activities on the implementation of professionally oriented projects.

If a teacher creates a team in Microsoft Teams, a Microsoft 365 group is automatically created with all its components: inbox, shared calendar, SharePoint document library, shared OneNote digital notebook, SharePoint group site, and planner (Figure 3).

Group members use the Inbox component to communicate via Outlook, as this folder contains the e-mail addresses of all registered participants within the educational institution, and it is also possible to additionally configure the receipt of messages from people outside a certain institution. The interaction of participants in the educational process during distance learning using Outlook and Teams services is presented in Figure 4.

Figure 3. Microsoft 365 group components and Teams cluster (Trilogy Solutions, Inc.)

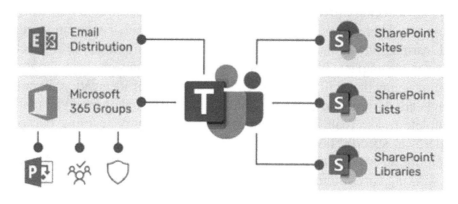

Figure 4. Educational interaction using Outlook and Teams

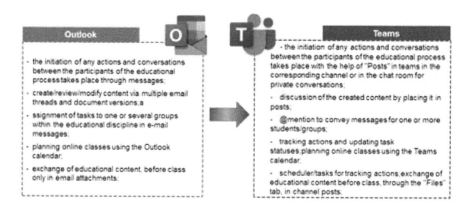

Participants in the educational process can use the Group calendar to plan meetings and group tasks. For storing and sharing files between group members, and delivering various types of educational content the SharePoint document library can be used. The teacher can deliver educational content to learners using a shared OneNote digital notebook. Learners can collect ideas in a joint OneNote digital notebook, and accumulate data for conducting various types of research. The SharePoint group site can be used as a central repository. Teachers can collect information and links to external resources, group content, and save various types of educational content. To assign and manage individual or project tasks for group members can be used the Planner service.

When creating a team channels can be automatically created. Channels can be added as a separate section in the team. In these channels, conversations can be organized by topics, modules, academic disciplines, collective projects, or any other category determined by the teacher. All team members can have open conversations in Teams channels, as they are open to all connected participants. Additional channels can be added manually by the user.

All teams include a "General" channel, which is used by any team as a space to post announcements, introduce members, and share a variety of content that is newly added or frequently used. This channel is available both for general use by all team members and only for viewing content, posts, and announcements posted by the teacher.

Teachers can organize collaboration environments for a separate category of learners, for example, a separate academic group studying a discipline or a team working on a group project. It is possible to organize a separate channel for each of them. In this way, learners can view both the content of the "General" channel and a separate channel within the team to which they are attached.

When transitioning to blended or distant learning, schools are forced to design learning environments and create virtual learning spaces for teachers and learners. Microsoft Teams is an ideal tool for ensuring continuity and flexibility of learning as a digital hub for a hybrid learning environment. Microsoft Teams allows teachers to communicate with learners through Teams calls, create and collect assignments, share resources, and facilitate learner collaboration, whether or not they are personally present in the classroom or connected remotely. The capabilities of Microsoft Teams tools for personal and virtual interaction between teachers and learners are listed in Table 1.

When transitioning to blended or distance learning, the teacher uses a virtual educational environment for synchronous and asynchronous learning and should evaluate its functionality and available tools for different educational activities, in particular, designing and delivering diverse educational content, taking into account synchronous or asynchronous interaction between teachers and learners.

Microsoft Teams is a powerful tool for digitalizing education, and organizing synchronous and asynchronous interaction between students in the learning process. With its help, teachers can easily organize video conferences, communicate with students through chats, conduct assessments, and collect feedback. Integration with other Microsoft 365 tools makes it easy to work together to complete assignments and share additional learning materials. Nevertheless, Microsoft Teams has some drawbacks for organizing synchronous and asynchronous learning. Microsoft Teams may require the adaptation of traditional teaching methods to effectively utilize its features, which can be challenging for instructors. Asynchronous learning can be challenging to ensure student engagement and participation in the absence of direct supervision. There is a possibility that teachers use Teams in different ways, which can create unpredictability for students and complicate the organization of the learning process. It is also important to take into account the technical requirements and capabilities of users, as well as to conduct effective training for teachers and students to maximize their ability to use this tool. With the need to learn the new interface and understand all the available features, Teams can be a powerful tool to support learning and collaboration in a remote format. The advantages and disadvantages of using Microsoft Teams for synchronous interaction during remote (hybrid) activities are shown in Table 2.

Table 1. Microsoft Teams: a digital hub for the hybrid learning environment

Personal Interaction	Virtual Interaction
Posts tab	
● daily interaction; ● talks; ● question-and-answer sessions;	● learners and teachers can engage in conversation and collaboration on the Posts tab; ● teachers can pose prompts or discussion questions for learners to engage with throughout the week; ● learners are encouraged to seek clarification on any aspect of the content or assigned task; ● a platform for peer-to-peer interaction and exchange of original thoughts is provided;
Teams Meetings (Raise your hand; Chat; Share Screen; Whiteboard)	
● conducting lectures; ● screen demonstration; ● teamwork; ● dialogue;	● remote classes and online consultations are facilitated through Microsoft Teams, where both learners and teachers can participate; ● learners have multiple channels for engagement within Teams. They can raise their hand virtually, utilize the chat function, or respond directly to the teacher's inquiries; ● visual aids are incorporated into the learning experience through features such as screen sharing and digital whiteboards, enriching content delivery for learners;
Files tab	
● provision of educational materials to learners; ● encouragement of collaboration between learners;	● teaching resources and read-only materials are readily available for both teachers and learners in the dedicated Learning Materials folder within the Files tab; ● Word, PowerPoint, Excel, and Visio files housed in the Files tab facilitate collaborative learning experiences. learners and teachers can co-edit documents, offer comments directly on the files, and engage in context-specific discussions through the built-in chat feature;

continues on following page

Digitalization of Education in a School on the Basis of Microsoft Teams

Table 1. Continued

Personal Interaction	Virtual Interaction
Class Notebook tab	
● dissemination of educational materials and supplementary electronic resources to learners is facilitated through a robust platform; ● a dedicated virtual workspace is offered to foster learner engagement and collaboration; ● strategies are implemented to encourage peer-to-peer learning and teamwork among learners;	● teachers can leverage the Notebook content library to curate a rich ecosystem of learning materials and resources for learners to explore and engage with. Additionally, they can create individualized workspaces tailored to specific assignments and projects; ● the Digital Notebook collaboration space fosters vibrant peer-to-peer learning experiences through joint project work and seamless resource sharing among learners; ● equipped with their workspace, learners gain autonomy in note-taking, learning material organization, and assignment completion, fostering an independent learning mindset;
Tasks tab	
● assignments are distributed to learners through a secure and efficient platform; ● completed works are uploaded to a designated repository for review and grading; ● feedback is provided on learner work to support their learning and development;	● teachers facilitate seamless assignment distribution and collection through the dedicated Tasks tab. They can easily attach OneNote pages for learners to populate with links and files, simplifying digital content integration; ● learners conveniently submit their completed work directly within the Task Response section. This enables efficient workflow and streamlined assessment for instructors; ● instructors retain flexibility in reviewing learner work. They can provide valuable feedback and allow for revisions based on feedback or proceed with final grading directly;
Grades tab	
● communication of task assessment outcomes;	● learners can access their assessment scores on the "Grades" tab; ● assessment results are available for learners on the "Grades" tab; ● the "Grades" tab provides learners with their assessment scores; ● learners can view their assessment performance on the "Grades" tab;
Channels	
● the development of educational centers and/or organizational materials and resources for learners;	● teachers can structure their virtual learning environment using channels, categorizing them by week, topic, or task; ● through channels, teachers can organize their virtual classrooms by week, topic, or activity, resulting in a well-defined course structure; ● by leveraging channels and arranging them by theme, timeframe, or assignment, teachers can establish a clear framework for their online courses;
Insights	
● Online activity monitoring	● a live dashboard keeps educators in the loop, presenting immediate feedback on learner involvement in discussions, meeting attendance, and completion of assignments
Microsoft Stream	
● lectures; demonstrations	● teachers can bring educational videos and demos to Teams seamlessly by uploading them to the Stream channel and adding them as a dedicated tab
Microsoft Forms	
● quizzes; surveys	● teachers can seamlessly weave Forms quizzes into their video lessons, enabling feedback collection through embedded surveys; ● educational videos and Forms quizzes go hand-in-hand. Teachers can easily connect videos to assessments or create video-inspired surveys with ease

Table 2. Advantages and disadvantages of using Microsoft Teams for synchronous collaboration

Advantages of Use	Disadvantages of Use
Organization of various types of online learning activities: - the ability to conduct classes in synchronous mode using video conferencing - the possibility of establishing communication between participants in the educational process (chatting, video meetings, etc.) - the ability to ensure interaction between participants in the educational process in real-time	*Unstable operation and dependence on Internet access:* - technical problems with the devices used for connection - unstable Internet, no or limited access to the Internet, which prevents synchronous interaction between participants in the educational process in real-time - technical problems with the functioning of the tool
Organization of effective cooperation: - the ability of participants in the educational process to collaborate on group projects using the joint creation, editing, and commenting of various types of documents - ability to track changes (availability of a version log) - the ability to increase productivity in the organization of various types of educational activities	*Inconvenience of use on mobile devices:* - limited functionality compared to the version on a computer - insufficient convenience of displaying different types of educational content
Providing access to various types of educational content: - possibility to distribute different types of educational content for online and offline study - ability to set up different access rights to educational content - ability to adapt learning content to the dominant learning style of students	*The need for skills to use the tool:* - insufficient knowledge of the tool and its functionality - insufficient level of practical skills in working with the tool - insufficient level of competence in using the tool to organize various types of educational activities
Organization of reflection and evaluation: - the ability to conduct reflection in real-time during various types of learning activities - the ability to test and evaluate students during synchronous interaction using special tools - the ability to demonstrate and track the progress of students	*Difficulties for teachers:* - significant time spent on creating and delivering different types of educational content to students - adaptation of traditional teaching methods - time spent on developing assessment elements ensuring student engagement

Organization of Synchronous Interaction in Microsoft Teams

Introducing Microsoft 365 services into the learning process and using them to conduct video meetings and record video content is one of the methods that can be used to increase the effectiveness of blended (distance) learning.

The components of online learning in the Microsoft Teams environment, which are determined in the research by I. Sarerusaenye Ismail, Shahrinaz Ismail (2020) to be the most useful in the learning process, are (1) a meeting after recording; (2) form of quizzes; (3) flexible window chat; and (4) generic links using Microsoft (MS) programs. These four components have a significant impact on the learning process of participants in the educational process, which can be divided into five stages: (1) easy-to-understand instructions; (2) time management; (3) no delay in submitting course evaluations; (4) improve learner understanding (self-study); and (5) an effective manner of discussion and interaction.

During synchronous interaction, teachers and learners are involved in simultaneous learning in a single digital learning environment by following these steps: planning online meetings, creating educational content for presentation, conducting training sessions, providing feedback, and conducting additional consultations (Figure 5).

Figure 5. Scheme of synchronous interaction organization

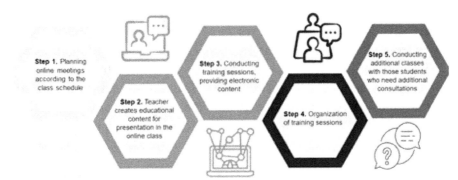

Step 1. Teachers Plan Online Meetings With Learners According to the Class Schedule

Microsoft Teams uses several ways to conduct online meetings, namely: meetings, webinars, and live broadcasts. A teacher who acts as an organizer during a webinar or broadcast has additional control over the event. During distance or blended learning, the teacher can choose different types of interaction between the participants of the educational process. Ensuring two-way interaction by organizing webinars, and managing questions and answers - broadcasts. These different types of interaction have different restrictions on the number and functionality of participants in these events. The main types of meetings that are recommended for different numbers of participants and the organization of interaction methods in between Microsoft Teams: Meetings, Webinar, and Events in real-time (Table 3).

Table 3. Main types of meetings organized in Microsoft Teams

Meeting Type	Interaction Type
Meetings (up to 10,000 participants)	- the first 1,000 participants are given the same educational process opportunities for organizing interactive interaction; - other participants are allowed to view
Webinar (up to 10,000 participants)	- if the number of participants does not exceed 1,000, they are provided with fully interactive opportunities; - customized interaction with the audience; - you can appoint the speakers
Events in real-time (up to 10,000 participants)	- broadcasting for large audiences; - moderated questions and answers for interaction with the audience; - you can specify organizers and speakers, including invited speakers; - support for extended capabilities of the working environment

Meetings hosted in Teams support audio and video and allow screencasting for an audience of up to 1,000 people and view-only for over 1,000 participants. Learners do not need to have a corporate account to join. Participants can join directly from the calendar invitation via the "Join Meeting" link or by voice call. The teacher can use this type of meeting in Teams to consult learners on performing laboratory (practical) work. The teacher can invite specialists from various fields of activity following the defined topic of the meeting, at which experienced specialists will act as speakers. The teacher, who will act as the organizer, can adjust the parameters of the meeting and determine which functions to enable. In addition to regularly scheduled meetings, participants can create meetings according to the study group channel, which allows all team members to see that meetings are taking place, join them, or use the chat for communication. Channel meetings allow the teacher to quickly invite all learners of the team to the scheduled meeting.

The teacher can organize Microsoft Teams video events. Events allow planning and conducting meetings that are broadcast to a large audience of learners on the Internet. Such video events can be created in two ways. The first way is to use the Teams tool and invite speakers and learner participants to join the discussion from their own devices. The second is to use an external hardware and software encoder via Microsoft Stream.

Another option for organizing meetings during distance learning with learners is holding webinars, where the role of each participant is clearly defined (Figure 6).

The main difference between webinars and Teams meetings is that webinars support pre-registration and collect participant activity data. A teacher can use Teams Webinars to host online meetings to share content, video, and audio content. Learners have the opportunity to view the offered educational content and, if necessary, ask the teacher questions. During the webinar, learners can actively participate in the discussion by reacting, posting messages in the chat, or answering survey questions. learners cannot share their audio, video, or other educational content.

Figure 6. Roles of participants during webinars

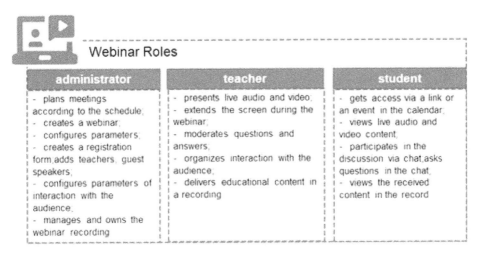

Teachers can arrange, plan, and deliver real-time events for large audiences. Such interaction with the audience during meetings involves managing questions and answers from engaged participants. The distribution of roles in events organized in real-time is shown in Figure 7. In Yammer or Microsoft Stream, broadcasts allow the teacher to schedule activities even for a larger number of participants.

Live events using Microsoft 365 take live video streaming to a new level. Such events encourage communication throughout the lifecycle of teacher-learner interactions before, during, and after such events. A teacher can create a live event wherever their audience, team, or community is with Microsoft Stream, Teams, or Yammer.

All participants in the educational process can collaborate in chat, phone calls, meetings, and live events. Learners can view the event live or recorded in Yammer, Teams, or Stream, and interact with teacher or guest speakers through a moderated Q&A or Yammer conversation. The process of holding events in real time using Microsoft 365 services is presented in Figure 8.

Figure 7. Distribution of roles in live events

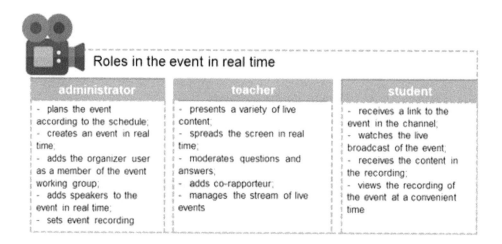

Figure 8. Conducting live events using Microsoft 365 services

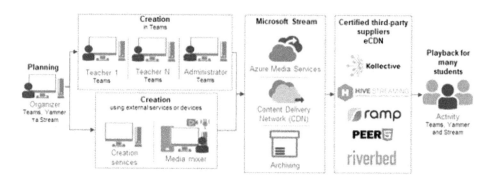

Before the beginning of the academic semester, an administrator or a teacher can personally plan a schedule in the Calendar service by adding a Teams meeting, inviting learners from the contact list, or organizing an educational environment in Teams to schedule a meeting directly in the team channel. The scheduled meeting in Teams will be posted both in the Calendar of each team member and in the posts of the channel.

A teacher can organize a meeting with learners through the Outlook service, namely a Call from Teams using three available connection options:

- download Teams (work or school account);
- continue in the same browser;

- open Teams (work or school account).

After creating or updating a live event, and adding presenters and learners (by adding team members), the meeting will appear in Outlook calendar and Teams calendar. In this case, the participants of the educational process have the opportunity to view both their own scheduled meetings and the meetings to which they have been invited, as well as react to such invitations: confirm or reject their participation in the meeting.

Teachers can send an invitation to the event via email to all participants. Learners who are attached to this channel will receive a notification in the channel posts. The teacher can also add notes to each training session in advance for learners to get acquainted with it.

Step 2. Teacher Creates Educational Content for Presentation in the Online Class

Creating and delivering different types of content to learners in synchronous learning involves using the interactive cloud service Microsoft Sway. The functionality of this service allows you to combine short videos (video content) without publishing them on additional resources, or gif animation in one tool, but you need to take into account the file size limitations.

Microsoft Sway can be used as a blended learning resource by using the ability to insert content from various resources (Figure 9).

Figure 9. Integration of different types of content into the Sway interactive service

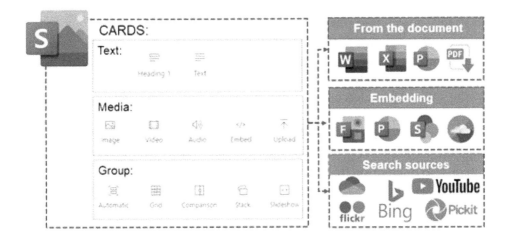

Using Microsoft Sway, teachers can quickly and easily create various learning materials (content) on all available devices. As a result, learners receive a web resource with learning content that is adapted to any device screen and can be accessed using a simple or visual link.

Microsoft Sway supports the ability to embed documents in various formats, such as Word, Excel, and PowerPoint, including individual charts and tables from Excel stored in OneDrive, or SharePoint by pasting the embed code for that document into Sway. This way, you can also integrate a wide variety of content (including images, maps, audio, and video) from multiple web resources into Sway.

Creating video content in the form of streaming video, which will be processed by learners in asynchronous mode, allows you to prepare educational video materials, screencasts, educational vlogs, video lectures, webinars, etc. Video streaming is the easiest and most affordable way to view video content hosted for learners in digital learning environments or on streaming services. Microsoft Stream service allows the sharing of already created video content in Teams, and Microsoft 365 applications such as SharePoint, Microsoft Teams, and Yammer. This tool is integrated with Microsoft 365 groups. It allows each group to have its own channel on which educational video content will be placed, which will further simplify content management among educational groups. Microsoft Stream uses embedded, encrypted video. Videos can be viewed easily and safely on any device and screens of any size, regardless of the location of each participant in the educational process. The use of streaming video in the educational process in combination with the capabilities of Microsoft Teams allows to organize the educational process according to the "flipped" learning model. Learners familiarize themselves with the content of the presented educational content at a convenient pace, from any device and place for a deeper study of the content. They follow interactive interaction with all sides of the educational process. Teachers can - increase learner involvement in the learning process using interactive elements, sound and feedback, joint work, and solving problem-oriented tasks. Using streaming video can also increase learners' motivation and organize mobile training effectively.

The combination of a series of videos, designed in the form of a video channel of a discipline, a separate topic, etc., with the possibilities of organizing interactive interaction through Microsoft Teams allows to consider complex practice-oriented tasks and to development of both learner autonomy and the expansion of opportunities to work in a team (group).

Step 3. Conduct Training Sessions

During various online meetings, the participants of the educational process can use the screen demonstration function and provide access to certain educational content. All the participants of the meeting can demonstrate their screen, a certain window, or an online whiteboard. During the demonstration, teachers can familiarize learners with the necessary educational material or organize its collective processing using an online board.

During such a video lesson, the teacher can share their desktop to discuss a certain material or present a PowerPoint presentation, a handwritten text on a OneNote digital notebook page, demonstrate the search for a solution to a given problem, or any other file on their device.

For reviewing the educational content that was shown to learners during the educational session, with the prior consent of the participants of the educational process, it can be recorded by the administrator or the teacher. Video recording will be available to all Teams members in chat posts.

When organizing live events, you can use any source for video, due to the capabilities of the Teams tool. To do this, you can use several means of capturing video content, one on each device used by the administrator or teachers, and change the camera, choosing the active video to broadcast in Teams to learners (Figure 10).

Figure 10. Creating a broadcast in Teams

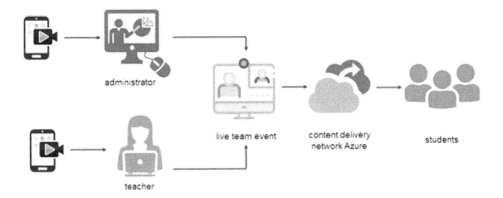

Moreover, if during an online meeting, a teacher needs to show data from an HDMI web feed that uses multiple desktops or other equipment fitted with multiple cameras and audio sources, then one environment in Teams will suffice: you either enter an event created in Teams using a capture card or key; or join directly via RTMP an event created using an external application or device (Figure 11).

Figure 11. Creating a broadcast using external devices

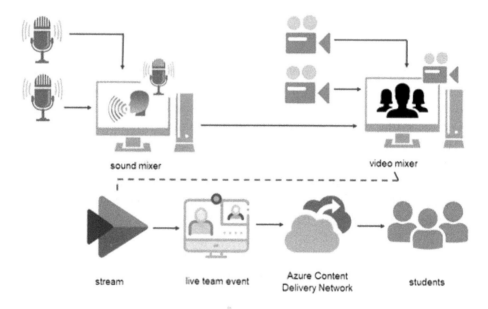

There are several options for participants in the educational process to join a meeting organized in Teams (Figure 12):

- as authorized users of Teams (includes desktop, mobile, and web clients of Teams);
- as unauthenticated anonymous users;
- through Communication Services user applications, when the users use the BYOI authentication model, i.e. create their own identity;
- through special Communication Services applications as Teams users using the Teams authentication model.

Digitalization of Education in a School on the Basis of Microsoft Teams

Figure 12. Ways to join a Teams meeting (Microsoft Learn, Interoperability do Teams, 2023)

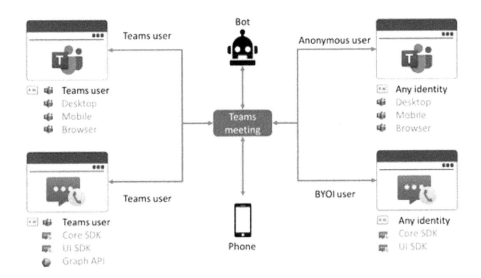

Using the identity authentication model, the Communication Services program allows Teams users to join calls with other users of this service from different devices (Figure 13).

Figure 13. Teams call schemes (Microsoft Learn, Interoperability do Teams, 2023)

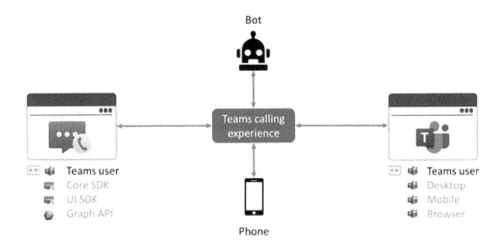

After the end of the video meeting, a report about its visit will be available in the channel posts. In such a report, the administrator and teacher can view both the number of participants who attended the meeting, the start and end times of the meeting, and information about the joined participants (personal data, time of joining, duration of connection, etc).

A teacher can create a meeting room and generate a password to share with all learners via email or invitation code. Regular classes can be lectures, lessons, discussions, and others. Each meeting room has different authorized access. Teachers can start uploading any documents and lecture slides a week before the exact date of the meeting in the publications section via Microsoft Teams. All learners who join the meeting room can download and view it at any time. Microsoft Teams offers an automatic recording function in the meeting function so that all session recordings can be directed to the learner's email (Ismail and others, 2020). The training scheme using Microsoft Teams is shown in Figure 14.

Figure 14. The study scheme using Microsoft Teams

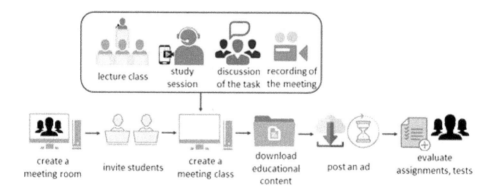

Interaction with the participants of the educational process is important for the effective organization of distance learning. The use of Microsoft 365 online services for conducting classes in the format of online meetings, and creating and delivering video content makes it easier to plan educational activities, ensure flexibility in learning, provide learners with access to the content of the curriculum, organize the educational process remotely and expands the possibilities of virtual interaction.

Step 4. Provide Feedback From Learners

During the *training sessions* learners perform and send tasks to the teacher, in turn, teachers provide feedback on completed tasks to learners and establish feedback with them with the help of online tools that are available in the educational environment Microsoft Teams.

Also, during online learning sessions, learners can show intermediate results of their work using the screen-sharing feature, and the teacher can provide comments and explanations.

Using the integrated Whiteboard service, the teacher can also organize learners' collective work in synchronous mode, tracking the activity and contribution of each learner.

Step 5. Conducting Additional Classes With Those Learners Who Need Additional Consultations

Providing additional instruction for learners who need extra help during synchronous learning is important to ensure that they understand the material and are successful. The teacher can develop an individual learning plan for each learner based on their needs. Prepare additional learning material to help learners better understand the topic of the lesson. For example, it can be an additional explanation, video, presentation, interactive tasks, or online resources for self-study.

Microsoft Teams provides a wide range of tools that allow teachers to interact with learners and provide additional learning material during synchronous learning.

Microsoft Teams Tools for Organizing Asynchronous Interaction Between Learners and Teachers

In the mode of asynchronous interaction, learners study a variety of educational content delivered to them according to a personally planned schedule, since teachers and learners do not study online every day. Teachers provide designed instructional material, presentations, video content, screencasts, and assignments that learners can review, work through, and complete relevant assignments within a specified period (a clear deadline is set for each assignment). During this time, learners can participate in various discussion panels, work together on various formats of documents for completing tasks, and view video instructions or relevant methodological recommendations. Teachers may host one or two online meetings per week where they address key issues around a specific topic and interact with the learning group as a whole. There can also be scheduled and configured virtual office hours for the teacher, where learners can get additional advice or ask questions about completing tasks for a certain week.

Accordingly, the asynchronous learning process is organized into 5 steps (Figure 15): planning and development of learning content, hosting and providing access to relevant resources, an independent study of the material by learners, communication and support from the teacher, evaluations, and feedback.

Figure 15. Scheme of organizing asynchronous interaction

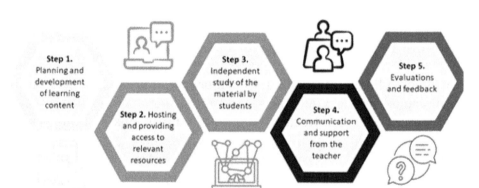

Step 1. Planning and Development of Different Types of Learning Content

It involves not only drawing up a calendar plan but also structuring the learning material, as well as choosing the type of content and the tool for creating it. Development of learning content such as video tutorials, interactive presentations, different types of tasks, etc.

Teachers can create different types of digital educational content. They should focus on the skills that the learners should acquire in the process of learning in various types of educational activities. The main capabilities of Microsoft 365 tools for creating and delivering such content in Teams are:

Digitalization of Education in a School on the Basis of Microsoft Teams

- instructions, methodological recommendations in Word, PowerPoint, Visio, or Excel can be delivered using OneDrive storage files or Teams tasks;
- online recording of live classes automatically stored in Stream with closed captions for learners to review and pause as needed if they are unable to attend a live lecture or laboratory (hands-on) according to the class schedule;
- pre-recording of training classes with embedded survey forms to organize interactive cooperation with learners;
- creation of interactive shared whiteboards for live interaction and the ability to export them in PDF formats for distribution to learners in a OneNote or Teams digital notebook.

To study the material during asynchronous classes, teachers can record video instructions and screencasts. To increase learner engagement, educators can add interactive content such as form-based quizzes or quizzes to a video by uploading it to Microsoft Stream.

In distance learning, educational materials are often presented to learners in the form of PowerPoint presentation files, which are convenient to use on various devices, including mobile ones.

Using the cloud version of the PowerPoint service, a teacher

- when creating educational content for classes, can add various content to PowerPoint and receive appropriate recommendations on slide design, work together with learners on the presentation by solving case studies, and add feedback;
- can place the educational material for the relevant subject as a set of files explaining the sequence of studying the material in a PowerPoint presentation file on their OneDrive storage or in a shared library. In doing so, the teacher can set up access parameters for viewing or editing the file, specifying an expiration date, or prohibiting downloads.
- by posting an online PowerPoint presentation in the Microsoft Teams channel, you can organize its collective processing or filling. When working collectively in such a file, the teacher can view the versions, as well as view the changes made by each learner;
- if it is necessary to create video content, the teacher can use PowerPoint to record a slideshow with video and voice explanations of the material presented on the slides. Exporting such a video allows you to get educational video content for further publication and distribution to learners in the Microsoft Stream cloud service. With the help of

Microsoft Forms tests and surveys, you can set up interactive forms of feedback and check the learning material, embed testing after watching video clips, etc.

- using pre-created surveys in the Forms service (for example, a feedback form) at the right time and place in the video, the teacher can embed the link in Microsoft Stream or directly into the presentation as a PowerPoint slide. The latter option involves creating the educational material as a .pptx file and distributing it through Microsoft Teams channels.

The use of various cloud services in the organization of learning activities, development of educational content, namely screen recording combined with teacher voice explanations, and the addition of interactivity, allows you to create a variety of educational video material that learners can view at their convenience and from any device.

Microsoft Stream uses built-in encryption and authenticated access to educational video content, which ensures that materials are shared only with a specific target audience (groups of learners within a particular subject).

Microsoft Stream training videos can be published using the educational institution's channels or in Microsoft 365, and separate channels can be created within a group. You can also share links to videos on SharePoint sites in custom web parts, in a closed Yammer social community, in Sway interactive presentations, or in OneDrive file storage. In Microsoft Teams, you can post a link to a single video or a video channel in a group channel, depending on the pedagogical purpose (for example, adding videos to a channel by different lecturers or guest speakers), followed by a group discussion using Microsoft Teams chat.

Step 2. Placement and Provision of Access to Relevant Resources

To make it easy for learners to access and search for the necessary materials, before posting content, it is necessary to create a unified learning environment in which participants in the educational process can learn asynchronously. Accordingly, after defining the course goals and creating the necessary content according to the curriculum, teachers need to focus on the channels of delivery of such content to learners, as well as develop interactive elements of interaction with it. In the created digital environment of Microsoft Teams, the teacher can plan and organize various tasks for learners, while receiving

Digitalization of Education in a School on the Basis of Microsoft Teams

data showing how the participants of the educational process interact in the group, including completed tasks, indicators of their activity, and evaluations.

Access to learning resources will ensure an effective and convenient learning process in this mode.

Precisely using Teams for online learning, educators can deliver classes by bringing conversations, content, and apps together in one digital environment. It allows teachers to organize learning more creatively by setting spaces for collaborative work in digital notebooks, to join other colleagues in professional learning communities, and to communicate with fellow teachers (Hasanah, Dewi, 2022). Digital notebook services such as OneNote, ClassNotebook, and StaffNotebook are integrated into this learning environment. The functionality of each of the services allows you to both post the necessary educational content and organize the interaction of participants in the educational process in an asynchronous mode.

In addition to the functionality already described, OneNote digital notebooks allow all participants in the educational process to organize digital notes conveniently, setting the necessary structure for their storage. To jointly develop new ideas, projects, and opportunities, or collectively design and develop educational content, teachers can use StaffNotebook, a digital notebook that effectively organizes collaboration and sets up a private workspace for each of them. The ClassNotebook digital notebook will allow you to design and develop an online course with a content library, which will distribute all the necessary educational content to learners, a workspace for each learner, check individual achievements, and organize an area for collaboration, discussion, and solving common problems. The types of digital notebooks and the possibilities of their use are shown in Figure 16.

Embedded OneNote Class Notebooks and end-to-end task management allow teachers to organize interactive educational sessions, to provide effective and timely feedback between all participants of the educational process. Class Notebook includes a content library for sharing learning content and teacher resources with learners, an interaction space where everyone can collaborate, and sections for learners to complete their assignments and for teachers to share feedback on their work. Using Class Notebook, the teacher can organize individual spaces for each learner to perform laboratory or practical work and control them, while feedback is provided both with a specific learner (chat) and with all Microsoft Teams tools that are learning, for example, during collective discussions.

In today's conditions, schools need solutions to ensure effective joint work, taking into account mobility. Such a solution can be the use of the OneNote Online digital notebook as a tab in the "General" channel of the Microsoft

Teams group. For learners who use the Teams environment based on OneNote Online in distance learning conditions the ability to communicate with all participants in the educational process, and plan tests or module tasks.

Figure 16. Microsoft 365 digital notebook capabilities

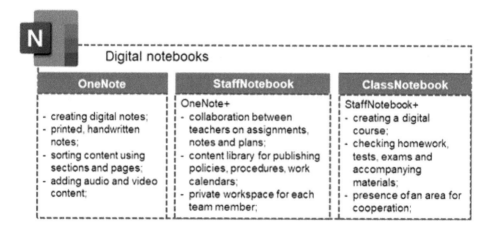

Staff Notebook provides a personal workspace for each teacher, a content library for storing public data, a space for collaboration with other users, and a space for managers. In a digital notebook, the teacher can place samples of visual materials with elements of video and audio content, instructions for using the tools of the Microsoft 365 cloud platform, examples of working with these services, etc., which apply to a certain educational institution, taking into account the latest innovations with the possibility of adding new one's educational materials.

Step 3. Independent Study of Educational Content by Learners

During independent learning in Microsoft Teams, learners have the opportunity to carry out learning activities following the curriculum developed by the teacher.

Each MS Team's team and channel has its repository that can be used not only to host learning content, but also to curate, co-create, and process it. In such a repository, all participants of the educational process can familiarize themselves with the content, post the results of their work, independently find useful materials and resources, and also work together on their creation.

Digitalization of Education in a School on the Basis of Microsoft Teams

This way you can create Word, Excel workbooks, PowerPoint presentations, OneNote, Visio drawings, and Excel forms.

For quick access to the content most often used by the learner in the educational process, it can be placed in the team or channel tabs. The learner can publish three types of educational content on the tab: educational content (OneNote, PowerPoint, Stream, content library, Wiki, SharePoint), areas for working together with other learners (Word, Excel, PowerPoint, Whiteboard), tools for tracking deadlines (Lists, Tasks with Planner and To-Do), etc.

Step 4. Communication and Support From the Teacher

Communication and teacher support are important aspects of asynchronous learning, as each participant in the educational process works on their own time. Teachers can send the necessary information to learners via email or the built-in messaging system in Teams.

In the Teams channel, you can add a tab for both collective filling and discussion, as well as personal tabs that all learners can work on independently. One tab that allows you to post learning materials for learners to read is the Wiki tab. Such a tab acts as an intelligent text editor, with the help of which not only teachers can place the necessary materials, but also learners can work together on different sections. In this way, the teacher can manage the work of learners in the Wiki in asynchronous mode and monitor their activities and, accordingly, the results of their activities.

To discuss posted materials or work results, the teacher and learners can start a conversation on each Wiki page in which to send a comment, emoji, sticker, request for material approval, attach a file, and also link to the video content posted in Stream. To maintain communication between all participants of the educational process in Teams, the chat on the Team Posts tab is key. The teacher can send short notes to learners, attach files with educational content, add links to external resources for additional processing of the material, @address mention, start a communication chain, or even react using emotions to quickly and effectively establish communication. In addition, the changes made in the command, such as an added tab or a posted task, will be automatically placed in the chat. The chat feature can be useful for asynchronous learning, as it allows you to send direct messages, use group chats, and channel conversations for all participants in the learning process. Chat also has a search function that allows you to track previous conversations by message type and keywords. Learners can save chat messages to return to them later and review the content presented. If there are learners in a study group who need one-on-one advice, the teacher can start a private chat with that learner at any time.

Using the Insights application in Microsoft Teams by a teacher, filling with data, it is possible to receive analytical information about learner activities, that allows analyzing joint work in groups, which are the main indicators of the interaction of participants in the educational process. The report on digital activities in Insights shows the activity of learners in Teams during a certain period, the educator can see the level of activity of each of the learners in the digital environment.

Data Mapping in Insights empowers learners to explore and share their feelings, fostering empathy and communication. This emotional awareness, backed by research, has proven to boost academic and behavioral performance for everyone involved, enriching both the learning journey.

The *Communication Data r*eport in Insights provides information about how learners communicate with each other, participate in conversations, post messages, and respond to each other. The progress status allows the teacher to track learners' progress, and assess where they need advice or reminders about deadlines. If the instructor selects a yellow or red segment of the chart, only those learners who still need to complete that stage of the assignment will be shown. The teacher can also select the name of any learner and send them a reminder message accordingly. When interacting with learners in the Team's digital environment, the teacher can track their communication activity, which provides information about the total number of posts, responses to them, reactions sent, and view such activity by day for a certain period of study: week, module, semester, etc.

A teacher, checking the completed tasks of the learners, has the opportunity to add files to the feedback to achieve constructive feedback and add a personal video with a comment. In such videos, the teacher can note the positive results of the task and offer learners to use the educational materials from the attached files to clarify the answers to the task. Such videos will be available for learners to view and download on their own devices and will be stored in the Microsoft Teams SharePoint site library. On the "Assessment" tab, the teacher evaluates learners' work and can further monitor the success of study groups in general or of each learner individually.

With the help of the Thanks function, the teacher can add badges to congratulate each of the learners of the study group on certain successes, and to express gratitude for active participation in completing tasks. Such achievements and corresponding thanks can be seen by all learners of the study group.

Another option for interaction in the educational process is quick questions and answers using a bot. In the Microsoft Teams ecosystem, all bots are built using the Microsoft Bot Framework. The Teams App Studio tool allows you to create a bot, deploy it, upload it, or send it to the Microsoft Teams team for review and addition to the store. It is also possible to organize the forwarding of messages between Telegram and Microsoft Teams using Power Automate, namely to set up a two-way exchange of text messages between these services. Thus, a message sent to the Telegram chat or several different chats will be sent to the Teams chat, in turn, messages from the Teams chat will be forwarded to Telegram. This is also relevant in modern conditions, as teachers and learners actively use Telegram channels for communication.

Step 5. Assessment and Feedback

Microsoft Teams offers a variety of ways to evaluate and collect feedback from learners in asynchronous learning. You can use various features in Teams to conduct assessments, surveys, or polls about learner perceptions of the various types of learning content you provide, its difficulty, and more.

Microsoft Class Teams allows teachers to collaborate with learners while integrating assignments, assessments, and various tools directly into the team they create. Such integration reduces the administrative burden on teachers and increases the efficiency and concentration of learners on the management of learners' educational activities.

One of the options for involving learners in class activity, as well as checking the level of mastery of the presented topic, are surveys, which can be created immediately in Teams using Pools or using the Forms service.

The Pools tool allows the instructor to create polls, quizzes, and word cloud polls both before and during the meeting, and to view learner responses in real-time. The teacher can create such a survey, send it in chat, and also show the results to learners.

Another option for conducting such learner surveys is the teacher's use of the Forms tool, which can also be attached to the team's posts.

Team tasks offer a comprehensive solution for managing practical training, formative assessment, and final evaluations. Teachers can create assignments, Q&A sessions, grades according to criteria, and more. They have granular control, setting instructions, deadlines, teams, evaluation criteria, and even adding resources for learner submissions.

An important element of task placement is the setting of their display parameters, which include the selection of a channel and calendars for task publication, as well as submission notifications upon completion of the due date. Tasks in the form of a test are created based on the Forms service, using which the teacher can create a new survey and attach an already created one.

Information about the created and posted tasks is published in the posts of the channel in the form of announcements and is also placed in the calendar of each learner. In this way, all learners can see changes in tasks, as well as plan their implementation, taking into account the deadlines set by the teacher.

For complex or group projects, learners must independently plan and break down the work into smaller steps. Tasks in Planner and To Do helps with this by letting you not only create tasks but also assign and track them.

Assignments and grades in Insights allow a teacher to identify support needs and track learner learning by reporting average and grade distribution, assignment status, and more. All the data received by the teacher can be organized at the level of the learning group, by individual learners, or based on tasks, which helps to adapt the strategy of teaching, creating, and delivering different types of content according to the learning styles of learners.

Figure 17. The structure of the educational hub based on Microsoft Teams

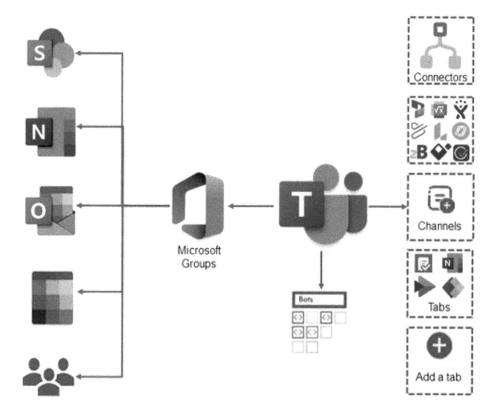

Digitalization of Education in a School on the Basis of Microsoft Teams

The created digital environment based on Microsoft Teams is also called a learning hub, which includes components of the Microsoft 365 group and created channels for managing learning activities. The structure of such an educational hub based on Microsoft Teams is presented in Figure 17.

Microsoft 365 groups allow you to integrate into MS Teams Hub such components for the communication of participants in the educational process as:

- email – for sending and receiving mail with members of the environment;
- joint calendar – for planning events related to participants of the educational process who cooperate in the same environment;
- SharePoint document library – a central place for storing educational content and sharing files;
- OneNote shared notebook – for collecting ideas, research data, and information;
- SharePoint group site – a central repository of information, links, and content related to educational activities;
- contacts – for managing the contacts of participants in the educational process.

Educational content is structured by distributing it to separate sections of the team (channels). The functionality of the channels can be expanded with the help of connectors and applications. Connectors act as an interface to integrate into the Teams learning hub of other services in or outside of the Microsoft Cloud and place them in channel tabs. In Teams, the teacher can integrate such support programs as Dynamics 365, Math, Jira, Powtoon, Nearpod, Lucidchart, zipBoard, Skillsoft Percipio, LMS365, Kahoot, Pear Deck, Polly or Flipgrid and others. Creating a distance learning environment, which is based on a dynamic and flexible tool, will help reduce cognitive load, and due to the integration of tools, ensure work with educational content in this environment throughout its life cycle. The teacher can also connect various add-ons for Microsoft 365 cloud services in the Teams environment, one of which is the Pear Deck add-on for PowerPoint, which allows you to make interaction with learners more active, in particular, turn static presentations into interactive ones.

Evaluating the Effectiveness of Microsoft Teams for Collaboration in Distance and Blended Learning

Based on the analysis of scientific works of scientists and our own experience of using Microsoft Teams for synchronous and asynchronous interaction in distance and hybrid learning, we conducted an expert assessment using a survey based on certain criteria and indicators. The presented performance evaluation indicators for each of the defined criteria (functionality, reliability, efficiency, interaction, accessibility, security and privacy, technical support, and assistance) are presented in Table 4.

Table 4. Evaluation of the effectiveness of Microsoft Teams for interaction in distance and hybrid learning

Indicators	Experts		
	Sum of Ranks	S	Weight
Functionality			
the ability to add up to 1000 participants to a video conference or more than 1000 to a webinar	319	17424	0,01
availability of tools for establishing interaction and cooperation (interactive whiteboard, screen sharing, various types of documents)	81	11236	0,08
availability of tools for establishing communication in synchronous and asynchronous modes	144	1849	0,06
Reliability			
reliability of the service functionality to ensure interaction in various types of learning activities	112	5625	0,07
correct operation of all available functions of the service, without delays or errors in real-time	287	10000	0,02
uninterrupted operation of the service (no technical problems and errors) in communication, interaction, and cooperation	225	1444	0,04
Performance			
efficiency of service functions to achieve the set tasks, their implementation in synchronous and asynchronous modes	173	196	0,05
the ability to interact with video and audio content to improve understanding and assimilation of educational material	57	16900	0,08
the ability to use an interactive whiteboard or other features of the service to distribute and interact with educational content	129	3364	0,06
Interaction			
availability of a function to organize and support interaction between participants in the educational process	31	326	0,09
the ability to set up different access rights for interacting with learning content	124	233	0,06
the ability to discuss and comment on available content in real-time	92	9025	0,07
Availability			
accessibility for users from both personal and corporate accounts	299	12544	0,02

continues on following page

Digitalization of Education in a School on the Basis of Microsoft Teams

Table 4. Continued

Indicators	Experts		
	Sum of Ranks	S	Weight
accessibility from different devices and operating systems	198	121	0,04
the ability to organize the interaction of participants in the educational process from any place and at any time	181	36	0,05
Security and privacy			
the ability to ensure the security and privacy of user data when exchanging data and content	249	3844	0,03
the ability to provide connection and data encryption	292	11025	0,02
the ability to control the level of access to video conferencing	176	121	0,05
the ability to control the level of access to documents distributed and filled by participants in the educational process	157	900	0,06
Technical support and assistance			
the ability to quickly get support and assistance in using the tool	267	6400	0,03
the ability to contact technical support in case of problems in real-time	317	16900	0,01
Total	3927	157529	1
Concordance ratio	0,71		
calculated	238,56		
tabular (k=20, α=0,05)	31,4		

A questionnaire was developed, in which teachers were asked to assess the degree of importance of each of the previously identified indicators of the environment in three categories separately. Experts assessed the degree of importance of the parameters by assigning them a rank number. The indicator given the highest score by an expert was assigned rank 1. To assess the level of coherence of experts' opinions, the concordance coefficient was calculated using the formula: , where, m – number of experts, n – number of factors. We calculated the weight of the parameters under consideration based on the obtained numbers of ranks.

When evaluating the effectiveness of Microsoft Teams tool support for interaction in distance and hybrid learning, it was determined that the availability of a function to organize and support interaction between participants in the educational process (0.09), the ability to interact with video and audio content to improve understanding and learning of educational material (0.08), and the availability of tools for establishing interaction and collaboration (interactive whiteboard, screen sharing, various types of documents) (0.08) are the most important factors. The concordance coefficient was 0.71, which indicates a high level of consistency in the experts' opinions.

The significance of the concordance coefficient was assessed using Pearson's correlation criterion. By comparing the calculated $\chi2$ (238,56) with the table value (31.4) for the number of degrees of freedom K=n-1=21-1=20 and at a given significance level of $\alpha=0.05$, we can conclude that W=0.71 is not a random value, and therefore the results are statistically significant.

The assessment of Microsoft Teams' capabilities for interaction in distance and hybrid learning shows that the availability of functions for organizing and supporting interaction between participants in the educational process (0.09), the ability to interact with video and audio content to improve understanding and learning of educational material (0.08), the availability of tools for establishing interaction and collaboration (interactive whiteboard, screen sharing, various types of documents) (0.08) are the most significant indicators when using this tool in distance and hybrid learning.

REFERENCES

Alameri, J., Masadeh, R., Hamadallah, E., Ismail, H. B., & Fakhouri, H. N. (2020). Students' Perceptions of E-learning platforms (Moodle, Microsoft Teams and Zoom platforms) in the University of Jordan Education and its Relation to self-study and Academic Achievement During COVID-19 pandemic. *Advanced Research & Studies Journal*, *11*(5), 21–33.

Ali, M., Zaid, K.M., & Shegunshi, S.A. (2021). Effective Online Teaching Tools and Comparison (MS Teams, Cisco WebEx Meetings, Zoom & Google Meet). *IJESC*, 28638-28650.

Buchal, R., & Songsore, E. (2019, June 9 -12). Using Microsoft Teams to support collaborative knowledge building in the context of sustainability assessment. In *Proc. 2019 Canadian Engineering Education Association (CEEA-ACEG19) Conf.* University of Ottawa.

Glazunova, O., Voloshyna, T., Gurzhii, A., Korolchuk, V., Parhomenko, O., Sayapina, T., & Semyhinivska, T. (2020). Cloud resources and services for the development of self-educational competence of future IT specialists: Business process modeling and examples of using. *CEUR Workshop Proceedings*.

Hasanah, D. R., & Dewi, D. N. (2022). Teachers Challenges and Strategies of Using Microsoft Office 365 in Teaching Online Classroom during Pandemic. *TEKNOSASTIK*, *20*(1), 57–65. doi:10.33365/ts.v20i1.1428

Herskowitz, N. (2021). *Gartner Recognises Microsoft as Leader in Unified Communications as a Service and Meetings Solutions.* Microsoft 365. https://www.microsoft.com/en-us/microsoft-365/blog/2021/10/2 5/gartner-recognizes-microsoft-as-leader-in-unified-communic ations-as-a-service-and-meetings-solutions/

Hlazunova, O., Korolchuk, V., & Voloshyna, T. (2022). The Strategy of Digital Competence Formation Using a Hybrid Learning Environment Based on Microsoft 365 Services: collective monograph. National University of Life and Environmental Sciences of Ukraine.

Ismail, S., & Ismail, S. (2020). Teaching Approach using Microsoft Teams: Case Study on Satisfaction versus Barriers in Online Learning Environment. *Journal of Physics: Conference Series*, *1874*(1), 012020. doi:10.1088/1742-6596/1874/1/012020

Ivankova, N., Ryzhov, O., & Androsov, O. (2020). Algorithm for the formation of a personal learning environment using structuring the educational space of the university based on Office365 and MS Teams services. *Electronic Scientific Professional Journal "Open Educational E-Environment of Modern University"*, *9*, 26-40. doi:10.28925/2414-0325.2020.9.3

Karthikeyan, D. (2020). Assessing the effectiveness of Microsoft Teams during COVID-19 for online learning: A learners' perceptive. *Efficacy of Microsoft Teams during COVID-19- Survey (London, England)*, 479–495.

Microsoft Learn. (2022). *Interoperabilidade do Teams.* https://learn.microsoft.c,om/pt-br/azure/communication-services/concepts/teams-interop

Microsoft Teams Planning & Migration Services. (n.d.). *Trilogy Solutions.* https://www.trilogysolutions.com/Services-Teams-Deployment.h tml

Olugbade, D., & Olurinola, O. (2021). Teachers' Perception of the Use of Microsoft Teams for Remote Learning in Southwestern Nigerian Schools. *African Journal of Teacher Education*, *10*(1), 265–281. doi:10.21083/ajote.v10i1.6645

Pham, A. T. V. (2023, Aug 15). Using Microsoft Teams as a Learning Management System in English Courses: A story from a Vocational School. *ICFET '23: Proceedings of the 2023 9th International Conference on Frontiers of Educational Technologies.* 10.1145/3606150.3606163

Poston, J., Apostel, S., & Richardson, K. (2020). Using Microsoft Teams to enhance engagement and learning with any class: It is fun and easy. *Pedagogicon Conference Proceedings*.

Rojabi, A. R. (2020). Exploring EFL learners' Perception of Online Learning via Microsoft Teams: University Level in Indonesia. *English Language Teaching Educational Journal, 3*(2), 163-173. https://files.eric.ed.gov/fulltext/EJ1268365.pdf

Sobaih, A. E. E., Salem, A. E., Hasanein, A. M., & Elnasr, A. E. A. (2021). Responses to COVID-19 in Higher Education: Learners' Learning Experience Using Microsoft Teams versus Social Network Sites. *Sustainability (Basel), 13*(18), 10036. doi:10.3390/su131810036

Zamora-Antuñano, M. A., Rodríguez-Reséndiz, J., Rodriguez Segura, L., Cruz Perez, M. A., Altamirano Corro, J. A., Paredes-Garcia, W. J., & Rodríguez-Reséndiz, H. (2021). Analysis of emergency remote education in COVID-19 crisis focused on the perception of the teachers. *Sustainability (Basel), 13*(7), 3820. doi:10.3390/su13073820

Compilation of References

Açıkalın, A. (1998). Üç rakamlı yıldönümlerine doğru. *Kuram ve Uygulamada Eğitim Yönetimi, 16*(16), 387–393.

Ahmad, M., & Dilshad, M. (2016). Leadership styles of public schools' heads in Punjab: A teachers' perspective. *Pakistan Journal of Social Sciences, 36*(2), 907–916.

Ainley, J., & Carstens, R. (2018). *Teaching and learning international survey (TALIS) 2018 conceptual framework*. OECD. doi:10.1787/799337c2-

Alameri, J., Masadeh, R., Hamadallah, E., Ismail, H. B., & Fakhouri, H. N. (2020). Students' Perceptions of E-learning platforms (Moodle, Microsoft Teams and Zoom platforms) in the University of Jordan Education and its Relation to self-study and Academic Achievement During COVID-19 pandemic. *Advanced Research & Studies Journal, 11*(5), 21–33.

Al-Delfi, A. M. H., & Salman, A. S. (2022). Investigating the Impact of Educational Space Design in Fostering Social Distancing: A Case Study of the University of Technology Buildings, Iraq. *Journal of Sustainable Architecture and Civil Engineering, 31*(2), 39–57. doi:10.5755/j01.sace.31.2.30746

Alexander, K., Clary-Muronda, V., Smith, J. M., & Ward, J. (2020). The relationship between past experience, empathy, and attitudes toward poverty. *The Journal of Nursing Education, 59*(3), 158–162. doi:10.3928/01484834-20200220-07 PMID:32130418

Ali, M., Zaid, K.M., & Shegunshi, S.A. (2021). Effective Online Teaching Tools and Comparison (MS Teams, Cisco WebEx Meetings, Zoom & Google Meet). *IJESC*, 28638-28650.

Allensworth, E., Bryk, A. S., Easton, J. Q., Luppescu, S., & Sebring, P. B. (2010). *Organizing schools for improvement: Lessons from Chicago*. University of Chicago Press.

Altunay, E., Arlı, D., & Yalçınkaya, M. (2012). İlköğretim okullarında değişim yönetimine ilişkin nitel bir çalışma. *Kuram ve Uygulamada Eğitim Bilimleri, 12*(2), 713–730.

Álvarez Vega, E., & Grande de Prado, M. (2023). Early Childhood Care in Spain before the lockdown. *Encyclopedia, 3*(4), 1306–1319. doi:10.3390/encyclopedia3040093

Amburgey, T. L., Dawn, K., & Barnett, W. P. (1993). The dynamics of organizational change and failure. *Administrative Science Quarterly, 38*(1), 51–73. doi:10.2307/2393254

Andree, A., Darling-Hammond, L., Orphanos, S., Richardson, N., & Wei, R. C. (2009). *Professional learning in the learning profession: A status report on teacher development in the United States and abroad*. National Staff Development Council.

Anne E. Casey Foundation. (2023). *Child poverty*. Retrieved from https://www.aecf.org/topics/child-poverty

Argon, T., & Özçelik, N. (2008). İlköğretim okulu yöneticilerinin değişimi yönetme yeterlikleri. *Mehmet Akif Ersoy Üniversitesi Eğitim Fakültesi Dergisi, 8*(16), 70–89.

Asal, V., & Blake, E. L. (2006). Creating simulations for political science education. *Journal of Political Science Education, 2*(1), 1–18. doi:10.1080/15512160500484119

Asher, J. J. (1968). The Total Physical Response Method for Second Language Learning. *The Clearing House: A Journal of Educational Strategies, Issues and Ideas*.

Atkinson, N. D. (1972). *Teaching Rhodesian: A history of educational policy in Rhodesia*. Longman.

Ausubel, D., Novak, J. D., & Hanesian, H. (1968). *Psicología educativa, un punto de vista cognoscitivo* [Educational psychology, a cognitive point of view]. Trillas.

Azer, S. A., Guerrero, A. P., & Walsh, A. (2013). Enhancing learning approaches: Practical tips for students and teachers. *Medical Teacher, 35*(6), 433–443. doi:10.3109/0142159X.2013.775413 PMID:23496121

Azieh, S. (2021). The Critical Period Hypothesis in Second Language Acquisition: A Review of the Literature. *International Journal of Research in Humanities and Social Studies, 8*(4), 20–26. doi:10.22259/2694-629.0804001

Baird, M. D., Hamilton, L. S., Pane, J. F., & Steiner, E. D. (2015). *Continued progress: Promising evidence on personalized learning*. RAND Corporation.

Ballesta, J., & Guardiola, P. (2021). *Escuela, familia y medios de comunicación* [School, family, and mass media means]. CCS.

Bangs, J., & Frost, D. (2012). *Teacher self-efficacy, voice and leadership: Towards a policy framework for educational international: A report on an international survey of the views of teachers and teacher union officials*. Education International Research Institute.

Barron, B., Cook-Harvey, C., Darling-Hammond, L., Flook, L., & Osher, D. (2020). Implications for educational practice of the science of learning and development. *Applied Developmental Science, 24*(2), 97–140. doi:10.1080/10888691.2018.1537791

Bass, B. M. (1998). The ethics of transformational leadership. In J. B. Ciulla (Ed.), *Ethics: The heart of leadership* (pp. 169–192). Praeger.

Bass, B. M., & Avolio, B. J. (1993). Transformational Leadership: A response to critiques. In M. M. Chemers & R. Ayman (Eds.), *Leadership theory and research: Perspectives and directions*. Academic Press Inc.

Compilation of References

Bassett, P. G. (1997). The theory and practice of adaptive reuse. In *Proceedings of the 1997 symposium on Software reusability* (pp. 2-9). 10.1145/258366.258371

Bates, C. C., & Morgan, D. N. (2018). Seven elements of effective professional development. *The Reading Teacher*, *71*(5), 623–626. doi:10.1002/trtr.1674

Baxter, P., & Jack, S. (2008). Qualitative case study methodology: Study design and implementation for novice researchers. *Qualitative Report*, *13*(4), 544–559.

Ben Ouahi, M., Lamri, D., Hassouni, T., Ibrahmi, A., & Mehdi, E. (2022). Science teachers' views on the use and effectiveness of interactive simulations in science teaching and learning. *International Journal of Instruction*, *15*(1), 277–292. doi:10.29333/iji.2022.15116a

Bennett, N., Harvey, J. A., Wise, C., & Woods, P. A. (2003). *Distributed Leadership: A Desk Study*. www.ncsl.org.uk/literaturereviews

Bennett, N., Crawford, M., & Riches, C. (Eds.). (1992). *Managing change in education: individual and organizational perspectives*. Sage.

Bennie, K., & Newstead, K. (1999). *Obstacles to implementing a new curriculum*. In M.J. Smit, & A.S. Jordaan (Eds.), *Proceedings of the National Subject Didactics Symposium* (pp.150-157). Stellenbosch: University of Stellenbosch.

Beycioğlu, K., & Aslan, M. (2010). Okul gelişiminde temel dinamik olarak değişim ve yenileşme: Okul yöneticileri ve öğretmenlerin rolleri. *Yüzüncü Yıl Üniversitesi Eğitim Fakültesi Dergisi*, *7*(1), 153–173.

Birasnav, M., Gantasala, S. B., Gantasala, V. P., & Singh, A. (2022). Total quality leadership and organizational innovativeness: The role of social capital development in American schools. *Benchmarking: An International Journal*. doi:10.1108/BIJ-08-2021-0470

Blase, J., & Blase, J. (1999). Implementation of shared governance for instructional improvement: Principals' perspectives. *Journal of Educational Administration*, *37*(5), 476–500. doi:10.1108/09578239910288450

Bliese, P. D. (2000). Within-group agreement, non-independence, and reliability: Implications for data aggregation and analysis. In *Multilevel theory, research, and methods in organizations: Foundations, extensions, and new directions* (pp. 349–381). Jossey-Bass/Wiley.

Blomeke, S., Nilsen, T., & Scherer, R. (2021). School innovativeness is associated with enhanced teacher collaboration, innovative classroom practices, and job satisfaction. *Journal of Educational Psychology*, *113*(8), 1645-1667. doi:10.1037/edu0000668

Boet, S., Bould, M. D., Layat Burn, C., & Reeves, S. (2014). Twelve tips for a successful interprofessional team-based high-fidelity simulation education session. *Medical Teacher*, *36*(10), 853–857. doi:10.3109/0142159X.2014.923558 PMID:25023765

Bolden, R. (2011). Distributed leadership in organizations: A review of theory and research. *International Journal of Management Reviews*, *13*(3), 251–269. doi:10.1111/j.1468-2370.2011.00306.x

Boss, S., & Krauss, J. (2017). *Reinventing project-based learning: Your field guide to real-world projects in the digital age*. ISTE.

Brauckmann, S., Pashiardis, P., & Ärlestig, H. (2020). Bringing context and educational leadership together: fostering the professional development of school principals. *Professional Development in Education*.

Broer, M., Bai, Y., & Fonseca, F. (2019). A Review of the Literature on Socioeconomic Status and Educational Achievement. In *Socioeconomic Inequality and Educational Outcomes. IEA Research for Education* (Vol. 5). Springer. doi:10.1007/978-3-030-11991-1_2

Bruner, J. (1984). *Acción, pensamiento y lenguaje* [Action, thought, and language]. Alianza Psicología.

Bryce, T. G., & Blown, E. J. (2023). Ausubel's meaningful learning re-visited. *Current Psychology (New Brunswick, N.J.)*, 1–21. doi:10.1007/s12144-023-04440-4 PMID:37359615

Bryk, A. S., Gomez, L. M., & Grunow, A. (2015). *Getting ideas into action: Building networked improvement communities in education*. Carnegie Foundation for the Advancement of Teaching.

Bryk, A. S., & Schneider, B. (2002). *Trust in schools: A core resource for improvement*. Russell Sage Foundation.

Buchal, R., & Songsore, E. (2019, June 9 -12). Using Microsoft Teams to support collaborative knowledge building in the context of sustainability assessment. In *Proc. 2019 Canadian Engineering Education Association (CEEA-ACEG19) Conf.* University of Ottawa.

Bullen, P. A., & Love, P. E. (2010). The rhetoric of adaptive reuse or reality of demolition: Views from the field. *Cities (London, England)*, *27*(4), 215–224. doi:10.1016/j.cities.2009.12.005

Bullen, P., & Love, P. (2011). Factors influencing the adaptive re-use of buildings. *Journal of Engineering. Design and Technology*, *9*(1), 32–46. doi:10.1108/17260531111121459

Burns, J. M. (1978). *Leadership*. Harper & Row.

Buske, R. (2018). The principal as a key actor in promoting teachers' innovativeness–analyzing the innovativeness of teaching staff with variance-based partial least square modeling. *School Effectiveness and School Improvement*, *29*(2), 262–284. doi:10.1080/09243453.2018.1427606

Buyukgoze, H., Caliskan, O., & Gümüş, S. (2022). Linking distributed leadership with collective teacher innovativeness: The mediating roles of job satisfaction and professional collaboration. *Educational Management Administration & Leadership*. doi:10.1177/17411432221130879

Compilation of References

Cahyani, I., & Yulindaria, L. (2018). The effectiveness of Discovery learning model in improving students' fiction writing. *Indonesian Journal of Learning and Instruction*, *1*(1), 37–45. doi:10.25134/ijli.v1i1.1281

Calabrese, R. L., & Shoho, A. (2000). Recating educational administration programs as learning organizations. *The Journal of Educational Management*, *14*(5), 210–218.

Cameron, E., & Green, M. (2004). *Making sense of change management*. Kogan Page.

Can, A. (2018). *SPSS ile bilimsel araştırma sürecinde nicel veri analizi*. Pegem.

Carnall, C. A. (2007). *Managing change in organizations* (5th ed.). Prentice Hall.

Castro Zubizarreta, A. (2020). La participación de los niños en el marco de la educación infantil: algunas coordenadas para su práctica efectiva. [Children's participation in Early Childhood Education: some coordinates for its effective practice]. *Dossier Revista del IICE*, *49*, 43–58. doi:10.34096/iice.n48

Ceyhan, E., & Summak, M. S. (1999). Haşlanmış kurbağa ve değişim yönetimi. *Kuram ve Uygulamada Eğitim Yönetimi*, *20*, 521–544.

Chernikova, O., Heitzmann, N., Stadler, M., Holzberger, D., Seidel, T., & Fischer, F. (2020, August). Simulation-based learning in higher education: A meta-analysis. *Review of Educational Research*, *90*(4), 499–541. doi:10.3102/0034654320933544

Choi, M., & Wendy, E. A. (2011). Individual readiness for organizational change and its implications for human resource and organization development. *Human Resource Development Review*, *10*(1), 46–73. doi:10.1177/1534484310384957

Ciriza Mendivil, C.D., Mendioroz, A., Hernández de la Cruz, J.M. & Rivero, P. (2023). Cultural Heritage in Early Childhood Education: An analysis of the perception of future teachers. *Social and Education History*, 1-18. https://doi.org/ doi:10.17583/hse.120525

Clarke, S., & O'Donoghue, T. (2017). Educational Leadership and Context: A Rendering of an Inseparable Relationship. *British Journal of Educational Studies*, *65*(2), 167–182. doi:10.1080/00071005.2016.1199772

Çoban, Ö., & Atasoy, R. (2020). Relationship between distributed leadership, teacher collaboration and organizational innovativeness. *International Journal of Evaluation and Research in Education*, *9*(4), 903-911. doi:10.11591/ijere.v9i4.20679

Coburn, C. E. (2003). Rethinking scale: Moving beyond numbers to deep and lasting change. *Educational Researcher*, *32*(6), 3–12. doi:10.3102/0013189X032006003

Cochran-Smith, M., & Villegas, A. M. (2016). Preparing teachers for diversity and high-poverty schools: A research-based perspective. In Lampert & Burnett (Eds.), Teacher Educa tion for high poverty schools (pp. 9-31). Springer International Publishing. doi:10.1007/978-3-319-22059-8_2

Coltart, D. (2012). Education for employment,developing skills for vocation. Speech at the African Innovation Summit, Cape Town, South Africa.

Compton, R. A., & Wagner, T. (2012). *Creating innovators: The making of young people who will change the world.* Scribner.

Creamer, J., Shrider, E. A., Burns, K., & Chen, F. (2021). U.S. Census Bureau, Current Population Reports, P60-277, Poverty in the United States. U.S. Government Publishing Office.

Creasy, T. (2007) *Defining management.* https://www.pro-sci.com/change-management/thught-leadership-library/change-management-definition

Crowe, S., Cresswell, K., Robertson, A., Huby, G., Avery, A., & Sheikh, A. (2011). The case study approach. *BMC Medical Research Methodology, 11*(1), 100. doi:10.1186/1471-2288-11-100 PMID:21707982

Daft, R. L. (2016). Organisational theory and design (12th ed.). South-Western Cengage Learning.

Dalinger, T., Thomas, K., Stansberry, S., & Xiu, Y. (2019). A mixed reality simulation offers strategic practice for pre-service teachers. *Computers & Education, 144.* Doi-10.1016/j.compedu.2019.103696.

Darling-Hammond, L., Hyler, M. E., & Gardner, M. (2017). Effective teacher professional development. Learning Policy Enstitute. http://creativecommons.org/licenses/by-nc/4.0/ doi:10.54300/122.311

Darling-Hammond, L. (2000). Teacher quality and student achievement: A review of state policy evidence. *Education Policy Analysis Archives, 8*(1), 1–44. doi:10.14507/epaa.v8n1.2000

Darling-Hammond, L. (2019). *A license to teach: Building a profession for 21st century schools.* Routledge. doi:10.4324/9780429039928

Day, C., Sammons, P., Hopkins, D., Harris, A., Leithwood, K., Gu, Q., & Brown, F. (2010). *10 Strong claims about successful school leadership.* https://assets.publishing.service.gov.uk/ government/uploads/system/uploads/attachment_data/ file/327938/10-strong-claims-about-successful-school-leadership.pdf

De Jager, P. (2001, May- June). Resistance to change: A new view of an old problem. *The Futurist, 53*(3), 24–27.

De Paris, S., Lacerda Lopes, C. N., & Neuenfeldt, A. Junior. (2022). The use of an analytic hierarchy process to evaluate the flexibility and adaptability in architecture. *Archnet-IJAR: International Journal of Architectural Research, 16*(1), 26–45. doi:10.1108/ARCH-05-2021-0148

Demers, C. (2007). *Organizational change theories: A synthesis.* Sage.

Deming, W. E. (1996). *Out of the crisis.* MIT Press.

Compilation of References

Deniz, U., & Demirkasimoğlu, N. (2022). The cultural dimensions of Pakistani teachers' zone of acceptance regarding school principals' authority. *International Journal of Leadership in Education*, 1–30. doi:10.1080/13603124.2022.2076288

Dent, E. B., & Goldberg, S. G. (1999). Challenging "resistance to change". *The Journal of Applied Behavioral Science*, *35*(1), 25–41. doi:10.1177/0021886399351003

Desimone, L. M. (2009). Improving impact studies of teachers' professional development: Toward better conceptualizations and measures. *Educational Researcher*, *38*(3), 181–199. doi:10.3102/0013189X08331140

Drucker, P. F. (2001) *Management Challenges for the 21ˢᵗ Century*. Harper Business.

DuFour, R., & Eaker, R. (2008). *Professional learning communities at work: Best practices for enhancing student achievement*. Solution Tree.

DuFour, R., & Marzano, R. J. (2011). *Leadership for differentiating schools & classrooms*. Solution Tree Press.

Durlak, J. A., Dymnicki, A. B., Pachan, M., Payton, J., Schellinger, K. B., Taylor, R. D., & Weissberg, R. P. (2008). *The positive impact of social and emotional learning for kindergarten to eighth-grade students: Findings from three scientific reviews. In Collaborative for Academic, Social, and Emotional Learning*. CASEL.

Durlak, J. A., Dymnicki, A. B., Schellinger, K. B., Taylor, R. D., & Weissberg, R. P. (2011). The impact of enhancing students' social and emotional learning: A meta-analysis of school-based universal interventions. *Child Development*, *82*(1), 405–432. doi:10.1111/j.1467-8624.2010.01564.x PMID:21291449

Dweck, C. S. (2006). *Mindset: The new psychology of success*. Random House.

Ellis, S. & Dick, P. (2003). Introduction to organizational behaviour. London: Mc Graw Hill.

Elmore, R. (2000). *Building a New Structure for School Leadership*. Albert Shanker Institute.

Erdoğan, İ. (2012). Eğitimde değişim yönetimi (3rd ed.). Ankara: Pegem Akademi.

Fadel, C., & Trilling, B. (2009). *21st century skills: Learning for life in our times*. Jossey-Bass.

Fernandes, V. (2019a). Disrupting the norm: implementing educational business improvement models in Pakistani public-private school partnerships. In V. Fernandes, & P. W. K. Chan (Eds.), Asia Pacific Education: Leadership, Governance and Administration (1st ed., pp. 187-204). Information Age Publishing.

Fernandes, V. (2019b). From the middle out: empowering transformational leadership capability of middle-level school leaders. In R. Chowdhury (Ed.), *Transformation and Empowerment through Education: Reconstructing our Relationship with Education* (1st ed., pp. 195–213). Routledge.

Fernandes, V. (2019c). The Case for Effectively Using Existing Business Improvement Models in Australian Schools. In A. Normore, L. Long, & M. Javidi (Eds.), *Handbook of Research on Effective Communication, Leadership, and Conflict Resolution* (2nd ed., pp. 98–124). Information Science.

Fernandes, V., Khan, F., Raj, L., & Thenabadu, S. (2019). Persistent inequality in female education within South Asia: comparing Bangladesh, India, Pakistan and Sri Lanka. In R. Chowdhury & L. K. Yazdanpanah (Eds.), *Identity, Equity and Social Justice in Asia Pacific Education* (1st ed., pp. 44–65). Monash University Publishing.

Fidan, T., & Balci, A. (2017). Managing schools as complex adaptive systems: A strategic perspective. *International Electronic Journal of Elementary Education, 10*(1), 11–26. doi:10.26822/iejee.2017131883

Fleta, T. (2019). *From research on child L2 acquisition of English to classroom practice*. De Gruyter.

Fletcher, J. K., & Kaufer, K. (2003). Shared leadership: Paradox and possibility. In C. J. Pearce & C. Conger (Eds.), Shared leadership: Reframing the how and whys of leadership (pp. 21–47). Sage.

Floyd, P. (2002). *Organizational change*. Capstone.

Fontenot, K., Semega, J., & Kollar, M. (2018). *Income and poverty in the United States: 2017.* U.S. Census Bureau, 60–263. Retrieved from https://www.census.gov/content/dam/Census/library/publications/2018/demo/p60-263.pdf

Frederking, B. (2005). Simulations and student learning. *Journal of Political Science Education, 1*(3), 385–93. doi:10.1080/15512160500261236

Fullan, M. (2001). *Leading in a culture of change*. Jossey-Bass.

Fullan, M. (2001). *New meaning of educational change* (3rd ed.). Teachers College Press. doi:10.4324/9780203986561

Fullan, M. (2006). *Change theory: A force for school improvement*. Centre for Strategic Education.

Fullan, M. (2007). *The new meaning of educational change* (4th ed.). Teachers College Press.

Fullan, M. (2014). *Leading in a Culture of Change*. John Wiley & Sons.

Fullan, M. (2016). *Indelible leadership: Always leave them learning*. Corwin Press.

Fullan, M., & Hargreaves, A. (1998). *What's worth fighting for out there?* Teachers College Press.

Fullan, M., & Hargreaves, A. (2012). *Professional capital: Transforming teaching in every school*. Teachers College Press.

Gabler, C. B., Richey, R. G. Jr, & Rapp, A. (2015). Developing an eco-capability through environmental orientation and organizational innovativeness. *Industrial Marketing Management, 45*, 151–161. doi:10.1016/j.indmarman.2015.02.014

Compilation of References

García Grau, P., Martínez Rico, G., McWilliam, R., & Grau, D. (2019). Early Intervention and Family-Centeredness in Spain: Description and Profile of Professional Practices. *Topics in Early Childhood Special Education, 41*(2), 160–172. doi:10.1177/0271121419846332

García Mayo, M. P. (2021). Research on EFL learning by young children in Spain. *Language Teaching for Young Learners, 3*(2), 181–188. doi:10.1075/ltyl.00022.edi

Gay, G. (2010). *Culturally responsive teaching: Theory, research, and practice.* Teachers College Press.

George, D., & Mallery, M. (2003). *Using SPSS for Windows step by step: A simple guide and reference.* Allyn & Bacon.

George, J. M., & Gareth, R. (2002). *Understanding and managing organizational behaviour.* Pearson.

Glazunova, O., Voloshyna, T., Gurzhii, A., Korolchuk, V., Parhomenko, O., Sayapina, T., & Semyhinivska, T. (2020). Cloud resources and services for the development of self-educational competence of future IT specialists: Business process modeling and examples of using. *CEUR Workshop Proceedings.*

Gökçe, F. (2004). Okulda değişmenin yönetimi. *Eğitim Fakültesi Dergisi, 17*(2), 211–226.

Gopalakrishnan, S., & Damanpour, F. (1997). A review of innovation research in economics, sociology and technology management. *Omega, 25*(1), 15-28. doi:10.1016/S0305-0483(96)00043-6

Gordon, D. (2005). Indicators of poverty & hunger. *Expert Group meeting on youth development indicators, 1*(1), 12–14. https://www.un.org/esa/socdev/unyin/documents/ydiDavidGordon_poverty.pdf

Gorski, P. C. (2008a). The myth of the 'culture of poverty.' *Educational Leadership, 65*(7), 32. https://www.researchgate.net/publication/228620924

Gorski, P. C. (2008b). Peddling poverty for profit: Elements of oppression in Ruby Payne's framework. *Equity & Excellence in Education, 41*(1), 130–148. doi:10.1080/10665680701761854

Gosen, J., & Washbush, J. (2004). A review of scholarship on assessing experiential learning effectiveness. *Simulation & Gaming, 35*(2), 270–293. doi:10.1177/1046878104263544

Graciela Torcomian, C. (2020). Infancia y aprendizaje: Experiencias de niña en la escuela pública [Childhood and Learning: Girl's experiences in a public school]. *Acta Académica, 66*, 67–90.

Graetz, F. (2000). Strategic change leadership. *Management Decision, 38*(8), 550–562. doi:10.1108/00251740010378282

Grobman, G. M. (2005). Complexity Theory: A New Way to Look at Organisational Change. *Public Administration Quarterly, 29*(3/4), 350–382.

Gronn, P. (2000). Distributed Properties: A New Architecture for Leadership. *Educational Management & Administration, 28*(3), 317–338. doi:10.1177/0263211X000283006

Gül, H. (2006). Çevresel baskı gruplarının okulun genel işleyişine etkileri (Kocaeli-İzmit örneği). *Kocaeli Üniversitesi Sosyal Bilimler Enstitüsü Dergisi, 11*(1), 71–84.

Güzelci, O. Z., Alaçam, S., Kocabay, S., & Akkuyu, E. (2020). Adaptability of primary and middle schools to post-pandemic reuse - a discussion in the context of flexibility. *Journal of Design Studio, 2*(2), 5–22. doi:10.46474/jds.776665

Güzelci, O. Z., Şen Bayram, A. K., Alaçam, S., Güzelci, H., Akkuyu, E. I., & Şencan, İ. (2021). Design tactics for enhancing the adaptability of primary and middle schools to the new needs of postpandemic reuse. *Archnet-IJAR: International Journal of Architectural Research, 15*(1), 148–166. doi:10.1108/ARCH-10-2020-0237

Hair, N. L., Hanson, J. L., Wolfe, B. L., & Pollak, S. D. (2015). Association of child poverty, brain development, and academic achievement. *JAMA Pediatrics, 169*(9), 822–829. doi:10.1001/jamapediatrics.2015.1475 PMID:26192216

Hajimia, H., Sarjit Singh, M. K., & Mariandavan Chethiyar, S. D. (2020). Second Language Acquisition: Krashen's Monitor Model and the Natural Approach. *People International Journal of Social Science, 6*(3), 87–99. doi:10.20319/pijss.2020.63.8799

Hakonsson, D. D., Klaas, P., & Carrol, T. N. (2012). The structural properties of sustainable, continuous change: Achieving reliability through flexibility. *The Journal of Applied Behavioral Science, 49*(2), 179–205. doi:10.1177/0021886312464520

Hall, G. E., & Hord, S. M. (2015). *Implementing Change: Patterns, Principles, and Potholes.* Pearson.

Hallinger, P. (2011). Leadership for learning: Lessons from 40 years of empirical research. *Journal of Educational Administration, 49*(2), 125–142. doi:10.1108/09578231111116699

Hallinger, P., & Heck, R. H. (1996). Reassessing the principal's role in school effectiveness: A review of empirical research, 1980-1995. *Educational Administration Quarterly, 32*(1), 5-44. doi:10.1177/0013161X96032001002

Han, P., Wang, L., Song, Y., & Zheng, X. (2022). Designing for the post-pandemic era: Trends, focuses, and strategies learned from architectural competitions based on a text analysis. *Frontiers in Public Health, 10*, 1084562. doi:10.3389/fpubh.2022.1084562 PMID:36568743

Hansen, M. T., & Birkinshaw, J. (2007). The innovation value chain. *Harvard Business Review, 85*(6), 121-130. PMID:17580654

Hargreaves, A. (2007). *Teaching in the knowledge society: Education in the age of insecurity.* Teachers College Press.

Hargreaves, A., & Shirley, D. (2009). *The fourth way: The inspiring future for educational change.* Corwin Press. doi:10.4135/9781452219523

Harris, A. (2009). Distributed leadership, studies in educational leadership. Springer.

Compilation of References

Harris, A. (2004). Distributed leadership and school improvement: Leading or misleading? *Educational Management Administration & Leadership*, *32*(1), 11–24. doi:10.1177/1741143204039297

Harris, A. (2008). Distributed leadership: According to the evidence. *Journal of Educational Administration*, *46*(2), 172–188. doi:10.1108/09578230810863253

Harris, A. (2013). *Distributed leadership matters: Perspectives, practicalities, and potential.* Corwin Press. doi:10.4324/9780203607909

Harris, A., Hopkins, D., & Leithwood, K. (2008). *Seven strong claims about successful school leadership*. National College for School Leadership.

Harris, A., & Muijs, D. (2004). *Improving schools through teacher leadership*. Open University Press.

Hasanah, D. R., & Dewi, D. N. (2022). Teachers Challenges and Strategies of Using Microsoft Office 365 in Teaching Online Classroom during Pandemic. *TEKNOSASTIK*, *20*(1), 57–65. doi:10.33365/ts.v20i1.1428

Hasnain, H., & Mohseni, F. (2018, March). Creative ideation and adaptive reuse: A solution to sustainable urban heritage conservation. *IOP Conference Series. Earth and Environmental Science*, *126*(1), 012075. doi:10.1088/1755-1315/126/1/012075

Hattie, J. (2009). *A synthesis of over 800 meta-analyses relating to achievement*. Routledge., doi:10.4324/9780203887332

Heck, R. H., & Hallinger, P. (2010). Testing a longitudinal model of distributed leadership effects on school improvement. *The Leadership Quarterly*, *21*(5), 867-885. doi:10.1016/j.leaqua.2010.07.013

Heckscher, C. (2007). *The collaborative enterprise: Managing speed and complexity in knowledge-based businesses*. Yale Books.

Heidrich, O., Kamara, J., Maltese, S., Re Cecconi, F., & Dejaco, M. C. (2017). A critical review of the developments in building adaptability. *International Journal of Building Pathology and Adaptation*, *35*(4), 284–303. doi:10.1108/IJBPA-03-2017-0018

Heifetz, R. A., & Linsky, M. (2004). A survival guide for leaders. *Harvard Business Review*, *82*(6), 65–74. PMID:12048995

Hellriegel, D., & Slocum, J. W. Jr. (2011). *Organizational behaviour*. Cengage Learning.

Herskowitz, N. (2021). *Gartner Recognises Microsoft as Leader in Unified Communications as a Service and Meetings Solutions*. Microsoft 365. https://www.microsoft.com/en-us/microsoft-365/blog/2021/10/25/gartner-recognizes-microsoft-as-leader-in-unified-communications-as-a-service-and-meetings-solutions/

Highfield, D., & Gorse, C. (2009). *Refurbishment and upgrading of buildings*. Routledge. doi:10.4324/9780203879160

Hlazunova, O., Korolchuk, V., & Voloshyna, T. (2022). The Strategy of Digital Competence Formation Using a Hybrid Learning Environment Based on Microsoft 365 Services: collective monograph. National University of Life and Environmental Sciences of Ukraine.

Hohepa, M., Lloyd, C., & Robinson, V. M. (2019). *School leadership and student outcomes: Identifying what works and why*. Australian Council for Educational Research (ACER).

Holland, J. H. (1998). *Emergence: From chaos to order*. Oxford University Press. doi:10.1093/oso/9780198504092.001.0001

Hopkins, D., & Jackson, D. (2002). Building the capacity for leading and learning. In A. Harris, C. Day, D. Hadfield, D. Hopkins, A. Hargreaves, & C. Chapman (Eds.), *Effective Leadership for school improvement* (pp. 84–105). Routledge.

Howard, T. C., & Rodriguez-Scheel, A. (2016). Difficult dialogues about race and poverty in teacher preparation. In Lampert & Burnett (Eds.), Teacher Education for High Schools (pp. 53–72). Springer. doi:10.1007/978-3-319-22059-8_4

Huberman, M. (1998). Teacher careers and school improvement. *Journal of Curriculum Studies*, *20*(2), 119–132. doi:10.1080/00220272.1988.11070783

Huerta Guerra, M. C., Cárdenas González, V. G., & León, D. (2020). Practices to foster learning to learn in Early Childhood Education. *Aula Abierta*, *49*(3), 261–278. doi:10.17811/rifie.49.3.2020.261-278

Hurley, R. F., Hult, G. T. M., & Knight, G. A. (2005). Innovativeness and capacity to innovate in a complexity of firm-level relationships: A response to Woodside (2004). *Industrial Marketing Management*, *34*(3), 281–283. doi:10.1016/j.indmarman.2004.07.006

Iandoli, L., & Zollo, G. (2008). *Organisational Cognition and Learning: Building Systems for the Learning Organization*. Idea Group Incorporated.

Ijla, A., & Broström, T. (2015). The sustainable viability of adaptive reuse of historic buildings: The experiences of two world heritage old cities; Bethlehem in Palestine and Visby in Sweden. *International Invention Journal of Arts and Social Sciences*, *2*(4), 52–66.

Institute of Social and Policy Sciences (ISAPS). (2010). *Private Sector Education in Pakistan – Mapping and Musing*. ISAPS.

Isaac, S. (2007). *Survey of ICT and education in Africa: Zimbabwe country report*. Retrieved from http/:www.infodev.org

İsmailoğlu, S., & Kulak Torun, E. (2022). Spatial Organization of Interior Design Studios in the Normalization Process. *Turkish Online Journal of Design Art and Communication*, *12*(2), 497–514. doi:10.7456/11202100/019

Ismail, S., & Ismail, S. (2020). Teaching Approach using Microsoft Teams: Case Study on Satisfaction versus Barriers in Online Learning Environment. *Journal of Physics: Conference Series*, *1874*(1), 012020. doi:10.1088/1742-6596/1874/1/012020

Compilation of References

Ivankova, N., Ryzhov, O., & Androsov, O. (2020). Algorithm for the formation of a personal learning environment using structuring the educational space of the university based on Office365 and MS Teams services. *Electronic Scientific Professional Journal "Open Educational E-Environment of Modern University", 9*, 26-40. doi:10.28925/2414-0325.2020.9.3

Jantzi, D., & Leithwood, K. (2005). A review of transformational school leadership research 1996–2005. *Leadership and Policy in Schools, 4*(3), 177–199. doi:10.1080/15700760500244769

Jehan, M. (2015). *High school principals' ethical decisions: A comparative analysis of sociocultural and structural contexts in Pakistan and United States* (Doctoral dissertation).

Johns, E. A. (1973). *The sociology of organizational change.* Pergamon.

Jønsson, T., Unterrainer, C., Jeppesen, H. J., & Jain, A. K. (2016). Measuring distributed leadership agency in a hospital context: Development and validation of a new scale. *Journal of Health Organization and Management, 30*(6), 908–926. doi:10.1108/JHOM-05-2015-0068 PMID:27681024

Karip, E. (2005). Daha bir eğitimde değişim tartışmaları. *Kuram ve Uygulamada Eğitim Yönetimi, 42*, 149–150.

Karthikeyan, D. (2020). Assessing the effectiveness of Microsoft Teams during COVID-19 for online learning: A learners' perceptive. *Efficacy of Microsoft Teams during COVID-19- Survey (London, England)*, 479–495.

Kaufman, D., & Ireland, A. (2016). Enhancing teacher education with simulations. *TechTrends, 60*(3), 260–267. doi:10.1007/s11528-016-0049-0

Keshavarz, N., Nutbeam, D., Rowling, R., & Khavarpour, F. (2010). Schools as social complex adaptive systems: A new way to understand the challenges of introducing the health promoting schools concept. *Social Science & Medicine, 70*(10), 1467–1474. doi:10.1016/j.socscimed.2010.01.034 PMID:20207059

Kezar, A. J. (2001). *Understanding and facilitating organizational change in the 21st century: Recent research and conceptualizations. ASHE-ERIC Hiigher Education Reports, 28(4)*.

Koh, G. A., & Askell-Williams, H. (2021). Sustainable school-improvement in complex adaptive systems: A scoping review. *Review of Education, 9*(1), 281–314. doi:10.1002/rev3.3246

Kotter, J. P. (1995, Mar.). Leading change: why transformation efforts fail. Harvard Business Review, 59-67.

Kotter, J. P. (1996). Leading change. Harvard Business School Press.

Kotter, J. P. (2006). *Leading change.* Harvard Business School Press.

Kotter, J. P., & Schlesinger, L. A. (1979). Choosing strategies for change. *Harvard Business Review, 57*(2), 106–114. PMID:10240501

Krashen, S. (1985). *The input hypothesis: issues and implications.* Longman.

Krashen, S. D., & Terrel, T. D. (1983). *The Natural Approach. Language acquisition in the classroom*. Pergamon.

Kurtz, C. F., & Snowden, D. J. (2003). The new dynamics of strategy: Sense-making in a complex and complicated world. *IBM Systems Journal, 42*(3), 462–483. doi:10.1147/sj.423.0462

Kutz, M. (2008). Toward a conceptual model of contextual intelligence. *Kravis Leadership Institute Leadership Review, 8*(8), 1–31.

Ladson-Billings, G. (2004). The Dreamkeepers: Successful Teachers of African American Children. *The Journal of Negro Education, 63*(4), 530–543.

Ladson-Billings, G. (2006). From the achievement gap to the education debt: Understanding achievement in U.S. schools. *Educational Researcher, 35*(7), 3–12. doi:10.3102/0013189X035007003

Langley, G. J., Moen, R. D., Nolan, K. M., Nolan, T. W., Norman, C. L., & Provost, L. P. (2009). *The improvement guide: A practical approach to enhancing organizational performance* (2nd ed.). Jossey-Bass.

Lanz, F., & Pendlebury, J. (2022). Adaptive reuse: A critical review. *Journal of Architecture (London), 27*(2-3), 441–462. doi:10.1080/13602365.2022.2105381

Lee, P. C., Lin, C. T., & Kang, H. H. (2016). The influence of open innovative teaching approach toward student satisfaction: A case of Si-Men Primary School. *Quality & Quantity, 50*(2), 491–507. doi:10.1007/s11135-015-0160-x

Lee, W., & Krayer, K. J. (2004). An integrated model for organizational change. *Performance Improvement, 43*(7), 22–26. doi:10.1002/pfi.4140430708

Leithwood, K., & Jantzi, D. (2000). The effects of different sources of leadership on student engagement in school. In K. Riley & K. Louis (Eds.), *Leadership for Change and School Reform* (pp. 50–66). Routledge.

Leithwood, K., & Louis, K. S. (2011). *Learning from leadership: Investigating the links to improved student learning*. Center for Applied Research and Educational Improvement.

Leithwood, K., Mascall, B., & Strauss, T. (2009). *Distributed leadership according to the evidence*. Routledge. doi:10.4324/9780203868539

Leithwood, K., Mascall, B., Strauss, T., Sacks, R., Memon, N., & Yashkina, A. (2007). Distributing Leadership to Make Schools Smarter: Taking the Ego Out of the System. *Leadership and Policy in Schools, 6*(1), 37–67. doi:10.1080/15700760601091267

Leithwood, K., & Riehl, C. (2003). *What we know about successful school leadership*. Laboratory for Student Success, Temple University.

Lenneberg, E. H. (1967). *Fundamentos biológicos del lenguaje* [Biological foundations of language]. Alianza Editorial.

Compilation of References

Leonard, H. S. (2013). The history and current status of organizational and systems change. In The Wiley-Blackwell handbook of the psychology of leadership, change, and organizational development (pp. 239-366). Oxford: John Wiley ve Sons, Ltd.

León, M., Palomene, D., Ibañez, Z., Martínez Virto, L., & Gabaldón Estevan, D. (2022). Between equal opportunities and work-life balance: Balancing institutional design in early years education in Spain. *Papers. Revista de Psicología*, *107*(3), 1–22.

Lewin, K. (1958). Group decisions and social change. In E. E. Maccobby, T.M. Newcomb, & E. L. Hartley (Eds.), Readings in Social Psychology (pp. 330-344). New York: Holt, Rinehart & Winston.

Lindqvist, S. M., & Reeves, S. (2007). Facilitators' perceptions of delivering interprofessional education: A qualitative study. *Medical Teacher*, *29*(4), 403–405. doi:10.1080/01421590701509662 PMID:17786761

Liu, X. (2023). The effect of affective filter hypothesis on college students' English writing teaching and its enlightment. *OAlib*, *10*(9), 1–9. doi:10.4236/oalib1110671

Li, Y., Zhao, L., Huang, J., & Law, A. (2021). Research frameworks, methodologies, and assessment methods concerning the adaptive reuse of architectural heritage: A review. *Built Heritage*, *5*(1), 1–19. doi:10.1186/s43238-021-00025-x

Lo Faro, A., & Miceli, A. (2019). Sustainable strategies for the adaptive reuse of religious heritage: A social opportunity. *Buildings*, *9*(10), 211. doi:10.3390/buildings9100211

López, G., & Rodríguez, M. T. (2019). *Reflexiones y propuestas para trabajar la lengua inglesa en Educación Infantil* [Reflections and proposal for working on the English language in Early Childhood Education]. Servicio de Publicaciones de la Universidad de Oviedo.

Louis, K. S., & Miles, M. B. (1990). *Improving the urban high school: What works and why*. Teachers College Press.

Lumpkin, G. T., & Dess, G. G. (1996). Clarifying the entrepreneurial orientation construct and linking it to performance. *Academy of Management Review*, *21*(1), 135–172. doi:10.2307/258632

Majoni, C. (2014). *Challenges facing university education in Zimbabwe*. Academic Press.

Mansoor, Z. (2015). The paradigm shift: Leadership challenges in the public sector schools in Pakistan. *Journal of Education and Practice*, *6*(19), 203–211.

Marishane, R. N. (2020). *Contextual intelligence in school leadership: Responding to the dynamics of change*. Brill Sense. doi:10.1163/9789004431263

Matas, A. (2019). El inglés y las nuevas tecnologías: motivar el alumnado con destrezas que conoce [English and new technologies: motivating students with skills they know]. *Cuadernos de Educación y desarrollo, 1*(7), 1-5.

Matsumoto, M., Mendoza, K., Gómez-Estern, B. M., & Poveda, D. (2023). Early Childhood Education and Care in Spain: A model to understand diverse conditions in the current system. *C&E, Cultura y Educación, 35*(1), 588–621. doi:10.1080/11356405.2023.2200593

Matuchniak, T., & Warschauer, M. (2010). New technology and digital worlds: Analyzing evidence of equity in access, use, and outcomes. *Review of Research in Education, 34*(1), 179–225. doi:10.3102/0091732X09349791

McFarland, J., Hussar, B., Zhang, J., Wang, X., Wang, K., Hein, S., Diliberti, M., Forrest Cataldi, E., Bullock Mann, F., & Barmer, A. (2019). *The Condition of Education 2019 (NCES 2019-144)*. U.S. Department of Education. Retrieved from https://nces.ed.gov/pubsearch/pubsinfo. asp?pubid=2019144

Merryfield, M. M. (2002). *Teaching about international conflicts: Education, theory, and practice*. Peter Lang.

Microsoft Learn. (2022). *Interoperabilidade do Teams*. https://learn.microsoft.c,om/pt-br/azure/communication-services/concepts/teams-interop

Microsoft Teams Planning & Migration Services. (n.d.). *Trilogy Solutions*. https://www.trilogysolutions.com/Services-Teams-Deployment.html

Midgley, S., Stringfield, S., & Wayman, J. C. (2007). *Leadership for data-based decision making: Collaborative educator teams*. Teachers College Press.

Miller, J., & Vick, C. (2022). An examination of the community action poverty simulation in rural education. *Alabama Journal of Educational Leadership, 9,* 133–141. https://eric.ed.gov/?id=EJ1362044

Missouri Association for Community Action Network (CAN). (2018). *Community Action Poverty Simulation*. Retrieved from https://www.communityaction.org/povertysimulations/

Moya, A. J., & Albentosa, J. I. (2023). *La enseñanza de la lengua extranjera en la Educación Infantil* [Foreign Language Teaching in Early Childhood Education]. Servicio de Publicaciones de la Universidad de Castilla-La Mancha.

Mubika, K., & Bukaliya, R. (2011). Teacher competence in ICT: Implications for Computer Education in Zimbabwean secondary schools. *International Journal of Social Sciences and Education, 1*.

Murado, J. L. (2020). *Didáctica del Inglés en Educación Infantil. Métodos para la enseñanza y el aprendizaje de la lengua inglesa* [Didactics of English in Early Childhood Education: Methods for Teaching and Learning the English Language]. Ideaspropias.

Mur, O. (2018). *Cómo introducir el inglés en Educación Infantil* [How to introduce English in Early Childhood Education]. Editorial Escuela Española.

Compilation of References

Nadeem, M., Arif, S., & Asghar, M. Z. (2019). Effectiveness of the teacher appraisal system in public higher secondary schools of Punjab (Pakistan). *Global Regional Review*, *4*(1), 194–208. doi:10.31703/grr.2019(IV-I).22

Nasreen, A., & Odhiambo, G. (2018). The Continuous Professional Development of School Principals: Current Practices in Pakistan. *Bulletin of Education and Research*, *40*(1), 259–280.

National Center for Education Statistics (NCES). (2015). *U.S. Department of Education report on the "condition of education 2015."* NCES. Retrieved from https://nces.ed.gov/programs/coe/pdf/Indicator_CCE/coe_cce_2015_05.pdf

National Center for Education Statistics (NCES). (2017). *U.S. Department of Education report on the "condition of education 2017."* NCES. Retrieved from https://nces.ed.gov/pubs2017/2017144.pdf

Navaratnam, K. K. (1997). Quality management in education must be a never-ending journey. In K. Watson, C. Modgil & S. Modgil (Eds.), Educational Dilemmas: Debate and Diversity, Vol. VI: Quality in Education. Cassell.

Nawab, A., & Asad, M. M. (2020). Leadership practices of school principal through a distributed leadership lens: A case study of a secondary school in urban Pakistan. *International Journal of Public Leadership*, *16*(4), 411–422. doi:10.1108/IJPL-08-2020-0081

Newmann, F. M., & Wehlage, G. G. (1995). *Successful School Restructuring: A Report to the Public and Educators*. American Federation of Teachers. https://eric.ed.gov/?id=ED387925

Niederhauser, D. S., Howard, S. K., Voogt, J., Agyei, D. D., Laferriere, T., Tondeur, J., & Cox, M. J. (2018). Sustainability and scalability in educational technology initiatives: Research-informed practice. *Technology. Knowledge and Learning*, *23*(3), 507–523. doi:10.1007/s10758-018-9382-z

Niesche, R. (2016). Perpetuating Inequality in Education: Valuing Purpose over Process in Educational Leadership. The Dark Side of Leadership: Identifying and Overcoming Unethical Practice in Organisations. *Advances in Educational Administration*, *26*, 235–252. doi:10.1108/S1479-366020160000026013

Ni, G., Xu, H., Cui, Q., Qiao, Y., Zhang, Z., Li, H., & Hickey, P. J. (2021). Influence mechanism of organizational flexibility on enterprise competitiveness: The mediating role of organizational innovation. *Sustainability (Basel)*, *13*(1), 1-23. doi:10.3390/su13010176

Noone, J., Sideras, S., Gubrud-Howe, P., Voss, H., & Mathews, L. R. (2012). Influence of a poverty simulation on nursing student attitudes toward poverty. *The Journal of Nursing Education*, *51*(11), 616–622. doi:10.3928/01484834-20120914-01 PMID:22978272

Northrup, A., Berro, E., Spang, C., & Brown, M. (2020). Teaching poverty: Evaluation of two simulated poverty teaching interventions with undergraduate nursing students. *The Journal of Nursing Education*, *59*(2), 83–87. doi:10.3928/01484834-20200122-05 PMID:32003847

Nurutdinova, A. R., Perchatkina, V. G., Zubkova, G. I., & Galeeva, F. T. (2016). Innovative teaching practice: Traditional and alternative methods (Challenges and Implications). *Science Education*, *11*(10), 3807–3819.

Nyagura, L. M. (1991b). *Multilevel Investigations of Effects of schools, Classrooms and Student Characteristics on Academic Achievements in Zimbabwe Primary Schools.* Human Resources Research Center: University of Zimbabwe.

Nyaruwata, L. T., Thomas, K. A., & Ndawi, V. E. (2013). Barriers to effective intergration of information and communication technology in Harare secondary schools. *International Journal of Science and Research, 2.* www.ijsr.net

Nziramasanga, C. T. (1999). *Report of the Presidential commission of inquiry into education and training.* Government Printers.

O'Connell, M. (2019). Is the impact of SES on educational performance overestimated? Evidence from the PISA survey. *Intelligence, 75,* 41–47. doi:10.1016/j.intell.2019.04.005

OECD. (2015). *Schools for 21st-century learners: Strong leaders, confident teachers, innovative approaches.* Organisation for Economic Co-operation and Development. https://www.oecd-ilibrary. org/education/schools-for-21st-century-learners_9789264231191-en

OECD. (2019). *TALIS 2018 technical report* [Research Report]. https://www.oecd.org/education/ talis/TALIS_2018_Technical_Report.pdf

Oloniram, S. O. (2016). *Revisiting UNESCO Four pillars of education and its implications for the 21st century teaching and learning.* http:www.UNESCO.org/delors/fourpil.htm

Olugbade, D., & Olurinola, O. (2021). Teachers' Perception of the Use of Microsoft Teams for Remote Learning in Southwestern Nigerian Schools. *African Journal of Teacher Education, 10*(1), 265–281. doi:10.21083/ajote.v10i1.6645

Örücü, D. (2013). Örgütsel değişimin yönetimi. In S. Özdemir (Ed.), Eğitim yönetiminde kuram ve uygulama (pp. 445-479). Ankara: Pegem Akademi.

Otero Mayer, A., González Benito, A., & Gutiérrez de Roza, B. (2022). Implicaciones emocionales en maestros de Educación Infantil y las familias en pandemia en España. [Emotional implications for Early Childhood Education Teachers and Families during the pandemic in Spain]. *Mendive. Review of Education, 20*(1), 255–269.

Owens, R. G. (2004). *Organizational behavior in education: Adaptive leadership and school reform.* Pearson.

Owojori, O. M., Okoro, C. S., & Chileshe, N. (2021). Current status and emerging trends on the adaptive reuse of buildings: A bibliometric analysis. *Sustainability (Basel), 13*(21), 11646. doi:10.3390/su132111646

Özdemir, S., & Cemaloğlu, N. (1999). Eğitimde değişimi uygulama modelleri. *Kuram ve Uygulamada Eğitim Yönetimi, 17*(17), 91–103.

Özmen, F., & Sönmez, Y. (2007). Değişim sürecinde eğitim örgütlerinde değişim ajanlarının rolleri. *Fırat Üniversitesi Sosyal Bilimler Dergisi, 17*(2), 177–198.

Compilation of References

Pakpahan, F. H., & Saragih, M. (2022). Theory of Cognitive Development by Jean Piaget. *Journal of Applied Linguistics*, *2*(2), 55–60. doi:10.52622/joal.v2i2.79

Partnership for 21st Century Learning. (2015). *P21 framework definitions*. Retrieved from https://www.p21.org/storage/documents/docs/P21_Framework_Definitions_New_Logo_2015.pdf

Patil, D. T., Patil, A., & Patil, J. (2021). The Decision-Making Criteria for Adaptive Reuse for Sustainable Development. In *Advances in Geotechnics and Structural Engineering: Select Proceedings of TRACE 2020*, 599-607. doi:10.1007/978-981-33-6969-6_52

Patterson, N., & Hulton, L. J. (2012). Enhancing nursing students' understanding of poverty through simulation. *Public Health Nursing (Boston, Mass.)*, *29*(2), 143–151. doi:10.1111/j.1525-1446.2011.00999.x PMID:22372451

Pearce, C. J., & Conger, C. (2003). *Shared leadership: Reframing the hows and whys of leadership*. Sage. doi:10.4135/9781452229539

Pedzisai, C., Tsvere, M., & Nkhonde, M. (2014). The Zimbabwe Two Pathway Education Curriculum: Insights into policy implementation challenges and opportunities. *International Journal of Advanced Research in Management and Social Science, 3*(5).

Pham, A. T. V. (2023, Aug 15). Using Microsoft Teams as a Learning Management System in English Courses: A story from a Vocational School. *ICFET '23: Proceedings of the 2023 9th International Conference on Frontiers of Educational Technologies*. 10.1145/3606150.3606163

Piaget, J. (1983). Piaget's Theory. In P. Mussen (Ed.), *Handbook of Child Psychology*. Wiley & Sons.

Pinder, J. A., Schmidt, R., Austin, S. A., Gibb, A., & Saker, J. (2017). What is meant by adaptability in buildings? *Facilities*, *35*(1/2), 2–20. doi:10.1108/F-07-2015-0053

Poole, M. S. (2004). Central issues in the study of change and innovation. In M. S. Poole, & A. H. Van de Ven (Eds.), Handbook of organizational change and innovation (pp. 3-31). New York: Oxford University Press.

Poston, J., Apostel, S., & Richardson, K. (2020). Using Microsoft Teams to enhance engagement and learning with any class: It is fun and easy. *Pedagogicon Conference Proceedings*.

Poverty in USA. (n.d.). *The Population of Poverty USA*. Poverty in USA. Retrieved from https://www.povertyusa.org/facts

Preiser, R., Struthers, P., Suraya, M., Cameron, N., & Lawrence, E. (2014). External stakeholders and health promoting schools: Complexity and practice in South Africa. *Health Education*, *114*(4), 260–270. doi:10.1108/HE-07-2013-0031

Prensky, M. (2001). Digital natives, digital immigrants part 1. *On the Horizon*, *9*(5), 1–6. doi:10.1108/10748120110424816

253

Putra, I. N. G. M. (2021). Analysis of Proposed Adaptation of Fostered Environment and Evaluation of Built Environment in Bali in Facing Covid-19. *Architectural Research Journal*, *1*(1), 26–34. doi:10.22225/arj.1.1.3299.26-34

Rambe, S. (2019). Total Physical Response. *English Education Journal for Teaching and Learning*, *7*(1), 45–58. doi:10.24952/ee.v7i01.1652

Raza, M., Gilani, N., & Waheed, S. A. (2021). School Leaders' Perspectives on Successful Leadership: A Mixed Methods Case Study of a Private School Network in Pakistan. *Frontiers in Education*, *6*, 656491. doi:10.3389/feduc.2021.656491

Reeves, D. (2008). *Leading change in your school: How to conquer myths, build commitment, and get results*. ASCD.

Reimer, T., Reiser, B. J., & Spillane, J. P. (2002). Policy implementation and cognition: Reframing and refocusing implementation research. *Review of Educational Research*, *72*(3), 387–431. doi:10.3102/00346543072003387

Retallick, J. (2005). Managing school success: A case study from Pakistan. *Leading & Managing*, *11*, 32–42.

Rizvi, M. (2008). The role of school principals in enhancing teacher professionalism: Lessons from Pakistan. *Educational Management Administration & Leadership*, *36*(1), 85–100. doi:10.1177/1741143207084062

Rodrigo Monche, M., & Gómez Redondo, C. (2023). El material no estructurado en la práctica educativa dentro de Educación Infantil [Unstructured material in educational practice within Early Childhood Education]. *Pulso. Review of Education*, *46*, 76–101. doi:10.58265/pulso.5884

Rodríguez, B. (2014). Técnicas metodológicas empleadas en la enseñanza del inglés en Educación Infantil: Estudio de caso. Didáctica [Methodological Techniques used in the teaching of English in Early Childhood Education: A case study]. *Lengua y Literatura*, *16*, 145–161.

Rodríguez-Triana, M. J., Prieto, L. P., Ley, T., de Jong, T., & Gillet, D. (2020). Social practices in teacher knowledge creation and innovation adoption: A large-scale study in an online instructional design community for inquiry learning. *International Journal of Computer-Supported Collaborative Learning*, *15*(4), 445–467. doi:10.1007/s11412-020-09331-5

Rojabi, A. R. (2020). Exploring EFL learners' Perception of Online Learning via Microsoft Teams: University Level in Indonesia. *English Language Teaching Educational Journal*, *3*(2), 163-173. https://files.eric.ed.gov/fulltext/EJ1268365.pdf

Rosas, S. R. (2017). Systems thinking and complexity: Considerations for health promoting schools. *Health Promotion International*, *32*, 301–311. PMID:26620709

Royal Decree 95/2022, of February 1, 2022, establishing the minimum teaching for the second cycle of Early Childhood Education. Official State Gazette, 28, 2022.

Compilation of References

Salfi, N. A. (2011). Successful leadership practices of head teachers for school improvement: Some evidence from Pakistan. *Journal of Educational Administration*, *49*(4), 414–432. doi:10.1108/09578231111146489

Salfi, N. A., Virk, N., & Hussain, A. (2014). Analysis of leadership styles of head teachers at secondary school level in Pakistan: Locale and gender comparison. *International Journal of Gender and Women's Studies*, *2*(2), 341–356.

Salim, Z. (2016). *Teachers' Roles in Shared Decision-Making in a Pakistani Community School* (Unpublished Thesis) George Mason University.

Sallis, E. (1993). *Total Quality Management in Education*. Kogan Page.

Sanko, J., Matsuda, Y., Salani, D., Tran, L., Reaves, R., & Gerber, K. (2021). A comparison of learning outcomes from two poverty simulation experiences. *Public Health Nursing (Boston, Mass.)*, *38*(1), 427–438. Advance online publication. doi:10.1111/phn.12853 PMID:33410560

Santoro, N. (2017). *Challenging racial silences in Australian schools*. Springer.

Schein, E. H., & Schein, P. A. (2016). Organisational Culture and Leadership (5th ed.). John Wiley and Sons, Inc.

Schein, E. H. (2010). *Organizational culture and leadership*. Jossey-Bass.

Schleicher, A. (2016). *Teaching excellence through professional learning and policy reform: Lessons from around the world. International Summit on the Teaching Profession*. OECD Publishing. doi:10.1787/9789264252059-en

Senge, P. M. (2010). *The fifth discipline: The art and practice of the learning organization*. Crown Publishing Group.

Senge, P. M. (2000). *The fifth discipline: The art and practice of the learning organization*. Doubleday/Currency.

Sergiovanni, T. J. (2001). *The principalship: A reflective practice perspective*. Allyn & Bacon.

Shah, S. (2018). *An Analysis of the Interaction of the Gender of Head teachers with their Leadership Styles in Secondary Schools in Pakistan: A Pragmatist Perspective* (Unpublished Thesis). University of Cambridge.

Shellman, S. M., & Turan, K. (2006). Do simulations enhance student learning? An empirical evaluation of an IR simulation. *Journal of Political Science Education*, *2*(1), 19–32. doi:10.1080/15512160500484168

Siahaan, F. (2022). The Critical Period Hypothesis of SLA Eric Lenneberg's. *Journal of Applied Linguistics*, *2*(2), 40–45. doi:10.52622/joal.v2i2.77

Silalahi, R. M. (2019). Understanding Vygotsky's Zone of Proximal Development for Learning. *Polyglot Jurnal Ilmiah*, *15*(2), 169–186. doi:10.19166/pji.v15i2.1544

Simkins, T., Garrett, V., Memon, M., & Ali, R. N. (1998). The role perceptions of government and non-government head teachers in Pakistan. *Educational Management and Administration, 26*(2), 131–146. doi:10.1177/0263211X98262003

Simkins, T., Sisum, C., & Memon, M. (2003). School leadership in Pakistan: Exploring the headteacher's role. *School Effectiveness and School Improvement, 14*(3), 275–291. doi:10.1076/sesi.14.3.275.15841

Şimşek, H., & Louis, K. S. (1994). Organizational change paadigm shift: An analysis of the change process in a large, puplic university. *The Journal of Higher Education, 65*(6), 670–695.

Smith-Carrier, T., Leacy, K., Bouck, M. S., Justrabo, J., & Decker Pierce, B. (2019). Living with poverty: A simulation. *Journal of Social Work, 19*(5), 642–663. doi:10.1177/1468017318766429

Smylie, M. A. (1995). Teacher learning in the workplace: Implications for school reform. In T. R. Guskey & M. Huberman (Eds.), *Professional development in education: New paradigms and practices* (pp. 199–218). Teachers College Press.

Sobaih, A. E. E., Salem, A. E., Hasanein, A. M., & Elnasr, A. E. A. (2021). Responses to COVID-19 in Higher Education: Learners' Learning Experience Using Microsoft Teams versus Social Network Sites. *Sustainability (Basel), 13*(18), 10036. doi:10.3390/su131810036

Solé, I. (2016). Las relaciones entre familia y escuela [Relationships between family and school]. *C&E, Cultura y Educación, 8*(4), 11–17. doi:10.1174/11356409660561241

Sottile, J., & Brozik, D. (2004). *The use of simulations in a teacher education program: The impact on student development* [A critical review]. Paper presented at the 2004 Hawaii International Conference on Education (HICE). Honolulu, HI. https://files.eric.ed.gov/fulltext/ED490383.pdf

Spennemann, D. H. (2021). Residential Architecture in a post-pandemic world: Implications of COVID-19 for new construction and for adapting heritage buildings. *Journal of Green Building, 16*(1), 199–215. doi:10.3992/jgb.16.1.199

Spillane, J. (2015). Leadership and Learning: Conceptualising Relations between School Administrative Practice and Instructional Practice. *Societies (Basel, Switzerland), 5*(2), 277–294. doi:10.3390/soc5020277

Spillane, J. P. (2006). *Distributed leadership*. Jossey-Bass.

Spillane, J. P., Halverson, R., & Diamond, J. B. (2004). Towards a theory of leadership practice: A distributed perspective. *Journal of Curriculum Studies, 36*(1), 3–34. doi:10.1080/0022027032000106726

Stake, R. E. (1995). The art of case study research. *Sage (Atlanta, Ga.)*.

Strasser, S., Smith, M. O., Pendrick Denney, D., Jackson, M. C., & Buckmaster, P. (2013). A poverty simulation to inform public health practice. *American Journal of Health Education, 44*(5), 259–264. doi:10.1080/19325037.2013.811366

Compilation of References

Şubesi, M. O. A. (2019). Mutlu Haber: Eski Arkeoloji Müzesi Kültür Varlığı Olarak Tescillendi. *Mimarlık*, *408*, 10–12.

Subramanian, A., & Nilakanta, S. (1996). Organizational innovativeness: Exploring the relationship between organizational determinants of innovation, types of innovations, and measures of organizational performance. *Omega*, *24*(6), 631-647. doi:10.1016/S0305-0483(96)00031-X

Supovitz, J. A., & Taylor, B. Y. (2005). The search for productive professional development. *Phi Delta Kappan*, *87*(3), 194–200.

Sykes, G. (1996). Reform of and as professional development. *Phi Delta Kappan*, *77*(7), 464-489.

Tajik, M. A., & Wali, A. (2020). Principals' strategies for increasing students' participation in school leadership in a rural, mountainous region in Pakistan. *Improving Schools*, *23*(3), 245–263. doi:10.1177/1365480220923413

Taş, A. (2009). Ortaöğretim okulu müdürlerinin değişimi yönetme davranışlarına ilişkin öğretmen algılarının değerlendirilmesi. *İnönü Üniversitesi Eğitim Fakültesi Dergisi, 10*(2), 1-18.

The World Bank. (2023). *Poverty and Shared Prosperity 2022 Correcting Course.* The World Bank. Retrieved from https://www.worldbank.org/en/publication/poverty-and-shared-prosperity

The World Bank. (n.d.). *Poverty.* The World Bank. Retrieved from https://www.worldbank.org/en/topic/poverty/overview

Thomas, J. W. (2010). *A review of research on project-based learning.* Autodesk Foundation.

Thurlings, M., Evers, A. T., & Vermeulen, M. (2015). Toward a model of explaining teachers' innovative behavior: A literature review. *Review of Educational Research*, *85*(3), 430–471. doi:10.3102/0034654314557949

Tomlinson, C. A. (2014). *The differentiated classroom: Responding to the needs of all learners.* ASCD.

Töremen, F. (2002). Eğitim örgütlerinde değişimin engel ve nedenleri. *Fırat Üniversitesi Sosyal Bilimler Dergisi*, *12*(1), 185–202.

Trask, S., Charteris, J., Edwards, F., Cowie, B., & Anderson, J. (2023). Innovative learning environments and student orientation to learning: A kaleidoscopic framework. *Learning Environments Research*, *26*(3), 727–741. doi:10.1007/s10984-022-09449-3

Türk Dil Kurumu. (2022). *Değişim.* https://sozluk.gov.tr/

Tyerman, J., Luctkar-Flude, M., Graham, L., Coffey, S., & Olsen-Lynch, E. (2016). Pre-simulation preparation and briefing practices for healthcare professionals and students: A systematic review protocol. *JBI Database of Systematic Reviews and Implementation Reports*, *14*(8), 80–89. doi:10.11124/JBISRIR-2016-003055 PMID:27635748

Uhl-Bien, M., Marion, R., & McKelvey, B. (2007). Complexity leadership theory: Shifting leadership from the industrial age to the knowledge era. *The Leadership Quarterly, 18*(4), 298–318. doi:10.1016/j.leaqua.2007.04.002

United States Census Bureau. (2020). *Poverty thresholds by size of family and number of children.* Census.gov/data/tables/time-series/demo/income-poverty/historical-poverty-thresholds.html

Vafaie, F., Remøy, H., & Gruis, V. (2023). Adaptive reuse of heritage buildings; a systematic literature review of success factors. *Habitat International, 142*, 102926. doi:10.1016/j. habitatint.2023.102926

Van de Ven, A. H., & Poole, M. S. (1995). Explaining development and change in organizations. *Academy of Management Review, 20*(3), 510–540. doi:10.2307/258786

van Oord, L. (2013). Towards transformative leadership in education. *International Journal of Leadership in Education, 16*(4), 419–434. doi:10.1080/13603124.2013.776116

Vardopoulos, I. (2023). Adaptive Reuse for Sustainable Development and Land Use: A Multivariate Linear Regression Analysis Estimating Key Determinants of Public Perceptions. *Heritage, 6*(2), 809–828. doi:10.3390/heritage6020045

Vila, I. (2018). *Familia, escuela y comunidad* [Family, school, and community]. Horsori.

Violante, R. (2018). Didáctica de la Educación Infantil: Reflexiones y Propuestas [Didactics of Early Childhood Education: Reflections and Proposals]. *Revista Senderos Pedagógicos, 9*(9), 131–150. doi:10.53995/sp.v9i9.961

Vygotsky, L. (1987). *Pensamiento y Lenguaje* [Thought and Language]. La Pléyade.

Wallace, M. (2002). Modelling distributed leadership and management effectiveness: Primary school senior management teams in England and Wales. *School Effectiveness and School Improvement, 13*(2), 163–186. doi:10.1076/sesi.13.2.163.3433

Webb, M., & Cox, M. (2004). A review of pedagogy related to information and communications technology. *Technology, Pedagogy and Education, 13*(3), 235–286. doi:10.1080/14759390400200183

Willower, D. J. (1963). Barriers to change in educational organizations. *Theory into Practice, 2*(5), 257–263. doi:10.1080/00405846309541873

Wong, L. (2016). *Adaptive reuse: extending the lives of buildings.* Birkhäuser. doi:10.1515/9783038213130

Wright, T., Nankin, I., Boonstra, K., & Blair, E. (2019). Changing through relationships and reflection: An exploratory investigation of pre-service teachers' perceptions of young children experiencing homelessness. *Early Childhood Education Journal, 47*(3), 297–308. doi:10.1007/s10643-018-0921-y

Compilation of References

Yatmo, Y. A., & Atmodiwirjo, P. (2022). Open Learning Spaces: Redefining School Design in a Post-Pandemic World. In Architectural Factors for Infection and Disease Control (pp. 245-257). Routledge.

Yılmaz, D., Kılıçoğlu, G., & Turan, S. (2014). Örgütsel değişim. In S. Turan (Ed.), Eğitim yönetimi: Teori, araştırma ve uygulama (pp. 253-292). Ankara: Pegem Akademi.

Yosso, T. J. (2005). Whose culture has capital? A critical race theory discussion of community cultural wealth. *Race, Ethnicity and Education*, *8*(1), 69–91. doi:10.1080/1361332052000341006

Zamora-Antuñano, M. A., Rodríguez-Reséndiz, J., Rodriguez Segura, L., Cruz Perez, M. A., Altamirano Corro, J. A., Paredes-Garcia, W. J., & Rodríguez-Reséndiz, H. (2021). Analysis of emergency remote education in COVID-19 crisis focused on the perception of the teachers. *Sustainability (Basel)*, *13*(7), 3820. doi:10.3390/su13073820

Zhang, R. (2023). The characteristics of Early Childhood Education in Spain. *Journal of Education and Educational Research*, *6*(1), 8–10. doi:10.54097/jeer.v6i1.14124

Zindi, F. (1997). *Special education in Africa*. Tasalls.

Zvobgo, R. J. (1996). *Transforming Education the Zimbabwean experiences*. Bulawayo.

Related References

To continue our tradition of advancing academic research, we have compiled a list of recommended IGI Global readings. These references will provide additional information and guidance to further enrich your knowledge and assist you with your own research and future publications.

Aburezeq, I. M., & Dweikat, F. F. (2017). Cloud Applications in Language Teaching: Examining Pre-Service Teachers' Expertise, Perceptions and Integration. *International Journal of Distance Education Technologies, 15*(4), 39–60. doi:10.4018/IJDET.2017100103

Acharjya, B., & Das, S. (2022). Adoption of E-Learning During the COVID-19 Pandemic: The Moderating Role of Age and Gender. *International Journal of Web-Based Learning and Teaching Technologies, 17*(2), 1–14. https://doi.org/10.4018/IJWLTT.20220301.oa4

Adams, J. L., & Thomas, S. K. (2022). Non-Linear Curriculum Experiences for Student Learning and Work Design: What Is the Maximum Potential of a Chat Bot? In S. Ramlall, T. Cross, & M. Love (Eds.), *Handbook of Research on Future of Work and Education: Implications for Curriculum Delivery and Work Design* (pp. 299–306). IGI Global. https://doi.org/10.4018/978-1-7998-8275-6.ch018

Adera, B. (2017). Supporting Language and Literacy Development for English Language Learners. In J. Keengwe (Ed.), *Handbook of Research on Promoting Cross-Cultural Competence and Social Justice in Teacher Education* (pp. 339–354). Hershey, PA: IGI Global. doi:10.4018/978-1-5225-0897-7.ch018

Related References

Ahamer, G. (2017). Quality Assurance for a Developmental "Global Studies" (GS) Curriculum. In I. Management Association (Ed.), Educational Leadership and Administration: Concepts, Methodologies, Tools, and Applications (pp. 438-477). Hershey, PA: IGI Global. https://doi.org/ doi:10.4018/978-1-5225-1624-8.ch023

Akayoğlu, S., & Seferoğlu, G. (2019). An Analysis of Negotiation of Meaning Functions of Advanced EFL Learners in Second Life: Negotiation of Meaning in Second Life. In M. Kruk (Ed.), *Assessing the Effectiveness of Virtual Technologies in Foreign and Second Language Instruction* (pp. 61–85). IGI Global. https://doi.org/10.4018/978-1-5225-7286-2.ch003

Akella, N. R. (2022). Unravelling the Web of Qualitative Dissertation Writing!: A Student Reflects. In A. Zimmerman (Ed.), *Methodological Innovations in Research and Academic Writing* (pp. 260–282). IGI Global. https://doi.org/10.4018/978-1-7998-8283-1.ch014

Alegre de la Rosa, O. M., & Angulo, L. M. (2017). Social Inclusion and Intercultural Values in a School of Education. In S. Mukerji & P. Tripathi (Eds.), *Handbook of Research on Administration, Policy, and Leadership in Higher Education* (pp. 518–531). Hershey, PA: IGI Global. doi:10.4018/978-1-5225-0672-0.ch020

Alexander, C. (2019). Using Gamification Strategies to Cultivate and Measure Professional Educator Dispositions. *International Journal of Game-Based Learning*, 9(1), 15–29. https://doi.org/10.4018/IJGBL.2019010102

Anderson, K. M. (2017). Preparing Teachers in the Age of Equity and Inclusion. In I. Management Association (Ed.), Medical Education and Ethics: Concepts, Methodologies, Tools, and Applications (pp. 1532-1554). Hershey, PA: IGI Global. doi:10.4018/978-1-5225-0978-3.ch069

Awdziej, M. (2017). Case Study as a Teaching Method in Marketing. In D. Latusek (Ed.), *Case Studies as a Teaching Tool in Management Education* (pp. 244–263). Hershey, PA: IGI Global. doi:10.4018/978-1-5225-0770-3.ch013

Bakos, J. (2019). Sociolinguistic Factors Influencing English Language Learning. In N. Erdogan & M. Wei (Eds.), *Applied Linguistics for Teachers of Culturally and Linguistically Diverse Learners* (pp. 403–424). IGI Global. https://doi.org/10.4018/978-1-5225-8467-4.ch017

Banas, J. R., & York, C. S. (2017). Pre-Service Teachers' Motivation to Use Technology and the Impact of Authentic Learning Exercises. In L. Tomei (Ed.), *Exploring the New Era of Technology-Infused Education* (pp. 121–140). Hershey, PA: IGI Global. doi:10.4018/978-1-5225-1709-2.ch008

Barton, T. P. (2021). Empowering Educator Allyship by Exploring Racial Trauma and the Disengagement of Black Students. In C. Reneau & M. Villarreal (Eds.), *Handbook of Research on Leading Higher Education Transformation With Social Justice, Equity, and Inclusion* (pp. 186–197). IGI Global. https://doi.org/10.4018/978-1-7998-7152-1.ch013

Benhima, M. (2021). Moroccan English Department Student Attitudes Towards the Use of Distance Education During COVID-19: Moulay Ismail University as a Case Study. *International Journal of Information and Communication Technology Education*, *17*(3), 105–122. https://doi.org/10.4018/IJICTE.20210701.oa7

Beycioglu, K., & Wildy, H. (2017). Principal Preparation: The Case of Novice Principals in Turkey. In I. Management Association (Ed.), Educational Leadership and Administration: Concepts, Methodologies, Tools, and Applications (pp. 1152-1169). Hershey, PA: IGI Global. https://doi.org/ doi:10.4018/978-1-5225-1624-8.ch054

Bharwani, S., & Musunuri, D. (2018). Reflection as a Process From Theory to Practice. In M. Khosrow-Pour, D.B.A. (Ed.), Encyclopedia of Information Science and Technology, Fourth Edition (pp. 1529-1539). Hershey, PA: IGI Global. doi:10.4018/978-1-5225-2255-3.ch132

Bhushan, A., Garza, K. B., Perumal, O., Das, S. K., Feola, D. J., Farrell, D., & Birnbaum, A. (2022). Lessons Learned From the COVID-19 Pandemic and the Implications for Pharmaceutical Graduate Education and Research. In C. Ford & K. Garza (Eds.), *Handbook of Research on Updating and Innovating Health Professions Education: Post-Pandemic Perspectives* (pp. 324–345). IGI Global. https://doi.org/10.4018/978-1-7998-7623-6.ch014

Bintz, W., Ciecierski, L. M., & Royan, E. (2021). Using Picture Books With Instructional Strategies to Address New Challenges and Teach Literacy Skills in a Digital World. In L. Haas & J. Tussey (Eds.), *Connecting Disciplinary Literacy and Digital Storytelling in K-12 Education* (pp. 38–58). IGI Global. https://doi.org/10.4018/978-1-7998-5770-9.ch003

Bohjanen, S. L., Cameron-Standerford, A., & Meidl, T. D. (2018). Capacity Building Pedagogy for Diverse Learners. In J. Keengwe (Ed.), *Handbook of Research on Pedagogical Models for Next-Generation Teaching and Learning* (pp. 195–212). Hershey, PA: IGI Global. doi:10.4018/978-1-5225-3873-8.ch011

Brewer, J. C. (2018). Measuring Text Readability Using Reading Level. In M. Khosrow-Pour, D.B.A. (Ed.), Encyclopedia of Information Science and Technology, Fourth Edition (pp. 1499-1507). Hershey, PA: IGI Global. doi:10.4018/978-1-5225-2255-3.ch129

Related References

Brookbanks, B. C. (2022). Student Perspectives on Business Education in the USA: Current Attitudes and Necessary Changes in an Age of Disruption. In A. Zhuplev & R. Koepp (Eds.), *Global Trends, Dynamics, and Imperatives for Strategic Development in Business Education in an Age of Disruption* (pp. 214–231). IGI Global. doi:10.4018/978-1-7998-7548-2.ch011

Brown, L. V., Dari, T., & Spencer, N. (2019). Addressing the Impact of Trauma in High Poverty Elementary Schools: An Ecological Model for School Counseling. In K. Daniels & K. Billingsley (Eds.), *Creating Caring and Supportive Educational Environments for Meaningful Learning* (pp. 135–153). IGI Global. https://doi.org/10.4018/978-1-5225-5748-7.ch008

Brown, S. L. (2017). A Case Study of Strategic Leadership and Research in Practice: Principal Preparation Programs that Work – An Educational Administration Perspective of Best Practices for Master's Degree Programs for Principal Preparation. In V. Wang (Ed.), *Encyclopedia of Strategic Leadership and Management* (pp. 1226–1244). Hershey, PA: IGI Global. doi:10.4018/978-1-5225-1049-9.ch086

Brzozowski, M., & Ferster, I. (2017). Educational Management Leadership: High School Principal's Management Style and Parental Involvement in School Management in Israel. In V. Potocan, M. Üngan, & Z. Nedelko (Eds.), *Handbook of Research on Managerial Solutions in Non-Profit Organizations* (pp. 55–74). Hershey, PA: IGI Global. doi:10.4018/978-1-5225-0731-4.ch003

Cahapay, M. B. (2020). Delphi Technique in the Development of Emerging Contents in High School Science Curriculum. *International Journal of Curriculum Development and Learning Measurement, 1*(2), 1–9. https://doi.org/10.4018/IJCDLM.2020070101

Camacho, L. F., & Leon Guerrero, A. E. (2022). Indigenous Student Experience in Higher Education: Implementation of Culturally Sensitive Support. In P. Pangelinan & T. McVey (Eds.), *Learning and Reconciliation Through Indigenous Education in Oceania* (pp. 254–266). IGI Global. https://doi.org/10.4018/978-1-7998-7736-3.ch016

Cannaday, J. (2017). The Masking Effect: Hidden Gifts and Disabilities of 2e Students. In P. Dickenson, P. Keough, & J. Courduff (Eds.), *Preparing Pre-Service Teachers for the Inclusive Classroom* (pp. 220–231). Hershey, PA: IGI Global. doi:10.4018/978-1-5225-1753-5.ch011

Cederquist, S., Fishman, B., & Teasley, S. D. (2022). What's Missing From the College Transcript?: How Employers Make Sense of Student Skills. In Y. Huang (Ed.), *Handbook of Research on Credential Innovations for Inclusive Pathways to Professions* (pp. 234–253). IGI Global. https://doi.org/10.4018/978-1-7998-3820-3.ch012

Cockrell, P., & Gibson, T. (2019). The Untold Stories of Black and Brown Student Experiences in Historically White Fraternities and Sororities. In P. Hoffman-Miller, M. James, & D. Hermond (Eds.), *African American Suburbanization and the Consequential Loss of Identity* (pp. 153–171). IGI Global. https://doi.org/10.4018/978-1-5225-7835-2.ch009

Cohen, M. (2022). Leveraging Content Creation to Boost Student Engagement. In T. Driscoll III, (Ed.), *Designing Effective Distance and Blended Learning Environments in K-12* (pp. 223–239). IGI Global. https://doi.org/10.4018/978-1-7998-6829-3.ch013

Contreras, E. C., & Contreras, I. I. (2018). Development of Communication Skills through Auditory Training Software in Special Education. In M. Khosrow-Pour, D.B.A. (Ed.), Encyclopedia of Information Science and Technology, Fourth Edition (pp. 2431-2441). Hershey, PA: IGI Global. doi:10.4018/978-1-5225-2255-3.ch212

Cooke, L., Schugar, J., Schugar, H., Penny, C., & Bruning, H. (2020). Can Everyone Code?: Preparing Teachers to Teach Computer Languages as a Literacy. In J. Mitchell & E. Vaughn (Eds.), *Participatory Literacy Practices for P-12 Classrooms in the Digital Age* (pp. 163–183). IGI Global. https://doi.org/10.4018/978-1-7998-0000-2.ch009

Cooley, D., & Whitten, E. (2017). Special Education Leadership and the Implementation of Response to Intervention. In F. Topor (Ed.), *Handbook of Research on Individualism and Identity in the Globalized Digital Age* (pp. 265–286). Hershey, PA: IGI Global. doi:10.4018/978-1-5225-0522-8.ch012

Cosner, S., Tozer, S., & Zavitkovsky, P. (2017). Enacting a Cycle of Inquiry Capstone Research Project in Doctoral-Level Leadership Preparation. In I. Management Association (Ed.), Educational Leadership and Administration: Concepts, Methodologies, Tools, and Applications (pp. 1460-1481). Hershey, PA: IGI Global. doi:10.4018/978-1-5225-1624-8.ch067

Crawford, C. M. (2018). Instructional Real World Community Engagement. In M. Khosrow-Pour, D.B.A. (Ed.), Encyclopedia of Information Science and Technology, Fourth Edition (pp. 1474-1486). Hershey, PA: IGI Global. doi:10.4018/978-1-5225-2255-3.ch127

Related References

Crosby-Cooper, T., & Pacis, D. (2017). Implementing Effective Student Support Teams. In P. Dickenson, P. Keough, & J. Courduff (Eds.), *Preparing Pre-Service Teachers for the Inclusive Classroom* (pp. 248–262). Hershey, PA: IGI Global. doi:10.4018/978-1-5225-1753-5.ch013

Curran, C. M., & Hawbaker, B. W. (2017). Cultivating Communities of Inclusive Practice: Professional Development for Educators – Research and Practice. In C. Curran & A. Petersen (Eds.), *Handbook of Research on Classroom Diversity and Inclusive Education Practice* (pp. 120–153). Hershey, PA: IGI Global. doi:10.4018/978-1-5225-2520-2.ch006

Dass, S., & Dabbagh, N. (2018). Faculty Adoption of 3D Avatar-Based Virtual World Learning Environments: An Exploratory Case Study. In I. Management Association (Ed.), Technology Adoption and Social Issues: Concepts, Methodologies, Tools, and Applications (pp. 1000-1033). Hershey, PA: IGI Global. https://doi.org/ doi:10.4018/978-1-5225-5201-7.ch045

Davison, A. M., & Scholl, K. G. (2017). Inclusive Recreation as Part of the IEP Process. In C. Curran & A. Petersen (Eds.), *Handbook of Research on Classroom Diversity and Inclusive Education Practice* (pp. 311–330). Hershey, PA: IGI Global. doi:10.4018/978-1-5225-2520-2.ch013

DeCoito, I. (2018). Addressing Digital Competencies, Curriculum Development, and Instructional Design in Science Teacher Education. In M. Khosrow-Pour, D.B.A. (Ed.), Encyclopedia of Information Science and Technology, Fourth Edition (pp. 1420-1431). Hershey, PA: IGI Global. https://doi.org/ doi:10.4018/978-1-5225-2255-3.ch122

DeCoito, I., & Richardson, T. (2017). Beyond Angry Birds™: Using Web-Based Tools to Engage Learners and Promote Inquiry in STEM Learning. In I. Levin & D. Tsybulsky (Eds.), *Digital Tools and Solutions for Inquiry-Based STEM Learning* (pp. 166–196). Hershey, PA: IGI Global. doi:10.4018/978-1-5225-2525-7.ch007

Delmas, P. M. (2017). Research-Based Leadership for Next-Generation Leaders. In R. Styron Jr & J. Styron (Eds.), *Comprehensive Problem-Solving and Skill Development for Next-Generation Leaders* (pp. 1–39). Hershey, PA: IGI Global. doi:10.4018/978-1-5225-1968-3.ch001

Demiray, U., & Ekren, G. (2018). Administrative-Related Evaluation for Distance Education Institutions in Turkey. In K. Buyuk, S. Kocdar, & A. Bozkurt (Eds.), *Administrative Leadership in Open and Distance Learning Programs* (pp. 263–288). Hershey, PA: IGI Global. doi:10.4018/978-1-5225-2645-2.ch011

Related References

Dickenson, P. (2017). What do we Know and Where Can We Grow?: Teachers Preparation for the Inclusive Classroom. In P. Dickenson, P. Keough, & J. Courduff (Eds.), *Preparing Pre-Service Teachers for the Inclusive Classroom* (pp. 1–22). Hershey, PA: IGI Global. doi:10.4018/978-1-5225-1753-5.ch001

Ding, Q., & Zhu, H. (2021). Flipping the Classroom in STEM Education. In J. Keengwe (Ed.), *Handbook of Research on Innovations in Non-Traditional Educational Practices* (pp. 155–173). IGI Global. https://doi.org/10.4018/978-1-7998-4360-3.ch008

Dixon, T., & Christison, M. (2021). Teaching English Grammar in a Hybrid Academic ESL Course: A Mixed Methods Study. In K. Kelch, P. Byun, S. Safavi, & S. Cervantes (Eds.), *CALL Theory Applications for Online TESOL Education* (pp. 229–251). IGI Global. https://doi.org/10.4018/978-1-7998-6609-1.ch010

Donne, V., & Hansen, M. (2017). Teachers' Use of Assistive Technologies in Education. In L. Tomei (Ed.), *Exploring the New Era of Technology-Infused Education* (pp. 86–101). Hershey, PA: IGI Global. doi:10.4018/978-1-5225-1709-2.ch006

Donne, V., & Hansen, M. A. (2018). Business and Technology Educators: Practices for Inclusion. In I. Management Association (Ed.), Business Education and Ethics: Concepts, Methodologies, Tools, and Applications (pp. 471-484). Hershey, PA: IGI Global. https://doi.org/ doi:10.4018/978-1-5225-3153-1.ch026

Dos Santos, L. M. (2022). Completing Student-Teaching Internships Online: Instructional Changes During the COVID-19 Pandemic. In M. Alaali (Ed.), *Assessing University Governance and Policies in Relation to the COVID-19 Pandemic* (pp. 106–127). IGI Global. https://doi.org/10.4018/978-1-7998-8279-4.ch007

Dreon, O., Shettel, J., & Bower, K. M. (2017). Preparing Next Generation Elementary Teachers for the Tools of Tomorrow. In M. Grassetti & S. Brookby (Eds.), *Advancing Next-Generation Teacher Education through Digital Tools and Applications* (pp. 143–159). Hershey, PA: IGI Global. doi:10.4018/978-1-5225-0965-3.ch008

Durak, H. Y., & Güyer, T. (2018). Design and Development of an Instructional Program for Teaching Programming Processes to Gifted Students Using Scratch. In J. Cannaday (Ed.), *Curriculum Development for Gifted Education Programs* (pp. 61–99). Hershey, PA: IGI Global. doi:10.4018/978-1-5225-3041-1.ch004

Egorkina, E., Ivanov, M., & Valyavskiy, A. Y. (2018). Students' Research Competence Formation of the Quality of Open and Distance Learning. In V. Mkrttchian & L. Belyanina (Eds.), *Handbook of Research on Students' Research Competence in Modern Educational Contexts* (pp. 364–384). Hershey, PA: IGI Global. doi:10.4018/978-1-5225-3485-3.ch019

Related References

Ekren, G., Karataş, S., & Demiray, U. (2017). Understanding of Leadership in Distance Education Management. In I. Management Association (Ed.), Educational Leadership and Administration: Concepts, Methodologies, Tools, and Applications (pp. 34-50). Hershey, PA: IGI Global. https://doi.org/ doi:10.4018/978-1-5225-1624-8.ch003

Elmore, W. M., Young, J. K., Harris, S., & Mason, D. (2017). The Relationship between Individual Student Attributes and Online Course Completion. In K. Shelton & K. Pedersen (Eds.), *Handbook of Research on Building, Growing, and Sustaining Quality E-Learning Programs* (pp. 151–173). Hershey, PA: IGI Global. doi:10.4018/978-1-5225-0877-9.ch008

Ercegovac, I. R., Alfirević, N., & Koludrović, M. (2017). School Principals' Communication and Co-Operation Assessment: The Croatian Experience. In I. Management Association (Ed.), Educational Leadership and Administration: Concepts, Methodologies, Tools, and Applications (pp. 1568-1589). Hershey, PA: IGI Global. https://doi.org/ doi:10.4018/978-1-5225-1624-8.ch072

Everhart, D., & Seymour, D. M. (2017). Challenges and Opportunities in the Currency of Higher Education. In K. Rasmussen, P. Northrup, & R. Colson (Eds.), *Handbook of Research on Competency-Based Education in University Settings* (pp. 41–65). Hershey, PA: IGI Global. doi:10.4018/978-1-5225-0932-5.ch003

Farmer, L. S. (2017). Managing Portable Technologies for Special Education. In V. Wang (Ed.), *Encyclopedia of Strategic Leadership and Management* (pp. 977–987). Hershey, PA: IGI Global. doi:10.4018/978-1-5225-1049-9.ch068

Farmer, L. S. (2018). Optimizing OERs for Optimal ICT Literacy in Higher Education. In J. Keengwe (Ed.), *Handbook of Research on Mobile Technology, Constructivism, and Meaningful Learning* (pp. 366–390). Hershey, PA: IGI Global. doi:10.4018/978-1-5225-3949-0.ch020

Ferguson, B. T. (2019). Supporting Affective Development of Children With Disabilities Through Moral Dilemmas. In S. Ikuta (Ed.), *Handmade Teaching Materials for Students With Disabilities* (pp. 253–275). IGI Global. doi:10.4018/978-1-5225-6240-5.ch011

Fındık, L. Y. (2017). Self-Assessment of Principals Based on Leadership in Complexity. In I. Management Association (Ed.), Educational Leadership and Administration: Concepts, Methodologies, Tools, and Applications (pp. 978-991). Hershey, PA: IGI Global. https://doi.org/ doi:10.4018/978-1-5225-1624-8.ch047

Related References

Flor, A. G., & Gonzalez-Flor, B. (2018). Dysfunctional Digital Demeanors: Tales From (and Policy Implications of) eLearning's Dark Side. In I. Management Association (Ed.), The Dark Web: Breakthroughs in Research and Practice (pp. 37-50). Hershey, PA: IGI Global. https://doi.org/ doi:10.4018/978-1-5225-3163-0.ch003

Floyd, K. K., & Shambaugh, N. (2017). Instructional Design for Simulations in Special Education Virtual Learning Spaces. In T. Kidd & L. Morris Jr., (Eds.), *Handbook of Research on Instructional Systems and Educational Technology* (pp. 202–215). Hershey, PA: IGI Global. doi:10.4018/978-1-5225-2399-4.ch018

Freeland, S. F. (2020). Community Schools: Improving Academic Achievement Through Meaningful Engagement. In R. Kronick (Ed.), *Emerging Perspectives on Community Schools and the Engaged University* (pp. 132–144). IGI Global. https://doi.org/10.4018/978-1-7998-0280-8.ch008

Ghanbarzadeh, R., & Ghapanchi, A. H. (2019). Applied Areas of Three Dimensional Virtual Worlds in Learning and Teaching: A Review of Higher Education. In I. Management Association (Ed.), *Virtual Reality in Education: Breakthroughs in Research and Practice* (pp. 172-192). IGI Global. https://doi.org/10.4018/978-1-5225-8179-6.ch008

Giovannini, J. M. (2017). Technology Integration in Preservice Teacher Education Programs: Research-based Recommendations. In M. Grassetti & S. Brookby (Eds.), *Advancing Next-Generation Teacher Education through Digital Tools and Applications* (pp. 82–102). Hershey, PA: IGI Global. doi:10.4018/978-1-5225-0965-3.ch005

Good, S., & Clarke, V. B. (2017). An Integral Analysis of One Urban School System's Efforts to Support Student-Centered Teaching. In J. Keengwe & G. Onchwari (Eds.), *Handbook of Research on Learner-Centered Pedagogy in Teacher Education and Professional Development* (pp. 45–68). Hershey, PA: IGI Global. doi:10.4018/978-1-5225-0892-2.ch003

Guetzoian, E. (2022). Gamification Strategies for Higher Education Student Worker Training. In C. Lane (Ed.), *Handbook of Research on Acquiring 21st Century Literacy Skills Through Game-Based Learning* (pp. 164–179). IGI Global. https://doi.org/10.4018/978-1-7998-7271-9.ch009

Hamidi, F., Owuor, P. M., Hynie, M., Baljko, M., & McGrath, S. (2017). Potentials of Digital Assistive Technology and Special Education in Kenya. In C. Ayo & V. Mbarika (Eds.), *Sustainable ICT Adoption and Integration for Socio-Economic Development* (pp. 125–151). Hershey, PA: IGI Global. doi:10.4018/978-1-5225-2565-3.ch006

Related References

Hamim, T., Benabbou, F., & Sael, N. (2022). Student Profile Modeling Using Boosting Algorithms. *International Journal of Web-Based Learning and Teaching Technologies*, *17*(5), 1–13. https://doi.org/10.4018/IJWLTT.20220901.oa4

Henderson, L. K. (2017). Meltdown at Fukushima: Global Catastrophic Events, Visual Literacy, and Art Education. In R. Shin (Ed.), *Convergence of Contemporary Art, Visual Culture, and Global Civic Engagement* (pp. 80–99). Hershey, PA: IGI Global. doi:10.4018/978-1-5225-1665-1.ch005

Hudgins, T., & Holland, J. L. (2018). Digital Badges: Tracking Knowledge Acquisition Within an Innovation Framework. In I. Management Association (Ed.), Wearable Technologies: Concepts, Methodologies, Tools, and Applications (pp. 1118-1132). Hershey, PA: IGI Global. https://doi.org/ doi:10.4018/978-1-5225-5484-4.ch051

Hwang, R., Lin, H., Sun, J. C., & Wu, J. (2019). Improving Learning Achievement in Science Education for Elementary School Students via Blended Learning. *International Journal of Online Pedagogy and Course Design*, *9*(2), 44–62. https://doi.org/10.4018/IJOPCD.2019040104

Jančec, L., & Vodopivec, J. L. (2019). The Implicit Pedagogy and the Hidden Curriculum in Postmodern Education. In J. Vodopivec, L. Jančec, & T. Štemberger (Eds.), *Implicit Pedagogy for Optimized Learning in Contemporary Education* (pp. 41–59). IGI Global. https://doi.org/10.4018/978-1-5225-5799-9.ch003

Janus, M., & Siddiqua, A. (2018). Challenges for Children With Special Health Needs at the Time of Transition to School. In I. Management Association (Ed.), Autism Spectrum Disorders: Breakthroughs in Research and Practice (pp. 339-371). Hershey, PA: IGI Global. doi:10.4018/978-1-5225-3827-1.ch018

Jesus, R. A. (2018). Screencasts and Learning Styles. In M. Khosrow-Pour, D.B.A. (Ed.), Encyclopedia of Information Science and Technology, Fourth Edition (pp. 1548-1558). Hershey, PA: IGI Global. doi:10.4018/978-1-5225-2255-3.ch134

John, G., Francis, N., & Santhakumar, A. B. (2022). Student Engagement: Past, Present, and Future. In S. Ramlall, T. Cross, & M. Love (Eds.), *Handbook of Research on Future of Work and Education: Implications for Curriculum Delivery and Work Design* (pp. 329–341). IGI Global. https://doi.org/10.4018/978-1-7998-8275-6.ch020

Karpinski, A. C., D'Agostino, J. V., Williams, A. K., Highland, S. A., & Mellott, J. A. (2018). The Relationship Between Online Formative Assessment and State Test Scores Using Multilevel Modeling. In M. Khosrow-Pour, D.B.A. (Ed.), Encyclopedia of Information Science and Technology, Fourth Edition (pp. 5183-5192). Hershey, PA: IGI Global. doi:10.4018/978-1-5225-2255-3.ch450

Kats, Y. (2017). Educational Leadership and Integrated Support for Students with Autism Spectrum Disorders. In I. Management Association (Ed.), Educational Leadership and Administration: Concepts, Methodologies, Tools, and Applications (pp. 101-114). Hershey, PA: IGI Global. https://doi.org/ doi:10.4018/978-1-5225-1624-8.ch007

Kaya, G., & Altun, A. (2018). Educational Ontology Development. In M. Khosrow-Pour, D.B.A. (Ed.), Encyclopedia of Information Science and Technology, Fourth Edition (pp. 1441-1450). Hershey, PA: IGI Global. doi:10.4018/978-1-5225-2255-3.ch124

Keough, P. D., & Pacis, D. (2017). Best Practices Implementing Special Education Curriculum and Common Core State Standards using UDL. In P. Dickenson, P. Keough, & J. Courduff (Eds.), *Preparing Pre-Service Teachers for the Inclusive Classroom* (pp. 107–123). Hershey, PA: IGI Global. doi:10.4018/978-1-5225-1753-5.ch006

Kilburn, M., Henckell, M., & Starrett, D. (2018). Factors Contributing to the Effectiveness of Online Students and Instructors. In M. Khosrow-Pour, D.B.A. (Ed.), Encyclopedia of Information Science and Technology, Fourth Edition (pp. 1451-1462). Hershey, PA: IGI Global. doi:10.4018/978-1-5225-2255-3.ch125

Koban Koç, D. (2021). Gender and Language: A Sociolinguistic Analysis of Second Language Writing. In E. Hancı-Azizoglu & N. Kavaklı (Eds.), *Futuristic and Linguistic Perspectives on Teaching Writing to Second Language Students* (pp. 161–177). IGI Global. https://doi.org/10.4018/978-1-7998-6508-7.ch010

Konecny, L. T. (2017). Hybrid, Online, and Flipped Classrooms in Health Science: Enhanced Learning Environments. In I. Management Association (Ed.), Flipped Instruction: Breakthroughs in Research and Practice (pp. 355-370). Hershey, PA: IGI Global. https://doi.org/ doi:10.4018/978-1-5225-1803-7.ch020

Kupietz, K. D. (2021). Gaming and Simulation in Public Education: Teaching Others to Help Themselves and Their Neighbors. In N. Drumhiller, T. Wilkin, & K. Srba (Eds.), *Simulation and Game-Based Learning in Emergency and Disaster Management* (pp. 41–62). IGI Global. https://doi.org/10.4018/978-1-7998-4087-9.ch003

Kwee, C. T. (2022). Assessing the International Student Enrolment Strategies in Australian Universities: A Case Study During the COVID-19 Pandemic. In M. Alaali (Ed.), *Assessing University Governance and Policies in Relation to the COVID-19 Pandemic* (pp. 162–188). IGI Global. https://doi.org/10.4018/978-1-7998-8279-4.ch010

Related References

Lauricella, S., & McArthur, F. A. (2022). Taking a Student-Centred Approach to Alternative Digital Credentials: Multiple Pathways Toward the Acquisition of Microcredentials. In D. Piedra (Ed.), *Innovations in the Design and Application of Alternative Digital Credentials* (pp. 57–69). IGI Global. https://doi.org/10.4018/978-1-7998-7697-7.ch003

Llamas, M. F. (2019). Intercultural Awareness in Teaching English for Early Childhood: A Film-Based Approach. In E. Domínguez Romero, J. Bobkina, & S. Stefanova (Eds.), *Teaching Literature and Language Through Multimodal Texts* (pp. 54–68). IGI Global. https://doi.org/10.4018/978-1-5225-5796-8.ch004

Lokhtina, I., & Kkese, E. T. (2022). Reflecting and Adapting to an Academic Workplace Before and After the Lockdown in Greek-Speaking Cyprus: Opportunities and Challenges. In A. Zhuplev & R. Koepp (Eds.), *Global Trends, Dynamics, and Imperatives for Strategic Development in Business Education in an Age of Disruption* (pp. 126–148). IGI Global. https://doi.org/10.4018/978-1-7998-7548-2.ch007

Lovell, K. L. (2017). Development and Evaluation of Neuroscience Computer-Based Modules for Medical Students: Instructional Design Principles and Effectiveness. In J. Stefaniak (Ed.), *Advancing Medical Education Through Strategic Instructional Design* (pp. 262–276). Hershey, PA: IGI Global. doi:10.4018/978-1-5225-2098-6.ch013

Maher, D. (2019). The Use of Course Management Systems in Pre-Service Teacher Education. In J. Keengwe (Ed.), *Handbook of Research on Blended Learning Pedagogies and Professional Development in Higher Education* (pp. 196–213). IGI Global. https://doi.org/10.4018/978-1-5225-5557-5.ch011

Makewa, L. N. (2019). Teacher Technology Competence Base. In L. Makewa, B. Ngussa, & J. Kuboja (Eds.), *Technology-Supported Teaching and Research Methods for Educators* (pp. 247–267). IGI Global. https://doi.org/10.4018/978-1-5225-5915-3.ch014

Mallett, C. A. (2022). School Resource (Police) Officers in Schools: Impact on Campus Safety, Student Discipline, and Learning. In G. Crews (Ed.), *Impact of School Shootings on Classroom Culture, Curriculum, and Learning* (pp. 53–70). IGI Global. https://doi.org/10.4018/978-1-7998-5200-1.ch004

Marinho, J. E., Freitas, I. R., Leão, I. B., Pacheco, L. O., Gonçalves, M. P., Castro, M. J., Silva, P. D., & Moreira, R. J. (2022). Project-Based Learning Application in Higher Education: Student Experiences and Perspectives. In A. Alves & N. van Hattum-Janssen (Eds.), *Training Engineering Students for Modern Technological Advancement* (pp. 146–164). IGI Global. https://doi.org/10.4018/978-1-7998-8816-1.ch007

McCleskey, J. A., & Melton, R. M. (2022). Rolling With the Flow: Online Faculty and Student Presence in a Post-COVID-19 World. In S. Ramlall, T. Cross, & M. Love (Eds.), *Handbook of Research on Future of Work and Education: Implications for Curriculum Delivery and Work Design* (pp. 307–328). IGI Global. https://doi.org/10.4018/978-1-7998-8275-6.ch019

McCormack, V. F., Stauffer, M., Fishley, K., Hohenbrink, J., Mascazine, J. R., & Zigler, T. (2018). Designing a Dual Licensure Path for Middle Childhood and Special Education Teacher Candidates. In D. Polly, M. Putman, T. Petty, & A. Good (Eds.), *Innovative Practices in Teacher Preparation and Graduate-Level Teacher Education Programs* (pp. 21–36). Hershey, PA: IGI Global. doi:10.4018/978-1-5225-3068-8.ch002

McDaniel, R. (2017). Strategic Leadership in Instructional Design: Applying the Principles of Instructional Design through the Lens of Strategic Leadership to Distance Education. In V. Wang (Ed.), *Encyclopedia of Strategic Leadership and Management* (pp. 1570–1584). Hershey, PA: IGI Global. doi:10.4018/978-1-5225-1049-9.ch109

McKinney, R. E., Halli-Tierney, A. D., Gold, A. E., Allen, R. S., & Carroll, D. G. (2022). Interprofessional Education: Using Standardized Cases in Face-to-Face and Remote Learning Settings. In C. Ford & K. Garza (Eds.), *Handbook of Research on Updating and Innovating Health Professions Education: Post-Pandemic Perspectives* (pp. 24–42). IGI Global. https://doi.org/10.4018/978-1-7998-7623-6.ch002

Meintjes, H. H. (2021). Learner Views of a Facebook Page as a Supportive Digital Pedagogical Tool at a Public South African School in a Grade 12 Business Studies Class. *International Journal of Smart Education and Urban Society, 12*(2), 32–45. https://doi.org/10.4018/IJSEUS.2021040104

Melero-García, F. (2022). Training Bilingual Interpreters in Healthcare Settings: Student Perceptions of Online Learning. In J. LeLoup & P. Swanson (Eds.), *Handbook of Research on Effective Online Language Teaching in a Disruptive Environment* (pp. 288–310). IGI Global. https://doi.org/10.4018/978-1-7998-7720-2.ch015

Related References

Meletiadou, E. (2022). The Use of Peer Assessment as an Inclusive Learning Strategy in Higher Education Institutions: Enhancing Student Writing Skills and Motivation. In E. Meletiadou (Ed.), *Handbook of Research on Policies and Practices for Assessing Inclusive Teaching and Learning* (pp. 1–26). IGI Global. https://doi.org/10.4018/978-1-7998-8579-5.ch001

Memon, R. N., Ahmad, R., & Salim, S. S. (2018). Critical Issues in Requirements Engineering Education. In I. Management Association (Ed.), Computer Systems and Software Engineering: Concepts, Methodologies, Tools, and Applications (pp. 1953-1976). Hershey, PA: IGI Global. doi:10.4018/978-1-5225-3923-0.ch081

Mendenhall, R. (2017). Western Governors University: CBE Innovator and National Model. In K. Rasmussen, P. Northrup, & R. Colson (Eds.), *Handbook of Research on Competency-Based Education in University Settings* (pp. 379–400). Hershey, PA: IGI Global. doi:10.4018/978-1-5225-0932-5.ch019

Mense, E. G., Griggs, D. M., & Shanks, J. N. (2018). School Leaders in a Time of Accountability and Data Use: Preparing Our Future School Leaders in Leadership Preparation Programs. In E. Mense & M. Crain-Dorough (Eds.), *Data Leadership for K-12 Schools in a Time of Accountability* (pp. 235–259). Hershey, PA: IGI Global. doi:10.4018/978-1-5225-3188-3.ch012

Mense, E. G., Griggs, D. M., & Shanks, J. N. (2018). School Leaders in a Time of Accountability and Data Use: Preparing Our Future School Leaders in Leadership Preparation Programs. In E. Mense & M. Crain-Dorough (Eds.), *Data Leadership for K-12 Schools in a Time of Accountability* (pp. 235–259). Hershey, PA: IGI Global. doi:10.4018/978-1-5225-3188-3.ch012

Mestry, R., & Naicker, S. R. (2017). Exploring Distributive Leadership in South African Public Primary Schools in the Soweto Region. In I. Management Association (Ed.), Educational Leadership and Administration: Concepts, Methodologies, Tools, and Applications (pp. 1041-1064). Hershey, PA: IGI Global. doi:10.4018/978-1-5225-1624-8.ch050

Monaghan, C. H., & Boboc, M. (2017). (Re) Defining Leadership in Higher Education in the U.S. In V. Wang (Ed.), *Encyclopedia of Strategic Leadership and Management* (pp. 567–579). Hershey, PA: IGI Global. doi:10.4018/978-1-5225-1049-9.ch040

Morall, M. B. (2021). Reimagining Mobile Phones: Multiple Literacies and Digital Media Compositions. In C. Moran (Eds.), *Affordances and Constraints of Mobile Phone Use in English Language Arts Classrooms* (pp. 41-53). IGI Global. https://doi.org/10.4018/978-1-7998-5805-8.ch003

Mthethwa, V. (2022). Student Governance and the Academic Minefield During COVID-19 Lockdown in South Africa. In M. Alaali (Ed.), *Assessing University Governance and Policies in Relation to the COVID-19 Pandemic* (pp. 255–276). IGI Global. https://doi.org/10.4018/978-1-7998-8279-4.ch015

Muthee, J. M., & Murungi, C. G. (2018). Relationship Among Intelligence, Achievement Motivation, Type of School, and Academic Performance of Kenyan Urban Primary School Pupils. In M. Khosrow-Pour, D.B.A. (Ed.), Encyclopedia of Information Science and Technology, Fourth Edition (pp. 1540-1547). Hershey, PA: IGI Global. https://doi.org/ doi:10.4018/978-1-5225-2255-3.ch133

Naranjo, J. (2018). Meeting the Need for Inclusive Educators Online: Teacher Education in Inclusive Special Education and Dual-Certification. In D. Polly, M. Putman, T. Petty, & A. Good (Eds.), *Innovative Practices in Teacher Preparation and Graduate-Level Teacher Education Programs* (pp. 106–122). Hershey, PA: IGI Global. doi:10.4018/978-1-5225-3068-8.ch007

Nkabinde, Z. P. (2017). Multiculturalism in Special Education: Perspectives of Minority Children in Urban Schools. In J. Keengwe (Ed.), *Handbook of Research on Promoting Cross-Cultural Competence and Social Justice in Teacher Education* (pp. 382–397). Hershey, PA: IGI Global. doi:10.4018/978-1-5225-0897-7.ch020

Nkabinde, Z. P. (2018). Online Instruction: Is the Quality the Same as Face-to-Face Instruction? In J. Keengwe (Ed.), *Handbook of Research on Digital Content, Mobile Learning, and Technology Integration Models in Teacher Education* (pp. 300–314). Hershey, PA: IGI Global. doi:10.4018/978-1-5225-2953-8.ch016

Nugroho, A., & Albusaidi, S. S. (2022). Internationalization of Higher Education: The Methodological Critiques on the Research Related to Study Overseas and International Experience. In H. Magd & S. Kunjumuhammed (Eds.), *Global Perspectives on Quality Assurance and Accreditation in Higher Education Institutions* (pp. 75–89). IGI Global. https://doi.org/10.4018/978-1-7998-8085-1.ch005

Nulty, Z., & West, S. G. (2022). Student Engagement and Supporting Students With Accommodations. In P. Bull & G. Patterson (Eds.), *Redefining Teacher Education and Teacher Preparation Programs in the Post-COVID-19 Era* (pp. 99–116). IGI Global. https://doi.org/10.4018/978-1-7998-8298-5.ch006

O'Connor, J. R. Jr, & Jackson, K. N. (2017). The Use of iPad® Devices and "Apps" for ASD Students in Special Education and Speech Therapy. In Y. Kats (Ed.), *Supporting the Education of Children with Autism Spectrum Disorders* (pp. 267–283). Hershey, PA: IGI Global. doi:10.4018/978-1-5225-0816-8.ch014

Related References

Okolie, U. C., & Yasin, A. M. (2017). TVET in Developing Nations and Human Development. In U. Okolie & A. Yasin (Eds.), *Technical Education and Vocational Training in Developing Nations* (pp. 1–25). Hershey, PA: IGI Global. doi:10.4018/978-1-5225-1811-2.ch001

Pack, A., & Barrett, A. (2021). A Review of Virtual Reality and English for Academic Purposes: Understanding Where to Start. *International Journal of Computer-Assisted Language Learning and Teaching*, *11*(1), 72–80. https://doi.org/10.4018/IJCALLT.2021010105

Pashollari, E. (2019). Building Sustainability Through Environmental Education: Education for Sustainable Development. In L. Wilson, & C. Stevenson (Eds.), *Building Sustainability Through Environmental Education* (pp. 72-88). IGI Global. https://doi.org/10.4018/978-1-5225-7727-0.ch004

Paulson, E. N. (2017). Adapting and Advocating for an Online EdD Program in Changing Times and "Sacred" Cultures. In I. Management Association (Ed.), Educational Leadership and Administration: Concepts, Methodologies, Tools, and Applications (pp. 1849-1876). Hershey, PA: IGI Global. https://doi.org/doi:10.4018/978-1-5225-1624-8.ch085

Petersen, A. J., Elser, C. F., Al Nassir, M. N., Stakey, J., & Everson, K. (2017). The Year of Teaching Inclusively: Building an Elementary Classroom for All Students. In C. Curran & A. Petersen (Eds.), *Handbook of Research on Classroom Diversity and Inclusive Education Practice* (pp. 332–348). Hershey, PA: IGI Global. doi:10.4018/978-1-5225-2520-2.ch014

Pfannenstiel, K. H., & Sanders, J. (2017). Characteristics and Instructional Strategies for Students With Mathematical Difficulties: In the Inclusive Classroom. In C. Curran & A. Petersen (Eds.), *Handbook of Research on Classroom Diversity and Inclusive Education Practice* (pp. 250–281). Hershey, PA: IGI Global. doi:10.4018/978-1-5225-2520-2.ch011

Phan, A. N. (2022). Quality Assurance of Higher Education From the Glonacal Agency Heuristic: An Example From Vietnam. In H. Magd & S. Kunjumuhammed (Eds.), *Global Perspectives on Quality Assurance and Accreditation in Higher Education Institutions* (pp. 136–155). IGI Global. https://doi.org/10.4018/978-1-7998-8085-1.ch008

Preast, J. L., Bowman, N., & Rose, C. A. (2017). Creating Inclusive Classroom Communities Through Social and Emotional Learning to Reduce Social Marginalization Among Students. In C. Curran & A. Petersen (Eds.), *Handbook of Research on Classroom Diversity and Inclusive Education Practice* (pp. 183–200). Hershey, PA: IGI Global. doi:10.4018/978-1-5225-2520-2.ch008

Randolph, K. M., & Brady, M. P. (2018). Evolution of Covert Coaching as an Evidence-Based Practice in Professional Development and Preparation of Teachers. In V. Bryan, A. Musgrove, & J. Powers (Eds.), *Handbook of Research on Human Development in the Digital Age* (pp. 281–299). Hershey, PA: IGI Global. doi:10.4018/978-1-5225-2838-8.ch013

Rell, A. B., Puig, R. A., Roll, F., Valles, V., Espinoza, M., & Duque, A. L. (2017). Addressing Cultural Diversity and Global Competence: The Dual Language Framework. In L. Leavitt, S. Wisdom, & K. Leavitt (Eds.), *Cultural Awareness and Competency Development in Higher Education* (pp. 111–131). Hershey, PA: IGI Global. doi:10.4018/978-1-5225-2145-7.ch007

Richards, M., & Guzman, I. R. (2020). Academic Assessment of Critical Thinking in Distance Education Information Technology Programs. In I. Management Association (Ed.), *Learning and Performance Assessment: Concepts, Methodologies, Tools, and Applications* (pp. 1-19). IGI Global. https://doi.org/10.4018/978-1-7998-0420-8.ch001

Riel, J., Lawless, K. A., & Brown, S. W. (2017). Defining and Designing Responsive Online Professional Development (ROPD): A Framework to Support Curriculum Implementation. In T. Kidd & L. Morris Jr., (Eds.), *Handbook of Research on Instructional Systems and Educational Technology* (pp. 104–115). Hershey, PA: IGI Global. doi:10.4018/978-1-5225-2399-4.ch010

Roberts, C. (2017). Advancing Women Leaders in Academe: Creating a Culture of Inclusion. In S. Mukerji & P. Tripathi (Eds.), *Handbook of Research on Administration, Policy, and Leadership in Higher Education* (pp. 256–273). Hershey, PA: IGI Global. doi:10.4018/978-1-5225-0672-0.ch012

Rodgers, W. J., Kennedy, M. J., Alves, K. D., & Romig, J. E. (2017). A Multimedia Tool for Teacher Education and Professional Development. In C. Martin & D. Polly (Eds.), *Handbook of Research on Teacher Education and Professional Development* (pp. 285–296). Hershey, PA: IGI Global. doi:10.4018/978-1-5225-1067-3.ch015

Related References

Romanowski, M. H. (2017). Qatar's Educational Reform: Critical Issues Facing Principals. In I. Management Association (Ed.), Educational Leadership and Administration: Concepts, Methodologies, Tools, and Applications (pp. 1758-1773). Hershey, PA: IGI Global. https://doi.org/ doi:10.4018/978-1-5225-1624-8.ch080

Ruffin, T. R., Hawkins, D. P., & Lee, D. I. (2018). Increasing Student Engagement and Participation Through Course Methodology. In M. Khosrow-Pour, D.B.A. (Ed.), Encyclopedia of Information Science and Technology, Fourth Edition (pp. 1463-1473). Hershey, PA: IGI Global. doi:10.4018/978-1-5225-2255-3.ch126

Sabina, L. L., Curry, K. A., Harris, E. L., Krumm, B. L., & Vencill, V. (2017). Assessing the Performance of a Cohort-Based Model Using Domestic and International Practices. In I. Management Association (Ed.), Educational Leadership and Administration: Concepts, Methodologies, Tools, and Applications(pp. 913-929). Hershey, PA: IGI Global. https://doi.org/ doi:10.4018/978-1-5225-1624-8.ch044

Samkian, A., Pascarella, J., & Slayton, J. (2022). Towards an Anti-Racist, Culturally Responsive, and LGBTQ+ Inclusive Education: Developing Critically-Conscious Educational Leaders. In E. Cain-Sanschagrin, R. Filback, & J. Crawford (Eds.), *Cases on Academic Program Redesign for Greater Racial and Social Justice* (pp. 150–175). IGI Global. https://doi.org/10.4018/978-1-7998-8463-7.ch007

Santamaría, A. P., Webber, M., & Santamaría, L. J. (2017). Effective School Leadership for Māori Achievement: Building Capacity through Indigenous, National, and International Cross-Cultural Collaboration. In I. Management Association (Ed.), Educational Leadership and Administration: Concepts, Methodologies, Tools, and Applications (pp. 1547-1567). Hershey, PA: IGI Global. https://doi.org/ doi:10.4018/978-1-5225-1624-8.ch071

Santamaría, L. J. (2017). Culturally Responsive Educational Leadership in Cross-Cultural International Contexts. In I. Management Association (Ed.), Educational Leadership and Administration: Concepts, Methodologies, Tools, and Applications (pp. 1380-1400). Hershey, PA: IGI Global. https://doi.org/ doi:10.4018/978-1-5225-1624-8.ch064

Segredo, M. R., Cistone, P. J., & Reio, T. G. (2017). Relationships Between Emotional Intelligence, Leadership Style, and School Culture. *International Journal of Adult Vocational Education and Technology*, 8(3), 25–43. doi:10.4018/IJAVET.2017070103

Shalev, N. (2017). Empathy and Leadership From the Organizational Perspective. In Z. Nedelko & M. Brzozowski (Eds.), *Exploring the Influence of Personal Values and Cultures in the Workplace* (pp. 348–363). Hershey, PA: IGI Global. doi:10.4018/978-1-5225-2480-9.ch018

Siamak, M., Fathi, S., & Isfandyari-Moghaddam, A. (2018). Assessment and Measurement of Education Programs of Information Literacy. In R. Bhardwaj (Ed.), *Digitizing the Modern Library and the Transition From Print to Electronic* (pp. 164–192). Hershey, PA: IGI Global. doi:10.4018/978-1-5225-2119-8.ch007

Siu, K. W., & García, G. J. (2017). Disruptive Technologies and Education: Is There Any Disruption After All? In I. Management Association (Ed.), Educational Leadership and Administration: Concepts, Methodologies, Tools, and Applications (pp. 757-778). Hershey, PA: IGI Global. https://doi.org/ doi:10.4018/978-1-5225-1624-8.ch037

Slagter van Tryon, P. J. (2017). The Nurse Educator's Role in Designing Instruction and Instructional Strategies for Academic and Clinical Settings. In J. Stefaniak (Ed.), *Advancing Medical Education Through Strategic Instructional Design* (pp. 133–149). Hershey, PA: IGI Global. doi:10.4018/978-1-5225-2098-6.ch006

Slattery, C. A. (2018). Literacy Intervention and the Differentiated Plan of Instruction. In *Developing Effective Literacy Intervention Strategies: Emerging Research and Opportunities* (pp. 41–62). Hershey, PA: IGI Global. doi:10.4018/978-1-5225-5007-5.ch003

Smith, A. R. (2017). Ensuring Quality: The Faculty Role in Online Higher Education. In K. Shelton & K. Pedersen (Eds.), *Handbook of Research on Building, Growing, and Sustaining Quality E-Learning Programs* (pp. 210–231). Hershey, PA: IGI Global. doi:10.4018/978-1-5225-0877-9.ch011

Souders, T. M. (2017). Understanding Your Learner: Conducting a Learner Analysis. In J. Stefaniak (Ed.), *Advancing Medical Education Through Strategic Instructional Design* (pp. 1–29). Hershey, PA: IGI Global. doi:10.4018/978-1-5225-2098-6.ch001

Spring, K. J., Graham, C. R., & Ikahihifo, T. B. (2018). Learner Engagement in Blended Learning. In M. Khosrow-Pour, D.B.A. (Ed.), Encyclopedia of Information Science and Technology, Fourth Edition (pp. 1487-1498). Hershey, PA: IGI Global. doi:10.4018/978-1-5225-2255-3.ch128

Storey, V. A., Anthony, A. K., & Wahid, P. (2017). Gender-Based Leadership Barriers: Advancement of Female Faculty to Leadership Positions in Higher Education. In V. Wang (Ed.), *Encyclopedia of Strategic Leadership and Management* (pp. 244–258). Hershey, PA: IGI Global. doi:10.4018/978-1-5225-1049-9.ch018

Stottlemyer, D. (2018). Develop a Teaching Model Plan for a Differentiated Learning Approach. In *Differentiated Instructional Design for Multicultural Environments: Emerging Research and Opportunities* (pp. 106–130). Hershey, PA: IGI Global. doi:10.4018/978-1-5225-5106-5.ch005

Related References

Stottlemyer, D. (2018). Developing a Multicultural Environment. In *Differentiated Instructional Design for Multicultural Environments: Emerging Research and Opportunities* (pp. 1–27). Hershey, PA: IGI Global. doi:10.4018/978-1-5225-5106-5.ch001

Swagerty, T. (2022). Digital Access to Culturally Relevant Curricula: The Impact on the Native and Indigenous Student. In E. Reeves & C. McIntyre (Eds.), *Multidisciplinary Perspectives on Diversity and Equity in a Virtual World* (pp. 99–113). IGI Global. https://doi.org/10.4018/978-1-7998-8028-8.ch006

Swami, B. N., Gobona, T., & Tsimako, J. J. (2017). Academic Leadership: A Case Study of the University of Botswana. In N. Baporikar (Ed.), *Innovation and Shifting Perspectives in Management Education* (pp. 1–32). Hershey, PA: IGI Global. doi:10.4018/978-1-5225-1019-2.ch001

Swanson, K. W., & Collins, G. (2018). Designing Engaging Instruction for the Adult Learners. In M. Khosrow-Pour, D.B.A. (Ed.), Encyclopedia of Information Science and Technology, Fourth Edition (pp. 1432-1440). Hershey, PA: IGI Global. doi:10.4018/978-1-5225-2255-3.ch123

Swartz, B. A., Lynch, J. M., & Lynch, S. D. (2018). Embedding Elementary Teacher Education Coursework in Local Classrooms: Examples in Mathematics and Special Education. In D. Polly, M. Putman, T. Petty, & A. Good (Eds.), *Innovative Practices in Teacher Preparation and Graduate-Level Teacher Education Programs* (pp. 262–292). Hershey, PA: IGI Global. doi:10.4018/978-1-5225-3068-8.ch015

Taliadorou, N., & Pashiardis, P. (2017). Emotional Intelligence and Political Skill Really Matter in Educational Leadership. In I. Management Association (Ed.), Educational Leadership and Administration: Concepts, Methodologies, Tools, and Applications (pp. 1274-1303). Hershey, PA: IGI Global. https://doi.org/doi:10.4018/978-1-5225-1624-8.ch060

Tandoh, K. A., & Ebe-Arthur, J. E. (2018). Effective Educational Leadership in the Digital Age: An Examination of Professional Qualities and Best Practices. In J. Keengwe (Ed.), *Handbook of Research on Digital Content, Mobile Learning, and Technology Integration Models in Teacher Education* (pp. 244–265). Hershey, PA: IGI Global. doi:10.4018/978-1-5225-2953-8.ch013

Tobin, M. T. (2018). Multimodal Literacy. In M. Khosrow-Pour, D.B.A. (Ed.), Encyclopedia of Information Science and Technology, Fourth Edition (pp. 1508-1516). Hershey, PA: IGI Global. doi:10.4018/978-1-5225-2255-3.ch130

Torres, K. M., Arrastia-Chisholm, M. C., & Tackett, S. (2019). A Phenomenological Study of Pre-Service Teachers' Perceptions of Completing ESOL Field Placements. *International Journal of Teacher Education and Professional Development*, 2(2), 85–101. https://doi.org/10.4018/IJTEPD.2019070106

Torres, M. C., Salamanca, Y. N., Cely, J. P., & Aguilar, J. L. (2020). All We Need is a Boost! Using Multimodal Tools and the Translanguaging Strategy: Strengthening Speaking in the EFL Classroom. *International Journal of Computer-Assisted Language Learning and Teaching*, 10(3), 28–47. doi:10.4018/IJCALLT.2020070103

Torres, M. L., & Ramos, V. J. (2018). Music Therapy: A Pedagogical Alternative for ASD and ID Students in Regular Classrooms. In P. Epler (Ed.), *Instructional Strategies in General Education and Putting the Individuals With Disabilities Act (IDEA) Into Practice* (pp. 222–244). Hershey, PA: IGI Global. doi:10.4018/978-1-5225-3111-1.ch008

Toulassi, B. (2017). Educational Administration and Leadership in Francophone Africa: 5 Dynamics to Change Education. In S. Mukerji & P. Tripathi (Eds.), *Handbook of Research on Administration, Policy, and Leadership in Higher Education* (pp. 20–45). Hershey, PA: IGI Global. doi:10.4018/978-1-5225-0672-0.ch002

Umair, S., & Sharif, M. M. (2018). Predicting Students Grades Using Artificial Neural Networks and Support Vector Machine. In M. Khosrow-Pour, D.B.A. (Ed.), Encyclopedia of Information Science and Technology, Fourth Edition (pp. 5169-5182). Hershey, PA: IGI Global. doi:10.4018/978-1-5225-2255-3.ch449

Vettraino, L., Castello, V., Guspini, M., & Guglielman, E. (2018). Self-Awareness and Motivation Contrasting ESL and NEET Using the SAVE System. In M. Khosrow-Pour, D.B.A. (Ed.), Encyclopedia of Information Science and Technology, Fourth Edition (pp. 1559-1568). Hershey, PA: IGI Global. doi:10.4018/978-1-5225-2255-3.ch135

Wiemelt, J. (2017). Critical Bilingual Leadership for Emergent Bilingual Students. In I. Management Association (Ed.), Educational Leadership and Administration: Concepts, Methodologies, Tools, and Applications (pp. 1606-1631). Hershey, PA: IGI Global. doi:10.4018/978-1-5225-1624-8.ch074

Wolf, F., Seyfarth, F. C., & Pflaum, E. (2018). Scalable Capacity-Building for Geographically Dispersed Learners: Designing the MOOC "Sustainable Energy in Small Island Developing States (SIDS)". In U. Pandey & V. Indrakanti (Eds.), *Open and Distance Learning Initiatives for Sustainable Development* (pp. 58–83). Hershey, PA: IGI Global. doi:10.4018/978-1-5225-2621-6.ch003

Related References

Woodley, X. M., Mucundanyi, G., & Lockard, M. (2017). Designing Counter-Narratives: Constructing Culturally Responsive Curriculum Online. *International Journal of Online Pedagogy and Course Design*, 7(1), 43–56. doi:10.4018/IJOPCD.2017010104

Yell, M. L., & Christle, C. A. (2017). The Foundation of Inclusion in Federal Legislation and Litigation. In C. Curran & A. Petersen (Eds.), *Handbook of Research on Classroom Diversity and Inclusive Education Practice* (pp. 27–52). Hershey, PA: IGI Global. doi:10.4018/978-1-5225-2520-2.ch002

Zinner, L. (2019). Fostering Academic Citizenship With a Shared Leadership Approach. In C. Zhu & M. Zayim-Kurtay (Eds.), *University Governance and Academic Leadership in the EU and China* (pp. 99–117). IGI Global. https://doi.org/10.4018/978-1-5225-7441-5.ch007

About the Contributors

Nadire Gülçin Yildiz received, from the University of Iowa, her Ph.D. in the Counselor Education program in 2011, her M.A. in School Counseling in 2003 and her M.A. in Social Foundations of Education in 2004. Since 2003, Dr. Yildiz has been a licensed K-12 School Counselor for State of Iowa and, since 2009, a National Certified Counselor in the USA.Nadire Gülçin Yildiz currently works at the Counseling and Psychological Guidance, Istanbul Medipol University. Nadire does research in Social Policy, Qualitative Social Research. Their most recent publication is 'School Counselors' Partnerships With Linguistically Diverse Families: An Exploratory Study'.

* * *

Ramazan Atasoy is currently an associate professor at Harran University. He received his PhD in Educational Administration from Gazi University. His research interests include leadership, quality of education, education policy, PIAAC adult competency, literacy skills, numeracy skills and problem-solving skills in technology-rich environments, and organizational culture.

Damla Aydug is a Doctor of Philosophy in Educational Management, Inspection, Planning and Economy. Her academic research interests are organizational health, organizational trust, school evaluation, organizational behaviors, organizational learning and forgetting and school development. She has published articles in internationally indexed journals, submitted to and presented papers at international meetings, conferences, seminars, etc. She has contributed one international and three national research projects.

Alan Bruce is CEO and Director of Universal Learning Systems – an international consultancy firm specializing in research, training and project management. It has offices in Ireland, Barcelona, Helsinki, Sao Paulo and Chicago. Dr Bruce is a sociologist who studied and taught in universities in Los Angeles, Galway,

About the Contributors

Amsterdam and Hull. In 2016 he was appointed as Visiting Professor for Global Learning in the National Changhua University of Education in Taiwan. In 2016 he was course author for the Master in Online, Open and Distance Learning for Charles Sturt University, Australia. He is Academic Coordinator for the Conflicts of Interest program validated by Queens University Belfast. A member of the Association for Historical Dialogue and Research in Cyprus, he has lectured in Kosovo, Bosnia, Romania, Cyprus and Northern Ireland on conflict transformation, human rights and innovative learning. In 2018 he was appointed as External Expert for the European Commission in Brussels on migration policy. He was also appointed as Learning Design Expert with Universidad Nacional de Educación (UNAE) in Ecuador.

Özcan Doğan was born in Manisa, Turkey in 1977. He got the master of arts in educational administration from Eskişehir Osmangazi University in 2009. He is a PhD student in Anadolu University in the field of educational administration, evaluation, planning and economics. He has been an English lecturer at Eskişehir Osmangazi University since 1999. His research interests include teacher education, image management, occupational image and corporate image.

Venesser Fernandes is an internationally recognised expert in research on educational leadership studies, especially in the areas of Continuous Improvement Systems, Data-Improved Decision-making Processes, Evidence-based Educational Improvement Systems, Equitable School Systems and Educational Policy Analysis and Development. She teaches Masters courses in Education and Educational Leadership at Monash University. She is an international consultant on school effectiveness and improvement working with system leaders, school leaders and teachers on sustaining and improving educational quality.

Olena Glazunova (Doctor sciences in Pedagogic, specialty: Information Communication Technologies in Education) possesses an expertise in the development and use of information technologies in educational process, design and development of e-learning environment, e-learning courses. She has experience in creating educational cluster University, development of managing procedures of electronic educational environment based on ISO 9001, integration of Microsoft's cloud services with e-learning environment, guidelines of creating e-learning courses, provision of attestation e-learning courses. She also initiated three International conferences in the field of e-education. She took part in three research projects commissioned by the Ministry Education and Science of Ukraine (Models of Distance Learning (2008-2010), Certification of e-learning courses (2010-2012), Creating a hybrid cloud-based information and educational environment of the university of agrarian profile (2016-2017)) and three international TEMPUS projects (TEM-

PUS JEP 271362006 IMBASA « Implementation of basic and advanced scientific techniques to master and postgraduate curricula of agricultural direction » (2008-2010), ENAGRA - The curriculum of the specialty "Environmental Protection" in agricultural universities" (2010-2013), TEMPUS IV QANTUS - Qualifications Framework for Environmental Science of Ukrainian Universities" (2013-2016)). She has more then 90 publications, 3 of them – in Scopus DB.

Orkan Zeynel Güzelci received B.Arch. (2010) degree in Architecture from Istanbul Kultur University (IKU), M.Sc. (2012) degree in Architectural Design Program, Ph.D. (2018) degree in Architectural Design Computing Program from Istanbul Technical University (ITU), and Post Doctoral certificate (2021) from University of Porto. Currently, he is an associate professor at ITU and a researcher at FAUP+DFL/CEAU.

Antonio D. Juan Rubio has a degree in English Studies from the University of Murcia and a PhD from the National University of Distance Education (UNED) with the positive accreditation by the ANECA body, being given the Extraordinary Doctorate Award. He is currently working as a professor at the University of Granada. He has been awarded a scholarship by University College (Cork, Ireland), the Franklin Institute (University of Alcala de Henares, Spain) and the Radcliffe Institute for Advanced Study (Harvard University, USA), where he conducted a pre-doctoral research visit in the year 2012. He is currently a member of the scientific committee of several national and international journals as well as a member of the editorial board of several international journals. He also belongs to the organizing and scientific committee of several conferences organized by the Athens Institute for Education and Research (Greece). Among his main lines of research we can emphasize the following aspects: cultural studies in the United States; gender issues associated with the role of women in the Anglo-American literature; or the teaching practice and process of English.

Haruni Machumu (PhD) has an interest in educational leadership and management as well as quality issues in educational technology integration. He has been a faculty member and a prolific thinker in the Department of Educational Foundations and Teaching Management at the Faculty of Social Sciences – Mzumbe University since 2008. He has a PhD in educational sciences from Vrije Universiteit Brussel (VUB), Belgium. His PhD research situated in the area of educational technology integration (blended learning, e-learning and online learning). His research interests lie in the area of research methodology in education, ICT in Education and Pedagogy, human communication, e-learning theory, design and implementation. He has collaborated actively with researchers on students and teachers exchange

About the Contributors

programme, project write-up and implementation. Machumu is the instructor for popular research methods in education course to undergraduate students. Machumu supervises undergraduate, Master and PhD candidates. He has prolifically published in both international and local journals.

Raymond J. Schmidt has served as an education professional for 30 years. He began his teaching career in Chicago in 1993 and that experience carried him to Arizona and then Alaska. During that time, he ascertained his Master's Degree in Education and began teaching aspiring educators at university and in the classroom. By 2009, Dr. Schmidt began his first official education leadership position as an advisor to principals in Abu Dhabi, UAE. From there he served as an instructional coach in Sao Paulo, Brazil. Those opportunities ignited a passion for enhancing his leadership skills and he returned to the U.S. to complete his Administrative Services Credentials. While completing said coursework, he served first as an executive director and middle school principal and then as a lower school principal in L.A. In 2018, he accepted a lower school head position at Colegio Americano de Guatemala in Guatemala City. While serving the CAG community, he completed his doctorate degree in educational leadership and published peer-reviewed research on leadership decision-making. Currently, he is serving as the Superintendent at Escuela Internacional Sampedrana in San Pedro Sula, Honduras.

Margaret-Mary Sulentic Dowell, PhD, is Cecil "Pete" Taylor Endowed Professor of Literacy, Leadership, and Urban Education at Louisiana State University, Baton Rouge, USA. She is Director of the LSU Writing Project & Coordinator of the Educational Leadership PhD program in the School of Education. Her research agenda includes three strands focused on literacy in urban settings, specifically investigating the complexities of literacy leadership, examining service-learning as a pedagogical pathway to preparing pre-service teachers to teach literacy in urban environments, and exploring ways to provide access to literature, writing, and the arts (arts integration) in urban environs. Sulentic Dowell has published widely, and she has been nationally recognized for scholarship and teaching. Sulentic Dowell is a career educator & fierce public education advocate, spending the majority of her 20-year public school teaching experience in Iowa schools, but also possessing experience in northern Minnesota and southern Mississippi. She served public education as Assistant Superintendent of 64 elementary campuses in the East Baton Rouge Parish School System in Louisiana (2002-2006).

About the Contributors

Mehmet Tufan Yalçın is an Assistant Professor at Çankırı Karatekin University in Turkey. His research interests include leadership, school administration, instructional capacity, teacher professional learning, school climate, and organizational learning.

Index

A

Adaptability 1, 5, 17, 174, 177, 181, 183, 191, 194-195
Adaptive Reuse 173-178, 191-196
Advancement 21
Alignment 52, 90, 139
Architectural Heritage 173, 195
Asynchronous Learning 198, 205-206, 220, 225, 227

B

Blended Learning 209, 213, 229

C

Capacity 1-2, 6, 11-12, 14-17, 20, 34, 52, 54, 58, 66-67, 77, 82-84, 87, 96, 150, 158, 165-166, 177
Change 1-3, 5-16, 18-24, 26-27, 30, 32-34, 36-42, 44-45, 47-60, 62-74, 77-78, 82-87, 94-95, 97, 103-104, 106, 111, 114, 121-124, 127-129, 131-133, 135, 137-140, 142-143, 155, 157, 159, 161, 176, 196, 215
Change Models 49, 51, 59, 71
Collaboration 2, 4-6, 8-10, 12-20, 35, 60, 77, 79, 83, 85, 94, 114, 139-140, 153, 162, 182-184, 201, 205-206, 208, 223-224, 229, 231-232
Community 2, 6-11, 15-19, 31, 33, 40, 42, 44-45, 66, 82, 98-99, 102, 104-105, 108-109, 112-116, 118, 120, 124-126, 128, 144, 163, 172, 179, 182, 203, 211, 222

D

Digital Educational Environment 199, 201
Digitalization of Education 198
Distance Learning 199-201, 203, 205, 210, 218, 221, 224, 229
Distributed Leadership 2, 6, 14-15, 23, 25, 75-78, 81-87, 89, 91-98, 122, 125, 127, 132, 143

E

Early Childhood Education 120, 146-148, 150-151, 153, 155-158, 160-161, 164, 167-172
Educational Organizations 51, 54, 65-66, 68-69, 74, 84-85, 87
Educational Strategies 135, 169, 192
Engagement 1, 3, 8-9, 11-12, 18-20, 78, 85, 97, 113, 189, 200, 206, 221, 234
English 102, 129, 146-147, 151-152, 155, 159-165, 167-172, 200, 233-234
Experiential Learning 99, 107, 118, 182, 185

F

Family 67, 100, 103, 108-109, 120, 148, 152-154, 160, 162, 169, 172
Flexibility 6, 12, 43, 55, 66, 73, 97, 174, 177, 184, 186, 188-189, 191, 194, 196-197, 205, 218

G

Global Integration 146

I

Implementation 1, 5, 8-9, 13-14, 24, 28, 30, 32, 40-42, 45, 48-50, 57, 62, 67, 69, 79, 81, 93, 120, 136, 141, 147, 158-159, 165, 186, 192, 200, 203, 228

Initiatives 3, 5-6, 10-11, 13-16, 18-19, 65, 85-86, 97, 123, 139-140, 176, 185

Innovation 1-2, 5, 7, 12, 15-20, 42-43, 49, 64, 67, 74, 76-77, 83-87, 89, 95, 97-98

K

K-12 Schools 1-5, 7, 9-15, 17-20, 121

M

Microsoft 365 Services 201, 208, 211-212, 233

Microsoft Teams-Based Platform 199

N

New Technologies 35, 43, 146, 150-151, 158-159, 164, 171

O

Organisational Culture 39, 121-128, 131, 139-140, 144

Organizational Change 51-54, 56, 59-63, 65-67, 69-74, 77, 82-83, 86

Organizational Innovativeness 75-78, 83-87, 89, 91-95, 98

P

Pakistani K-12 Schools 121

Pedagogical Approaches 3, 16, 182, 192

Post-Pandemic Reuse 173-174, 176-177, 194

Poverty 99-110, 112-114, 116-120, 153

Preservice Teachers 99, 102

Primary School Design 173

Professional Development 1, 5-9, 11-12, 14-15, 18-19, 24-25, 47, 75-81, 85-86, 89-94, 98, 101, 105, 126-127, 137-138, 140-141, 143

Project 9, 99, 103-105, 107, 125, 146-149, 151, 154, 156-159, 164-168, 175, 177-179, 184, 186-193, 200, 203-205

Purposeful 57, 60

S

School Improvement 1-2, 10, 20, 23, 72, 76-78, 82, 86-87, 94-96, 98, 121-122, 124-125, 127-128, 133, 135-137, 139-140, 144

School Leadership 23-24, 77, 81, 86, 94-95, 124-125, 127-129, 132, 140, 143-145

Simulation 60-61, 99, 103-104, 106-120

Strategies 1-2, 7-9, 11-13, 15, 19-20, 23, 64, 79, 84, 122-123, 126, 131, 134-136, 138, 140, 145, 155, 158, 165, 169, 173, 177, 182-183, 185, 192, 194-195, 201-202, 232

Students Living in Poverty 99, 102-107, 109, 111-113, 116

Synchronous Learning 213, 219

T

Transformation 1, 28, 30, 45, 49-50, 59, 81, 137, 140, 142, 173-175, 181, 198

V

Vision 1-2, 5, 10, 14-15, 18-19, 34, 38-39, 41-42, 45, 60, 64-65, 86-87, 125, 127, 139, 185-186, 189

Recommended Reference Books

IGI Global's reference books are available in three unique pricing formats:
Print Only, E-Book Only, or Print + E-Book.
Order direct through IGI Global's Online Bookstore at www.igi-global.com or through your preferred provider.

Online Distance Learning Course Design and Multimedia in E-Learning

ISBN: 9781799897064
EISBN: 9781799897088
© 2022; 302 pp.
List Price: US$ 215

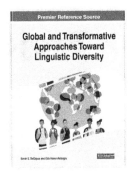

Global and Transformative Approaches Toward Linguistic Diversity

ISBN: 9781799889854
EISBN: 9781799889878
© 2022; 383 pp.
List Price: US$ 215

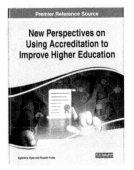

New Perspectives on Using Accreditation to Improve Higher Education

ISBN: 9781668451953
EISBN: 9781668451960
© 2022; 300 pp.
List Price: US$ 215

Impact of School Shootings on Classroom Culture, Curriculum, and Learning

ISBN: 9781799852001
EISBN: 9781799852018
© 2022; 355 pp.
List Price: US$ 215

Modern Reading Practices and Collaboration Between Schools, Family, and Community

ISBN: 9781799897507
EISBN: 9781799897521
© 2022; 304 pp.
List Price: US$ 215

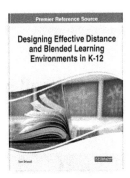

Designing Effective Distance and Blended Learning Environments in K-12

ISBN: 9781799868293
EISBN: 9781799868316
© 2022; 389 pp.
List Price: US$ 215

Do you want to stay current on the latest research trends, product announcements, news, and special offers?
Join IGI Global's mailing list to receive customized recommendations, exclusive discounts, and more.
Sign up at: www.igi-global.com/newsletters.

Publisher of Timely, Peer-Reviewed Inclusive Research Since 1988

www.igi-global.com   Sign up at www.igi-global.com/newsletters   facebook.com/igiglobal   twitter.com/igiglobal

Ensure Quality Research is Introduced to the Academic Community

Become an Evaluator for IGI Global Authored Book Projects

   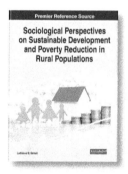

The overall success of an authored book project is dependent on quality and timely manuscript evaluations.

Applications and Inquiries may be sent to:
development@igi-global.com

Applicants must have a doctorate (or equivalent degree) as well as publishing, research, and reviewing experience. Authored Book Evaluators are appointed for one-year terms and are expected to complete at least three evaluations per term. Upon successful completion of this term, evaluators can be considered for an additional term.

If you have a colleague that may be interested in this opportunity, we encourage you to share this information with them.

Easily Identify, Acquire, and Utilize Published Peer-Reviewed Findings in Support of Your Current Research

IGI Global OnDemand

Purchase Individual IGI Global OnDemand Book Chapters and Journal Articles

For More Information:
www.igi-global.com/e-resources/ondemand/

Browse through 150,000+ Articles and Chapters!

Find specific research related to your current studies and projects that have been contributed by international researchers from prestigious institutions, including:

- Accurate and Advanced Search
- Affordably Acquire Research
- Instantly Access Your Content
- Benefit from the InfoSci Platform Features

> *It really provides* an excellent entry into the research literature of the field. *It presents a manageable number of* highly relevant sources *on topics of interest to a wide range of researchers. The sources are* scholarly, but also accessible *to 'practitioners'.*

- Ms. Lisa Stimatz, MLS, University of North Carolina at Chapel Hill, USA

Interested in Additional Savings?

Subscribe to

IGI Global OnDemand *Plus*

Learn More

Acquire content from over 128,000+ research-focused book chapters and 33,000+ scholarly journal articles for as low as US$ 5 per article/chapter (original retail price for an article/chapter: US$ 37.50).

7,300+ E-BOOKS.
ADVANCED RESEARCH.
INCLUSIVE & AFFORDABLE.

IGI Global e-Book Collection

- **Flexible Purchasing Options** (Perpetual, Subscription, EBA, etc.)
- Multi-Year Agreements with **No Price Increases** Guaranteed
- **No Additional Charge** for Multi-User Licensing
- No Maintenance, Hosting, or Archiving Fees
- Continually Enhanced & Innovated **Accessibility Compliance Features** (WCAG)

Handbook of Research on Digital Transformation, Industry Use Cases, and the Impact of Disruptive Technologies
ISBN: 9781799877127
EISBN: 9781799877141

Handbook of Research on New Investigations in Artificial Life, AI, and Machine Learning
ISBN: 9781799886860
EISBN: 9781799886877

Handbook of Research on Future of Work and Education
ISBN: 9781799882756
EISBN: 9781799882770

Research Anthology on Physical and Intellectual Disabilities in an Inclusive Society (4 Vols.)
ISBN: 9781668435427
EISBN: 9781668435434

Innovative Economic, Social, and Environmental Practices for Progressing Future Sustainability
ISBN: 9781799895909
EISBN: 9781799895923

Applied Guide for Event Study Research in Supply Chain Management
ISBN: 9781799889694
EISBN: 9781799889717

Mental Health and Wellness in Healthcare Workers
ISBN: 9781799888130
EISBN: 9781799888147

Clean Technologies and Sustainable Development in Civil Engineering
ISBN: 9781799898108
EISBN: 9781799898122

Request More Information, or Recommend the IGI Global e-Book Collection to Your Institution's Librarian

---

For More Information or to Request a Free Trial, Contact IGI Global's e-Collections Team: eresources@igi-global.com | 1-866-342-6657 ext. 100 | 717-533-8845 ext. 100

Are You Ready to Publish Your Research

IGI Global offers book authorship and editorship opportunities across 11 subject areas, including business, computer science, education, science and engineering, social sciences, and more!

Benefits of Publishing with IGI Global:

- Free one-on-one editorial and promotional support.
- Expedited publishing timelines that can take your book from start to finish in less than one (1) year.
- Choose from a variety of formats, including Edited and Authored References, Handbooks of Research, Encyclopedias, and Research Insights.
- Utilize IGI Global's eEditorial Discovery® submission system in support of conducting the submission and double-blind peer review process.
- IGI Global maintains a strict adherence to ethical practices due in part to our full membership with the Committee on Publication Ethics (COPE).
- Indexing potential in prestigious indices such as Scopus®, Web of Science™, PsycINFO®, and ERIC – Education Resources Information Center.
- Ability to connect your ORCID iD to your IGI Global publications.
- Earn honorariums and royalties on your full book publications as well as complimentary content and exclusive discounts.

Join Your Colleagues from Prestigious Institutions, Including:

Learn More at: www.igi-global.com/publish
or by Contacting the Acquisitions Department at: acquisition@igi-global.com

Individual Article & Chapter Downloads
US$ 29.50/each

Easily Identify, Acquire, and Utilize Published Peer-Reviewed Findings in Support of Your Current Research

- Browse Over **170,000+ Articles & Chapters**
- **Accurate & Advanced** Search
- Affordably Acquire **International Research**
- **Instantly Access** Your Content
- Benefit from the **InfoSci® Platform Features**

THE UNIVERSITY of NORTH CAROLINA at CHAPEL HILL

> "It really provides *an excellent entry into the research literature of the field.* It presents a manageable number of *highly relevant sources* on topics of interest to a wide range of researchers. The sources are *scholarly, but also accessible* to 'practitioners'."
>
> - Ms. Lisa Stimatz, MLS, University of North Carolina at Chapel Hill, USA

Interested in Additional Savings?

Subscribe to **IGI Global OnDemand *Plus***

Learn More

Acquire content from over 128,000+ research-focused book chapters and 33,000+ scholarly journal articles for as low as US$ 5 per article/chapter (original retail price for an article/chapter: US$ 37.50).

Printed in the USA
CPSIA information can be obtained
at www.ICGtesting.com
LVHW081756041124
795688LV00005B/610